W9-BXP-451

OPERA, LIBERALISM, AND ANTISEMITISM
IN NINETEENTH-CENTURY FRANCE
The Politics of Halévy's *La Juive*

This is the first comprehensive critical study of the nineteenth-century
French grand opera *La Juive* (Paris Opéra, 1835), a powerful and
successful work by the leading dramatist and librettist Eugène Scribe
and Conservatoire- trained composer Fromental Halévy. Hallman
explores the politically charged messages of the opera within the
context of French social and cultural history. The book addresses the
opera's portrayal of religious intolerance and Jewish–Christian conflict
in subject, setting, and characterization, viewing the anticlerical thrust
of its critique as a reminder of the historical abuses of an autocratic
Church and State and as a reflection of the liberal ideology of the July
Monarchy. It also considers the portrayal of the central Jewish
characters in light of literary stereotypes, Jewish "emancipation" and
acculturation, and contradictory, antisemitic attitudes toward Jews in
French society.

Diana Hallman is Associate Professor of Musicology at the University
of Kentucky. She is a contributing author to the forthcoming *Cambridge
Companion to Grand Opera* edited by David Charlton, and has written
articles and reviews concerning Halévy and the politics of French
grand opera, as well as an article on the librettist Ludovic Halévy in the
Dictionary of Literary Biography, 1998. She was a featured speaker for
the BBC's live broadcast of *La Juive* from the Vienna Staatsoper, 1999.
Dr. Hallman's research interests also include the history of American
concert life and performance, and she is completing a book on
turn-of-the-century Austrian-American pianist Fannie Bloomfield
Zeisler.

| CAMBRIDGE STUDIES IN OPERA

Series editor: Arthur Groos, *Cornell University*

Volumes for *Cambridge Studies in Opera* explore the cultural, political, and social influences of the genre. As a cultural art form, opera is not produced in a vacuum. Rather, it is influenced, whether directly or in more subtle ways, by its social and political environment. In turn, opera leaves its mark on society and contributes to shaping the cultural climate. Studies to be included in the series will look at these various relationships including the politics and economics of opera, the operatic representation of women or the singers who portrayed them, the history of opera as theatre, and the evolution of the opera house.

Editorial Board

Tim Carter, *University of North Carolina at Chapel Hill*

John Deathridge, *King's College, University of London*

James Hepokoski, *Yale University*

Paul Robinson, *Stanford University*

Ellen Rosand, *Yale University*

Already published

Opera Buffa in Mozart's Vienna
Edited by Mary Hunter and James Webster

Johann Strauss and Vienna: Operetta and the Politics of Popular Culture
Camille Crittenden

German Opera: From the Beginnings to Wagner
John Warrack

Opera and Drama in Eighteenth-Century London: The King's Theatre, Garrick and the Business of Performance
Ian Woodfield

Aesthetics of Opera in the Ancien Régime, 1647–1785
Downing A. Thomas

Opera, Liberalism, and Antisemitism in Nineteenth-Century France

The Politics of Halévy's *La Juive*

Diana R. Hallman

CAMBRIDGE
UNIVERSITY PRESS

PUBLISHED BY THE PRESS SYNDICATE OF THE UNIVERSITY OF CAMBRIDGE
The Pitt Building, Trumpington Street, Cambridge, United Kingdom

CAMBRIDGE UNIVERSITY PRESS
The Edinburgh Building, Cambridge CB2 2RU, UK
40 West 20th Street, New York, NY 10011-4211, USA
477 Williamstown Road, Port Melbourne, VIC 3207, Australia
Ruiz de Alarcón 13, 28014 Madrid, Spain
Dock House, The Waterfront, Cape Town 8001, South Africa

http://www.cambridge.org

© Diana R. Hallman 2002

This book is in copyright. Subject to statutory exception
and to the provisions of relevant collective licensing agreements,
no reproduction of any part may take place without
the written permission of Cambridge University Press.

First published 2002

Printed in the United Kingdom at the University Press, Cambridge

Typeface Dante MT 10.75/14 pt   *System* LATEX 2ε   [TB]

A catalogue record for this book is available from the British Library

Library of Congress Cataloguing in Publication data
Hallman, Diana R.
Opera, liberalism, and antisemitism in nineteenth-century France: the politics
of Halévy's La Juive / by Diana R. Hallman.
      p.   cm. – (Cambridge studies in opera)
Includes bibliographical references and index.
ISBN 0 521 65086 0
1. Halévy, F., 1799–1862. Juive.   2. Opera – France – 19th century.
3. Antisemitism – France – History – 19th century.   4. Liberalism – France –
History – 19th century.   I. Title.   II. Series.
ML410.H17 H35   2002   782.1 – dc21   2001052446

ISBN 0 521 65086 0 hardback

To Gordon and to my family

CONTENTS

ILLUSTRATIONS

PREFACE

La Juive (*The Jewess*) first captivated me as a doctoral student drawn to
the study of nineteenth-century opera – particularly neglected works
of the French theatre – and the interrelationships of opera with a larger
culture. As I turned to this central work of Parisian *grand opéra*, one of
a small body of operas that remained in the core repertoire in Paris and
other European musical capitals throughout the century, I began with
the simple query: why would a work so titled and featuring Jewish–
Christian antagonisms appear and succeed on the stage of the Paris
Opéra in 1835? Searching for answers to this basic question took me
well beyond the operatic stage and provided me with deep insights into
social, religious, and political realities of France in the early nineteenth
century. This exploration convinced me that a focus on the music and
drama solely within operatic traditions would not reveal the cultural
meanings of *La Juive* as deeply and broadly as a "thick" historical reading. In this study, I have chosen to view the work within some of the
rich contexts that made it a moving, evocative commentary, combining
with the power and beauty of its music and drama and the appeal of its
visual spectacle. This reading is only one of many that this provocative
work invites. Recent studies have shown how varied and multifaceted
the approaches to *grand opéra* can be, and this multiplicity seems especially fitting for a genre that represented the largest-scale fusing of
theatrical arts before Wagner, "the principal alternative to the Italian
tradition," as David Charlton states in his prospectus for the forthcoming *Cambridge Companion to Grand Opera*, and a genre closely bound
to the intriguing political era of the July Monarchy (1830–48) and a
rapidly urbanizing Europe. Inevitably, my interpretations of *La Juive*,
particularly its treatment of Jewish–Christian conflict and characterization, are mediated by my own sensibilities in a post-Holocaust age

(as they undoubtedly will be for my readers), my own cultural values and biases, and perhaps my belief that this work holds great relevance for our world today.

Lexington, Kentucky
February 2001

ACKNOWLEDGMENTS

In the development and refinement of this study I have been helped by many people. In its beginnings as a dissertation, it was advised and judiciously read by CUNY professors L. Michael Griffel, Allan W. Atlas, Leo Treitler, John M. Graziano, and Ora Frischberg Saloman, and greatly aided by M. Elizabeth C. Bartlet, who has continued to offer expert counsel and support with a generosity that is unflagging. Among many other colleagues who have enriched my work, I would especially like to thank Halévy scholar Karl Leich-Galland for his informed responses to my dissertation and his boundless enthusiasm, and Steven Huebner and Lesley A. Wright for key pieces of advice and assistance. I am indeed very grateful to Cambridge editor Victoria L. Cooper for her interest and encouragement, and for her many contributions toward making this book a reality, as well as to my two anonymous Cambridge readers, series editor Arthur Groos, and copy editor Laura Davey for their helpful, insightful suggestions. I thank Raymond La Charité for his skillful pruning of my French translations, Larry Nelson for his careful preparation of music examples, Vickie Steele for her pleasurable collaboration in organizing the index, and Richard Domek for his ready advice. Of the many library staff members who have helped me throughout my years of research, I offer my sincere appreciation to Catherine Massip, Nicole Wild, Martine Kahane, Romain Feist, Florence Callu, and Urbain Kouadio of the Bibliothèque Nationale, and to Odile Krakovitch of the Archives Nationales, as well as to the librarians and assistants of the New York Public Library (particularly of the Jewish Division and Performing Arts Library), the Pierpont Morgan Library, and the Library of Congress. Among the friends and acquaintances who made my visits to Paris so stimulating and refreshing, I thank Howard Haskin and Joshua Sigal, who graciously welcomed me into their beautiful home even when they were busy with their own concerns, and Jean-Louis Tamvaco, who granted me access to his dissertation and to his vast knowledge of Opéra iconography. I am grateful to my colleagues at the University of Kentucky for their uplifting camaraderie and their guidance in the formidable task of juggling university demands and writing deadlines. Finally, from the bottom of my heart, I thank my beloved partner of many years, Gordon Hawkins, who shared the pressures and struggles of seeing this project to its completion, my circle of dear, supportive friends, Vickie Steele, Jeannie Hinson, Kevin Stogner, Elisa Moskowitz, Keith Walters, Ivan Mills, Colette Valentine, Jocelyn Stewart, Ron Cappon, Causton Toney, and Muriel Ferris, and my loving, steadfast family, Anna, Bill, Stewart, and Janice Hallman, for their much-needed sustenance and care.

ABBREVIATIONS

F-Pan	Archives Nationales, Paris
F-Pa	Bibliothèque Nationale de France, Bibliothèque de l'Arsenal, Paris
F-Pn	Bibliothèque Nationale de France, Paris
F-Pn, Ms.	Bibliothèque Nationale de France, Département des Manuscrits, Paris
F-Pn, Mus.	Bibliothèque Nationale de France, Département de la Musique, Paris
F-Po	Bibliothèque Nationale de France Bibliothèque-Musée de l'Opéra, Paris
US NYp	New York Public Library, Performing Arts Division, Research Library, New York, NY
US NYpm	Pierpont Morgan Library, New York, NY

Introduction

Within a few years of the Revolution of 1830 and the advent of the July Monarchy, the renowned dramatist Eugène Scribe (1791–1861) began to sketch ideas and verse for a five-act *grand opéra* destined for the stage of the Académie royale de musique, or Paris Opéra. At the head of his draft synopsis, Scribe placed the words "Rachel ou L'auto-da-fe," but later opted for a simpler title, *La Juive* (*The Jewess*). After showing his plan to Opéra director Louis Véron (1798–1867), Scribe signed a contract for future completion of his libretto and began searching for a composer. He first sought out Giacomo Meyerbeer (1791–1864), his collaborator on the highly successful *Robert le diable* of 1831, but the German composer declined. Scribe then turned – somewhat reluctantly – to Fromental Halévy (1799–1862), a young Frenchman whom he knew primarily as *chef de chant* at the Opéra.[1] As Prix de Rome winner, Conservatoire professor, and composer of several *opéras comiques*, Halévy clearly had a solid reputation, but he had never written a *grand opéra* for the prestigious lyrical stage that he knew so well behind the scenes. It was a golden moment for the aspiring composer, one that Halévy would recall years later:

[1] Nicole Wild, *Dictionnaire des théâtres parisiens au XIXe siècle: Les Théâtres et la musique* (Paris: Aux Amateurs de Livres, 1989), 312–13, places Halévy as the third-ranked ("3e") *chef* or *maître de chant* at the Opéra, 1829–33, a position that entailed rehearsing and overseeing the chorus. Although Wild notes that the positions of *chef de choeur* and *chef de chant* were not clearly designated before 1840, Halévy's advancement to *premier chef de chant* in 1833 at the death of Hérold, and until 1840, involved a change in status as well as responsibility. In this position, Halévy rehearsed soloists, aided composers in rehearsals, and worked with other *chefs* when combined forces were rehearsed, as suggested in a letter of 1835 from Meyerbeer asking Halévy to call the chorus of *femmes* to rehearse the second and third acts of *Les Huguenots* with soloists. See *Fromental Halévy: Lettres*, ed. Marthe Galland (Heilbronn: Musik-Edition Lucie Galland, 1999), 12.

It was a beautiful summer evening in Montalais Park when M. Scribe first told me the subject of *La Juive*, which moved me deeply. I shall always remember this conversation, which was associated with one of the most interesting epochs in my life as an artist.[2]

With the powerful success of the opera that would grow from this collaboration, beginning with its première on 23 February 1835, Halévy's life as an artist blossomed more than he probably could have imagined on that evening at Montalais, Scribe's summer home near Meudon. His election to the Académie des beaux-arts the following year would prove to be only one demonstration of the new stature that *La Juive* would bring. During the meeting, Halévy undoubtedly reflected on the potential career benefits of working with this established dramatist and librettist and the artistic challenge of trying his hand at such a large-scale work. But perhaps dominating his thoughts was the scenario that Scribe related, the subject that moved him so profoundly. Certainly the title alone would have intrigued this young Jewish composer, son of a Talmudic scholar. The centering of an opera around not one but two Jewish characters, in a story of religious conflict, persecution, and doomed love, seems to have stimulated strong emotions in Halévy: his brother recalled that he wrote the score "with enthusiasm and passion . . . in a state of feverish anxiety."[3]

The setting that the theatrically astute Scribe had ultimately chosen and that Halévy endorsed, the early fifteenth-century Council of Constance (Konstanz), promised to satisfy popular taste in its evocation of the distant past. Historical settings, with vivid portrayals of a vast array of characters, detailed presentations of scene and costume, and an ambience of authenticity, continued to enthrall the French public

---

[2] (Jacques-François-) Fromental (-Elie) Halévy, *Derniers Souvenirs et portraits* (Paris: Michel Lévy Frères, 1863), 166: "C'est par une belle soirée d'été, dans le parc de Montalais, que M. Scribe me conta pour la première fois le sujet de *la Juive*, qui m'émut profondément, et je conserverai toujours le souvenir de cet entretien qui se rattache à une des époques les plus intéressantes pour moi de ma vie d'artiste." Henceforth, the original French of substantial quotations will be supplied for sources not readily available. All unattributed translations are mine, with editing by M. Elizabeth C. Bartlet and Raymond La Charité.

[3] Léon Halévy, *F. Halévy: Sa Vie et ses oeuvres*, 2d ed. (Paris: Heugel et Cie, 1863), 26: "d'entraînement et de passion . . . dans un état de fébrile anxiété."

in the theatre as in the novels of Sir Walter Scott, Victor Hugo, and Alexandre Dumas. Scribe's setting evoked scenes of visual splendor and ceremonial pomp significant to the new genre of *grand opéra*. But in his choice of a religious convocation, the inclusion of the historical figure Cardinal Jean-François Brogni, and a concluding *auto-da-fé* called for by the Church Council, Scribe was venturing into a provocative dramatic arena. The incorporation of religion, especially Catholicism, into French theatre, although not unprecedented, remained controversial.

Scribe again touched on popular trends in his partial modeling of the central Jewish characters of *La Juive*, Eléazar and Rachel, on the literary stereotypes of the mercenary, persecuted Shylock and his beautiful daughter. These stock types were known in France, particularly by contemporary writers, through editions and performances of Shakespeare, as well as through recastings in such popular works as Scott's *Ivanhoe* – one of the most widely read novels in France in the later 1820s. Like Scott's characterization of Rebecca, Rachel carries elements of exoticism that fascinated early nineteenth-century readers and audiences. Yet the librettist's choice to feature Jewish characters in a large theatrical work during one of the most significant periods in modern Jewish history in France – beginning with the granting of civil rights to French Jews shortly after the Revolution of 1789 and continuing with the establishment of a new legal equality after the Revolution of 1830 – suggests a historical immediacy of social and political import.

The Jewish–Christian amalgam of *La Juive* raises a number of interesting questions, particularly in light of the fact that Scribe was renowned for his adeptness at capturing public opinion and taste in his works. Moreover, as many scholars have determined, French *grands opéras* in essence melded art and politics, serving as vehicles for social and political critique and captivating audiences with the topical resonance of their subjects.[4] The strength of *grand opéra* hinged on

---

[4] See William L. Crosten, *French Grand Opera: An Art and a Business* (New York: King's Crown Press, 1948); Jane F. Fulcher, *The Nation's Image: French Grand Opera as Politics and Politicized Art* (Cambridge: Cambridge University Press, 1987). Fulcher emphasizes the political bases of *grand opéra* subjects in relation to the

the manner in which it addressed controversial issues or "powerful historical interests," as Véron described in his memoirs.[5] With these ideas in mind, *La Juive* promises strong connections to the social, political, and religious contexts of one of the most fascinating historical periods in France – the July Monarchy.[6]

government that subsidized the Académie royale de musique. See also her articles "French Grand Opera and the Quest for a National Image: An Approach to the Study of Government-Sponsored Art," *Current Musicology* 35 (1983): 34–45, and "Meyerbeer and the Music of Society," *Musical Quarterly* 67, no. 2 (April 1981): 213–29. Carl Dahlhaus, in *Nineteenth-Century Music*, trans. J. Bradford Robinson (Berkeley, Los Angeles: University of California Press, 1989), 114–15, states that the *Zeitgeist* of the era of *grand opéra* called for a "fusion of art and politics" and refers to Meyerbeer's *Les Huguenots* and *Le Prophète* as "musicopolitical concoction[s]." M. Elizabeth C. Bartlet generally refers to the genre's use of provocative subjects in "Grand opéra," in *The New Grove Dictionary of Opera*, ed. Stanley Sadie, 4 vols. (London: Macmillan, 1992), vol. II, 512–14. See also the forthcoming *Cambridge Companion to Grand Opera*, ed. David Charlton; Sieghart Döhring and Sabine Henze-Döhring, *Oper und Musikdrama im 19. Jahrhundert* (Laaber: Laaber-Verlag, 1997); Anselm Gerhard, *Die Verstädterung der Oper: Paris und das Musiktheater des 19. Jahrhunderts* (Stuttgart: J. B. Metzler, 1992), and its translation, *The Urbanization of Opera: Music Theater in Paris in the Nineteenth Century*, trans. Mary Whittall (Chicago and London: The University of Chicago Press, 1998); Rey M. Longyear, "Political and Social Criticism in French Opera, 1827–1920," in *Essays on Bach and Other Matters: A Tribute to Gerhard Herz*, ed. Robert L. Weaver (Louisville, KY: University of Kentucky Press, 1981), 245–54; Sonia Slatin, "Opera and Revolution: 'La Muette de Portici' and the Belgian Revolution of 1830 Revisited," *Journal of Musicological Research* 3 (1979): 45–62; and other publications listed in Anselm Gerhard, "Die französische 'Grand Opéra' in der Forschung seit 1945," *Acta musicologica* 59, no. 3 (1987): 220–70.

[5] Louis Véron, *Mémoires d'un bourgeois de Paris comprenant la fin de l'empire, la restauration, la monarchie de juillet, la république, jusqu'au rétablissement de l'empire*, 6 vols. (Paris: Libraire Nouvelle, 1856–7), vol. III, 181.

[6] Brief discussions of *La Juive*'s social relevance are offered by Crosten, *French Grand Opera*, and Fulcher, *The Nation's Image*. Also see Karl Leich-Galland, "*La Juive*: Commentaire musical et littéraire," *L'Avant-scène opéra* 100 (July 1987): 32–87; Hélène Pierrakos, "Chrétienté, judaïté et la musique," *L'Avant-scène opéra* 100 (July 1987): 20–23; Leich-Galland's introduction to Eugène Scribe, *La Juive: Opéra en cinq actes d'Eugène Scribe, musique de Fromental Halévy*, ed. Marthe Galland (Saarbrücken: Musik-Edition Lucie Galland, 1990), viii, and his essay, "'Scheut Ihr die Erinnerung?' Zur Wirkung von Halévy's *La Juive*," in *Halévy: La Juive*, program booklet for the 1999/2000 production of *La Juive* at the Vienna Staatsoper, 19–26; Alexander Gruber, "Gang der Handlung," in *Halévy, Die Jüdin*, program booklet for the 1989/90 production of *La Juive* by Bühnen der Stadt Bielefeld, ed. Heiner Bruns (Bielefeld: Kramer Druck, 1989), 16–29.

The political and philosophical liberalism that defines this era, particularly in its idealized revolutionary beginnings, emerges strongly in the subject of *La Juive*. At its core lies the polemic, central to French thought since the eighteenth century, between the principles of individual liberty and human rights and the principle of traditional authority – namely, authority emblematic of the absolutist *ancien régime*, Restoration monarchies, and the Catholic Church inextricably linked to them. Although metaphors of authority are treated ambiguously, the opera serves primarily as a critique of the intolerance and despotism of political and religious institutions – Voltairean themes that were espoused anew by a young, reform-minded generation generally opposed to the Bourbon monarchies of Louis XVIII and Charles X and supportive of the July Revolution and, at least initially, the Orléanist regime of Louis-Philippe.

This liberal, Voltairean critique inspires the opera's religious conflict, its setting at the Council of Constance, its concluding *auto-da-fé*, and – integral to the commentary – its use of Jewish characters as symbols of oppression. Echoing anticlerical sentiments that intensified during the Restoration after 1825, incited by a series of actions by ultraroyalists (extremely right-wing royalists), the opera most strongly illustrates and condemns the intolerance and abuse of power of the Catholic Church and political factions supportive of the Church. Without undermining its anticlerical slant, the opera moves somewhat beyond a tale of Christian oppressors and victimized Jews to a more universal, ambiguously told story. In the Voltairean tradition, the opera aims its criticism at any political or religious group that is unwilling to accept others with different beliefs and philosophies, including the Jews: in the language of the day, it points out the errors of the *fanatique* and of institutionalized fanaticism.

The opera's early reception in Paris points to its ideological stance. A review of the première in the legitimist paper *La Gazette de France* labeled it a "truly little masterpiece in the Voltairean genre" and an anachronistic example "of the most well-honed Voltairean philosophy."[7] This basis appears more concrete if the opera's setting is viewed

---

[7] *Fromental Halévy, "La Juive": Dossier de presse parisienne (1835)*, ed. Karl Leich-Galland (Saarbrücken: Musik-Edition Lucie Galland, 1987), 50. *La Gazette*

in light of the philosopher's own historical account of the Council of Constance in his widely published *Essai sur les moeurs et l'esprit des nations*.[8] In his narrative, Voltaire rebukes the Council's execution of the religious reformers Jan Hus (or Huss) and Jerome of Prague – whom he portrays as independent, rational thinkers – as well as the endorsement of this action by political authority. The Council of *La Juive*, rather than burning at the stake these real-life "heretic" reformers, condemns to death the "heretic" *juif* and *juive*.

The opera's anticlericalism resonates with other dramatic treatments of Catholic symbols and clergy in the early 1830s that carried political overtones, often serving as criticism of the power of the Church and pro-Church regimes. Many depictions were overtly unflattering and, in the minds of some, profane. Shortly after the banning of theatrical censorship by the Charte (Constitutional Charter) of 1830, villainous, murderous, and licentious Church figures began to appear in anticlerical satires such as *Le Mariage du capucin*, *Le Jésuite*, and *Le Te Deum et le tocsin*. In a similar vein, Scribe and Meyerbeer's *Robert le diable* smacks of sacrilege in the dancing of "debauched nuns." By comparison, *La Juive* presented a milder form of anticlericalism.

Voltairean interpretations and ideals fundamental to the work are further underscored by Scribe's parallel use of another Enlightenment symbol of religious and political tyranny in Meyerbeer's *Les Huguenots*, the Paris Opéra's new production of the following year (1836). Featured in its background and foreground is Saint-Barthélemy, or Saint Bartholomew's Eve, a sensational event of French history in which thousands of Huguenots were massacred by Catholic forces in 1572. This event had long served as a storm center of religious polemics and political theories, but Voltaire and other Enlightenment thinkers enhanced its mythological status in the eighteenth century.

backed the cause of legitimists (*légitimistes*), supporters of legitimism, a political movement devoted to returning the older branch of the Bourbon dynasty to the throne after its 1830 overthrow.

[8] François-Marie Arouet de Voltaire, *Oeuvres complètes de Voltaire*, 11 vols. (Paris: Chez Th. Desoer Libraire, 1817), vol. IV, 411–22.

Liberal voices of the 1820s and 1830s followed suit, adopting Voltaire's use of Saint-Barthélemy (in *Essai sur les guerres civiles de France*) to denounce the intolerance of the Catholic Church or the French Catholic monarchy. In the appropriation of Saint-Barthélemy and the Council of Constance, Voltairean mythology was realized by Scribe, Halévy, and Meyerbeer on the stage of the Paris Opéra.

The portrayal of Jewish intolerance in *La Juive*, as embodied in the character Eléazar, might ironically be linked to a cultural bias inherited from Enlightenment thinkers. In contrast to the symbolism of Semitic persecution and in contradiction to their calls for religious openmindedness, the French *philosophes* exhibited a harsh skepticism about Jews and Judaism. According to Jay Berkovitz, such attitudes were influenced by English Deists, whose academic analyses reflected the belief that Jews were superstitious, barbaric, fanatical, and, therefore, deserving of denigration.[9] The *philosophes*, particularly Voltaire, took the Deist invectives and pronouncements on early Judaism to another level, linking the ancient Hebrews more explicitly with contemporary Jews through character traits deemed permanent and unchanging. They harshly criticized the Talmud as a source of Jewish superstition and immorality and the rabbinic tradition as a hindrance to a much-needed intellectual, religious, or social reform of Jews. Montesquieu, despite his endorsement of biblical Judaism and his active denunciation of the Spanish Inquisition and other examples of religious persecution, criticized rabbinic Judaism as detrimental to Jewish character.[10] The belief that Jews and the Jewish religion were "morally deficient" lay at the foundation of Abbé Grégoire's influential late eighteenth-century *Essai sur la régénération physique, morale et politique des juifs*, which argued for Jewish civil rights and equality as the first steps toward *régénération*. Influenced by Montesquieu, Grégoire believed that Jews were not to be blamed for their perceived deficiencies, since these had developed in response to environments over

---

[9] Jay R. Berkovitz, *The Shaping of Jewish Identity in Nineteenth-Century France* (Detroit: Wayne State University Press, 1989), 34.

[10] Ibid., 35–6, 255, n. 36; Pierre Auberry, "Montesquieu et les Juifs," *Studies on Voltaire and the Eighteenth Century* 87 (1972): 87–99.

which they had no control.[11] Although interlaced with paradox, the arguments of the *philosophes* helped to bring about the "emancipation" of French Jews in 1791.

In a wide historical framework, the opera's presentation of Jewish elements – the characterizations of Eléazar and Rachel, the depiction of a Passover service, the religious confrontations, and the death sentences of the Jews – touches on the age-old conflict between the Christian and Jewish faiths. (Ernest Newman identified the central theme as "the eternal antagonism of Christian and Jew."[12]) This conflict, although set in a distant age, also bears on contemporary religious tensions and debates, and offers insight into attitudes toward and within French Jewish communities, exposing antisemitic strands of thought woven through the liberalism of this era. Following the granting of basic civil rights to French Jews, and a series of subsequent measures both positive and restrictive during the Empire and Restoration, the era of the "Citizen-King" Louis-Philippe brought about a significant change in the status of the Jewish community that was tied to ideals of political and religious freedom promoted by the early Monarchy, as well as to its official position toward the Catholic Church. Some historians have recognized the July Monarchy as the first period of absolute legal equality for French Jews, evidenced by a modification in the government's stance toward Judaism. Although the promise of religious freedom found in Article 5 of the 1830 Charte had already appeared in the 1814 Charte (also Article 5), the succinct declaration of Catholicism as the religion of state in the earlier document (Article 6) was removed. As one governmental spokesman proclaimed, with this omission "the state ceased to be identified with the Catholic religion."[13] Instead, the 1830 Charte specifies a commitment understood in Article 6 of the

---

[11] Berkovitz, *Jewish Identity*, 30–31.

[12] Ernest Newman, *More Stories of Famous Operas* (New York: Alfred A. Knopf, 1968), 323.

[13] *Archives parlementaires de 1787 à 1860: Recueil complet des débats législatifs et politiques des chambres françaises, seconde série*, ed. J. Mavidal and M. E. Laurent (Paris: Société d'Imprimerie et librairie administrative / Paul Dupont, 1887), vol. LXV, 313.

1814 Charte – that of governmental subsidy for priests of the Catholic religion "professed by the majority of French people." A law of 8 February 1831, however, extended governmental support to rabbis, or "les ministres du culte israélite," who would receive stipends (though not full salaries) from the "trésor public" (public revenues). Along with this legal signifying of religious acceptance came a stronger presence of Jews in French institutions and in positions of social and political prominence. Notables included Max Cerf-Berr, Adolphe Crémieux, and Achille Fould, deputies of France, Gustave Halphen, *consul-général* of Turkey in Paris, and Jacques Javal, member of the Conseil général des manufactures. Halévy's election to the Académie des beaux-arts figured in this new distinction.

The debates surrounding the passage of the 1831 law in the governmental houses, the Chambre des députés and Chambre des pairs, touch on questions that seem encapsulated in *La Juive*: questions about the meaning and extent of religious freedom, associations between the Catholic Church and the state, governmental tolerance and protection of religions other than Catholicism, and the social integration of Jews and Christians in France. In proposing the law, Joseph Mérilhou, the Ministre de l'Instruction publique et des cultes who had worked to suppress the law of sacrilege and the extremely clerical Société des missions de France, reminded his colleagues of the indignity of retaining the "rust of the Middle Ages" in an "enlightened century" and appealed to them: "Let us erase these distinctions that exist between our neighbors, let us erase these last vestiges of an oppression that must never be reborn, and let us ensure that in France there are only French citizens, rather than *religionnaires* divided by their religion."[14]

[14] *Ibid.*, 317: "Effaçons ces distinctions qui existent encore chez les peuples nos voisins, effaçons ces derniers vestiges d'une oppression qui ne doit plus renaître, et faisons qu'il n'y ait en France que des Français citoyens, et nullement des religionnaires divisés par leur culte." During the Restoration, Mérilhou belonged to the Carbonari, a radically oppositional society, acted as defense counsel for *Le Courrier français* and individual authors accused of sacrilege by the government, and played an instrumental role in organizing the resistance to Charles X's *ordonnances* (see pp. 18 and 50 below).

Another supporter cited the law as a consecration of "the great principle of tolerance" that would mark not only "the progress of public reason," but also the advancement of the principle established by the 1789 Revolution and Assemblée constituante; through this law, the Revolution and government of 1830 would *protect all religions* from intolerance.[15] Although the majority agreed with him through their votes of passage, those who opposed argued that citizens should not be asked to pay for such governmental subsidy, that it would be insulting to rabbis, and that it would result in hatred of the government within both "enlightened" and "unenlightened" regions; some argued that, despite past governmental efforts, no alliance between *les juifs* and *les chrétiens* existed in France, and to reward Jews for being true French citizens when most were not was inappropriate. These polemical voices, including those in the forum of the press, speak in *La Juive*: the theocratic, the reactionary, the liberal and *philosophe*-inspired. But it is the overruling voices that dominate the opera's critique, endorsing the government's stance that society should be swayed not by the power of tradition but by the principles of religious, and political, tolerance and freedom.

Social fears and prejudices revealed or referred to in these debates and period writings illustrate that, despite legal and social advances, antisemitism existed in overt and latent forms in the early July Monarchy. Although most French Jews lived in modest or even impoverished conditions, old, suppressed anxieties about Jewish usury resurfaced as the financial clout of Baron James de Rothschild (1792–1868) and other banking notables grew more powerful. With the partial decline of aristocratic and clerical power and the rise of bourgeois elites after the Revolution of 1830, concerns about the consequences of unchecked capitalism and industrialization often took the form of accusations against Jewish (as well as Protestant) bankers, manufacturers, and merchants. By the 1840s, an "anti-capitalist antisemitism," as defined by historian Roger Berg, had clearly emerged.[16]

---

[15] M. Vaucelles, *ibid.*, 318.
[16] Roger Berg, *Histoire des juifs à Paris de Chilpéric à Jacques Chirac* (Paris: Les Editions du Cerf, 1997), 155.

Adding to the opera's topicality are the conflicts about national-religious identity within Jewish communities themselves that continued unresolved from earlier decades. Liberal, socially progressive Jews, many of whom were the first generation to benefit from education in the nation's *lycées* and universities, pressed for full integration into the French Christian world, while seeking ways to make their heritage and new identity compatible. Calling themselves *israélites* to signify a changed identity and to rid themselves of the prejudices attached to the term *juif*, they believed in social reform as well as modifications to Judaic religious services; some called for the replacement of Hebrew with French, change of the Jewish Sabbath to Sunday, and modifications in worship. Orthodox Jews, who had once opposed emancipation for its threat to Jewish nationality, endorsed civil and military union with Christian citizens while still insisting on complete religious separation. They interpreted the reformers' appeals to replace Hebrew, for example, as sacrilegious, while some Reform Jews, adopting the views of their *philosophe* forbears, labeled Orthodox believers as fanatical *séparatistes*. Conversion or marriage outside the faith moved other French Jews even farther away from traditional Judaism.

These early nineteenth-century controversies bearing on the religious, political, and social merging of majority and minority communities with different histories, beliefs, and assumptions undoubtedly augmented the affective power of *La Juive*. The opera's Jewish characters are caught between political symbol, social projection, and literary stereotype, for they clearly correspond to images in literature but also to those depicted in non-fiction essays, caricatures, personal chronicles, and correspondence of the period. The complex and at times incongruent characterization of Eléazar particularly lurches between symbol and type. He appears as a somewhat miserly, vengeful *fanatique*, simultaneously touching the Shylock stereotype as well as the post-Enlightenment depiction of the Jew as oppressed pariah. His occupation as goldsmith-jeweller and his portrayed love of profit resonate with contemporary antisemitic portrayals of avaricious merchants and bankers. His struggle with Cardinal Brogni, as fathers of differing religions and competing fathers of the same daughter, alludes to longstanding doctrinal divergences as well as to the divided views about the status of Judaism as a religion more fully endorsed by the French state. Set against this struggle and the confrontations between Catholic crowds and Jewish characters, Eléazar's leading of a seder in Act II may be seen as an affirmation of Jewish presence in France and a dramatic allusion to the pro-Judaic law of 1831. Scribe's first thought of characterizing Eléazar as a rabbi makes the latter allusion even more probable, but with the retention of his name – that of a son of the biblical Aaron, of the line of Hebrew priests – the innuendo remains.

Contemporary ideas about Jewish identity are also embedded in Rachel's characterization: ideas of acculturation and assimilation, of *régénération* and *fusion*, that were actively being debated by Jewish and non-Jewish writers. Her dual religious identity manifests ambivalences that existed in both Christian and Jewish communities about the role of Jewish citizens within modern French society. Her romance, "betrothal," and near marriage to the Christian prince Léopold, although staple interactions of romantic opera, bear upon the question of Jewish assimilation, since Jewish–Christian intermarriage in early nineteenth-century France was sometimes viewed as a symbol of democracy. Her emotional leaning toward Cardinal Brogni and near-Christian identity (both stronger in Scribe's early plans for the work) subtly extend from the literary stereotype of the Shylockian daughter. In its broadest historical dimension, Rachel's religious duality is rooted in a centuries-old dilemma: as Ruth Jordan writes, "there had always been a conflict between loyalty to the ancient faith and the instinct to survive by embracing Christianity."[17] Yet more closely relevant to *La Juive* of 1835, her duality speaks to the efforts of French Jewish citizens to adapt to a state whose political and educational systems were still bound to Catholicism – despite the expanded governmental protection of Judaism – and to the greater acceptance of Jews who showed a willingness to assimilate.

As "la juive," Rachel carries literary and historical associations with the Western view of the Orient and Oriental Other, whether Muslim,

17 Ruth Jordan, *Fromental Halévy: His Life and Music, 1799–1862* (London: Kahn and Averill, 1994; New York: Proscenium Publishers, 1996), 46.

Ottoman, Arab, or Semite. Like Rebecca in *Ivanhoe,* her characterization belongs to a "virtual epidemic of Orientalia" that infected "every
major poet, essayist, and philosopher of the period" from approximately 1765 to 1850.[18] Victor Hugo, one writer touched by this "fever,"
observed: "In the century of Louis XIV, people were Hellenists, now
they are Orientalists."[19] Literary Orientalia or "Orientalism" ran parallel with a variety of attempts by western Europeans (primarily French
and British) to exert cultural dominance over the foreign, distant,
and exotic Orient. Edward Said, who generally defines Orientalism as
"a way of coming to terms with the Orient," explains that it encom-
passed and was affected by political conquests – from the Napoleonic
invasion of Egypt in 1798 to the French entry into Algeria in 1830
– scientific discoveries and codifications of the Orient, and a general
enthusiasm for anything Asiatic.[20]

Scribe's final choice of title, with its Orientalist inflection, actually
returns to a variant of "la belle juive," his idea in an early plot outline.
His conspicuous use of "juive," and its counterpart "juif," while calling attention to the romantic Jewish character, veers away from the
anticlericalism baldly suggested in *Rachel; ou, L'Auto-da-fé.* The use of
"israélite" would have been non-literary, perhaps, and anachronistic.
And to have highlighted Eléazar's centrality with such a title as "Le Juif
de Constance" – bearing a parallel to *Le Juif de Venise (The Merchant
of Venice)* – would have triggered even sharper connotations weighted
in the masculine form *juif.* One wonders whether the use of *juive* and
juif in title and libretto simply followed literary convention or every-
day language, or whether Scribe toyed with contemporary distinctions
between *juif* and *israélite.*

Significant to this study of the opera's multivalent meanings within
political and social contexts are the authors' own motivations and roles
as creators, or mediators, of this public art form. There are many who
would propose that these works are not personal expressions at all,

---

[18] Edward W. Said, *Orientalism* (New York: Vintage Books, 1979), 51, citing
Raymond Schwab, *La Renaissance orientale* (Paris: Payot, 1950).
[19] Said, *Orientalism*, 51, citing Hugo's *Oeuvres poétiques* ("Au siècle de Louis XIV on
était helléniste, maintenant on est orientaliste.").
[20] Said, *Orientalism*, 1, 42, 51.

only formulaic responses to "external" powers or forces. Borrowing the arguments of Jane Fulcher, in her provocative study *The Nation's Image: French Grand Opera as Politics and Politicized Art*, one could view Scribe, Halévy, and their collaborators primarily as "tools of the state," or as theatrical mouthpieces for Louis-Philippe, or the government-appointed administrative board of the Opéra. It is in fact clear that the authors responded in some way to the guidelines of the Commission de Surveillance, which functioned under the Ministre de l'Intérieur (the comte de Montalivet), despite the fact that this body carried no official censorship powers during the "years of liberty" (1831–5) in which theatrical censorship was banned.[21] One may also consider the influence of Louis Véron, *Directeur-Entrepreneur* of the Paris Opéra from 1831 to 1835, who, as William Crosten and others believe, helped to define this emerging genre through approval of works, artistic suggestions, and powerful leadership; Véron himself stated his resolute intentions to entertain the "victorious bourgeoisie" of the July Revolution.[22] Carl Dahlhaus writes that Véron held "astonishingly precise visions of the 'Gesamtkunstwerk' whose spectacular success he calculated."[23] If one adopts Crosten's view of the Opéra of this era as primarily a capitalistic enterprise, as well as Anselm Gerhard's emphasis on librettists and composers as capitalistic creators of artistic products, the authors might be seen as opportunists responding to public interests.[24] Adding to the complexities of such a genre – this "new synthesis of theatrical arts" as Pendle and Wilkins write – are the creative contributions of artists other than librettist and composer: taking the most expansive look involves examining the collaborations of *metteur en scène*, set designer, painters, machinists, choreographer, singers, dancers, conductor, and others important to the realization of

---

[21] Fulcher, *The Nation's Image*, 2.
[22] Crosten, *French Grand Opera*, 2; Véron, *Mémoires*, vol. III, 171.
[23] Dahlhaus, *Nineteenth-Century Music*, 125. Echoing Crosten further, Dahlhaus designates the scene designer's role as crucial to the artistic whole, stating that "the decorative displays of splendor and pomp ... of Duponchel's stage machinery were intimately connected with the dramaturgical core of a pictorial genre such as grand opera" (126).
[24] Gerhard, *The Urbanization of Opera*, 36–40.

grand opéra.[25] Not all influences came from behind or on the stage: the forces of the Parisian press and audiences at times affected a work's shape (indeed, cuts made in *La Juive* following its première may have been encouraged by several sharp critical responses and perhaps hints of flagging interest in the theatre). Without doubt, the fullest truths can be gained through a consideration of, and negotiation between, the responsibilities and motivations of many contributors and the effects of a range of forces on the creative work.

While acknowledging the complexity of opera creation, and agreeing with many scholars that notions of "work" and "authority" in *grand opéra* should continue to expand beyond those consistently used, I approach this study with the more traditional centering on librettist and composer as the primary determiners of the basic meanings of their opera, despite the vastly different strategies and exceptions represented throughout the century. My interpretations will focus on the authorship of Scribe and Halévy, along with two others of the creative team (to be mentioned below), but not with the intention of excluding other collaborators. Other interpretations may follow, enrich, and undoubtedly challenge what I am setting out here. While I believe these authors were indeed influenced by external forces, I do not view them as mindless and valueless manipulators of public taste or governmental values. Particularly in this moment of comparatively laissez-faire administrative supervision, the creative artists likely played a greater role in developing works that complied with their own philosophies. Undoubtedly Scribe, Halévy, and other artists adapted their work to fit

---

[25] See Karin Pendle and Stephen Wilkins, "Paradise Found: The Salle le Peletier and French Grand Opera," in *Opera in Context: Essays on Historical Staging from the Late Renaissance to the Time of Puccini*, ed. Mark A. Radice (Portland: Amadeus Press, 1998), 171–2. The authors note, for example, that it was *metteur en scène* Duponchel who proposed the cloister scene of *Robert le diable* (183). See also Mark Everist, "Giacomo Meyerbeer, the Théâtre Royal de l'Odéon, and Music Drama in Restoration Paris," *Nineteenth-Century Music* 17, no. 2 (fall 1993): 125; and the new interpretations of *grand opéra* in Maribeth Clark, "Understanding French Grand Opera through Dance" (Ph.D. diss., University of Pennsylvania, 1998), and Cormac Newark, "Staging Grand Opéra: History and the Imagination in Nineteenth-Century Paris" (Ph.D. diss., University of Oxford, 1999).

the overt or unspoken expectations of the director, Opéra Commission and the government it represented, the audiences, and the press, but, as I will argue, they were also guided by their own beliefs, attitudes, and responses to a changing sociopolitical milieu.

If one accepts the general, but narrow, view of Scribe as a predominantly commercial, apolitical dramatist and librettist, it would follow that he originated the subject of *La Juive* solely to exploit the government in power or the interests of the public for his own monetary gain. Scribe's success under different regimes as well as his own testimony seem to lend weight to the supposition of political indifference, yet contradictory biographical statements, personal associations, and recurring themes in many works suggest an affinity with the ideology behind the libretto of *La Juive*. Although Scribe did not participate in the Revolution of 1830 and commented on his dislike of governmental upheaval, he believed strongly in the democratic principle of individual liberty, as illustrated in his battles for authorial freedom and control. Themes and symbols of religious intolerance and anticlerical diatribes recur in travel journals of the late 1820s, and, from his early years as a Restoration dramatist, Scribe revealed his alignment to Voltairean principles and never wavered from calling himself a "liberal." What he meant by this label is difficult to pinpoint, however.

The terms "liberal" and "liberalism" carry a range of contemporary meanings, and historians disagree on their interpretation as they do with the equally vague terms "bourgeois" and "bourgeoisie." These terms are often intertwined in assessments of this period, with the 1830 Revolution seen as a triumph of liberal ideals as well as a triumph of the bourgeoisie. With the betrayal of or backing away from central liberal principles – freedom of thought, speech, press, religion, individual equality, and legal protection of individuals – by Louis-Philippe and by some members of the bourgeoisie, many historians have come to view the July Monarchy as a facade of liberalism and the bourgeoisie as exploiters of the Revolution to serve their own capitalistic ends. Christopher Greene notes that the Monarchy has routinely been maligned as "a materialistic, unprincipled and socially repressive regime dominated by financial elites who justified their self-interest with the rhetoric of individual liberalism."[26] Most often the dominant liberalism of this era is defined in terms of *le juste milieu* (the happy medium), promoted by Louis-Philippe as a middle ground between "the tyrannical despotism of sovereigns" and "the despotism of the multitude" and linked with an aversion to political conflict.[27] One might speak of this brand of liberalism as centrist, conservative, or bourgeois. Other forms leaned farther to the left, more strongly infused with republican, Jacobin, and revolutionary ideals.

Scribe's liberal identity most likely fits under the general label of bourgeois liberalism of *le juste milieu*, but, in my view, he held more strongly to the liberal articles of faith than many interpreters allow. In fundamental ideology, Scribe found a cohort in his collaborator Fromental Halévy, as well as in two contributors to the opera's developing text: Léon Halévy (1802–83), the composer's brother and "soulmate," who revised the libretto as the composer wrote the score, and Adolphe Nourrit (1802–39), the tenor who not only created the role of Eléazar, but reworked the text of his character's central aria and developed the opera's *mise en scène*.[28] While the contributions of Léon Halévy and Nourrit are documented primarily through first- and second-hand accounts, an exploration of their roles appears crucial. As his brother's confidant, contributor to the opera, and writer and voice of his generation, Léon especially helps penetrate the composer's mind and world; one senses that he is an Aaron to his brother's Moses as he articulates beliefs and ideals seemingly shared by both. An examination

[26] Christopher Greene, "Romanticism, Cultural Nationalism and Politics in the July Monarchy: The Contribution of Ludovic Vitet," *French History* 4, no. 4 (December 1990): 487.

[27] Gerhard, *The Urbanization of Opera*, 213–14.

[28] Nourrit was among the most influential performers at the Paris Opéra during this period. In addition to creating the role of Eléazar, he introduced Masaniello (*La Muette de Portici*, 1828), Arnold (*Guillaume Tell*, 1829), Robert (*Robert le diable*, 1831), and Raoul (*Les Huguenots*, 1836). Because Halévy, Auber, and Meyerbeer continued the practice of adapting their lyrical writing to suit the skills and preferences of individual singers, Nourrit affected both the composition and the interpretation of roles created for him. But he went a step further by directly contributing to the libretti, music, and staging of a number of operas other than *La Juive*.

of the philosophies and attitudes of these collaborators, particularly those of the principal authors, reveals a profound correspondence between them and the work that was realized on the stage of the Paris Opéra in 1835. Although with varied nuances, all of these artists held to the liberal, humanist, democratic principles that had gained renewed strength in opposition to the Restoration. As Scribe, the Halévys, and Nourrit matured, they witnessed first-hand the repressive measures of the Bourbon governments and clergy, including the suspension of the popular lecturer Victor Cousin from the Sorbonne for views deemed threatening by Louis XVIII's regime, attempted prosecutions of the liberal papers *Le Courrier français* and *Le Constitutionnel* for their attacks on religion, clerical refusal of burial to liberals or Jansenists, proposals to revoke the guarantee of religious freedom and impose a sacrilege law that threatened the death penalty, and, finally, Charles X's fateful suspension of the Chambre des députés in July 1830.[29] Although there were a number of articulate young men of their generation who exhibited royalist leanings and sentimental views on religion during this decade prior to the appearance of *La Juive*, the most influential voices opposed clerical control of government and supported a society built on Enlightenment rationalism and the principles of equality, justice, and freedom inherited from the 1789 Revolution. They saw the Restoration as a step backward and the Revolution of 1830 as a turn toward a more just, inclusive society.

The Halévys, who were among the first generation of French Jews born after the granting of Jewish citizenship, viewed conservative, clerical regimes as naturally antagonistic to the civil liberties of Jews and other individuals whose intellectual and religious beliefs stood outside French traditional culture. Like their father, who saw the benefits of supporting the government in power, both were admirers of Napoleon for his role in the expansion of Jewish civil rights, despite his flagrant, contradictory attacks on Jewish communities. Both were supporters of the Revolution of 1830 and wrote works honoring the days of July, but

---

[29] See discussions in Alan B. Spitzer, *The French Generation of 1820* (Princeton: Princeton University Press, 1987), and David H. Pinkney, *The French Revolution of 1830* (Princeton: Princeton University Press, 1972).

their concerns for reform led them away from the bourgeois liberalism of Scribe toward views more progressive and republican.

A politically active early follower of Saint-Simon (Claude-Henri de Rouvroy, comte de Saint-Simon, 1760–1825), Léon Halévy penned numerous essays and dramas imbued with reformist, Saint-Simonian ideals, even after he had formally split from the movement in the late 1820s over philosophical differences. With a variety of approaches, Halévy attacked intolerance, narrow-mindedness, and oppression in French society of the past and present and lauded the intellectual vision and progressive ideas of the eighteenth-century *philosophes*, Saint-Simon, and early reformers. While we cannot assume a total alignment of thought between Fromental and Léon, their lifelong intimacy, mutual friends and associates, and operatic collaborations point to an artistic, intellectual, and political solidarity.[30] Reputedly, Fromental enthusiastically participated in the early Saint-Simonian circle.

Both the Revolution of 1830 and the Saint-Simonian movement loomed large in Nourrit's short, ill-fated life. (He committed suicide two years after his unhappy departure from the Paris Opéra in 1837.) As Halévy himself recounted, Nourrit was more than a passive supporter of the Revolution; after having played revolutionary heroes on the stage, he realized a similar role in the streets of Paris, marching at the head of a company with sword in hand and running from theatre to theatre leading crowds in passionate renderings of patriotic songs.[31] Nourrit's blending of theatrical and social roles actualized a belief in the mission of artists as leaders in social reform that was espoused by Saint-Simonians – including the singer. The Halévys shared and articulated this belief, in conjunction with ideas about the power of the theatre as a forum for ameliorating society.

[30] See correspondence from Fromental to Léon in the Pierpont Morgan Library, Koch 681 (Box 98, Folder 1), this and other correspondence transcribed in Marthe Galland's *Fromental Halévy: Lettres*, Léon's biography of his brother, *F. Halévy: Sa Vie et ses oeuvres*, and his tribute, *Hommage à F. Halévy: Intermède lyrique exécuté sur le théâtre impérial de l'Opéra-comique, le 27 mai 1864, pour l'anniversaire de la naissance d'Halévy* (Paris: Heugel et Cie, 1864).

[31] Halévy, *Derniers Souvenirs*, 155–7.

In response to the Jewish elements of the opera, the composer, along with his brother, most likely bore the strongest personal feelings among the collaborators. The excitement about Scribe's initial ideas that fueled Halévy's work on the score undoubtedly extended in part from an eagerness to treat these aspects of subject, setting, and characterization. And he did not stay removed from "Jewish subjects" after *La Juive* – but devoted himself to two other operas directly or indirectly linked to Jewish history or myth. Although the strength of Halévy's ties to his Jewish heritage has been questioned, like many liberal French Jews of his time he was both drawn to and repulsed by traditional Judaic practices. While he respected Judaic devotion and gravitated toward the synagogue and the Talmudic teachings of his father, Elie Halévy, he later made clear statements about his distrust of Orthodoxy and rabbinic wisdom. The composer's own conflicted Jewish identity and his relationship with his co-religionists undoubtedly influenced the treatment of the opera's characters and dramatic development. An empathy with Jewish persecution, conceivably colored by his own suffering, seems to permeate his intense musical realization of the vicious Christian attacks on Rachel and Eléazar. Likely, too, is the effect that the composer's sensitivity about Jewish maltreatment may have had on the deletion of overt passages showing Jewish greed and anti-Jewish contempt in the opera's genesis. Other changes strengthening the opera's commentary on religion suggest his input or at least endorsement, and his setting of the Act II Passover scene appears informed by a basic knowledge of Judaic practice, easily obtained through his father's teachings or early experiences.

The composer's ambivalence about his heritage comes through most strongly in his approach to Eléazar as both character and symbol. While he writes music passionately evoking the love Eléazar feels toward his faith and his daughter, the composer later refers to him as a "Juif fanatique."[32] In this reference he reveals a certain aversion to the old image of the socially separate Jew that was clearly articulated by his brother in two publications on Jewish history of the late 1820s. In these historical studies Léon Halévy not only advocates assimilation

[32] *Ibid.*, 168.

but makes strong statements about Jewish fanaticism and superstition that reflect the mistrust of traditional Judaism expressed by eighteenth-century *philosophes*, as well as by many Reform Jews.

Unlike their counterparts in the twentieth century, writers and musicians of the nineteenth century generally viewed *La Juive* as a "Jewish opera" – for better or worse – with some recognizing a certain ethnic aura as well as personal connections of the composer to its subject. In 1845 Philarète Chasles referred to it as "the Jewish symbol of the nineteenth century."[33] Charles-Ernest Beulé, in eulogizing the composer at his death, spoke of the "religious and oriental color of biblical gravity" of the Passover scene that transported one "beneath the tents erected at the foot of Sinai."[34] Wagner, who held a lifelong admiration for the work and its composer despite his well-chronicled antisemitism, found such power and purity of expression in the opera that he believed that "a sort of fatality led the artist's footsteps to this 'book,' predestined to incite him to employment of his every force." Through it Halévy found his musical-dramatic destiny as he tapped into "the inmost and most puissant depths of human nature." Wagner writes: "I speak of that faculty of strong emotion, incisive and profound, quickening and convulsing the moral world of every age. 'Tis it that constitutes the magic element in this score of *La Juive*, the source whence spring alike the fanaticism of Eléazar – that rage so fierce and sombre, yet sending forth at times such blinding flames – and the dolorous love that consumes the heart of Rachel."[35] As noted by Cosima Wagner in her diary on 25 May 1875, she, and presumably her husband, thought of the opera as a *Judenoper*: "In the evening he takes up *La Juive*, pleasure in the great style of this work – a quite different use of Jewish sounds from that in present-day Jewish operas (*Die Maccabäer*, *Die Königin von Saba*)."[36]

---

[33] Leich-Galland, "'Scheut Ihr die Erinnerung?,'" 25.

[34] Charles-Ernest Beulé, "Eloge de F. Halévy à l'Institut de France," *Les Archives israélites* 23, no. 2 (November 1862): 643.

[35] *Wagner: Prose Works*, trans. W. A. Ellis (New York: Broude Bros., 1969), vol. VIII, 179–80.

[36] *Cosima Wagner's Diaries*, ed. Martin Gregor-Dellin and Dietrich Mack, trans. Geoffrey Skelton, 2 vols. (New York and London: Harcourt Brace Jovanovich, 1978–[80]), vol. I (1869–77), 848.

Twentieth-century interpreters have generally disagreed with Beulé and Wagner, with some emphasizing Halévy's religious indifference or lack of responsibility in originating subject, plot, and characterization, while others categorize the opera's Jewish elements solely as local color or twists on a fundamentally conventional plot. Although John Klein in the *Musical Times* praises Halévy for his creation of "a genuinely Jewish atmosphere, a remarkable feat in 1835" (in the Passover scene), a more common assessment is that of Mina Curtiss.[37] In her 1953 article on Halévy in the *Musical Quarterly*, Curtiss concludes that the religious conflict represents a stock operatic situation irrevelant to Halévy's identity, stating that the composer "seems either to have lacked or evaded any awareness of his inheritance, either social or religious."[38] While avoiding such a bald conclusion, Cormac Newark warns that "defining a Jewish composer only, or even principally, in terms of his Jewishness would be precisely the kind of racial essentialism *La Juive* calls into question."[39] Among the few studies of the last several decades to accept a strong, though clouded, connection between the composer's Jewish identity and his creation of *La Juive* are the dissertation on which the present book is based and Jordan's recent biography of Halévy.[40] Leich-Galland, who has spoken insightfully on

[37] John William Klein, "Halévy's *La Juive*," *Musical Times* 114, no. 1560 (February 1973): 141. Klein (140) views Halévy's ethnicity as a source of inspiration, particularly "the theme of racial persecution which appealed to some secret spring in Halévy's own complex nature."

[38] Mina Curtiss, "Fromental Halévy," *Musical Quarterly* 39 (1953): 197. See also her biography on Halévy's student and son-in-law, Georges Bizet, *Bizet and His World* (New York: Alfred A. Knopf, 1958). Hugh Macdonald echoes Curtiss's view in his brief entries "(Jacques-François-) Fromental [Fromentin] (-Elie) [-Elias] Halévy," in *The New Grove Dictionary of Music and Musicians*, ed. Stanley Sadie, 20 vols. (London: Macmillan, 1980), vol. VIII, 43–6, and "(Jacques-François) Fromental (-Elie) [Fromentin (-Elias)] Halévy," in *The New Grove Dictionary of Opera*, ed. Sadie, vol. II, 598–600. In "Grandest of the Grand," notes to the 1989 Philips recording of *La Juive* (CD 420 190–2), 20, Macdonald states that Halévy "had no strong awareness of his Jewish blood and sought to make no particular statement in setting 'La Juive.'"

[39] Cormac Newark, "Ceremony, Celebration and Spectacle in *La Juive*," in *Reading Critics Reading: Opera and Ballet Criticism in France from the Revolution to 1848*, ed. Roger Parker and Mary Ann Smart (Oxford: Oxford University Press, 2001), 174.

[40] Diana R. Hallman, "The French Grand Opera *La Juive* (1835): A Socio-Historical Study," 2 vols. (Ph.D. diss., City University of New York, 1995); Jordan, *Fromental*

the historical relevance of the opera's treatment of Judaism, makes a few statements linking this treatment to the composer's religious positions.[41]

In my search for fundamental meanings of La Juive within the early nineteenth century, I begin with a look at the pertinent biographies, working relationships, and ideologies of the primary authors and two significant collaborators, followed by chapters linking the opera to relevant literary, theatrical, and sociopolitical contexts of the July Monarchy. Through these contextualizations the rich significance of the opera's controversial and paradoxical messages will emerge from behind the mask of theatrical convention, exposing a powerful vehicle for social and political commentary. With the captivating language of grand opéra in its golden age – its mixture of poignancy and violent shocks in music and plot, the dramatic power and vocal beauty of its singer-actors, skillful dancers, opulent costumes, and awe-inspiring scenic-musical tableaux – the opera's messages were projected in an affecting theatrical synthesis.

As this exploration will reveal, the subject of La Juive reverberated with contemporary clashes in religious and political systems of belief. As it echoed Voltairean denunciations of religious and political intolerance, anticlericalism, and sympathy for Jewish persecution, the opera served as a theatrical realization of liberalism and a condemnation of symbols of theocratic regimes. Its alignment with the Monarchy's stated concerns for protection of religious and political freedom and expanded acceptance of Jews and Judaism within the state shows an allegiance to governmental values – or governmental symbols, as Fulcher would argue. At the same time, its Jewish characterization, while central to its sociopolitical critique, touched on the ambivalent, post-emancipation views of French society toward its Jewish citizens.

Halévy. Hans Ulrich Becker, "'Dieu de nos pères': Grosse Oper auf authentischem Hintergrund," in Halévy: La Juive, program booklet for the 1999/2000 production of La Juive at the Vienna Staatsoper, 36–42, links the composer's treatment of Jewish worship in the opera with Jewish traditions at Fürth (Bavaria), the birthplace of Halévy's father (see pp. 75 and 177 below).

[41] Leich-Galland, "La Juive: Commentaire musical et littéraire," 34; "Fromental Halévy et l'âge d'or de l'opéra français," in Entre le théâtre et l'histoire: La Famille Halévy (1760–1960), ed. Henri Loyrette (Paris: Librairie Arthème Fayard, 1996), 75.

The use of Jewish stereotypes in the midst of an ideologically liberal, anticlerical opera was not an anomaly, as attested in a variety of period writings, but a true reflection of contradictions within the society and in the minds of the work's authors. The assimilationist message embodied in the recasting of these stereotypes, that "unenlightened" Jewish practices were socially and politically destructive, reflected contradictions in the Voltairean philosophy undergirding its theme of intolerance. In its portrayal of Jewish–Christian antagonisms on the stage of the Paris Opéra, *La Juive* offered a vivid manifestation of the liberal ideology that inspired a second French revolution in 1830 as it embraced conflicts and paradoxes in the society and culture of the July Monarchy.

The collaboration and rapprochement of the authors of La Juive

EARLY NEGOTIATIONS AND ARTISTIC RELATIONSHIPS

As Halévy set about composing *La Juive* during the fall of 1833, he undoubtedly approached Scribe with a certain apprehension, for the dramatist and librettist held extraordinary power and was even known by some to be a "great tyrant" in musical collaborations of the previous decade.[1] Others viewed Scribe as an amiable, conciliatory collaborator. Without letters to trace composer–librettist exchanges during the genesis of *La Juive*,[2] few details of artistic interactions can be gleaned (music and libretto sources offer hard evidence of various stages of the opera's creation, but little about the balance of power or motivations for alterations). Basic facts about the early dealings and professional status of the primary authors suggest that the librettist wielded greater authority, at least at the beginning of the collaboration – but the picture is far from clear. Scribe's initial hesitancy in selecting Halévy to write the score, together with the composer's comparatively junior position, points to an imbalance of power: seemingly if any conciliation was called for, it would have been Halévy's place to acquiesce.

Among the produced works to the composer's credit were the opera semiseria *Clari* (1828), the ballet *Manon Lescaut* (1830), the *ballet-opéra*

[1] Louis Marie Quicherat, *Adolphe Nourrit: Sa Vie, son talent, son caractère, sa correspondance*, 3 vols. (Paris: L. Hachette, 1867), vol. I, 53.

[2] No letters have been found pertaining to the development of *La Juive*; none appears in archival collections viewed by this author, nor in Marthe Galland's *Fromental Halévy: Lettres*. It is possible that unseen, privately held letters contain pertinent clues (for example, one or two of the letters itemized in the "Fichier des lettres vendues," F-Pn, Mus., although the dates and annotations do not suggest relevancy), but just as likely that composer and librettist did not correspond while working in such close proximity. Furthermore, Halévy did not make notes directly onto libretto manuscripts, as Meyerbeer did, for example, on the *Huguenots* prose draft (F-Pn, Ms., n.a.fr. 22502, vol. XXIII, 2°:2°).

La Tentation (1832), and several *opéras comiques*, *Le Roi et le batelier* (1827), *L'Artisan* (1827), *Le Dilettante d'Avignon* (1829), *Attendre et courir* (1830), *La Langue musicale* (1830), *Les Souvenirs de Lafleur* (1833), and *Ludovic* (1833), which he partially wrote after it had been left incomplete by Ferdinand Hérold (1791–1833) at his death.[3] While his one clear success at this point was *Dilettante*, his completion of *Ludovic* and replacement of Hérold as *premier chef de chant* clearly enhanced his status at the Opéra. Halévy had in fact already worked with Scribe on *Manon Lescaut*, writing music to the ballet's dramatic plot developed by the librettist and Pierre Aumer. But with such a comparatively paltry record against Scribe's hundreds of dramas and operas, many of which were public triumphs, and with his prior contacts dictated by the subservience to librettists and composers built into his role as *chef*, it is hard to imagine a different artistic dynamic.

Halévy had eagerly negotiated for the "poem," soliciting the help of both director Véron and publisher Maurice Schlesinger (1798–1871), who wrote to Meyerbeer a few days before Scribe signed the Opéra contract on 25 August 1833 – a contract that stipulated payments and deadlines for completion of the libretto, but excluded the name of a composer.[4] (See the contract's transcription and translation in

---

[3] According to Léon Halévy, *Sa Vie*, 19, Hérold had written the overture and most of the first act of *Ludovic*; Halévy contributed a quartet to the first act and composed the entire second act. Mark Everist offered further detail of attribution in "Halévy, opéra comique et naissance d'une carrière," presented at the Colloque Halévy, Paris Conservatoire, 16 November 2000, and soon to be published. In these early works Halévy's collaborators included the librettists Jules-Henri Vernoy de Saint-Georges, P. F. A. Carmouche, de Courcy, and his brother, as well as the Italian poet P[ietro] Giannone on *Clari*, performed at the Théâtre-Italien. With others, he had written four early unproduced works, *Les Bohémiennes*, *Marco Curzio*, *Pygmalion*, *Les Deux Pavillons*, and an incomplete *Erostraste*.

[4] This exclusion suggests further that the composer had not been chosen by the time of the contract's signing, as many *traités* of the 1830s included composers' names. It is possible, however, that Halévy was already approved by 25 August but went unnamed because he was an Opéra employee. According to M. Elizabeth C. Bartlet, such an omission would represent a continuity of the practice of the 1820s, when composers with Opéra affiliations were rarely included in contracts (private communication). See Gerhard's comments on the comparative status of librettist and composer in these and later decades, *The Urbanization of Opera*, 36–7.

1 Portrait of Fromental Halévy (1799–1862) by Belliard (Cliché Musée de Carnavalet: © PMVP/Moser)

Appendix C and a rough chronology of the opera's stages of development in Appendix D.) Schlesinger alerted Meyerbeer, who seemed to be on the verge of returning the partial libretto that Scribe had sent him – most likely a detailed scenario and some draft verse – and gingerly reported Halévy's interest in securing it. In a letter of 21 August, Schlesinger tiptoes carefully as he mentions Halévy's report of Véron's contacting him about writing the score for *La Juive*.

Schlesinger's wording makes clear that both publisher and director hesitate to endorse Halévy until they are certain that Meyerbeer, whose *Robert le diable* continued to reap profits, has completely relinquished the project. Speaking of Véron's apprehension, Schlesinger gently appeals to Meyerbeer to come to Paris and help settle the matter: "[Y]our presence here, were it only for twenty-four hours, could be most beneficial."[5] The visit was apparently never made, and Meyerbeer, absorbed in completing the score of *Les Huguenots*, returned Scribe's poem.[6] Edouard Monnais (1798–1868), a writer and editor who became acquainted with Halévy at the Villemain salon in the early 1830s, emphasized more strongly than Schlesinger that the director had encouraged the young French composer to ask Scribe for the libretto.[7] Véron, aware of Meyerbeer's delay in finishing *Les Huguenots*, was undoubtedly nervous about having a new opera ready to produce.[8]

When Halévy broached the subject with Scribe, the librettist's initial condescension is palpable in a sharp rebuff conveying that he was busy with many profitable ventures and not to be bothered with trivialities. As Halévy had reported to Monnais, Scribe remarked: "'Is it urgent?' – 'Why yes, answered the musician,' and the poet once again, thinking about the usual fee: 'If it is urgent, you know, it is more expensive;

---

[5] Letter from Schlesinger in Paris to Meyerbeer in Frankfurt in *Giacomo Meyerbeer: Briefwechsel und Tagebücher*, ed. Heinz Becker, Gudrun Becker, and Sabine Henze-Döhring, 5 vols. (Berlin: Walter de Gruyter & Co., 1960–99), vol. II, 330–31. Herbert Weinstock, *Rossini: A Biography* (New York: Alfred A. Knopf, 1968), 160, claims, without evidence, that Rossini was offered the libretto. My dating of Scribe's early work on the scenario renders this claim doubtful. Véron, *Mémoires*, vol. III, 177, mentions that Rossini was first offered *Gustave III*, with no similar reference to *La Juive*.

[6] While the collaboration on *Les Huguenots* began in 1832, Meyerbeer wrote to Scribe on 2 July 1834 about changes to the libretto. *Giacomo Meyerbeer: A Life in Letters*, ed. Heinz Becker and Gudrun Becker, trans. Mark Violette (Portland: Amadeus Press, 1989), 56–7, 62–4, and *Giacomo Meyerbeer: Briefwechsel*, ed. Becker, Becker, and Henze-Döhring, vol. II, 376–8.

[7] Edouard Monnais, *F. Halévy: Souvenirs d'un ami pour joindre à ceux d'un frère* (Paris: Imprimerie Centrale des Chemins de Fer, 1863), 9, 13–14.

[8] Katharine Ellis, *Music Criticism in Nineteenth-Century France: La Revue et gazette musicale de Paris, 1834–80* (Cambridge: Cambridge University Press, 1995), 184, comments on the sluggish pace of Meyerbeer's collaboration, noting that "his demands on various directors of the Opéra were such that a work could take several years to reach the stage."

I have several works already begun, collaborators who are waiting.'"[9]
In Halévy's own memoirs, there is no hint of early negotiations or
struggles – only the composer's warm reminiscence of the moment
when Scribe told him the story of *La Juive*. The early wariness of Scribe,
and of Véron and Schlesinger, implies that Halévy's authority did not
approach that of Meyerbeer. Contemporary descriptions of Halévy
depict an affable, diplomatic, and peace-loving man who, one could
speculate, would have easily bowed to Scribe's will in making decisions
about the developing work.[10]

Viewed in another light, Halévy's creative authority may have been
greater than his status would suggest. Weighed against implications
of a power imbalance are Halévy's later influence and role as "acting
director" under Véron's successor Edmond Duponchel, Scribe's long
experience in collaborating, and the librettist's own reputed conciliatory manner and willingness to cede control to creative partners.
As a seasoned writer for many Parisian theatres by the early 1830s,
Scribe often relied on other writers, even to work out text destined
for non-musical theatre, which would not entail adapting to fit a composer's needs. Collaborators for operatic and non-operatic theatre who
were recognized as co-authors include Germain Delavigne (1790–1868),
Casimir Delavigne (1793–1843), Charles Duveyrier-Mélesville (1803–
66), Jean-François Bayard (1796–1853), and Jules-Henri Vernoy de Saint-
Georges (1783–1855); others went unnamed, acting as contributing
"ghost-writers."[11] The librettist himself explains that he was not simply being pragmatic in seeking the help of others. In a preface to an
early edition of collected works, written as a homage to his co-authors,

---

[9] Monnais, *F. Halévy*, 13–14: "'Est-ce pressé?–Mais oui, répondit le musicien'; et le
poëte de reprendre, en songeant à la prime d'usage: 'C'est que, vous concevez,
si c'est pressé, c'est plus cher; j'ai des ouvrages commencés, des collaborateurs
qui attendent.'"

[10] Véron, *Mémoires*, vol. III, 174, described Halévy's diplomatic advice in the
handling of singers – for example, in deciding whether Dorus-Gras or Falcon
was to sing the role of Alice in *Robert* on a particular day. Halévy was also
consulted about who could go on in place of Nourrit when the tenor was injured
during a performance of *Robert*, but Halévy left this decision to the director.

[11] F-Pn, Ms., n.a.fr. 22584, vol. XXXIV, fol. 64ᵛ. Karin Pendle, *Eugène Scribe and French
Opera of the Nineteenth Century* (Ann Arbor, MI: UMI Research Press, 1977),
13–16, notes that Scribe worked with approximately 130 literary collaborators.

Scribe modestly claims not to have had "the mind or the talent" to be a sole creator and, more significantly, describes collaboration a pleasure but working alone drudgery.[12]

Undoubtedly the nature of Scribe's artistic relationships varied with each personality and work, though some working habits remained constant. From his tyrannical dealings with musicians alluded to by Louis Quicherat, he was said to have been "converted" to accept the respective dominance of each art by the time of his collaboration with Auber on *La Muette de Portici* (1828).[13] In reference to changes in the role of Marcel in *Les Huguenots*, Meyerbeer portrays a very pliable librettist as he reminds Scribe of his earlier comments: "You responded that you would leave it up to me to make any changes I desired, with or without any mutual discussion of the matter. You also stated that you would allow me to make changes in the entire work provided that I request this of you only at a time when everything could be taken care of at once and when the score was complete."[14] In Alan Armstrong's careful examination of the Meyerbeer–Scribe creation of *Le Prophète*, he agrees with the general view that Meyerbeer exerted artistic control over the librettist, asking Scribe to rewrite to fit his rhythmic needs or dramatic concepts. Armstrong concludes that Scribe complied with most of Meyerbeer's demands, although he did not yield in several instances in which Meyerbeer stepped over Scribe's desires by rewriting the text himself or getting another writer to do so.[15]

In the collaboration on *La Juive*, Scribe appears both strict and flexible in accounts of opera insiders. As Halévy composed, Scribe took care that deadlines were met: Monnais recalls that, as each act was due, "the librettist came looking for the musician backstage in order

---

[12] Preface to the 1828 edition of his collected works, *Théâtre de Eugène Scribe dédié par lui à ses collaborateurs*, 10 vols. (Paris: Bezou & Aimé André).

[13] Quicherat, *Nourrit*, vol. I, 53.

[14] Letter from Baden-Baden, dated 2 July 1834, in *Giacomo Meyerbeer: A Life in Letters*, ed. Becker and Becker, 63. Also see *Correspondance d'Eugène Scribe et de Daniel-François-Esprit Auber*, ed. Herbert Schneider (Sprimont, Belgium: Mardaga, 1998).

[15] Alan Armstrong, "Meyerbeer's *Le Prophète*: A History of its Composition and Early Performances," 4 vols. (Ph.D. diss., Ohio State University, 1990), 192, n. 94, notes that when Meyerbeer altered the text, Scribe "retained his original version in the printed libretto."

to confirm that he was legally exact in his commitments."[16] In reworkings of text to comply with the composer's musical demands, according to Léon Halévy, Scribe proved quite malleable and even distanced himself from the intricate process of revision. In a rich account of the opera's complex history sketched in his 1862 biography of the composer, Léon emphasizes the librettist's ease in accepting others' contributions, while never questioning his role as primary author and approver of all revisions. Although undoubtedly a biased chronicler keen on securing Halévy's place in history (as well as his own), he suggests that the composer played a significant part in altering the text and drama, while he and Nourrit helped to make substantive and minor modifications. He writes: "How many times my brother and he [Nourrit] came to discuss and sort out with me these modifications agreed to by Scribe, who, understanding with exquisite tact the true role of the dramatic poet at the Opéra, would step aside in order to give way to the inspirations of the composer and to those of eminent artists, his interpreters!"[17] (See Appendix E for a fuller excerpt.)

Scribe's active schedule seemingly contributed to his collaborative pliancy. As Léon notes, because Scribe was typically overloaded with contracted pieces at several theatres at once, he preferred, or pragmatically chose, to concentrate on the initial preparation of a libretto rather than the year-long revisions that followed. In a similar vein, Quicherat points out that "nothing was more disagreeable" to the overworked Scribe than to revisit a piece while "the seeds of several others worked in his brain."[18] Léon explains that as *La Juive* developed Scribe welcomed his own contributions, in part because he felt indebted to him for having supplied documents and anecdotes for Scribe's acceptance speech before the Académie française. Scribe used these to prepare a tribute to his predecessor Antoine-Vincent Arnault (1766–1834), whom Léon had assisted at the Ecole polytechnique, and Léon claims that he never forgot this favor linked to such a significant event in his career.[19]

---

[16] Monnais, *F. Halévy*, 14: "le poëte, cherchant le musicien dans les coulisses, afin de constater légalement qu'il était exact à ses échéances."
[17] Léon Halévy, *Sa Vie*, 23.   [18] Quicherat, *Nourrit*, vol. i, 197.
[19] Léon Halévy, *Sa Vie*, 25.

The younger Halévy downplays his own role, emphasizing that it was that of facilitator – or *coopérateur* – rather than *collaborateur*. He describes helping his brother with detailed alterations of prosody and verse length, without laying claim to the full text of any number in *La Juive*, as he did for "Pendant la fête une inconnue" in *Guido et Ginevra*, Halévy's *grand opéra* of 1838, and "Quand de la nuit l'épais nuage" in *L'Eclair*, the *opéra comique* that appeared the same year as *La Juive*. As he reports on the librettists' approval of his "ghost-writing" these numbers, he underscores a certain authorial distance on their part and implies that the composer, using his brother to realize his wishes, often had the final word.[20] Léon portrays himself as the composer's trusted

[20] *Ibid.*, 25–6. Léon writes: "Seated near Halévy at one of the rehearsals of *Guido*, hearing for the first time the romance 'Pendant la fête une inconnue' sung in such a ravishing manner by Duprez, he [Scribe] cried out with naive surprise and sincere joy: 'Ah! What an exquisite piece! But I did not write those words! Where is your brother so that I can thank him?' I will also do justice to [F. A. E.] Planard, to whom the Opéra-Comique owes such a great number of excellent libretti, and who wrote *L'Eclair* with M. de Saint-Georges, the skillful and fortunate collaborator of my brother. Never was a man more agreeably surprised than he when he heard, at one of the rehearsals of *L'Eclair*, a charming melody which had seemed tedious in a duet of the second act moved to the beginning of the third, set to new words that my brother had asked of me the day before and I wrote during the night. It was the celebrated romance 'Quand de la nuit l'épais nuage,' whose music has become so popular. The two authors of the verse shook my hand; they would have written well also, even better, no doubt about it: but I was there near the composer's piano, and when I was adapting my verse to his melodies, I believed I was taking down his dictation." ("Placé près d'Halévy à l'une des répétitions de *Guido*, et entendant pour la première fois la romance: *Pendant la fête une inconnue*, chantée d'une manière si ravissante par Duprez, il [Scribe] s'écria avec un étonnement naïf et une joie sincère: 'Oh! le délicieux morceau! mais je n'ai pas fait ces paroles-là! Où est donc votre frère pour que je le remercie?' Je rendrai la même justice à Planard, à qui l'Opéra-Comique doit un si grand nombre d'excellents poëmes, et qui a fait *L'Eclair* avec M. de Saint-Georges, l'habile et heureux collaborateur de mon frère. Jamais homme ne fut plus agréablement surpris que lui, lorsqu'à l'une des répétitions de *L'Eclair* il entendit une mélodie charmante, qui avait paru faire longueur dans un duo du second acte, transportée au commencement du troisième, sur des paroles nouvelles que mon frère m'avait demandées la veille, et que je lui avais faites dans la nuit. C'était la célèbre romance: *Quand de la nuit l'épais nuage*, dont la musique est devenue si populaire. Les deux auteurs du poëme me serrèrent la main; ils auraient fait aussi bien, mieux sans doute: mais j'étais là près du piano du compositeur, et, quand j'adaptais mes vers à ses mélodies, je croyais écrire sous sa dictée.")

work companion who sat at his side at the piano and "freed the fecund and ingenious writer from a great care"; in return, as he writes, "I deeply appreciated the freedom to contribute to the success of works that were dear to me."[21]

In assessing what appears to be a sincere and diplomatic autobiographical account of Léon Halévy's contributions, we must consider that he set down these words after the death of Scribe, when the librettist could not dispute them. Since *La Juive* remained the *chef-d'oeuvre* of Fromental, Léon's claims may have been motivated by a self-serving desire to gild his own reputation, diminished since his early years of promise. The hand of Léon Halévy, or other clear traces of his work on *La Juive*, is not evident in libretto and music sources, although future research may lead to new discoveries.[22] But his statements are largely backed up by Monnais, who worked with the composer at the Opéra after being hired as assistant director in 1839.[23] Although personal loyalties may also have biased his corroborations, Monnais speaks emphatically about Léon's unheralded contributions to the libretti of his brother's operas, including the text for the same *air* from *L'Eclair* cited by Léon as well as others that had become popular. The credited librettists were thankful for Léon's services, Monnais writes, "but the public knew nothing about them."[24] Other than the cantatas *Les Plages du Nil* (1846) and *Prométhée enchaîné* (1849), Léon was primary librettist for only one other large-scale vocal work completed by his brother, *Le Dilettante d'Avignon*. Monnais infers that his secondary role in Fromental's operas was not by choice, but because "strange

[21] *Ibid.*, 25. See Appendix E.

[22] Of two notes containing libretto text (F-Pn, Ms., n.a.fr. 22502, vol. xxiii, 1°:1°) in unidentified hands, neither is in Scribe's hand, nor clearly in Léon Halévy's. One includes verse for the Act I chorus "Hâtons nous"; the other contains verse for the Act III numbers abandoned after the première (see pp. 112 and 228–30 below).

[23] Monnais, *F. Halévy*, 33. This account, dedicated to Léon Halévy, was intended as a companion piece to his own biography of the composer. At some point after *La Juive*, strong friendships developed between both Halévys and Monnais. At the composer's funeral in 1862, Monnais delivered a eulogy ("Obsèques de M. F. Halévy" [24 March 1862], F-Po, Dossier d'artiste: Fromental Halévy), and, under the pseudonym Paul Smith, wrote the article "F. Halévy," *La Revue et gazette musicale de Paris* 29, no. 12 (23 March 1862): 93.

[24] Monnais, *F. Halévy*, 33.

conditions that exist in the arrangements of the theatre" prevented Léon's being granted a larger, acknowledged role.[25] He hints that this lack of opportunity and lack of public recognition issued from the monopoly of power exerted by Scribe and other Opéra librettists and very likely implies that Léon's "tacit agreement" was intended to protect Scribe's authority as well as his royalties.[26] In one particularly emphatic statement, Monnais asserts Léon's artistic importance to the composer: "Throughout his career, your brother has known only three collaborators. M. de Saint-Georges and Scribe in public, and you in private."[27]

Contributions by Nourrit comprise his choosing and developing the role of Eléazar, originally destined for the bass Nicolas Levasseur (1791–1871), writing – or refining – the text of the famous aria "Rachel, quand du Seigneur," and determining its replacement of the choral finale planned for Act IV.[28] Moreover, he is credited with developing the *mise en scène* of *La Juive*.[29] Although this latter role goes unmentioned in the composer's memoirs, Halévy does confirm Nourrit's work on the aria, and Scribe's conciliation:

> Nourrit gave us excellent advice. There was a [choral] finale in the fourth act; he asked us to replace it with an aria. I wrote the music of the aria on the given situation; Nourrit asked Scribe for the authorization to write the words of the aria, whose music was written. He wanted to choose the syllables that were the most sonorous and the most suitable for his voice. M. Scribe, generous because of his wealth, lent himself with good grace

[25] *Ibid.*: "les bizarres conditions qui président aux arrangements de théâtre s'y opposaient toujours."

[26] For *La Juive*, for example, librettist and composer received equal royalties for performances.

[27] Monnais, *F. Halévy*, 33: "Dans toute sa carrière, votre frère n'a guère connu que trois collaborateurs. M. de Saint-Georges et Scribe pour le public, et vous pour l'intimité."

[28] The redistribution of roles is discussed by Léon Halévy, Monnais, Véron, and other contemporary writers – and by the composer himself. See Fromental Halévy, *Derniers Souvenirs*, 166–7, and Monnais, *F. Halévy*, 14; see also Appendix E.

[29] Stéphane Wolff, *L'Opéra au Palais Garnier (1875–1962): Les Oeuvres, les interprètes* (Paris: Déposé au journal *L'Entr'acte*, n.d.). I have not yet found documents that trace Nourrit's work on the *mise en scène*.

2 Portrait of Adolphe Nourrit (1802–39) by Vigneron

to the desire of the singer, and a few days later Nourrit brought us the
words of the aria "Rachel, quand du Seigneur la grâce tutélaire."[30]

---

[30] Fromental Halévy, *Derniers Souvenirs*, 167: "Nourrit nous donna d'excellents
conseils. Il y avait au quatrième acte un finale; il nous demanda de le remplacer
par un air. Je fis la musique de l'air sur la situation donnée; Nourrit demanda à
M. Scribe l'autorisation de faire lui-même les paroles de l'air dont la musique
était faite. Il voulait choisir les syllabes les plus sonores, les plus favorables à sa
voix. M. Scribe, généreux, parce qu'il est riche, se prêta de bonne grâce au désir

Libretto sources appear to back up this account and suggest that Nourrit at least revised the aria's text.[31] Loyalty to the singer, particularly after his tragic suicide in 1839 (which many blamed on the Opéra administration), may have biased Halévy and other writers to give Nourrit more credit than was due him, yet reports abound of Nourrit's extensive artistic responsibilities that went well beyond his meticulous role preparation. As Halévy points out, Nourrit also developed the scenario of the ballet *La Sylphide* (1832) and adapted Shakespeare's *Tempest* for the ballet *La Tempête* (1834).[32] Quicherat writes of Nourrit's demand to change what he felt was an ineffective end to the fourth act of *Les Huguenots*, calling instead for a duet between Valentine and Raoul; despite Meyerbeer's willingness to respond to the singer's ideas, Scribe was reluctant and too fatigued to write new verse.[33] In this case,

du chanteur, et Nourrit nous apporta peu de jours après les paroles de l'air: 'Rachel, quand du Seigneur la grâce tutélaire.'"

[31] The draft verse in Scribe's hand (F-Pn, Ms., n.a.fr. 22562) includes text for the choral finale, but not Eléazar's aria. The aria first appears in the copyist's libretto, F-Pan, AJ[13]202, in Act IV, Scene vii, beginning with the words "Lorsque d'un dieu puissant, la grâce tutélaire." Other manuscript evidence shows variants of early-layer text: the autograph, F-Po, A.509a, vol. II, 462ff., and a partbook for Eléazar, F-Po, Mat. 19e [315 (13), fol. 145[v], include a variant of the initial words in the copyist's libretto, "Hélas lorsque de dieu," which was replaced by "Rachel, quand du Seigneur." This evidence does not prove definitively Halévy's claim of Nourrit's authorship of the entire text, but neither does it refute it.

[32] Fromental Halévy, *Derniers Souvenirs*, 153–4, 162. Concerning *La Tempête*, Halévy (162, n. 1) wrote that "only the title, the original idea, and several details of this ballet were borrowed from Shakespeare. All the rest was the invention of Nourrit" ("[l]e titre, l'idée première et quelques détails seulement de ce ballet étaient empruntés à Shakspeare [sic]. Tout le reste était de l'invention de Nourrit."). Janet Lynn Johnson, "Rossini in Bologna and Paris during the Early 1830s: New Letters," *Revue de musicologie* 79, no. 1 (1993): 73, claims that Rossini thought of Nourrit, his Arnold in *Guillaume Tell*, as his "poëte adjoint"; Johnson also notes that the composer gave Opéra director Emile Lubbert (Véron's predecessor) and the librettist the liberty to make cuts in *Tell* during his absence, provided Nourrit was consulted.

[33] Quicherat, *Nourrit*, vol. I, 197. Meyerbeer's respect for Nourrit's artistry is evident in a letter to Alexandre Dumas *père* dated 23 May 1832, when he wrote that "[t]ogether, you and Nourrit could write half an opera in three weeks." See *Giacomo Meyerbeer: A Life in Letters*, ed. Becker and Becker, 54.

Quicherat claims that he allowed Emile Deschamps to act as secondary librettist, although Nourrit may have helped as well.[34]

At various stages of the genesis of *La Juive*, a certain "territorialism" and creative opposition undoubtedly arose among the collaborators as their individual roles overlapped. (Véron speaks of the artistic battles surrounding suppressions and cuts that typically went on in the final meeting prior to an opera's première.[35]) Scribe held onto final approval of text revisions, as Léon Halévy reports, yet it cannot be assumed that Scribe did not bend to the composer's preferences: it appears that what may have begun as a librettist-led collaboration had developed into a relatively balanced and cordial partnership – even if Scribe's relinquishing of some control was due mainly to fatigue or disinterest. A glimpse of artistic exchanges between Halévy and Scribe several years and operas later shows the composer as a persuasive, confident negotiator: in Halévy's letter of 20 June 1848, he tells Scribe of director Duponchel's requests to rework the already shortened *Guido et Ginevra*, and asks the librettist to write "a beautiful scene" as denouement to the fourth and then final act. His suggestions indicate that he does not limit himself to musical ideas, and reveal his attraction (and undoubtedly Duponchel's) to climactic scenes: "Couldn't one have a beautiful spectacle there? A fire, whose idea begins to take root at the end of the fourth act? In the middle of this fire, the arrival of Médicis with troops, all his court, all the clergy, all the people. Be good enough to give us a magnificent denouement, with torches, tocsin and *arc-en-ciel* [rainbow]."[36]

The portrait of amiability among *La Juive* collaborators depicted by Léon is enhanced by the composer's own references to Scribe's generosity in accommodating Nourrit, and by the congenial manner in which composer and librettist addressed each other publicly and

---

[34] Quicherat, *Nourrit*, vol. I, 198. A letter from Nourrit to Scribe in F-Pn, Ms., n.a.fr. 22502, vol. xxiii, 2°:4°, includes text for the Valentine–Raoul Act IV duet in his hand, with a note saying, "Here is the duet as we are singing it" and indicating that he will meet the composer the following day to discuss it.

[35] Véron, *Mémoires*, vol. iii, 162.

[36] *Fromental Halévy: Lettres*, ed. Galland, 61–2. According to Galland, this reworked version was not realized at the Opéra.

privately. Although civil, deferent expression is a key feature of French correspondence, particularly formal correspondence, genuine warmth and respect exude from their post-*Juive* letters; Scribe and Halévy use such phrases as "Mon cher maître," "Mon cher voisin et collaborateur," or "Mon cher et illustre collaborateur," with Halévy sometimes emphasizing "cher" with "très" and adding "ami" to the phrase; he also ends one letter of 1848 with "votre dévoué et affectionné collaborateur, confrère et ami."[37] To Nourrit, Halévy appears rather intimate in letters of the 1830s, addressing him as "Mon cher Adolphe" or "Mon cher ami" and signing off, "Votre bien dévoué." (See Appendix 1–2.) Although Halévy would play a role in hiring the tenor Gilbert-Louis Duprez at the Opéra, an action which severely wounded Nourrit's pride, he cared deeply for the singer; Quicherat sensed a "great familiarity" when he saw them together.[38] Although future research will undoubtedly offer a more distinct portrait of this central creative team, its flexible division of labor and seeming collaborative ease allows for an enticing range of interpretations as we examine the opera's subject and contexts.

THE LIBERALISM OF THE AUTHORS AND THEIR GENERATION

Beyond this basic collaborative accord, the authors of *La Juive* shared generational ideals that touched and inspired their work. It is in the liberalism of their "Generation of 1820" (so labeled by Alan Spitzer and other historians) that the socio-religio-political meanings of *La Juive* took root. Maturing after the fall of the Empire, this generation demonstrated extraordinary cohesion in its opposition to the Restoration governments, ultraroyalist, clerical actions, and established elites, and

---

[37] See, for example, letters from Halévy to Scribe dated 1 May 1848 (F-Pn, Ms., n.a.fr. 22547, fol. 296), 20 June 1848 (n.a.fr. 22547, fol. 298), and 5 January 1849 (F-Pn, Mus., "Lettres autographes," vol. L, No. 6); from Scribe to Halévy dated 3 January 1848, 17 January 1852, and 6 July (no year) (F-Pn, Ms., n.a.fr. 14347, fols. 59–60, fols. 65–6, and fols. 89–90), and 6 December 1848 (F-Pn, Ms., n.a.fr. 22547, fol. 300); see *Fromental Halévy: Lettres*, ed. Galland, 60–62, 65–8, 71–2, 96–9.

[38] Quicherat, *Nourrit*, vol. I, 230–31.

in its embrace of the principles of liberty, equality, and social progress.[39]
Charles-Augustin Sainte-Beuve (1804–69) sketched its rise to power:

> There is a generation composed of those born at the end of the last
> century, still children or too young under the Empire, which liberated
> itself to don manly garb in the midst of the storms of 1814 and 1815. This
> generation . . . who fought with virtual unanimity under the Restoration
> against the political and religious *ancien régime*, today occupies the
> summits of power and science in business, the Chambers and the
> Academies. The Revolution of 1830, to which this generation had so
> greatly contributed by its fifteen years of struggle, was made for it to a
> considerable extent and was the harbinger of its accession.[40]

Honoré de Balzac (1799–1850), one of the generation's most lumin-
ous members, captured its zealous idealism in *Sténie; ou, Les Erreurs
philosophiques*, as he called on the "children of the century and of
liberty, to speed the dawning of happiness among nations, to make
the security of thrones coincide with the freedom of peoples."[41] Léon
Halévy added to the self-affirmations, characterizing the period as "one
of those epochs of sharp transition where the emerging generations
are separated from their predecessors to such a degree that in the same
country, in the same century, we exist as citizens of two nations and
contemporaries of two eras."[42]

---

[39] Spitzer, *1820*, 3–4, 9. The specific designation of the generation varies, as well as
its age span and makeup – with most historians defining it in terms of a brilliant
group of educated, predominantly middle-class males. Spitzer's label
corresponds to the "Restoration generation" preferred by some writers. See his
references, 3–4, to Albert Thibaudet, "La Génération de 1820," in *Histoire de la
littérature française*, part 2 (Paris: Stock, 1936), 105–292; Charles Bruneau, "La
Génération de 1820," in *Histoire de la langue française des origines à nos jours*,
ed. Ferdinand Brunot (Paris: A. Colin, 1968), vol. II, 103–15; Robert Brown, "The
Generation of 1820 during the Bourbon Restoration in France: A Biographical
and Intellectual Portrait of the First Wave, 1814–1824" (Ph.D. diss., Duke
University, 1979); Henri Peyre, *Les Générations littéraires* (Paris: Boivin, 1948);
and François A. Isambert, *De la Charbonnerie au Saint-Simonisme: Etude sur la
jeunesse de Buchez* (Paris: Les Editions de Minuit, 1966).
[40] Cited in translation in Spitzer, *1820*, 5–6.
[41] Cited in translation in *ibid.*, frontispiece. Spitzer also includes characterizations
of the generation by Félicité-Robert de Lamennais, François-René, vicomte de
Chateaubriand, and Benjamin Constant (4–5).
[42] *Le Producteur* I (1825): 275, cited in translation in Spitzer, *1820*, 30.

The collapse of the Empire and return of the Bourbons stimulated powerful responses in the generation, but its collective *mentalité* was also galvanized by common schooling in *lycées* established under the Empire (the Imperial, Napoléon, Charlemagne, and Bonaparte, known as Louis-le-Grand, Henri IV, Charlemagne, and Bourbon under the Restoration), the Ecole normale, and the *collège* Sainte-Barbe; participation in literary salons and the founding of journals; and membership in such associations as the *normaliens*, students of the Ecole normale and other young intellectuals inspired by the political philosophy of Victor Cousin (1792–1867), the Carbonari, a group of political activists founded by Saint-Amand Bazard (1791–1852), and the Saint-Simonians.[43] For many of this generation, the 1830 Revolution was an epochal event and, as Sainte-Beuve wrote, the "harbinger of its accession." Although generational unity quickly dissolved as Louis-Philippe's government began to take on less revolutionary and more absolutist tones – as in the 1831–2 repression of republican resistance and workers' uprisings – liberal ideals continued to hold sway in the 1830s, albeit with increasing divisions of thought.

The generation's revolutionary, humanitarian spirit and anticlerical, anti-absolutist views influenced the authors of *La Juive*, although with varied nuances. Scribe, whose birthyear of 1791 places him slightly outside Spitzer's dating for the generation (the birthdates from 1792 to 1803 as *terminus a quo* and *ad quem*),[44] appears the most distant from the politics of this period, but he nevertheless shared many of its ideals. Both the Halévys and Nourrit fit its profile: the composer was born in 1799, the year of Balzac's birth, his brother and Nourrit in 1802, the year of Hugo's. Scribe attended the *lycée* Napoléon (Henri IV) and the *collège* Sainte-Barbe; Nourrit also attended Sainte-Barbe. Léon Halévy

---

[43] See Spitzer, *1820*, 3–34, for a more comprehensive discussion of the education, activities, and networks of this generation or "cohort." Its articulate *hommes de lettres* whose writings made a public mark in the 1820s included such men as Alfred de Vigny (1797–1863), Adolphe Thiers (1797–1877), Jules Michelet (1798–1874), and Auguste Comte (1798–1857).

[44] Spitzer, *1820*, 6, recognizes the arbitrariness of these dates and allows for some lack of clarity at these limits. He also refers to other boundaries – for example, the birthdates of 1795 and 1805 chosen by Peyre (4, n. 2).

studied at Charlemagne, winning its *concours général* in 1816–17 and thus a place among a brilliant elite.[45] Fromental's musical talents led him, from the time he was almost ten, to the Paris Conservatoire. Léon became a leading generational spokesman (one of the nearly 200 subjects used in Spitzer's study), a role that makes him a valuable informant for this study.

From Scribe's school experience emerged a lifelong association with important generational voices, particularly the brothers Casimir and Germain Delavigne, who as schoolmates with Scribe were nicknamed "the inseparables."[46] Casimir became a revered writer who was propelled into the Académie on the immense success of his poems mourning the fall of Napoleon, the *Messéniennes*. Memorized by countless youths who were "frantic liberals and frantic Bonapartists," Delavigne's poems gave him a reputation as a patriot and a god-like figure to French youths.[47] As a dramatist, he wrote works of political and philosophical import. Scribe collaborated with both Delavignes on theatre pieces, notably *La Muette de Portici* with Germain, and was influenced by both.[48] According to Ernest Legouvé, Scribe "confided everything" in Casimir,[49] who would remain a consultant and confidant even after their collaborative efforts ceased; moreover, Scribe's wife remembered that her husband never presented a theatrical work without having first read it before Germain.[50] (The brothers, particularly Casimir, also worked with Halévy on *Charles VI* of 1843.)

[45] F-Pan, Minutier central, Etude cxvii/1058, Dossier Halévy, letter of recommendation by Alexandre Dumas *père*, 20 October 1820, speaks of Léon's "brillantes études."

[46] Jean-Claude Yon, "Eugène Scribe, la fortune et la liberté" (Ph.D. diss., Université de Paris-Sorbonne, 1993), vol. I, 31.

[47] Ernest Legouvé, *Sixty Years of Recollections*, trans. Albert D. Vandam, 2 vols. (London: Eden, Remington & Co., 1893), vol. I, 16–17.

[48] Scribe worked with Germain Delavigne on *Thibault, comte de Champagne* (1813), the one-act *comédie Le Valet de son rival* (1816), and *La Somnambule* (1818). In 1819, he wrote a parody on Casimir's successful play of 1818, *Les Vêpres siciliennes* (which he would later rework as a libretto for Verdi).

[49] Legouvé, *Recollections*, vol. I, 30–31.

[50] Yon, "Eugène Scribe," vol. I, 31. As cited by Paul Bonnefon, "Scribe sous l'Empire et sous la Restauration d'après des documents inédits," *Revue d'histoire littéraire de la France* 27 (1920): 336, Scribe alludes to this close friendship in 1818, telling of a "charming season" of work and relaxation with the brothers in the country.

Among the watershed events that changed the lives of this generation, the return of the Bourbons produced a sharp reaction in Scribe
and left a deep imprint on the Halévys. At the end of 1814, shortly after
Louis XVIII came to power, the twenty-three-year-old Scribe displayed
anti-Bourbon fervor, writing a brief but telling summation of the year:
"This year . . . has not been happy, neither for me nor for France. The Al-
lies have come; Paris has been taken; the country ransomed; the Bourbons established on the throne: all the misfortunes at the same time."[51]
His anti-Bourbon feelings continue as he states his newly realized intention to make the theatre his profession in order "to be free and independent, and not to have to solicit jobs, help, or pensions from a government that I detest and despise."[52] In the biography of his brother,
Léon describes more personal experiences during the 1814 surrender
of Paris, which he cites as a major source of the brothers' mutual patriotism and love of liberty. On 30 March, as the British-led Allied forces
pushed to defeat Napoleon, the young Halévys were thrilled to hear of
the "heroic defense of Paris by the students of the Ecole polytechnique
on the hills of Saint-Chaumont";[53] on 1 April, shortly after the surrender, they observed from a tiny window on the rue Michel-Lepelletier an
enemy squadron of "savage-looking" Cossacks slowly marching past
and sensed the mournful, silent pall that fell on the streets of Paris. As
witnesses to this "painful" and "ill-fated" day, that would be followed by
Napoleon's abdication and exile ten days later, the adolescent Halévys
"never forgot the profound impression this scene produced."[54]

During the Restoration, the anticlericalism that arose in opposition to the increased influence of the Church touched Scribe and the
Halévys. All expressed anticlerical sentiments linked with views of individual and political freedom espoused in liberal newspapers of the
day. In his travel journals, Scribe makes a number of statements that
are overtly anti-absolutist, anticlerical, and revolutionary in spirit; he

---

[51] Bonnefon, "Scribe sous l'Empire," 327.
[52] *Ibid.*, cited in Pendle, *Eugène Scribe*, 4.
[53] Léon Halévy, *Sa Vie*, 12: "l'héroïque défense de Paris par les élèves de l'Ecole
polytechnique sur les buttes Saint-Chaumont."
[54] *Ibid.*: "n'oubliâmes jamais l'impression profonde qu'avait produite sur nous
cette scène."

also laments over inhuman conditions that he witnesses or that are brought to mind by historical relics seen during his journeys.[55] As he describes a visit to the church and abbey of St. Gall on 31 July 1826, Scribe characterizes the priests as "uneasy and unruly prelates who have always sown disorder among the Swiss people."[56] In writing of Avignon in 1827, and again in 1846, he condemns past abuses of the Church and wonders whether this early violence had set a precedent for more recent tragedies among the Avignonais, including the muti-lation of sixty-six "unfortunates" by "the good inhabitants of the Midi" during the Revolution and the 1815 assassination of the Napoleonic marshal Guillaume Marie-Anne Brune by royalists.[57] Such "habitual ferocity" had been inherited by the Avignonais from ancestors who had sought asylum in Avignon when it was under papal control; in the 1846 entry, Scribe identifies these descendants as "the *légitimiste* Avignonaise population."[58] Although almost twenty years separate these visits, Scribe speaks passionately of tortures and massacres linked with Avi-gnon on both occasions; during the 1846 visit, he remarks: "such is the ensemble of the minor measures of conviction that were used in earlier times to enlighten and convert those who refused to believe."[59] He concludes that "a temple to political and religious freedom" should be erected in Avignon, the site of so many injustices.[60]

[55] Writing in a journal of an 1827 trip to the South of France (F-Pn, Ms., n.a.fr. 22584, vol. II, fol. 33^r), Scribe deplores the sight of a procession of chained slaves: "What a horrible, dreadful sight! Four thousand galley slaves chained two by two passing as if in a parade . . . these condemned in perpetuity – in perpetuity . . . Ah! What a recollection! What degradation of human nature! I will never forget this awful scene and all day and all night in my dreams I saw marching past this long, immense column of infamy of all types." ("[O] l'horrible, l'effroyable spectacle! Quatre milles galériens enchaînés deux à deux passant ainsi une revue . . . ceux condamnés à perpétuité – à perpétuité . . . ah! quel souvenir! quelle dégradation de la nature humaine! Je n'oublierai jamais cette horrible scène et toute la journée, toute la nuit dans mes rèves je voyais défiler cette longue et immense colonne de forfait de toute espèce.")

[56] F-Pn, Ms., n.a.fr. 22584, vol. I, fol. 16^r: "prélats inquiets et turbulents qui ont toujours jeté le desordre dans la suisse."

[57] *Ibid.*, vol. II, fol. 20^r.   [58] *Ibid.*, vol. II, fol. 20^r; vol. V, fol. 7^r.

[59] *Ibid.*, vol. V, fol. 7^r: "tel est l'ensemble des petits moyens de conviction employés autrefois pour éclairer et convertir ceux qui refusaient de croire."

[60] *Ibid.*, fol. 7^v: "un temple à la liberté politique et religieuse."

Scribe's interest in revolutionary heroes also inspired a portion of his travel agenda of the late 1820s. In Zurich, Scribe paid homage to Guillaume Tell, the Swiss hero so popular in contemporary dramas and soon to be memorialized in Rossini's opera (libretto by Etienne de Jouy and Hippolyte-Louis Bis) at the Académie royale. Scribe visited an arsenal (where he placed Tell's quiver on his shoulder) and the site on Lake Lucerne where Tell's chapel was erected. At the chapel, he was moved to write down an inscription expressing generational spirit: "[H]ere ended the tyranny of Gesler and began the freedom of the Swiss people."[61] (See pp. 110–12 and 114–16 below for further discussion of this travel commentary.)

Léon Halévy more directly and publicly condemned the Catholic Church and clerical factions. In his *Résumé de l'histoire des juifs modernes* (1828), he speaks, although with little elaboration, of the treatment of French Jews by the "parti-prêtre" (priest or clerical party), referring to "the hidden scheming and the active, pernicious influence by which the clerical party has constantly threatened their political existence, has encouraged apostasy and shameful defections among them, and, until today, has excluded them from public employment and especially from university offices."[62] In the latter statement, Halévy may have been recalling the purging of the clergy-led University of 1822, when professors and administrators believed to be liberal or anticlerical were dismissed, together with a portion of secondary school teachers. And he was undoubtedly remembering that his Jewish heritage prevented him from obtaining a teaching position,[63] despite his brilliant record at Charlemagne (but see pp. 105–6 below). Such an experience would have sharpened his awareness of the Catholic hegemony and undoubtedly fueled a desire to vent his frustrations.

---

[61] *Ibid.*, vol. 1, fols. 11ᵛ, 35ʳ: "[I]ci a fini la tyrannie de Gesler et commencé la liberté de la suisse."

[62] Léon Halévy, *Résumé de l'histoire des juifs modernes* (Paris: Lecointe et Durey, 1828), 317: "des sourdes menées, de l'influence active et pernicieuse par laquelle le parti-prêtre a constamment menacé leur existence politique, a encouragé parmi eux l'apostasie et les défections honteuses, et les a exclus jusqu'à ce jour des emplois publics et notamment des fonctions universitaires."

[63] *Ibid.*, 82.

Shortly after this publication, the royalist paper *La Gazette de France* denounced an anticlerical poem by Halévy that was printed, without attribution, in its liberal nemesis *Le Courrier français* on 22 June 1829. Halévy's poem, "L'Extradition," which focuses on the "meurtre juridique" (legal murder) of the Italian patriot Galotti, extradited from France to Naples, is undeniably provocative. Halévy seemingly quotes Galotti on his path to the gallows in defiant phrases of liberal rhetoric, including "Tyranny is always prompt in its justice!" Its anticlericalism becomes sharpest in the final verses excerpted by the *Gazette*, which the paper found insulting to the Catholic Church and faith.[64] Halévy describes the encounter of "la victime" with "le prêtre," who in promising absolution reminds the condemned, "Man is saved by death and faith!" Rather than confessing, Galotti dramatically accuses the priest of disturbing his prayer, and shouts, "I can speak to God without you!" Despite these words, which the priest finds arrogant and the *Gazette* blasphemous, the priest continues to seek Galotti's confession. As Brogni will do in Act I of *La Juive*, the priest then questions his crime. Galotti's reply of resistance, "Among this base flock of slaves / I have pronounced the name of *liberté*!," prompts the priest's accusation of sedition and blasphemy and his sudden denial of absolution.

Halévy's treatment was not the only one condemned by the *Gazette*, which decried other discussions of Galotti's extradition in newspapers "of the liberal faction."[65] But in its rebuff of the poet, whom it accuses of supporting sedition, working to bring down religion and royalty, and denying Catholics religious freedom, it alludes to his Jewish identity. In its accusation, there is an uncanny foreshadowing of Eléazar's situation in Act I of the opera, and of the *Gazette*'s response to it (see pp. 159–62 and 170 below):

> In the middle of the most solemn ceremonies of the Catholic religion an impious voice insulted the faith of our fathers, the Church, and its ministers! The author, already guilty of having rhymed in detestable

---

[64] General statements about Galotti and the liberal press appear in "Sur l'affaire de Galotti," *La Gazette de France* (23 June 1829): 1–2, and the poem's denunciation on 24 June (1–2).

[65] "Sur l'affaire de Galotti," 1–2.

verses what he does not understand nor is in a state to understand, insults in his trivial work what the law ordains him to respect, and offends religious freedom itself in delivering to derision and scorn what the charter has consecrated as the state religion and what it has promised to *protect*. I do not think that a single Catholic would dare speak of the rites of the religion of Moses in such terms.[66]

The *Gazette* reminds the poet that in having the dying Galotti reject a priest's intercession, he is ruling out the need for rabbis and (Protestant) ministers as well as Catholic priests. In a letter of response to the paper, Halévy sharply denied that he had insulted the Christian faith: he found the *Gazette*'s accusations "false and slanderous" and viewed its references to his being "non chrétien" as underhanded, and undoubtedly antisemitic.[67]

No comparably intense anti-Catholic statements penned by Fromental have been found, particularly not public ones. In his curiosity about the treatment of Jews during his 1822 visit to Rome, "the capital of the Christian world," and his description of Rome's impoverished, ghettoized Jewish community (see pp. 89–91 below), for example, he does not draw a direct association between Jewish misery and Catholic dominance. But he does write warily about the Catholics of Italy, finding them corrupt and superstitious:

The first thing that strikes the foreigner when he arrives in Italy is the extreme superstition and corruption of the people . . . that is the state of the people in Rome, and especially in Naples; an abundance of priests, monks,

---

[66] *La Gazette de France* (24 June 1829): 2: "C'est au milieu des pompes les plus solennelles du culte catholique qu'une bouche impie insultait à la foi de nos pères, à l'église et à ses ministres! L'auteur, déjà coupable d'avoir rimé en détestables vers ce qu'il ne comprend pas et n'est pas en état de comprendre, outrage dans son oeuvre triviale ce que la loi ordonne de respecter, et blesse la liberté religieuse elle-même en livrant à la dérision et au mépris ce que la charte a consacré comme religion de l'état, ce qu'elle a promis de *protéger*. Je ne pense pas qu'aucun catholique osât s'exprimer en pareils termes sur les rites du culte de Moïse."

[67] See this letter in Pierre Guiral's chapter "Léon Halévy," in *La Famille Halévy*, ed. Loyrette, 84–5.

and madonnas, crosses on all street corners, indulgences attached to the adoration of these madonnas, that is what is responsible for their plight.[68]

During the 1820s, both Halévys were led further into liberal thought through the philosophy of Saint-Simon, a doctrine that Léon described as *"the most radical* and the most complete liberalism," and one that offered "all the elements of social prosperity."[69] Léon Halévy served as the philosopher's personal secretary from 1823 to 1825 and, before his formal split with the movement *circa* 1827, Léon penned influential writings; significant among them is the introduction to the Saint-Simonian *Opinions littéraires, philosophiques et industrielles* (1825), which resounds with generational optimism in its call to Frenchmen to unite, put the past behind, and march "as one man" toward a future earthly paradise.[70] He also contributed to two periodicals representative of Saint-Simonian thought: the short-lived *Le Producteur* (October 1825–October 1826), and the more successful *Le Globe*, established in 1824 by former Carbonarists and *normaliens* and read by Heine. Léon was among the ten founders of *Le Producteur*, who included Olinde Rodrigues (1795–1851), the man usually credited with beginning the Saint-Simonian movement, Prosper Enfantin (1796–1864), Benjamin-Philippe Buchez (1796–1865), and Saint-Amand Bazard. In collaboration with the older, liberally minded Arnault, he edited *L'Opinion: Journal des moeurs, de la littérature, des arts, des théâtres et de l'industrie*, a periodical established in December 1825. Among his signed contributions

---

[68] Fromental Halévy, journal, F-Pn, Ms., n.a.fr. 14349, fol. 3ʳ: "La première chose qui frappe l'étranger à son arrivée en Italie, c'est l'extrême superstition du peuple & son extrême corruption . . . voilà le peuple à Rome, & surtout à Naples; beaucoup de prêtres, de moines, de madonnes, des croix à tous les coins de rues, des indulgences attachés à l'adoration de ces madonnes, voilà la cause de cet état du peuple."

[69] "Souvenirs de Saint-Simon," *La France littéraire* 1 (1832): 525: "[l]e libéralisme *le plus radical*, le plus complet"; "tous les élémens de prospérité sociale."

[70] Cte. Claude-Henri de Saint-Simon, Léon Halévy, Olinde Rodrigues, *et al. Opinions littéraires, philosophiques et industrielles* (Paris: Galerie de Bossange Père, Libraire de S. A. R. Mᵒⁿ le duc d'Orléans, 1825), 21–2. Léon also claims authorship of essays under "Mélanges"; see his "Souvenirs de Saint-Simon," 538, and Victor R. Emanuel, "Léon Halévy," in *The Jewish Encyclopedia*, 12 vols. (New York: Ktav Publishing House, 1976–82), vol. vi, 169.

are articles heavily weighted in Enlightenment and Saint-Simonian philosophy.

Although Fromental Halévy did not become a full-fledged disciple, he did associate with the Saint-Simonian circle, which was solidified through familial ties as well as a common Jewish heritage. In the apartment building of the two brothers on the rue Montholon lived Olinde Rodrigues, who had, in fact, introduced Léon to Saint-Simon;[71] his father, of a Jewish merchant family from Bordeaux, had been a close friend of Elie Halévy before the death of the latter in 1826. Rodrigues hosted gatherings of the Saint-Simonians, many of whom were young Jewish recruits, including his brother Eugène Rodrigues, the brothers Edouard and Henri Rodrigues (unrelated to him), the brothers Emile and Isaac Pereire, and Gustave d'Eichthal.[72] The friendship of the Halévys with Rodrigues as well as d'Eichthal, who belonged to a family of bankers originating from Bavaria, was later strengthened by Fromental's 1842 marriage to Léonie Rodrigues-Henriques, a cousin of Olinde and sister of Cécile, d'Eichthal's future wife.[73] Another marriage further enhanced the group's cohesiveness: Emile Pereire, of a Sephardic Jewish family from Bordeaux related to the Rodrigues family, married one of Olinde's sisters.[74]

According to Léon Halévy, Fromental not only joined this "intelligent and passionate society" but revelled in its midst, "where his

[71] In "Souvenirs de Saint-Simon," 522, Léon describes his excitement at meeting the philosopher in the Palais-Royal garden and visiting him in his apartment a few days later, escorted by Rodrigues.

[72] Zosa Szajkowski, "The Jewish Saint-Simonians and Socialist Antisemites in France," *Jewish Social Studies* 9, no. 1 (January 1947): 37, notes that the number of active and influential Jewish members did not exceed a dozen, but because the group was small their participation was conspicuous and powerful.

[73] F-Pa, Ms. 14379/41; see also letters of Gustave's son, Eugène d'Eichthal, mentioning contact with Fromental's daughter, Geneviève Halévy-Bizet, F-Pa, Ms. 14404/6, 14404/112; letter of Halévy-Bizet, F-Pa, Ms. 14379/42; and *Fromental Halévy: Lettres*, ed. Galland, 127–8. The Rodrigues connection between the composer and d'Eichthal appears to have bound the families together in later decades.

[74] Emile remained a close family friend; after Fromental's death, he was named, along with Léon, a member of a "family council" who would act on behalf of the composer's daughters (F-Pan, Minutier central, Etude cxvii/1058, Dossier Halévy).

judgment and wit shone."[75] It was not disinterest that kept him from fuller participation, Léon notes, but his time-consuming Conservatoire and theatre positions. Yet he implies that the composer absorbed fundamental ideas in his early and continuing contact with group members. Ralph Locke supports a more vital role for the composer, writing that he "holds an entirely neglected place in the history of music among the Saint-Simonians."[76] While he does not name him a disciple, Locke recognizes the group's strong influence: he writes that Fromental's interactions with the Rodrigues–Pereire circle "may well have stimulated – although one cannot safely say to what degree – his social awareness and his interest in intellectual matters."[77] Among Halévy's activities most overtly connected to Saint-Simonian efforts was his later collaboration on an encyclopedia (*L'Encyclopédie nouvelle*) begun in the early 1860s by former Saint-Simonians, including Michel Chevalier, Duveyrier, and the Pereires;[78] a copy of Saint-Simon's *Doctrine* remained in his library until the end of his life.[79]

The Jewish circle that met at Rodrigues's home and helped to shape the movement was exceptional in its public appeals for social and political reform. Despite the changes in social and political status since civil emancipation, and the antisemitic actions during the Restoration, few Jews were politically active; according to Zosa Szajkowski, Jews as a group did not participate in the Bourbon opposition nor in the

---

[75] Léon Halévy, *Sa Vie*, 17: "société intelligente et passionnée"; "où brillaient son jugement et son esprit."

[76] Ralph P. Locke, *Music, Musicians and the Saint-Simonians* (Chicago: University of Chicago Press, 1986), 94. Other writers have included the composer among the early Saint-Simonians, but Szajkowski, "Jewish Saint-Simonians," 35, n. 13, considers his inclusion erroneous.

[77] Locke, *Saint-Simonians*, 95.

[78] Halévy was chosen by the editorial committee to write the article on music, but he never completed it, and the encylopedia never reached publication (F-Pa, Ms. 7860/2, Michel Chevalier *et al.*, "Encyclopédie, Procès-verbaux des séances du comité séance du 26 déc. 1862"; F-Pa, Ms. 7860/3–9, Michel Chevalier; F-Pa, Ms. 7860/18, "Musique par F. Halévy"). In the extant partial offprint, Halévy discusses the effect society and culture have on music, rather than its social uses. Locke, *Saint-Simonians*, 96–7, assesses the encyclopedia and Halévy's contribution.

[79] F-Pan, Minutier central, Etude cxvII/1288, De la Palme papers, inventory of Halévy's estate.

1830 Revolution.[80] Remembering Napoleon's reversal of certain civil liberties, Jews were reluctant to state openly radical, even liberal, opinions for fear of reprisal; moreover, many oppositional societies were closed to them.[81] But a number of young Jews, including the Halévys, were drawn to Saint-Simonism for its inclusiveness and promises for a new social order: its prescriptions for the elimination of hereditary rights, widespread industrialization, and economic, intellectual, and moral uplifting of the working class undoubtedly suggested ways in which post-emancipation Jews could forge more widely accepted, influential societal roles. Its emphasis on the special role of artists drew musicians and writers, including Liszt, Berlioz, Heine, and Nourrit, to the group's public lectures and gatherings – Nourrit was drawn as early as October 1830, if not before.[82]

The Halévys' liberalism put them most at odds with the monarchy of the pro-Church Charles X and led them to embrace *les trois glorieuses* (the three glorious days) of July. After Charles passed the ordinances demanding press censorship and dissolution of a newly elected Chamber on 26 July, a spontaneously merged coalition of workers, liberal bourgeois, students (many from the Ecole polytechnique), war veterans, and a reconstituted Garde nationale (National Guard) marched in the streets of Paris and formed barricades to fight off the government's troops. The composer's enthusiastic description of one of these impulsive uprisings, and of Nourrit's part in it, appears to expose his sympathies, although one might cynically presume that Halévy is indulging in a bit of myth-making. As he remembers, thirty years after the event, the *Guillaume Tell* rehearsal of 26 July, he portrays a scene that he notes had remained etched in memory. With the sounding

---

[80] Zosa Szajkowski, "French Jews during the Revolution of 1830 and the July Monarchy," *Historia Judaica* 22 (1960): 1022.

[81] *Ibid.* Szajkowski notes that "with few exceptions Jews were not as yet accepted on equal terms by the Christian population, even by liberals."

[82] Locke, *Saint-Simonians*, 98. Locke reports that a letter of Enfantin, dated 26 October 1830, refers to Nourrit's involvement; the recollections of Hippolyte Carnot, *Sur le Saint-Simonisme: Lecture faite à l'Académie des sciences morales et politiques* (Paris: Alphonse Picard, 1887), 25–6, speak of Nourrit attending the Saint-Simonian salons during 1830–31. See the communications between Nourrit and *Le Globe* in F-Pa, Ms. 7817/121 (10 December 1830) and Ms. 7817/183 (8 January 1831).

of Guillaume's words in the trio, "Either independence or death!,"
"a shiver ran through the theatre, and men who were at the back of
the stage or who filled the wings, actors, musicians, machinists, su-
pernumeraries, guards, who were struck with a sudden spark, rushed
forward and repeated the cry of Guillaume."[83] The effect was so spon-
taneous and powerful that "no movement designed by a skillful *metteur
en scène* was ever executed with so much fervor and unity."[84] An order
soon came for the rehearsal to stop, and the theatre was closed. As
Halévy recalls in detail, stage and boulevard continued to merge as
Nourrit acted as inspirational leader of what the composer calls "the
victory of the people":

> [T]he theater is silent for eleven days. And then, all that makes the
> strength and talent of Nourrit is put to the service of reality. The forum
> replaces the stage and the singer's voice rings out in the public square.
> From the top of the barricades, he sings *La Marseillaise*. Carrying the
> honors of the national militia, he marches, sword in hand, at the head of
> a company. Then the theatre reasserts its rights and opens its doors. On
> 4 August Nourrit reappears in the role of Masaniello in *La Muette*, having
> become the opera of occasion; the same day, he sings *La Parisienne*. To
> satisfy the popular wish, he runs from theatre to theatre and sings
> patriotic songs that the public repeats in chorus with an enthusiasm so
> great that it neglects accuracy and gets ahead of the tempo. It is no
> longer a role that Nourrit plays: it is he, himself. Poet, artist, citizen, he
> sings and celebrates the victory of the people.[85]

[83] Halévy, *Derniers Souvenirs*, 155: "un frémissement parcourut le théâtre, et les
hommes qui se tenaient au fond de la scène ou qui remplissaient les coulisses,
acteurs, musiciens, machinistes, comparses, soldats de garde, frappés d'une
étincelle soudaine, accoururent et répétèrent le cri de Guillaume."

[84] *Ibid.*: "Jamais mouvement réglé par un habile metteur en scène ne fut exécuté
avec autant de chaleur et d'ensemble."

[85] *Ibid.*, 155–7: "Alors, pendant onze jours, le théâtre est muet. Alors aussi, tout ce
qui fait la force et le talent de Nourrit se met au service de la réalité. Le forum
remplace la scène, et la voix du chanteur retentit sur la place publique. Du haut
des barricades, il chante *la Marseillaise*. Porté aux honneurs de la milice
nationale, il marche, l'épée à la main, à la tête d'une compagnie. Puis le théâtre
reprend ses droits et ouvre ses portes. Le 4 août, Nourrit reparaît dans le rôle de
Masaniello de *la Muette*, devenue opéra de circonstance; le même jour, il chante
la Parisienne. Pour satisfaire au voeu populaire, il court de théâtre en théâtre et
fait entendre des chants patriotiques, que le public répète en choeur avec un
enthousiasme si grand, qu'il s'affranchit de la justesse et qu'il devance le mesure.

According to his biographer Quicherat, Nourrit not only sang but helped to create *La Parisienne*, the song that became the special rallying cry of the July Revolution.[86] Quicherat writes that Nourrit was so moved by verses penned by Casimir Delavigne that he searched for appropriate music to fit them. (Quicherat, as well as the author of an 1848 article in *La Revue et gazette musicale*, identifies this music as a Prussian or Hanoverian march.[87]) As Nourrit himself wrote to a friend, he "squalled" the song so often in the span of two months, along with *La Marseillaise, Guillaume Tell,* and *Muette,* that he suffered a severe inflammation of his larynx.[88] He sang it again at the 1831 anniversary ceremony honoring the Revolution, held at the Panthéon with Louis-Philippe in attendance. It includes seven verses of revolutionary sentiment; the text of its first verse and refrain are as follows:[89]

Peuple Français, peuple de braves,	Frenchmen, brave people,
La liberté rouvre ses bras;	Liberty reopens its arms;
On nous disait: soyez esclaves!	They told us: be slaves!
Nous avons dit: soyons soldats!	We said: be soldiers!
Soudain Paris dans sa mémoire	Suddenly Paris in its memory
A retrouvé son cri de gloire:	Has found again its cry of glory:
Refrain	*Refrain*
En avant, marchons	Forward, let's march
Contre leurs canons	Against their cannons
A travers le fer,	By the sword,
Le feu des bataillons,	The battalion's fire,
Courons à la victoire.	Let's rush to victory.

Ce n'est plus un rôle que joue Nourrit, il est lui-même. Poëte, artiste, citoyen, il chante et célèbre la victoire du peuple."

[86] Quicherat, *Nourrit*, vol. I, 80–81.

[87] *Ibid.*; Georges Kastner, "La Marseillaise et les autres chants nationaux de Rouget de Lisle," *La Revue et gazette musicale* 15, no. 15 (9 April 1848): 109, recognizes the irony of a revolutionary song being based on a German-derived tune. Auber is often recognized as the music's composer, as in Fulcher, *The Nation's Image*, 212, n. 9.

[88] Letter to M. "Ed. P.," Le Havre, from Nourrit, Paris, 22 September 1830, in Quicherat, *Nourrit*, vol. III, 3.

[89] *La Parisienne, marche nationale. Paroles de Mʳ Casimir Delavigne. Chanté à l'Opéra et sur différens théâtres par A. Nourrit* (Paris: Chez Ph. Petit, n.d.) (F-Pn, Mus., Vmg. 19545).

At the anniversary the crowd pressed Nourrit to repeat the sixth verse, opening with the words "Soldier of the tricolor, /D'Orléans, you who have carried it!"[90]

Nourrit and Scribe were members of the Paris branch of the National Guard, a creation of the 1789 Revolution that was not permanently dissolved until 1871. During the Restoration the Guard retained some revolutionary and anticlerical spirit, for in April 1827 when Charles X reviewed the troops he was met with cries of "Vive la Charte! à bas les ministres! à bas les jésuites!" ("Long live the Charter! Down with the ministers! Down with the Jesuits!") In response to this challenge, the monarch dissolved the Guard; it would not reform until the days of July, when it fought to oust him. In the following years it became a symbol of the July Monarchy, although at times acting as a force of anti-republican repression. When Nourrit went to Naples after leaving the Opéra, his participation in the Revolution as well as his high National Guard rank made him a suspect of the Italian government; it believed him to be a Carbonarist, but he was able to convince officials that he was not.[91]

Both Halévys showed their support for the July Revolution and Monarchy, in part through works honoring the July uprising. A choral work by the composer entitled "Juillet 1830" begins with a recitative set to a text imbued with revolutionary sentiment:[92]

Voici la grande nuit sublime anniversaire,	Here is the grand, sublime anniversary night,
Amis, vous souvient-il de ces nuits sans sommeil	Friends, you remember these sleepless nights
Où nos braves, pensifs, l'oeil fixé sur la terre,	When our brave, thoughtful ones, with eyes fixed on the earth,
Pour combattre et mourir attendaient le soleil.	To fight and to die waited for the sun.

---

[90] Quicherat, *Nourrit*, vol. 1, 81–2: "Soldat du drapeau tricolore,/D'Orléans, toi qui l'as porté!" Quicherat notes that Louis-Philippe thought highly of the singer, and regretted Nourrit's loss of position at the Opéra in 1837 (301).

[91] *Ibid.*, 389.

[92] F-Pn, Mus., Ms. 14264, series of manuscript bifolios in Halévy's hand.

Léon also wrote a new *Marseillaise* dedicated to the National Guard,[93] as well as a *Hymne national en l'honneur des morts et des blessés des grandes journées de juillet 1830.* The latter is a poem of seven verses and refrain which opens in patriotic and belligerent tones:[94]

En avant! marchons camarades!	Onward! March, comrades!
Et s'ils ont soif de notre sang,	And if they are thirsty for our blood,
Qu'il coule sur nos barricades,	Let it flow on our barricades,
Rendons-leur le pavé glissant!	And give them a slippery path!

References to the "tricolor" and to "France's cry, suppressed for fourteen years!" clearly demonstrate an anti-Restoration, pro-Napoleonic stance typical of the 1820 generation. The text underscores a belief that Louis-Philippe, who was crowned as king "by the Will of the People," offers a return to citizens' rights disregarded under the Bourbons:

Le peuple a vengé son injure,	The people have avenged their injury,
De ses droits il veut le maintien,	They demand the preservation of their rights
Et brisant un sceptre parjure,	And, breaking a false sceptre,
Il couronne un roi-citoyen.	They crown a citizen-king.

Léon's drama *Les Trois Jours d'un grand peuple*, which premiered at the Théâtre-Français on 9 September 1830, captures this same optimism in another form.

Both Halévys had written and would write other "official" encomiums honoring different regimes, and these works may be viewed as dutiful gestures regardless of the principles embodied in the particular government.[95] They furthered their relationship with the monarchy in

---

[93] *La Marseillaise de 1830, dédiée à la Garde nationale* (Paris: Imprimerie de David, n.d.), cited in Eric C. Hansen, *Ludovic Halévy: A Study of Frivolity and Fatalism in Nineteenth-Century France* (Lanham, MD: University Press of America, 1987), 40, n. 88.

[94] Imprimerie de Pihan Delaforest (Morinval), n.d.

[95] In addition to his funeral march for the duc de Berry, Fromental wrote a "Marche funèbre pour le retour des cendres de Napoléon" (15 December 1840) (F-Pan, F^{21} 741–2).

later years – Fromental became musical director of the household of the duc d'Orléans, Louis-Philippe's eldest son, and warm admirer of the musical duchesse d'Orléans, and Léon addressed another hymn to the king at the duke's accidental death.[96] Although Eric Hansen acknowledges the composer's official affiliation with the duc d'Orléans, he does not believe that Léon enthusiastically supported the July Monarchy; similarly, Pierre Guiral believes that the younger Halévy was merely "posing" as the Monarchy's poet, yet he writes that in him was "a liberalism that never died, faith in the Orléans that will become the tradition of his family, a patriotism that was always aroused."[97] In essence, while the Halévys' Saint-Simonian and republican leanings differentiated them from many among the Orléanist bourgeoisie, their liberalism was in tune with the ideals that brought about the Monarchy and that the Monarchy loosely tried to hold onto, if only for public display. Significantly, Léon noted that, if his mentor Saint-Simon had lived to see the Revolution of 1830, he would have vigorously supported it.[98]

Contrary to Nourrit's passionate involvement with the July Revolution and the Halévys' clear endorsement of it was the political distance seemingly maintained by Scribe. While Nourrit stood at the top of the barricades, the librettist sheltered himself on his estate at Montalais, safely away from Paris. As he writes shortly after the Revolution, he appears more concerned with the value of maintaining diplomatic relations with those in power than with taking political sides:

> A great revolution has just broken out. I neither blame nor approve the causes of it. I have never been drawn by politics, but by literature, and it is only under this last report that I shall examine the consequences of a change which should be more bothersome than useful to me. From the time of the Restoration, whose shortcomings and ridicules I sang, I was pampered and feted by the opposition as well as those in power, well

[96] *Au roi: Ode sur la mort de S. A. R. Monseigneur le duc d'Orléans* (Paris: Maulde et Renou, 1842).
[97] Hansen, *Ludovic Halévy*, 9; Guiral, "Léon Halévy," in *La Famille Halévy*, ed. Loyrette, 84–5.
[98] Léon Halévy, "Souvenirs de Saint-Simon," 525.

considered by all, and I must record here all that I should acknowledge to
M. de Martignac, M. de Peyronnet, and M. d'Haussez, who have always
welcomed me so well.[99]

As if wanting to make a further point, Scribe adds "Il est vrai...,"
but trails off without completing the statement. He may have checked
himself by remembering the gratitude he owed the Restoration regimes under which he had earned close to a million francs, as Bonnefon
notes.[100] But Scribe clearly disapproved of abrupt political changes that
he saw as disruptive to the theatre, although realizing that, after the
initial phases of instability, they could "serve his interests."[101]

In an early twentieth-century study of the playwright, Neil Arvin
emphasizes Scribe's political independence, as do many writers (see
pp. 70–1 below);[102] in a more recent study, Jean-Claude Yon declares
that ideas born of the Revolution passed over Scribe.[103] These authors'
conclusions are certainly valid, for at the end of 1832, Scribe again
complained of the detrimental effects political events had on the theatre, describing the closing or abandonment of Paris theatres after the
republican and Carlist (supportive of Charles X) disturbances and the
excessively violent expressions that had "invaded" the French stage.
He railed against newspapers that exacerbated the anti-theatre climate and insulted him and his "poor Gymnase."[104] One of Scribe's

---

[99] Bonnefon, "Scribe sous l'Empire," 368; partially cited in translation by Pendle,
Eugène Scribe, 7. Jean-Baptiste-Silvère Gaye, vicomte de Martignac (1776–1832),
became Interior Minister in 1828, but was dismissed by Charles X in favor of
Polignac; Pierre-Denis Peyronnet (1778–1854), brought into power in 1829
under the retrogressive Polignac ministry, was responsible for the stringent
censorship law against the press of 1822. Charles Lemercher de Longpré, Baron
d'Haussez (1778–1854), oversaw the navy under Polignac.

[100] Bonnefon, "Scribe sous l'Empire," 368.   [101] *Ibid.*, 370.

[102] Neil Cole Arvin, *Eugène Scribe and the French Theatre, 1815–1860* (Cambridge,
MA: Harvard University Press, 1924), 7, notes that Scribe wrote no encomiums
to Napoleon during the Empire; however, he did contribute to the Napoleonic
fervor of the 1830s through theatrical portrayals of colonels, captains, and
lauriers.

[103] Yon, "Eugène Scribe," vol. I, 242.

[104] Paul Bonnefon, "Scribe sous la monarchie de Juillet d'après des documents
inédits," *Revue d'histoire littéraire de la France* 28 (1921): 65–6. The Gymnase,
established in 1820, served as the primary theatre of Scribe's *vaudevilles*; in 1824
it was renamed the Théâtre de S. A. R. Madame la Duchesse de Berry
(or Théâtre de Madame) to honor its new patron.

self-descriptions, however, seems to transform this political indifference into what may be closer to political (or one might say ideological)
moderation and an aversion to extremists – an aversion that is linked
to fears about his being an anachronistic, out-of-touch voice:

> I who have always remained faithful to my literary and patriotic
> principles. I who have not changed a bit for fifteen years and who have
> remained stationary when everyone else has moved forward, I now find
> myself behind the times and people call me *out of date, prejudiced old man,
> rococo*, etc. Liberal and classical in 1815, I am still liberal and classical in
> 1832. I therefore have against me the republicans, the Carlists, and the
> romantics, in a word the *ultras* of all types.[105]

Like Scribe, his friend Casimir Delavigne, as Binita Mehta writes,
"remained politically committed to liberal ideals while aesthetically
clinging to the bygone rules of classical theater";[106] despite his self-
labeling, Scribe absorbed aspects of Romantic drama, but nonetheless
felt bypassed by the Romantics. His expressed opposition to "the *ultras*
of all types" – both literary and political – illustrates Scribe's identity
with a more moderate, bourgeois liberalism than with that of republicans.[107] But his distance from the purely political might also be viewed
as a distrust of or cynicism about the ability and will of governments
to allow true freedom, particularly that of artistic expression.

Despite differences in individual liberal philosophies and political
involvement among these collaborators of *La Juive*, there was much
common ideological ground and shared experience among them, including an admiration for Enlightenment thought, an opposition to
the Restoration, and a belief in the basic principles promoted by the

---

[105] *Ibid.*, 65; cited in translation in Pendle, *Eugène Scribe*, 8.
[106] Binita Mehta, "Jean-François Casimir Delavigne (1793–1843)," in *Dictionary of
Literary Biography*, vol. CXCII: *French Dramatists, 1789–1914*, ed. Barbara T. Cooper
(Detroit, Washington, DC, and London: Gale Research, 1998), 70.
[107] Bonnefon, "Scribe sous la monarchie," 66. Scribe's criticism of the Romantics
and his Classicist stance does not completely accord with other statements or
with his works of the 1830s. He expressed admiration for Hugo, particularly for
Le Roi s'amuse. Scribe's works of the decade reflect an adoption of, and to some
degree an identification with, Romantic ideals, including the mystical aspects of
Robert le diable, the melodramatic shock effects and historical local color of his
grands opéras, and his borrowings from the novels and plays of Sir Walter Scott
and Shakespeare.

early July Monarchy. While the Halévys and Nourrit linked themselves closely to the Revolution of 1830 and the Halévys especially leaned toward republicanism and the "most progressive" liberalism of Saint-Simonism, Scribe reflected attitudes more typical of the Orléanist liberal bourgeoisie. Yet as their biographies and writings reveal, a fundamental bond of liberalism, one touched by the spirit of the Generation of 1820, united them as creators.

THE THEATRE AS SOCIAL AND POLITICAL FORCE

Further enhancing the rapprochement of these artists, and exposing individual theatrical aims, are their strong views about the power and freedom of the theatre and its use as a tool for the expression of important human concerns and sociopolitical ideas, and – particularly in the minds of the Halévys and Nourrit – for sociopolitical change. In Scribe's early years, as he defined a new seriousness about the theatrical profession, he revealed an interest in creating socially relevant works. In 1814, he displays an early wariness of governmental control of speech that would re-emerge more emphatically in later writings and activities. Although a distaste for law study turned him away from the law career envisioned by his mother, his anticipation of heavy Bourbon control of literary venues clearly steered him toward a theatrical career, an avenue that seemed auspicious for personal expression as well as financial success. He writes:

> With the reign that is commencing and under the heavy sceptre that is weighing on us, there will not be freedom of the press nor freedom of speech. On the contrary, the theatre can offer me a more certain career to make the most of. A revolution gives to society an entirely new face, with entirely new needs. Vaudeville, the only genre to which I am devoted, can be considered under another point of view than has been made up to the present. In place of following the paths of my colleagues and imitating them as I have done, I want to try to be myself, to have my own genre, style, and theatre.[108]

[108] Bonnefon, "Scribe sous l'Empire," 327; partially cited in Pendle, *Eugène Scribe*, 4.

The following year, he reiterates this interest, describing *Une Nuit de la Garde nationale*, a *comédie-vaudeville* written with Délestre-Poirson (Charles-Gaspard Poirson, 1790–1859), as "the first piece written according to my new ideas, a piece of the moment, a piece representing a corner of present-day society."[109] In the preface to *Le Combat des montagnes* (1817), Scribe again recognizes the topicality of *vaudevilles*, while noting their social and political evanescence.[110] As Douglas Cardwell writes, Scribe aimed to create fiction entertaining to his audience, but fiction with "the ring of truth";[111] comic, satiric aspects added to the ephemerality of these works, although many had an underlying serious core overlooked by critics.[112] Scribe sensed the profit-making potential of socially relevant works, an idea that was not new and certainly not unique to him, but his success came to taint his artistic standing among contemporary writers, even extending to historical assessments of his work.[113]

Scribe strongly believed that artists should be free to make controversial statements through the theatre, and he worked to give them this freedom by leading the Société des auteurs dramatiques. While stating early in his career that his goal was to write theatrical pieces that represented "a corner of society," in his speech on 28 January 1836 marking his induction into the Académie française, he offered the thesis – hotly contested by the revered historian Abel-François Villemain

[109] *Ibid.*, 330, cited in translation in Pendle, *Eugène Scribe*, 5.
[110] Cited in Helene Koon and Richard Switzer, *Eugène Scribe* (Boston: Twayne Publishers, 1980), 47.
[111] Douglas Cardwell, "Eugène Scribe (1791–1861)," in *Dictionary of Literary Biography*, vol. CXCII: *French Dramatists, 1789–1914*, ed. Barbara T. Cooper (Detroit, Washington, DC, and London: Gale Research, 1998), 368.
[112] "(Augustin-Eugène) Scribe," in Pierre Larousse, *Grand Dictionnaire universel du xixe siècle*, 17 vols. (Paris: Administration du Grand Dictionnaire universel, 1866–79. Reprint, Geneva and Paris: Slatkine, 1982), vol. XIV, 424. Koon and Switzer, *Scribe*, 84, describe his comedies with contemporary references as "moral comedies" instead of "social comedies" and characterize Scribe as an individual "concerned with the moral problems of his ever changing society."
[113] Koon and Switzer, *Scribe*, 327–8; Pendle, *Eugène Scribe*, 4–6. Beyond his desire to share in the profits of directors, he worked hard as president of the Société des auteurs dramatiques to obtain a bigger percentage of profits for all dramatic authors.

(1790–1870) – that theatre of earlier decades had not reflected political realities.[114] Paying tribute to his predecessor Arnault, Scribe passionately insisted on the independence of artists from governmental constraints and decried the curbing of liberty through abuse of power, intensifying sentiments expressed in his 1814 evaluation. He reminded the august body of Academicians how Arnault had been a pawn of the state and criticized the Académie itself for caving in to political pressure.[115] Because Arnault had aligned himself with the comte de Provence (later Louis XVIII) in the days when an *homme de lettres* needed the protection of a *grand seigneur*, he had to leave France in 1792 when the count was exiled.[116] Arnault was allowed to return, for he later became a favorite of Napoleon, who imposed his own literary preferences on at least one of the dramatist's works, the *tragédie Les Vénitiens*.[117] Because of Arnault's association with Napoleon, he was exiled again after the Hundred Days, dismissed from the Académie, and his works were suppressed. Scribe, in direct, acerbic statements, condemns the Académie's hypocritical and politically motivated action of expulsion and its declaration, "by virtue of an ordinance countersigned by a minister," that his great works *Marius à Minturnes* and *Les Vénitiens* "had never existed."[118] A fervent belief in authorial freedom and a distrust of governmental promises to ensure it fuel Scribe's words. His speech, coming several months after preventive censorship had been reinstated, provides insight into his arguments as Société president in support of this form of censorship, which he saw as less invasive than such arbitrary repressive censorship as the 1832 banning of Hugo's *Le Roi s'amuse*. Other liberal thinkers decried the reversal of the no-censorship promises of the 1830 Charte represented by both governmental actions.

[114] Eugène Scribe, "Discours de réception à l'Académie française, prononcé dans la séance du 28 janvier 1836," preface to *Oeuvres complètes de M. Eugène Scribe*, 5 vols., rev. ed. (Paris: Furne & Cie / Aimé André, 1840–41), vol. I, 1–14. Because Scribe took well over a year to write his speech, his formal address came much later than his election.

[115] Scribe, "Discours," 3.   [116] *Ibid.*, 4.

[117] *Ibid.* Scribe related how Napoleon, "whose literary opinions were just as fixed as his political opinions," dictated a change from the play's original happy ending to a tragic one.

[118] *Ibid.*, 5.

In paradoxical statements about the import of theatrical works, including his own *comédies*, Scribe argued that the theatre, as a vehicle for diversion, had commonly represented the opposite of social and political truths, unlike the boldly critical *chansons* that he saw as a truly activist art form.[119] Scribe in fact suggested that social reality lay in what was *not* said in the theatre:

> You run to the theatre, not to learn and improve yourselves, but to be distracted and amused . . . Thus, during the Terror, it was precisely because your eyes were offended by bloody scenes of carnage that you were happy to find in the theatre human values and goodness, as they could be found nowhere else at the time. In the same way, during the Restoration, when all of Europe had been oppressing you, you were reminded of the time when you made the laws of Europe, and the past became a consolation for the present.
>
> The theatre is quite rarely the expression of a society, or at least, as you have seen, it often provides an inverted image of it, and it is in what it does not say that one must look for or guess at what actually goes on.[120]

Scribe's focus on *comédie* was undoubtedly rooted in his extensive work in comedic genres and his reputation as a *"mere" vaudevilliste*, as he humbly introduced himself to the Académie audience.[121]

---

[119] In Arvin's interpretation, *French Theatre*, 23, Scribe "develops the paradox, contradicted by his own example, that comedy, in order to be successful, does not have to resemble society." Koon and Switzer, *Scribe*, 26, find Scribe's thesis curious since it was an indictment of the irrelevance of his own works.

[120] Scribe, "Discours," 9–10: "Vous courez au théâtre, non pour vous instruire ou vous corriger, mais pour vous distraire et vous divertir . . . Ainsi, dans la terreur, c'était justement parce que vos yeux étaient affligés par des scènes de sang et de carnage, que vous étiez heureux de retrouver au théâtre l'humanité et la bienfaisance, qui étaient alors des fictions. De même, sous la restauration, où l'Europe entière venait de vous opprimer, on vous rappelait le temps où vous donniez des lois à l'Europe, et le passé vous consolait du présent. Le théâtre est donc bien rarement l'expression de la société, ou du moins, et comme vous l'avez vu, il en est souvent l'expression inverse, et c'est dans ce qu'il ne dit pas qu'il faut chercher ou deviner ce qui existait." Cf. Gerhard's discussion of Bonald's aesthetic theory of tragedy as "faithful mirror of human life and society" in *The Urbanization of Opera*, 13.

[121] Scribe, "Discours," 3. Scribe portrays himself as "only" a *vaudevilliste* unworthy to follow a literary voice as powerful as Arnault, whose *tragédie Marius à*

In a formal response, Villemain contradicted Scribe's claims, charging that he had misjudged himself, that in fact he "had spent his entire life refuting the text that he supports," and then admonished him: "you are a historian in spite of yourself."[122] Villemain elaborated with an overview of French *comédie* to disprove Scribe's assertions, emphasizing that it, or theatre as a whole, serves as a supplement to history rather than a narrator as it "bears precious witness to the history of opinions and morals," including "the prejudices, the memories, and the regrets of a people."[123]

Scribe likely meant that, instead of being completely void of social or political content, *comédies* (and, perhaps by extension, *tragédies*) had typically reacted to societal changes anachronistically rather than motivating or embodying them. By beginning with commentary on the manipulation and rejection of Arnault's works, he clearly conveyed that censorship and autocratic political climates had not allowed dramas to explore directly and openly hard truths on the stage, at least not consistently. In his contrast of *comédies* with *chansons*, he implies a regret that the former could not be as politically frank as the latter. If Scribe's theory is applied, one might argue that the anticlerical critique represented by *La Juive* (see pp. 116ff.) would have had a more powerful political relevance and impact during the Restoration when the Church's power held full sway, rather than in the July Monarchy.

His impassioned statements about Arnault's fate and authorial freedom may provide a clue to his distance from political factions. His own experiences offer further insights. Although Scribe had been presented as an Académie candidate as early as 1830, he claims in a letter to a friend

---

Minturnes he admires greatly. It is likely that Scribe's public humility was laden with an unspoken sarcasm, for in another commentary on the success of *Bertrand et Raton* he scoffed at the childishness of the public in correlating the length of the work (five acts) with its importance and in undervaluing the comparatively lighter and shorter *vaudevilles* that made up the bulk of his output (Bonnefon, "Scribe sous la monarchie," 70).

[122] *Journal des débats* (30 January 1836): 3: "a passé toute sa vie à réfuter le texte qu'il soutient"; "vous êtes historien malgré vous." Véron notes that he witnessed Villemain's severe and ironic response to the speech (*Mémoires*, vol. III, 67).

[123] *Journal des débats* (30 January 1836): 3: "un témoin précieux pour l'histoire des opinions et des moeurs"; "les préjugés, les souvenirs, les regrets d'un peuple."

(6 October 1834) that his not being a "political man" had delayed his election; Arvin reports that clerical members of the Académie had voted against Scribe because of the irreligious nature of some of his plays, including *Madame de Sainte-Agnès; ou, La Femme à principes* (1829).[124] Throughout his theatrical career, Scribe had felt the weight of governmental censure. In 1812, his work *Marguerite de Valois*, written with Germain Delavigne, was prohibited by the imperial police, forcing Scribe to rename it *Thibault, comte de Champagne*.[125] In his debut years particularly, Scribe persisted despite the intrusion of imperial censors, notes Bonnefon, unlike playwright Charles Brifaut, who left the theatre after he was forced to turn his *Don Sanche d'Aragon* into *Ninus II* with a change of scene from Spain to Assyria.[126] But difficulties continued in his mature years, with the duchesse de Berry threatening to take away her patronage of the Théâtre de Madame over the performance of Scribe's *Avant, pendant et après* in 1828.[127] Censors also objected to Scribe's *La Manie des places; ou, La Folie du siècle* (1828), believing that it referred too closely to Martignac, the liberal minister then in power (ousted in 1829), but Scribe averted the banning of this work by writing directly to the minister, who gave his approval.[128]

Scribe's early libretti for *La Muette de Portici* and *Les Huguenots* contained revolutionary and anti-royalist material that was suppressed by censorship bodies. Although his collaborator Germain Delavigne wrote the first, three-act version of *La Muette*'s libretto, he undoubtedly approved of its content; when censors demanded that the libretto be purged of explicit revolutionary passages, Scribe answered their demands as he expanded the libretto to five acts.[129] The censors

---

[124] Bonnefon, "Scribe sous la monarchie," 72–3; Arvin, *French Theatre*, 23.
[125] Bonnefon, "Scribe sous l'Empire," 326.
[126] *Ibid.* But Brifaut returned to co-write the libretto for Spontini's *Olimpie* (1819) and *Charles de Navarre* (1820).
[127] *Ibid.*, 364.   [128] *Ibid.*
[129] Herbert Schneider, "La Muette de Portici," in *The New Grove Dictionary of Opera*, ed. Sadie, vol. III, 505. See the transcription of four libretto versions in *La Muette de Portici: Kritische Ausgabe des Librettos und Dokumentation der ersten Inszenierung*, eds. Herbert Schneider and Nicole Wild (Tübingen: Stauffenburg-Verlag, 1993). Gerhard, *The Urbanization of Opera*, 130, assesses the libretto as "unambivalently antirevolutionary."

also frowned on the implications of guilt of Church and Crown in the sixteenth-century massacre of Protestants, references that corresponded with Voltaire's historical treatment of the event and the views of later liberal historians. They particularly objected to the inclusion of Catherine de Médicis, as well as a verse originally given to Raoul in Act V, Scene ii, in which King Charles is described overseeing the massacre from a balcony.[130] The censors may also have disliked its original title, *St. Barthélemy*, a direct, conspicuously political reference to the well-known historical event and symbol.

As an articulator of early Saint-Simonian thought, Léon Halévy appears to have held a more idealistic view about theatre's role in society, at least its potential role. Prominent in his introduction to *Opinions littéraires*, as well as in the volume's final essay that Locke attributes to him, "L'Artiste, le savant, et l'industriel: Dialogue," is the belief that art could promote social and moral reform and that artists, along with industrialists and scientists, would be leaders in bringing this about. Artists are viewed as belonging to an influential avant-garde leading society in new directions, contributing to the common good, and propagating "timely," "generous" ideas.[131] With missionary zeal, Halévy appeals to fellow artists to produce works that benefit society rather than address the "imagination" alone and reminds them that theatrical works hold the utmost power to activate social change:

> It is we artists who will be your avant-garde: the power of the arts is in fact the most immediate and the most rapid. We have arms of all kinds: when we want to spread new ideas among mankind, we inscribe them on marble or canvas. We popularize them in poetry and song. We use in turn the lyre or the fife, the ode or the chanson, the historical account or the novel. *The dramatic stage is open to us, and it is there, above all, that we exert an electric and victorious influence* [my emphasis]. We address

---

[130] See the censors' libretto of *Les Huguenots*, F-Pan, F[18] 669.
[131] Locke, *Saint-Simonians*, 37. Rather than accepting the common view that the essay is one of the last writings of Saint-Simon, who then "regressed" from its ideas in *Le Nouveau christianisme*, Locke believes it represents one of the first of the Saint-Simonian movement, largely written by Léon Halévy, whom he assesses as "the first of the disciples to tackle the problem of enriching and aestheticizing Saint-Simon's view of the social role of art."

ourselves to the imagination and to the sentiments of mankind, we must therefore always exercise the most vivid and decisive action; and if our role appears to be nil or at least truly secondary today, it is because the arts were missing what is essential to their spirit and success, a common impulse and a widely shared idea.[132]

Although Fromental did not contribute to early Saint-Simonian publications or make public statements about the mission of the arts and theatre in years prior to *La Juive*, he did express ideas aligning with his brother's in the early days of the Second Republic.[133] As *citoyen* Halévy, he ran as candidate of the Association des artistes-musiciens for election to the Assemblée nationale (Constituent or National Assembly) on a slate with Victor Hugo and three other artists.[134] (In and of itself, the fact that artists were being put forward as governmental representatives appears a realization of Saint-Simonian goals.) At his election as candidate, Halévy promised that he "would demand the greatest freedom" for theatres, encourage wider access for all citizens to the "education" they offered, and make it possible for any citizen to open a theatre.[135] A public notice of his candidacy further points to his

[132] "L'Artiste, le savant, et l'industriel: Dialogue," in Saint-Simon *et al., Opinions littéraires*, 341–4, cited in translation in Locke, *Saint-Simonians*, 38–40. (See the fuller quotation, with the original French, in Appendix J.)

[133] In even later years the composer expressed views on the social application of the arts in a response to a publication by comte Léon de Laborde (1807–69) that he wrote as the Académie's *secrétaire perpétuel*; he also wrote for the choral society, the Orphéon, and published the singing primer *Leçons de lecture musicale* (1857) for use in Parisian schools. See Fromental Halévy, "Les Arts et l'industrie: Observations sur un ouvrage de M. le comte Léon de Laborde, membre de l'Institut," *Souvenirs et portraits: Etudes sur les beaux-arts* (Paris: Michel Lévy Frères, 1861), 307–38. Although the essay represents collective views of a nine-member Académie commission, and not strictly the composer's personal ideas, Halévy at least shared them and helped to shape them in his influential role. Included are endorsements of Laborde's suggestions to make art more than "a purely aristocratic pleasure," to make its study a part of general education, including that of the working classes, and to direct the work of skillful artists toward industry and national "progress," though Halévy disapproved of the author's promotion of art "of practical utility."

[134] Hansen, *Ludovic Halévy*, 34, n. 28.

[135] *La Revue et gazette musicale* 15, no. 17 (23 April 1848): 125–6. The *Revue* proposed to its readers thirty-four candidates, including Halévy, Hugo, the *chansonnier* Béranger, and the Ministre de l'Instruction publique Carnot.

belief in the social power of art. Although Halévy lost the election, the notice advocates that he and his fellow candidates from "[t]he humanities, the theatre, and the liberal arts" should represent the country because it was the "all-powerful ideas" of France that had inspired all of Europe.[136] The document also reveals the seriousness of Halévy's Saint-Simonian and/or republican intentions to uplift the working classes through the arts and to work for the good of the country. (See the transcription and translation of this notice in Appendix K.) In an address as candidate, Halévy makes his political stance crystal-clear, implying that while he has always been a believer in liberal and democratic principles, it is only after the February Revolution that he completely identifies himself as republican:

> I was not republican on 22 February. But what citizen is not loyally, sincerely republican today? Is the Republic not the last word of societies? For all good minds, the accession of the Republic was unassailably necessary . . . A thousand times more generous than the Republics of antiquity, the new Republic proclaims that all men are brothers. Before this magnificent teaching that France will keep noble and pure, all of Europe shuddered; the people are emancipated. France, like a radiant light, shows to all the path of true freedom. Who today would dare recommend that the country regress from this glorious course?[137]

According to Hansen, the Revolution of 1848 "troubled" Léon, but he honored the government's request to write a new *Marseillaise* ("La Marseillaise nouvelle"), and by 1852 was a committed republican.[138] This republicanism held throughout his later years; his son Ludovic

---

[136] As cited in translation in Hansen, *Ludovic Halévy*, 9–10.

[137] *La Revue et gazette musicale* 15, no. 17 (23 April 1848): 126: "Je n'étais pas républicain le 22 février. Mais quel citoyen n'est pas aujourd'hui loyalement, sincèrement républicain? La République n'est-elle pas le dernier mot des sociétés? Pour tous les bons esprits, l'avènement de la République était invinciblement nécessaire . . . Plus généreuse mille fois que les Républiques de l'antiquité, la République nouvelle proclame que tous les hommes sont frères. Devant ce magnifique enseignement que la France conservera noble et pur, l'Europe entière a tressailli; les peuples sont affranchis. La France, comme une lumière éclatante, montre à tous le chemin de la vraie liberté. Qui donc aujourd'hui oserait conseiller à la patrie de rétrograder dans cette route glorieuse?"

[138] Hansen, *Ludovic Halévy*, 23; 40, n. 90.

attested in 1870 that his father was "very republican, constantly urging revolution" and very much against the Empire of Napoleon III.[139]

Nourrit, too, had pointed things to say about the power of the theatre that merge with his own actions as an artist-leader during the 1830 Revolution and echo Saint-Simonian ideas. Although Nourrit's involvement seems to have come after Léon Halévy had officially left the movement, he, too, bears the influence of views the writer had helped articulate. Within the month following the première of *La Juive*, Nourrit enthuses in a letter to a friend that in art lies a greater potential for inducing societal changes than in government, noting that he "still believe[s] more in the future and the power of art than in the future and the power of the constitutional government" (a view seemingly shared by Scribe), and that, as an artist, he continues to work harder than ever for "individual progress" and "progress for all."[140] Another letter of 1836 responding to an article in *Le Temps* by Edouard Charton, a popular Saint-Simonian preacher, reflects the language found in the *Doctrine* and other writings by Léon: "Yes, the theater can and must be something other than a place for the idlers to divert themselves. Since an actor's effect is often powerful, it must become *useful*. To awake generous thoughts, to exalt the loving faculties – there's our mission!"[141] Having already realized the close interaction of theatre and politics in revolutionary days, Nourrit moved away from the purely political in his increasingly religious last years. Drawn to Barrault's and Enfantin's vision of an actor-priest who would transform the theatre, Nourrit dreamed that it could become a force for moral, and even religious, amelioration.[142]

The comparatively pragmatic Scribe, despite contradictory statements and censorship battles, attempted to realize his underlying desire

---

[139] Ludovic Halévy, *Carnets inédits*, vol. XXII, 177–8 (30 August 1870), quoted in *ibid.*, 40, n. 91.

[140] Quicherat, *Nourrit*, vol. III, 9–10: letter to M. "Ed. P.," Le Havre, 27 March 1835.

[141] Cited in translation by Locke, *Saint-Simonians*, 99.

[142] *Ibid.*, 98–101. Locke also discusses an article printed in the *Courrier de Lyon* after Nourrit's death in 1839 which articulated the singer's plans, including his emphasis on the "great choral masses and numerous performing artists" who would be a part of his theatre, as well as a school that would be attached to it (100).

that theatre should be free to express political truths and address con-troversial subjects. Works with political overtones appeared during 1828–9, under Martignac: other than *La Muette*, these included *Avant, pendant et après* (1828), a drama suffused with criticism of previous political eras, and *Madame de Sainte-Agnès; ou, La Femme à principes* (1829), whose protagonist resembled a feminine Tartuffe.[143] Follow-ing the political upheaval of the July Revolution, Scribe produced melodramas, historical plays, and operas with pronounced social, po-litical, and moral messages, after retrenching from his "rose-water comedy" of the Théâtre de Madame (with the exception of a few "diversionary" comedies).[144] By 1833, Scribe initiated a "new manner," as literary scholars have recognized, turning away from "indulgences" and moving toward the "decency and good taste" represented in his five-act political drama *Bertrand et Raton; ou, L'Art de conspirer*.[145] This work began his series of historical or political works performed at the Théâtre-Français, including *L'Ambitieux* (1834), *La Camaraderie* (1837), and *Les Indépendants* (1837).[146] In several dramas, themes of liberty, tolerance, individual rights, and portrayals of an anachronistic and sometimes corrupt aristocracy reflect liberal sentiments.

In the triptych *Avant, pendant et après*, Scribe takes a group of charac-ters through dramatic life changes in three separate historical periods as he satirizes political abuses and excesses within each.[147] In the *Avant* section, set in 1787, with the aristocracy in power, Scribe is critical of rigidly drawn class distinctions that obstruct the love of the charac-ters Gérard and Julie. In *Pendant*, Scribe condemns the violence of the revolutionary "Terror" and depicts a much-changed world surround-ing the central characters: servants are forbidden, names are changed, new laws are enacted, and the aristocracy is being hunted down. After witnessing a violent confrontation, an army general – a former

---

[143] Bonnefon, "Scribe sous l'Empire," 364.   [144] Arvin, *French Theatre*, 20–21.

[145] *Ibid.*, 21–2. Scribe repeated in 1833 (cited in Bonnefon, "Scribe sous la monarchie," 70) how he had profited from the public's fatigue of romantic excesses of bloody, incestuous, and adulterous plots centering on "shameless women" and prostitutes.

[146] "(Augustin-Eugène) Scribe," in Larousse, *Grand Dictionnaire*, vol. XIV, 424.

[147] Bonnefon, "Scribe sous l'Empire," 364.

chevalier – is given the clear voice of reason (perhaps the voice of Scribe himself?) in Scene viii: "Ah, do not confuse liberty with the excesses committed in its name. Liberty, as we understand it, is the friend of order and duty; it protects rights. It approves laws and institutions, not scaffolds."[148]

Of the three periods, Scribe depicts *Après*, the final period set in 1828, most optimistically. (This date corresponds to the time of the brief change to Martignac's liberal ministry.) Gone is the unjust, privileged aristocracy, but one old aristocrat, the vicomte de Morlière, returns as an anachronism after being marooned on a desert island for forty years; he is shocked at the changes in French society, particularly the taxing of citizens and the necessity to work for a living. The barriers between social classes have broken down and the merit of an individual depends more on skills and contributions and less on family background. The chevalier, revealing his adaptation to a changing social climate by accepting his daughter's suitor despite a lack of pedigree, represents the new era's credo, saying: "Let me not punish the children for the sins of their father; merit and honor, wherever they are found, have the right to our esteem."[149]

Scribe does not make the aristocracy his single target, as demonstrated in his sympathetic portrayal of the chevalier. But in several other plays, he treats royal and clerical figures harshly. In the two-act *comédie-vaudeville Le Moulin de Javelle* (1833), Scribe draws the main characters directly from French history during the Regency of 1718, boldly focusing on Philippe, duc d'Orléans, regent under Louis XV, and grandfather of Louis-Philippe, together with his confidant and advisor, l'abbé Dubois. He paints Philippe and Dubois as immoral, power-abusing individuals, along with the duchesse du Maine, who plots to assassinate the duke. Suggestions of an indolent, profligate lifestyle resonate with portrayals of aristocrats and clerics prominent in political literature of the revolutionary era, as well as the early July Monarchy. Scribe also dramatizes common liberal accusations of the lascivious behavior of clerics, including the maintaining of harems within the hallowed confines of the Church. But, as in *La Juive*, Scribe does not

---

[148] Cited in translation by Koon and Spitzer, *Scribe*, 90.   [149] *Ibid.*

his own works, suggest that he was not lacking in ideology. As attested by Villemain, Scribe contradicted his own self-judgments: in a number of ways, he appears guided by the principles of liberalism, albeit a conservative or moderate liberalism. His dramas and operas, whether comic or tragic, truly carry weight as historical documents reflective of shifts in political and social currents, although they must be viewed against the realities or threats of censorship and other external forces. Whether they represent an impersonal "exploitation" of current ideas and sentiments or an extension of Scribe's own values is debatable, but it is likely that they represent an amalgamation of both. His desire to produce relevant and sometimes provocative dramas, if set against the Halévys' and Nourrit's social views of the theatre, points to a collective desire to imbue *La Juive* with topical, thought-provoking messages. One might easily apply Fulcher's statement about the collaboration of *Robert le diable* to that of *La Juive*: it "was the result of a felicitous, indeed remarkable coordination of theatrical conceptions and aims."[158] Yes, the theatre could be a diversionary, profit-making arena, but for these authors it also represented a vehicle for advancing powerful ideas embraced by many of their generation, and those springing from their own convictions. And for the composer and his brother, these powerful ideas were ones tempered by the legacy of Judaism, as we shall see.

[158] Fulcher, *The Nation's Image*, 68.

What did it mean to be a Jew in the "land of promise" in the early nineteenth century, the land that had made gestures of *fraternité* and offered moments of *liberté* and *égalité*? To be one among the early generations of Jewish *citoyens* (citizens) in this French Catholic world, a world in which – in some corners – "juif" remained synonymous with "usurer"? Such rhetorical questions enter our minds as we look more closely at the composer and his brother, not only as *juifs* in France, but as *israélites* who embraced and promoted the principles of liberalism. In their stories and creative output can be felt a palpable tension in the balancing of their lives as *citoyens* and *israélites*, a tension that led to a certain ambivalence toward their heritage and the religion of their birth. Their experiences, and those of their father, offer "insider" views of the Jewish representations in *La Juive*, and cast at least a slender beam of light onto some of the composer's key musical choices and expressions. The brothers' philosophies, and their mediation between the public world of France and the private, sometimes internal world of their ancestors, begin in the beliefs and efforts of their devout, literary father, Elie Halphen Halévy (1760–1826), co-founder and chief editor of the first Jewish journal in France, *L'Israélite français: Ouvrage moral et littéraire* (1817–19).[1]

Encapsulating a view fundamental to Elie Halévy's literary and religious activities, and to post-revolutionary goals of reformist French

---

[1] Paris: Chez Poulet. In many sources, Elie Halévy is designated the founder and editor of the monthly journal, but only Mathis Dalmbert is designated as *éditeur-propriétaire* in the journal's first issue (title page). See Léon Halévy, *Sa Vie*, 5–7. Hansen, *Ludovic Halévy*, 3, mentions Dalmbert as the publisher; Patrick Girard, *Les Juifs de France de 1789 à 1860: De l'émancipation à l'égalité* (Paris: Calmann-Lévy, 1976), 87, lists Dalmbert and Germain Mathiot as co-founders with Halévy, who functioned with the support of the Consistoire central and the rabbi of Cologne.

Jews, is the journal's epigraph, drawn from Psalm 37, v. 3: "Tiens au pays, et conserve la foi" ("Hold to one's country, and keep to one's faith"). The epigraph embodies ideals Elie transmitted to his sons, although many biographical interpretations imply that both brothers held to the first part of their father's editorial maxim but not to the second. They are generally characterized as non-practicing, assimilated Jews, with little thought of their religious heritage; at times Léon's ties to Judaism are thought to be closer than Fromental's, while some authors believe those of the elder brother remained stronger. Entries in the *Encyclopaedia Judaica*, for example, describe the composer as having been "consciously neutral" to Judaic faith, while noting that Léon had "intermittent" connections with the Jewish community.[2] Eric Hansen, in his study of the composer's famous nephew, the librettist Ludovic Halévy (1834–1908), goes so far as to say that "[t]hrough Fromental Halévy the family severed all traditional ties with Hebrew beliefs and culture; if, by the time of the composer's earliest triumphs, his clan claimed any connection with its past, it was one in name only."[3]

Rather than ignoring, or being indifferent to, their Jewish heritage, both Halévys in fact strongly demonstrated identification with Jewish concerns.[4] Although they were clearly non-traditional Jews, it is misleading to speak of either as a Jew "in name only." Instead, they embody a changing identity among the first generation of educated, post-emancipation French Jews – the new *israélites* – who were eager to participate more fully as citizens while searching for alternative ways in which to retain their heritage. With their entry into institutions from which Jews had virtually been excluded, both Fromental and Léon became citizens in a fuller sense and advocates of an even more expansive assimilation into French Christian society than had been possible in previous generations. Yet at the same time they were drawn, both discreetly and overtly, to the traditions to which their father clung,

---

[2] Moshé Catane, "Halévy," and Josef Tal, "Jacques (François) Fromental Elie Halévy," in *Encyclopaedia Judaica*, 16 vols. (New York: Macmillan, 1971–2), vol. VII, 1181–2, 1184–5.

[3] Hansen, *Ludovic Halévy*, 3.

[4] Jordan, *Fromental Halévy*, offers insightful discussions on the significance of Halévy's roots.

and inspired by his attempts to align Judaism with the values and ideals of his adopted country, to increase awareness of Jewish history, and to combat religious narrow-mindedness.

The duality built into the prescription of *L'Israélite français*, paradoxical for Jews in countries that did not grant them civil rights, remained problematic for Fromental and Léon Halévy and other young French Jews of their generation. The equivocations and contradictions in the Halévys' public lives should be understood in the context of an age when complete equality for Jews was claimed while apostasy remained an avenue toward gaining ground socially and financially, when new Jewish identities were taking hold while antisemitism was palpable in both private and public. Fromental and Léon may have downplayed their Jewishness in their ambitious rise to the nation's intelligentsia, but they also created musical, literary, and dramatic works that point to affiliations with the Parisian Jewish community and interest in the ongoing debates about Jewish issues.

Behind their father's determination to "keep to one's faith" was his Orthodox Jewish upbringing as the eldest son of a rabbi, Jacob (Jaakov) Levy. Elie Halévy was born in Fürth, a Bavarian village immediately northwest of Nuremberg in which the Jewish population lived in a circumscribed area and interacted with the dominant Christian populace only in restricted commercial activities;[5] he then lived in the town of Würzburg. As a young man he moved to Metz, France, shortly before 1789, practically on the eve of the Revolution. Preceded by his brother, who returned to Germany to escape the violence, Elie remained in France, saying that "all this interests me."[6] Quite probably the promise of great social change drew Elie, for he soon became affiliated with a number of intellectual circles of reform-minded Jews in Metz. In 1798, aged thirty-eight, Elie married the seventeen-year-old Julie Mayer (1781–1819) of Lorraine,[7] and shortly afterward moved with

[5] Béatrice Philippe, "Elie Halévy," in *La Famille Halévy*, ed. Loyrette, 55. Becker, "'Dieu de nos pères,'" 36, states that Jews could in fact live and work in Christian neighborhoods in Fürth.

[6] Hansen, *Ludovic Halévy*, 2.

[7] *Ibid.*, 33, n. 8, cites the marriage license (24 June 1798), F-Pan, Minutier central, Etude cxvii/1058, Dossier Halévy.

her to Paris, where he set up household in a Jewish neighborhood on the rue Neuve-des-Mathurins. He first tried to earn a livelihood at commerce, but quickly lost money; upon the reopening of the synagogues after the Reign of Terror, he served as choirmaster for several Parisian synagogues, and, according to a number of sources, was later appointed cantor of the Central Synagogue in the rue de la Victoire.[8] On 27 May 1799, several months before Napoleon's *coup d'état*, Elie's first son was born and given, of several *prénoms*, the revolutionary name Fromental;[9] Léon's birth followed in 1802. The marriage also produced three daughters, Zélie (1801–24), Flore (1805–72), and Mélanie (1813–98).[10]

Besides his musical endeavors, Elie's Hebraic scholarship and poetry gave him a certain renown. Among works considered influential in modern Hebraic literature are poems that synthesize Judaic and French national spirit.[11] The work often designated as his most significant is *Ha-Shalom*, a poem written to commemorate the cease-fire between France and England in 1801.[12] Modeled after the Greco-Roman ode then popular in France, *Ha-Shalom* effuses patriotic rhetoric in its lauding of Napoleon's peacemaking efforts.[13] Halévy's praise extends to France itself, not only "the most beautiful nation" and "the garden of God," but the land where liberty and equality are available to all men,

[8] Hansen, *Ludovic Halévy*, 2. Elie Halévy goes unnamed as cantor for the Temple Sainte-Avoye in Gérard Ganvert, "La Musique synagogale à Paris à l'époque du premier Temple consistorial (1822–74)" (Ph.D. diss., Université de Paris-Sorbonne, 1984), 60–73. For this synagogue, Ganvert names the cantors Hayem Blos (or Plozky) (1797–1814), Isaac David (1815–18), and Israël Lovy (1818–33).

[9] The political leader Pierre Joxe, great-great-grandson of Léon Halévy and grandson of Daniel Halévy, spoke of the revolutionary significance of the name in a discussion aired on France-Musique, 22 April 2000, 7:30–8:00 p.m. Joxe, formerly the Ministre de l'Intérieur and Ministre de la Défense, was named president of la Cour des comptes in 1993.

[10] Léon notes in *Sa Vie*, 16, that Zélie died "in the full bloom of youth and beauty." The two youngest sisters never married and lived with Fromental and Léon after the death of their parents. See Jean-Pierre Halévy, "La Famille Halévy (1760–1960)," in *La Famille Halévy*, ed. Loyrette, 120–23.

[11] S[amuel] Cahen, "De la littérature hébraïque et juive en France," *Les Archives israélites* 1 (1840): 35, 38.

[12] *Ha-Shalom: Hymne à l'occasion de la paix par le Cen. Elie Lévy, chantée en hébreu et lue en français, dans la grande synagogue, à Paris, le 17 Brumaire An X* (Paris: Imprimerie de la République, An X [1801]).

[13] *Ibid.*, 16. Also referred to in Hansen, *Ludovic Halévy*, 3, 33, n. 9.

including the Jews.[14] In return, urges the poem, the Jews should join their compatriots in rebuilding France.

Halévy's *Ha-Shalom* reflects his own ready acceptance of a new allegiance – only a decade after the granting of emancipation to Jews in France – and perhaps that of the worshipers in the "Great Synagogue" of Paris, for whom it was first sung, or recited, in Hebrew on 8 November 1801, accompanied by a French translation. It soon spread to other synagogues and Christian churches throughout the country, bringing Halévy immediate recognition. The renowned Protestant minister Paul-Henri Marron (1754–1832) praised the author as a new David, "who has celebrated the return of peace in Hebraic verse in a brilliant manner."[15] The Orientalist Isaac Silvestre de Sacy (1758–1838) added to the enthusiastic reception, writing an adulatory letter that appeared as preface to the work's first edition in 1802.[16]

Halévy also worked as translator for the Consistoire central de Paris, the ruling body of the seven regional Consistoires organized under Napoleon in 1808 to administer Jewish congregations. Many Consistoire pronouncements translated by Halévy profess a keen admiration for the emperor, who both expanded and curbed Jewish civil rights during his reign, yet undoubtedly couched in effusive phrases is a diplomatic flattery useful for the preservation and advancement of the community. Among published translations is a *Discours* by a *grand rabbin* of the Consistoire central, presented on 25 December 1808 in the synagogue of the rue Sainte-Avoye to celebrate the surrender of Madrid to Napoleon.[17] In the *Discours*, the emperor is depicted as a conqueror as great as Alexander, Caesar, Scipio, and Charlemagne, a wise and compassionate legislator and father to his people, and the

---

[14] *Ha-Shalom*, 8, 11. Also in Hansen, *ibid.*

[15] This excerpt ("[q]ui a célébré d'une manière brillante en vers hébraïques le retour de la paix"), drawn from Marron's poetic tribute in Latin verse, is found in Léon Halévy's *Sa Vie*, along with a French translation (5, 6, n. 1). See the full review, F-Pan, Minutier central, Etude CXVII/1058, Dossier Halévy.

[16] Letter dated 11 November 1801 (20 Brumaire An X) in *Ha-Shalom*, 3; cited in Hansen, *Ludovic Halévy*, 3, 33, n. 11. De Sacy later wrote the young Léon Halévy a letter of recommendation, citing his school achievements and budding literary efforts, F-Pan, Minutier central, Etude CXVII/1058, Dossier Halévy.

[17] *Discours prononcé dans le Temple de la rue Ste.-Avoye* (Paris: De l'Imprimerie de Ballard, imprimeur du Consistoire central des israélites, 1808).

reincarnation of a Hebraic king ordained and sent by God. Another panegyric, from 1809, is a prayer to honor the "glorious battle" in which Napoleon defeated the Austrians at Wagram.[18]

Within the same two-year period (1808–9) in which Halévy was appointed Consistoire translator, he became permanent secretary of the Parisian Jewish community. Both positions were awarded on the strength of his Talmudic scholarship, language skills, and undoubtedly the reputation built on the success of *Ha-Shalom*. They also signal a certain moral and political authority, as one who reminded his co-religionists of their obligations to France. Although Halévy may never have become a citizen,[19] one overt, though involuntary, manifestation of his adaptation to French society was the change of his birth name, Levy, to Halévy in 1807. As his son Léon explained, French Jews were requested by the government, in concert with the Jewish leaders of the Grand Sanhédrin assembled by Napoleon, to change or modify their family names to avoid the confusing multiplicity of similar names on official registers.[20] (The resulting name was not Gallic, however; with

---

[18] *Discours prononcé par M. Abraham Cologna, Membre du Collège électoral des Savans du royaume d'Italie, Grand-Rabbin du Consistoire central des Israélites, le 13 mai 1809, dans le Temple de la rue Ste.-Avoie . . . suivi d'une prière composée en Hébreu, par M. le Prés. du dit Consistoire, D. Sintzheim, traduite par M. Elie Halévy* (Paris: De l'Imprimerie de Ballard, [1809]). Also see Cahen, "De la littérature hébraïque," 35. One prayer translated by Halévy marked the dedication of a synagogue in Lyon in 1813; delivered by Mardoché Roque-Martine, rabbi of the Circonscripion de Marseille, it is a homage to Napoleon as well as a blessing on local authority, in part to assure protection for community and synagogue. See the *Prière composée par M. Mardoché Roque-Martine Grand Rabbin de la Circonscription de Marseille. Pour être récitée à l'occasion de l'inauguration du nouveau Temple israélite de la ville de Lyon (en mars 1813) . . . traduite en Français par M. Elie Halévy, traducteur spécial du Consistoire central des israélites, et de celui de la Circonscription de Paris* (Paris: De l'Imprimerie des Langues Orientales de L.-P. Sétier Fils, 1813).

[19] Hansen, *Ludovic Halévy*, 2, 33, n. 5. Hansen cites evidence that Elie had not been naturalized before 1793: a document dated 28 August 1793 (F-Pan, Minutier central, Etude CXVII/1058, Dossier Halévy) granted Elie exemption from military service on the basis of his not being a citizen. Hansen also refers to Léon Halévy's letter of 18 July 1862 to Charles-Ernest Beulé reporting that he had not found any naturalization documents among his father's papers.

[20] Léon Halévy, *Sa Vie*, 6, n. 1, notes that "Halevy" was the name of several famous Talmudists. See also Zosa Szajkowski, "Judaica-Napoleonica: A Bibliography of Books, Pamphlets and Printed Documents, 1801–1815," *Studies in Bibliography and Booklore* 2, no. 3 (June 1956): 120.

the added prefix "Ha," Hebraic for "the," "Halévy" would translate as "the Levite."[21]) It is in Elie's writings, however, that we find the strongest evidence for his interest in revamping Jewish traditions to create a more amicable accord with French institutions and society.

The belief in a strong alliance between Jews and governmental authority, Napoleonic and otherwise, is clear in editorial statements of *L'Israélite français,* as in its epigraph. The preface to the first issue explains that the title "reminds Israelites of France of their most sacred duties: adherence to the laws and devotion to the country."[22] Respect for religious laws was built into Jewish tradition, but compliance with political laws of the countries Jews had inhabited as non-citizens had been a self-protective necessity. In response to social and political changes following emancipation, however, "devotion to the country" carried new meaning for French Jews. A principal goal of the periodical was to demonstrate the progress Jews had made as citizens and to encourage further intellectual and moral advancement.[23] As expressed in the preface, "moral improvement" ("perfectionnement moral") was necessary for Jews in France "to justify or merit the social advantages that they have obtained" and, for those outside France, to prepare for a similar future, awaiting "the wisdom of their governments."[24]

The choice of "israélite" in the title, rather than "juif," signifies this transformation of Jewish citizenry. The title reflects the attempts begun *circa* 1806 to suppress the use of the latter term because of its stereotypical associations.[25] Articles in *L'Israélite français* center on religious, political, historical, and literary topics, including translations of scriptural pieces and religious discourses, extracts from theological books, and biographies of prominent rabbis and such esteemed Jews as

---

[21] In biblical history, "Levite" meant an individual attached to the service of God or the sanctuary; in the later Temple period, Levites taught Torah, participated in the Temple service, and were in charge of music in worship.

[22] *L'Israélite français* 1 (1817): 2: "rappelle aux Israélites de France leurs obligations les plus sacrées: attachement aux lois, et dévouement à la patrie."

[23] *Ibid.*

[24] *Ibid.*: "de justifier ou de mériter les avantages sociaux qu'ils ont obtenus"; "la sagesse des gouvernemens."

[25] Berr-Isaac Berr (1744–1828) led the charge to replace "juif" with "israélite," or "hébreu." See Girard, *De l'émancipation à l'égalité,* 140.

Moses Mendelssohn. Political articles reveal concern for the universal condition of Jews and offer solutions for improving their civil and moral position in countries less "enlightened" than France; one noteworthy historical selection is an article on the Spanish Inquisition.[26] Included in the "Partie littéraire" is a lengthy examination of the legend of the "Juif errant" that found its way into French literature and drama of the next several decades, and into Fromental's opera (see pp. 95–6 below).[27]

A work by Halévy more theological in nature than his journal contributions is *Limmudei Dat u-Musar* (*Instruction religieuse et morale à l'usage de la jeunesse israélite*), a catechism of religious instruction for young Jews drawn from the *Pentateuque* (of the Torah, corresponding to the first five books of the Bible). Published in 1820, it reveals the strength of Halévy's devotion to Talmudic teachings, but again shows his determination to find common religious and social ground among Jews and their non-Jewish compatriots. Extracting from a Hebraic work by an anonymous "Levite" from Barcelona, Halévy presents some of the same basic precepts with his own commentary. Intended to guide the student as "homme et Israélite," the book repeatedly stresses the theme of dual devotion to faith and country. Central to this are the ideals of *fraternité* (in Talmudic and Revolutionary terms) and of Jewish *régénération* which permeate Halévy's preface, editorial notes, and selected extracts from Sanhédrin decisions. Halévy emphasizes in the preface that society is "divided only by the ways of worshipping our common Father," and encourages young Israelites to absorb divine precepts and learn "to fulfil all the duties of fraternity toward those to whom we owe our happiness and our own regeneration, that is, toward those nations that share with us the benefits of a wise and philanthropic constitution."[28]

---

[26] "Histoire critique de l'inquisition d'Espagne," 2 (1818): 33–46; see Elie Halévy's poems "La Mort de Goliath" and "Entrée du grand-prêtre au temple" among literary selections, 1 (1817): 28–34, 122–7, 127–8; 2 (1818): 10–20.

[27] C. L., "De l'histoire du juif errant," 1 (1817): 109–21.

[28] *Instruction religieuse et morale à l'usage de la jeunesse israélite* (Paris: Chez l'auteur; Metz: Chez Gerson-Lévy, 1820), 12: "divisés que par les manières d'adorer notre Père commun"; "à remplir tous les devoirs de la fraternité envers ceux à qui nous sommes redevables de notre bonheur et de notre propre régénération, je veux dire envers ces nations qui nous font partager les bienfaits d'une constitution sage et philanthropique."

In the pedagogical sections, which begin with the Ten Command-
ments ("le Décalogue"), he applies precepts to ideals of citizenship,
addressing various duties toward God and neighbor and reinforcing
the contemporary applicability of old Judaic principles with references
to the reformist Sanhédrin decisions printed at the end of the book:
Article IV, for example, is an extended passage on *fraternité*, in which
the Sanhédrin exhorts all Israelites to regard their Christian *concitoyens*
as brothers and "treat them in all civil and moral relations equivalent
to their *co-religionnaires.*" Not to do so would be "contrary to these
sacred maxims." In Article VI ("Rapports civils et politiques"), he pre-
scribes that Israelites are "scrupulously bound to . . . serve them, defend
them, obey their laws, and conform, in all their transactions, to the
requirements of the civil code."[29]

Among the maxims, Halévy includes several that refer to usury: in-
clusions undoubtedly intended to alert young Jews to avoid any practice that might inflame old Christian fears. He quotes Scripture that
warns against taking interest or "supplement" from a brother or needy
person and condemns this "illicit commerce" between individuals of
different religions as a transgression of divine law.[30] Again, Halévy
coordinates these maxims with Sanhédrin decisions, including a long
passage in Article VIII on the misinterpretation of the Hebrew word
for usury (*nechech*).[31]

Despite the clear message of cooperation with Christian society,
Halévy presents these guidelines and ideals with a dose of realism,
hoping that they will help combat "the ill will . . . so often voiced against
our laws" and steel the pupil against "the malignity of our detractors."[32]
In one extended note, he speaks of men "blinded by fanaticism and
prejudice" who would "raise doubts about the compatibility of Judaism
with the exercise of political rights and about the moral principles
practiced by the Israelites."[33]

[29] *Ibid.*, 20, n. 1; 82–3, n. 2; 111–12, 114.
[30] *Ibid.*, 92, 98 (Nos. 176, 177, 179, 189); Girard, *De l'émancipation à l'égalité*, 88.
[31] Halévy, *Instruction religieuse*, 117.
[32] *Ibid.*, 12: "la malveillance . . . si souvent publiée contre nos lois"; "la malignité de
   nos détracteurs."
[33] *Ibid.*, 110: "aveuglés par le fanatisme et les préjugés"; "élever des doutes sur la
   compatibilité du judaïsme avec l'exercice des droits politiques et sur les principes
   de morale pratiqués par les Israélites."

Halévy's catechism was approved, with minor modifications, by the Consistoire central.[34] Praised by French Jewish leaders, it became an influential guide in its adoption for use in Hebrew schools throughout France during the final years of the Restoration and the two decades of the July Monarchy. It even elicited support from the Ministre de l'Instruction publique, who found it "full of wisdom" and suitable for use in schools.[35] From this catechism, along with Halévy's pro-Napoleonic poetry, Talmudic interpretations, biblical poetry, unpublished writings, and work for *L'Israélite français*, emanates a passionate zeal for the intellectual and political fusion of Jews and non-Jews, balanced by a retention of Judaic faith.[36]

Elie Halévy's dual commitment also manifested itself in the education selected for his sons. The young Halévys were first sent to a *heder*, a strict synagogue school, where they learned the rudiments of Classical Hebrew and French grammar,[37] but their father then insisted that they receive a liberal education, even though his own Orthodox upbringing left him without the resources to oversee their work:

> Our father, very eager for the complete intellectual emancipation of his
> *co-religionnaires*, whom the Revolution had made citizens, did not take a
> direct part in our instruction (the specialization of his knowledge did not
> allow it); but he devoted himself entirely to our education, and despite
> being completely ruined by a bad business venture, he made the greatest
> sacrifices so that his two sons could devote themselves to their studies
> and to the liberal professions.[38]

---

[34] *Ibid*. The modifications, given at the end of the publication, are primarily word changes and clarifying phrases (Nos. 1–10).

[35] Letter from Simeon, Ministre de l'Instruction publique, to Elie Halévy, 16 November 1820 (F-Pan, Minutier central, Etude cxvii/1058, Dossier Halévy), cited in Hansen, *Ludovic Halévy*, 4, 34, n. 13.

[36] Léon Halévy, *Sa Vie*, 7, n. 1. Among writings he never completed are two ambitious projects that represent other cultural meshings: the first a Hebrew–French dictionary and the second a large study of Aesop's Fables. According to Léon, Elie considered the Proverbs of Solomon to be the moral bases for the Fables.

[37] Léon Halévy, *Sa Vie*, 8; Jordan, *Fromental Halévy*, 5.

[38] Léon Halévy, *Sa Vie*, 8: "Notre père, très-ardent pour la complète émancipation intellectuelle de ses coreligionnaires, que la révolution avait faits citoyens, ne prit pas à notre instruction une part directe (la spécialité de ses connaissances ne le

Such an education, according to the son of Samuel Cahen, founder of *Les Archives israélites*, was then a rarity in the Parisian Jewish community, at that time primarily composed of immigrants from Alsace-Lorraine who made their living as small traders and peddlers (*colporteurs*).[39] Following the *heder*, Halévy's sons became day pupils at a French boarding school, studying Latin, classic literature, and French essay writing; on 30 January 1809, a few months before his tenth birthday, Fromental entered the Conservatoire, while Léon later attended the lycée Charlemagne.[40] Despite the fact that his sons' "Gentile" education was disapproved of by less liberal Jews,[41] Elie was proud and vocal about their achievements. Included in the first volume of *L'Israélite français* is an early verse by the fifteen-year-old Léon Halévy, as well as short biographical paragraphs citing the sons' school honors. Léon's work, entitled "Egée, Scène lyrique," is identified as a "cantate" and includes text for recitative and aria.[42] In the paragraphs following "Egée," the honors mentioned for Léon include those won in the *concours général* in 1816 and "several first prizes" at Charlemagne the following year.[43] Noted as the achievement of Fromental, then Cherubini's pupil, is the *second* Prix de Rome won in both 1816 and 1817. The presence of the proud editor-father is strongly felt in the final paragraph: "Happy are the fathers who find, in the conduct and success of their children, the reward of the sacrifices they make to get a good education for them!"[44]

permettait pas); mais il se dévoua entièrement à notre éducation, et quoique complètement ruiné par une malheureuse entreprise commerciale, il fit les plus grands sacrifices pour vouer ses deux fils aux études et aux professions libérales."

[39] Isidore Cahen, "Actualités: Quelques Notes sur Léon Halévy," *Les Archives israélites* 44, no. 37 (13 September 1883): 296.

[40] Léon Halévy, *Sa Vie*, 8; Jordan, *Fromental Halévy*, 5. Some sources suggest that Fromental also attended Charlemagne; see, for example, Cahen, "Actualités," 296.

[41] Cahen, "Actualités," 296.

[42] *L'Israélite français* 1 (1817): 137–9. Accompanying commentary suggests that the eighteen-year-old Fromental intended to set the text – whether he did is unknown.

[43] *Ibid.*, 140.

[44] *Ibid.*: "Heureux les pères qui trouvent, dans la conduite et dans les succès de leurs enfans, la récompense des sacrifices qu'ils font pour leur procurer une bonne éducation!"

Such early achievements depict the young Halévys working to acquire the emblems and values of elite French society, and the successful careers that ensued further enhance the public portrait of fully assimilated Jews whose desire to be noteworthy French citizens outweighed their observance of Jewish customs and traditions. Fromental's musical career was full of honors. After being awarded the *premier* Prix de Rome in 1819 for his cantata *Herminie*, the composer later became professor of harmony and accompaniment at the Conservatoire in 1827, of counterpoint and fugue in 1833, and of composition in 1840. In addition to being *chef de chant* or *chef de choeur* at the Théâtre-Italien (1826–9) and at the Opéra (1829–40), Fromental composed for all three lyric stages, primarily the Opéra-Comique and the Opéra. The most appreciated of his twenty *opéras comiques*, in addition to his first success in the genre, *Le Dilettante d'Avignon* (1829), include *L'Eclair* (1835), *Le Guitarrero* (1841), *Les Mousquetaires de la reine* (1846), *Le Val d'Andorre* (1848), *La Fée aux roses* (1849), and *La Dame de pique* (1850). Among his six completed *grands opéras*, *La Reine de Chypre* (1841) and *Charles VI* (1843) held on in the Opéra repertoire, although the number of performances fell well below those of *La Juive*; *Guido et Ginevra* (1838) and *Le Juif errant* (1852) garnered the praise of many critics, but failed as sustaining repertoire pieces. His last produced *grand opéra*, *La Magicienne* (1858), was perhaps his least successful. Halévy also wrote two- and three-act works for the Opéra, *Le Drapier* (1840) and *Le Lazzarone* (1844). Following Halévy's 1836 election to the prestigious Académie des beaux-arts of the Institut de France – largely as a result of *La Juive* – he was appointed its *secrétaire perpétuel* in 1854, the first Jew to hold this distinguished position. Fromental was granted membership in the Légion d'honneur, and by the end of his life held the title Commandeur de l'ordre impérial.

Léon Halévy's active career produced fewer honors and less money than that of his older brother, but he established a strong reputation as an author. In 1831, he accepted the post of assistant professor of French literature at the Ecole polytechnique and later became chief of Le Bureau des sociétés scientifiques, attached to Le Ministère de l'Instruction publique. Besides the operatic collaborations with his brother, Léon wrote more than thirty-five *comédies, comédie-vaudevilles,* and *tragédies* produced at the Théâtre-Français, the Odéon, and other Parisian theatres. These include *Le Concert à la campagne* (1828), *Le Czar Démétrius* (1829), *Le Chevreuil* (1831), *Le Grand Seigneur et la paysanne, Une Leçon d'égalité* (1832), *Indiana* (1833), *Léone Léoni* (1840), *Un Mari s'il vous plaît* (1843), and *Le Mari aux épingles* (1856). Bringing him more renown than his political-philosophical writings (see pp. 47–8) were his translations of Euripides, Sophocles, and Horace, from the early *Odes d'Horace* of 1821–2 to the translations of his more mature years, *La Grèce tragique, chefs-d'oeuvre d'Eschyle, de Sophocle et d'Euripide.*[45] His *Recueil de fables* of 1844 was crowned by the Académie, but he was never elected to its exclusive *quarante.*

Bound to secular French society through education and an inculcated desire to succeed on its terms, both Halévy sons also made choices in their personal relationships that demonstrate simultaneous bonds to Jewish and Christian worlds. Fromental, in an 1842 ceremony that borrowed from Hebraic ritual,[46] married the wealthy Jewess Léonie Rodrigues-Henriques (1820–84), a member of the Rodrigues banking family of Bordeaux and twenty-one years his junior. This marriage, however, came on the heels of a decade-long liaison with a Catholic chorister at the Opéra with whom he reputedly had three illegimate children. Although the relationship goes unmentioned in family accounts and published biographies or memoirs, it was apparently known in Opéra circles, as implied in a gossip-filled account of backstage life by Opéra employee Jean-Pierre-Louis Gentil (1782–1857) (see pp. 274–80 below for further discussion of this account).[47] In 1837,

---

[45] Paris: Imprimerie de A. Bobée, 1821–2; Paris: J. Labitte, 1846–61.

[46] Léon Halévy, *Sa Vie,* 6, n. 2.

[47] "Chroniques de l'Académie royale de musique: Les Cancans de l'Opéra en 1836[–1848]. Extraits du journal tenu par une habilleuse concernans les choses qui sont venues à sa connaissance durant l'année 1836[–1848]," vols. I–III (F-Po, Rés. 658 (1)–(5)), vol. IV (US NYp, *MGZMB-Res). See the annotated transcription of this multivolume document, with a description of each volume, in Jean-Louis Tamvaco, "Les Cancans de l'Opéra: Première édition critique intégrale du manuscrit dit: 'Les Cancans de l'Opéra' ou 'Les Mémoires d'une habilleuse' de 1836 à 1845," 3 vols. (Ph.D. diss., Université de la Sorbonne Nouvelle [Paris III], Institut d'études théâtrales, 1995), and in Tamvaco's book

Gentil identifies a chorister named Proche as Halévy's "mistress of nine years," and speaks of the baptism of their third child in the church Notre-Dame-de-Lorette.[48] Gentil names Halévy's close friend Achille Guyardin as godfather, and baptismal records of this same church confirm that Guyardin acted as such to Léon-Achille Proche, born on 1 May 1836 to "Aimée Clothilde Proche" (no father is given, but it seems significant that one of the child's given names is that of Fromental's brother, while the other is that of the godfather).[49] It is likely, if Gentil's account is reliable, that two other children born to the same mother, living at the same address (rue Neuve Coquenard 13, then in the 2e arrondissement), and baptized in Notre-Dame-de-Lorette were also fathered by Halévy: Marie-Clémence-Félicie Proche, born on 20 July 1830 to "Catherine Clothilde Aimée Proche artiste," was baptized on 17 August 1837, a few months after Léon-Achille; Augustine-Marie-Clothilde, born to "Catharine Clothilde Proche, artiste dramatique" on 30 July 1833 had been baptized two years earlier, on 19 September 1835.[50]

Les Cancans de l'Opéra: Le Journal d'une habilleuse, 1836–1848, 2 vols. (Paris: CNRS Editions, 2000). Subsequent references to entries in this journal will be to the transcriptions in Tamvaco's book.

[48] "Madame Bardet, née Delphine de Montguyon," in Tamvaco, *Cancans*, vol. 1, 273. In a note to this entry, Tamvaco states that Halévy, while living in his apartment at the Opéra (see below), also shared a residence with Mlle Proche at rue Papillon 18, and, after leaving his post as *chef de chant*, lived with her at rue Grange Batelière 3.

[49] *Ibid.* Tamvaco (274, n. 6) identifies this *choriste* as Marie-Anne-Antoine (or Marie-Anne) Proche, born 14 January (actually, 13 January) 1785 (F-Pan, AJ¹³ 192); but he also discusses another Opéra employee, "Aglaé-Marie-Thérèse Proche," whom he identifies as a dancer born on the same date as the *choriste*. In two separate pension documents (F-Pan, AJ¹³ 176), Aglaé-Marie-Thérèse Proche is identified with the "ballet" as well as with "choeurs." According to birth records (Archives de Paris, "Naissances antérieur à 1860," 5 Mi 2/1002), Aglaé-Marie-Thérèse Proche was born [30] September 1780. Because the Proches that Tamvaco names would have been in their forties or fifties during the 1830s, it is unlikely that either was the mother of Halévy's children. In the baptismal record in Archives de Paris, Archevêché, Notre-Dame-de-Lorette, Registre 3337, the godmother is not Madame Bardet, as Gentil states. But Stéphanie Barder (or Bardet) does appear as godmother to another child baptized a few months later to "Catherine Aimée Proche artiste."

[50] Archives de Paris, Archevêché, Notre-Dame-de-Lorette, Registres 3335 and 3337. Birth records of the Archives (5 Mi 2/1002) give the birthdate of "Clemence Felicie Proche" as 3 July 1830. Despite name variants (common in such records), other corresponding details in the three records point to the same woman.

No birth records were found for Halévy's mistress, but a baptismal inventory indicates that Catherine-Clothilde Proche, an "enfant naturel" (natural child), was baptized 21 September 1812.[51] Therefore, she was likely sixteen or seventeen at the time Halévy, at twenty-nine or thirty, began a relationship with her (if Gentil's dating is correct), and eighteen at the birth of Marie in 1830.

Halévy's resistance to formalizing this relationship or publicly acknowledging the children born of it was typical of men of status or those seeking status in nineteenth-century France, especially if the woman were of a different religion or socioeconomic standing. Proche, like many choristers and dancers at the Opéra, was undoubtedly from the working class (several Proches of this time worked as *tapissiers*[52]) and, as an illegitimate child herself, even less desirable as a marriage partner. According to Gentil, the couple did not take up residence together – Halévy shared his Opéra quarters with Léon and two sisters – but he sardonically notes that the composer could often be found in Proche's apartment.[53] While the children's baptism may point further to Halévy's religious ambivalence, it speaks more strongly to his relinquishing responsibility for his out-of-wedlock children to their Catholic mother. It is likely that he took some financial responsibility, however, since years later his brother's dying mistress, Lucinde Paradol (1798–1843), solicited his support for her son with Léon.[54] An *obligation* that the composer signed with Guyardin in June 1840, in which he agrees to pay his friend 13,000 francs, guaranteed by his *droit d'auteur* for all works performed at the Opéra, Opéra-Comique, and provincial theatres, may very well have been a discreet way to ensure subsidy of Proche and children.[55] Unfortunately, because of vague wording – the debt is for "diverse advances" previously made by Guyardin – this document alone cannot establish whether Halévy's payments, or

[51] Archives de Paris, Archevêché, Notre-Dame-de-Lorette, Registre 3331.
[52] *Ibid.*, Registres 3333, 3337.
[53] "Etat des personnes logées à l'Opéra," in Tamvaco, *Cancans*, vol. II, 364.
[54] F-Pn, Ms., n.a.fr. 19914, fols. 138–9; cited in *La Famille Halévy*, ed. Loyrette, 19–20.
[55] F-Pan, Minutier central, Etude cxvii/1058, Dossier Halévy, "Obligation par M. Halévy à M. Guyardin," 23 June 1840. See letters that reveal a close association between Halévy and Guyardin, F-Pn, Ms., n.a.fr. 14346, fols. 263–4, 273, 350–51, 429–30.

Guyardin's loans, for that matter, had anything to do with caring for the Proche family, including Guyardin's godchild Léon-Achille.

His brother's affair with Paradol, a respected Comédie-Française actress (her religious status is uncertain), also produced a child, Anatole Prévost-Paradol (1829–70). Rather than being "hidden," he was raised in Léon's household, with Fromental's support, after his mother's early death. (Prévost-Paradol went on to become a prominent diplomat.) Unlike Fromental, Léon did not marry a Jewish woman. In 1832 he wed the Catholic Alexandrine Le Bas (1813–93), daughter of the prosperous architect Hippolyte Le Bas (1782–1867), designer of Notre-Dame-de-Lorette (the baptismal church of the Proche children) and member of the Institut de France from 1824.[56] Through Léon's marriage, his alleged conversion to Catholicism (see p. 291), and the baptism of his son Ludovic (the future librettist) two years after his birth in 1834, "Léon's branch ceased to be Jewish," writes descendant Jean-Pierre Halévy.[57] Such personal decisions, if set against his anticlerical statements of the late 1820s, among other contradictory expressions, suggest a complex self-identity.

While Fromental and Léon were bound to a non-Jewish world on many fronts, they also reveal active, even if intermittent, concern for Jewish issues through a significant number of their dramatic works and their writings. In them one can feel reverberations of their father's commitments to honor Judaic moral principles and culture and to seek compatibility between these and French Christian society. Signs of equivocation, of both apathy and attraction to Judaism, in part reflect the difficulties of conserving a traditionally Jewish identity in the face of civil empowerment.

An early journal entry by Fromental indicates a keen interest in Judaic customs and the condition of Jews outside France, although it seems, on the surface, to imply a lack of exposure to the Passover

---

[56] Pierre Pinon, "Les Vaudoyer et les Le Bas, dynasties d'architectes," in *La Famille Halévy*, ed. Loyrette, 88–9, notes that Léon's marriage aligned him with three generations of Parisian architects: Le Bas was the nephew of Antoine-Laurent-Thomas Vaudoyer (1756–1846) and the cousin of Léon Vaudoyer (1803–72).

[57] "La Famille Halévy (1760–1960)," in *La Famille Halévy*, ed. Loyrette, 25.

ritual that he later depicts in *La Juive*. Writing in the journal which he
kept in Italy during his Prix de Rome sojourn from the end of 1820
to the spring of 1822, Fromental pens an extensive narrative of his
visit to the Jewish ghetto in Rome.[58] On six of the thirty-five pages
devoted mainly to travel commentary, he carefully describes the experience: his happenstance stumbling on the ghetto, his entry into
a hidden synagogue located on the second floor of a house, his lis-
tening to the responsorial prayer between the bass cantor and the
worshipers, his interactions with a M. Issakhar, and, in most detail,
his observation of the Passover meal at Issakhar's house following
the synagogue service.[59] Throughout his detailed narrative, the composer never steps forward as a Jew who is interacting with his co-
religionists; instead, he introduces himself to his host as "a foreigner"
("un étranger") interested in learning unfamiliar customs. This lack of
personal connection could be interpreted as a type of "editorial distan-
cing," particularly since the description is written formally, in a manner
familiar in nineteenth-century journals intended to be read by others.
Moreover, Halévy, as Prix de Rome winner, was undoubtedly viewing
himself above all as a *Frenchman* in Italy. Although some biographers
have interpreted Halévy's passage as reflective of a complete denial
or ignorance of his heritage,[60] certain elements seem to "expose" the
composer as more intrigued by, and aware of, his roots than is often
acknowledged.

Halévy describes the piquing of his curiosity when he – by chance,
as he claims – walks near a guarded door leading into the ghetto.
While he had known beforehand that Jews lived in the city, nothing
had prodded him to seek them out. But at this moment he resolves

[58] This entry, like most, is undated (F-Pn, Ms., n.a.fr. 14349); the last entries are
dated late spring 1822. See a discussion of the ghetto visit in Jordan, *Fromental
Halévy*, 23–4.

[59] Journal, fols. 9^r–14^r.

[60] Curtiss, "Fromental Halévy," 197. Hansen, *Ludovic Halévy*, 7, states that by the
time Halévy wrote this journal account, he "had surrendered all awareness of
being Jewish"; he interprets Halévy's question, "What is a ghetto?" – which
Hansen uses as the epigraph for his first chapter – as a sign of a total lack of
Jewish identity.

"to take advantage of what chance was pointing out to me, and study the customs of this remainder of the twelve tribes a little, and the way in which they were treated in the capital of the Christian world."[61] After meticulously describing the decor in the synagogue, the meaning and placement of the tabernacle, and the service itself, Fromental paints a grim scene of poverty and wretched living conditions seen en route to M. Issakhar's home.[62] During the Passover meal, the young composer queries his host about the governmental treatment of the Jews:

> You see how we are treated, he said to me: the neighborhood that we live in, as you can judge by the streets that you walked with me, is an enclosure beyond which we cannot go – we are less miserable than our ancestors, he said, but our situation is still quite dismal. We can live only in this neighborhood, which the Romans call *ghetto*; but we have been given permission to establish our stores in the adjacent streets.[63]

Curiosity about Jews outside France and compassion for their hardships appear to be the most obvious motivations behind the composer's questioning. His interest, although a naturally humanitarian one, may very well have been stimulated by the historic-cultural explorations in his father's journal, in such entries as "Des Israélites du Malabar" or "Les Israélites de la Chine."[64] In this light, Fromental's detailed recounting of the synagogue service and Passover meal could be seen

[61] Journal, fol. 9ʳ: "profiter de l'avertissement que me donnais le hasard, et d'étudier un peu les moeurs de ce restant des douze tribus, et la manière dont on les traitait dans la capitale du monde chrétien."

[62] *Ibid.*, fols. 11ʳ⁻ᵛ: "Actually, we found ourselves in narrow passes that did not deserve to be called streets. The small, low, poorly lighted houses were full of women, of children, whose clothes attested to their extreme poverty." ("Effectivement, nous nous trouvions dans d'étroits défilés qui ne méritent pas le nom de rues. Les maisons petites, basses, mal éclairées, étaient remplies de femmes, d'enfants, dont les vêtements attestaient la misère.")

[63] *Ibid.*, fol. 14ʳ: "Vous voyez comment on nous traite, me répondit-il: le quartier que nous habitons & donc vous pouvez juger par les rues que vous avez traversées avec moi est une enceinte que nous ne pouvons franchir – nous sommes moins misérables que nos ancêtres, me répondit-il, mais notre sort est toujours bien triste. Nous ne pouvons habiter que ce quartier, que les Romains nomment *ghetto*, seulement, on nous a accordé la permission d'établir nos magasins dans les rues adjacentes."

[64] *L'Israélite français* 1 (1817): 14–34; 2 (1818): 93–108.

as his own "comparative study" of differences between the practices of Italian and French Jews, perhaps written with the expectation of reporting to his father. Although the young composer casts himself as a novitiate, it seems doubtful that he was newly encountering these basic rites.

Inside the synagogue, Fromental carefully describes the tabernacle and comments on the retention of traditional Hebrew prayers.[65] In Issakhar's home, he points out Hebraic writing above a door, but asks his host its meaning. And, as he sits down to the Passover meal, he appears to see and taste unleavened bread for the first time. Fromental carefully describes various foods used in the ritual that follows the prayer. He then writes:

> My host, who seemed to have a rather enlightened mind . . . told me: these preparations, necessary for our ceremonies, must appear very strange to you; but you undoubtedly know that our celebrations, like most celebrations of all peoples, were instituted only in order to perpetuate the remembrance of memorable events . . . All these objects whose presence here might seem ridiculous have an allegorical meaning and are to remind the Israelites of their deliverance and flight from Egypt.[66]

As one reads this portion of the account, the "disguised" Frenchman seems to foreshadow the disguised Samuel / Léopold in the seder scene of *La Juive*. Yet the composer's seeming lack of knowledge of the Hebrew language or of traditional rituals does not correspond with other biographical evidence. As noted above, Léon Halévy recalled that his brother and he were taught at least basic Hebrew as children.[67] Moreover, the inclusion in his father's catechism of numerous Talmudic

---

[65] Journal, fol. 10ᵛ.

[66] *Ibid.*, fol. 13ʳ: "Mon hôte, qui paraissait avoir un esprit assez éclairé . . . me dit: ces préparatifs, nécessaires à nos cérémonies doivent vous paraître bien bizarres; mais vous savez sans doute que nos fêtes, comme la plupart des fêtes de tous les peuples, n'ont été instituées que pour perpétuer le souvenir d'événements mémorables . . . Tous ces objets dont la présence ici pourraient paraître ridicule ont un sens allégorique et doivent rappeler aux israélites leur délivrance et leur sortie de l'Egypte."

[67] Léon Halévy, *Sa Vie*, 8.

directives pertaining to festivals (*fêtes*) of the Sabbath, New Year, Passover, Pentecost, and the Tabernacles (Chapter V, Nos. 63–94) implies that the meanings of traditional celebrations would have been familiar to Fromental by the time of his ghetto visit. The maxims relating to the celebration of Passover, for example, discuss the eating of unleavened bread, although without itemizing other symbolic foods. Immediately following Elie Halévy's passage prescribing the day that the unleavened bread (*pain azyme*) is to be eaten (No. 79, from Exodus 12:18) is the same precept from the traditional *Haggadah* (narration) of the Passover seder that Issakhar repeats: "On this day you will say to your son: this is done because of what the Lord did for me when I left Egypt" (No. 80, from Exodus 13:8).[68]

It seems unlikely that Elie Halévy would have allowed his sons to go without knowledge of the very rituals that he considered significant for his young readers, but conceivable that he produced his catechism upon realizing, in hindsight, the scantiness or inconsistency of the Judaic foundation given to his own children. Yet close to the time of the catechism's publication, Halévy showed interest in Jewish concerns in two meaningful ways. In the mid-1820s, he became a committee member of the Société israélite des amis du travail, a charity organization formed to support the training of indigent Jewish youth in industrial arts and crafts.[69] Even more significant, Halévy demonstrated a close association with his father's synagogue activities as well as some knowledge of Hebrew – shortly before his departure for Italy.

In the same manner in which Elie had written and translated commemorative poems, Fromental composed a psalm in Hebrew for the memorial service held at the Temple Sainte-Avoye for the duc de Berry, who had been killed at the Opéra on 13 February 1820. A *procès-verbal* of a Consistoire meeting (19 March 1820) preliminary to the memorial shows that Consistoire rabbis, after accepting Fromental's offer to set a psalm, selected Psalm 130, *De profundis*, and requested that he choose

---

[68] Elie Halévy, *Instruction religieuse*, 50.

[69] F-Pan, F^{19} 11013–14, "Culte israélite de France." Other committee members included manufacturers O. Lévy and R. Cohen and lawyer M. Picard; bureau members included the lawyers E. Halphen *fils* and A. Halphen *fils*.

"young Israelite musicians" to participate in the orchestra as well as direct it.[70] Halévy set the psalm for male chorus (tenor I, tenor II, bass) and solo bass (*basse-taille*), specifically for Israël Lovy, cantor of the Temple Sainte-Avoye from 1818 to 1833.[71] Dedicated to his teacher Cherubini, the work is scored for flute, pairs of oboes, clarinets, horns, and bassoons, three trombones, strings, and timpani. It begins with the fully instrumental *Marche funèbre* in F minor; the setting of the psalm follows in two numbers – the first for chorus and soloist in D minor and the second for bass solo in F major, accompanied by oboes, horns, and strings. Halévy wrote at least one more work for Lovy: he was invited "to compose a new Hallel" specifically for the singer as noted in the *procès-verbal* for another Consistoire meeting (2 October 1820), at which both Halévy and Lovy were present.[72]

Léon Halévy later characterized the 1820 *Marche funèbre et de profundis* as a work "imprinted with a profound religious color," and one that created a sensation.[73] Ganvert, in his study of nineteenth-century Parisian synagogal music, categorizes it as "one of the very first manifestations of learned synagogal music in Paris" and the first score of nineteenth-century French synagogue music to be printed.[74] Furthermore, he cites its use in the duc de Berry service as an important example of synagogal musical reform.

Since its establishment the Consistoire had considered "la musique occidentale" significant to synagogue worship, particularly for the commemorative services that became popular under the Empire (the types of services for which Elie Halévy translated poems).[75] Ganvert

---

70 Ganvert, "La Musique synagogale," 64 (from F-Pan, Reg. AA1^bis of Consistoire papers). Invitees for the orchestra include nine musicians, with eight string players and one clarinettist.

71 Ganvert's dates for Lovy; the dates given in Naumbourg's *Recueil de chants religieux et populaires* (see note 77 below), xxxix, are 1816–32.

72 Ganvert, "La Musique synagogale," 64–5, n. 3.   73 Léon Halévy, *Sa Vie,* 13.

74 Ganvert, "La Musique synagogale," 63, 107. *Marche funèbre et de profundis en Hébreu, à 3 voix et à grand orchestre (avec une traduction italienne et accompagnement de piano)* (Paris: Chez Ignaz Pleyel et Fils aîné, [1820]) (F-Pn, Mus., L. 1686).

75 Ganvert, "La Musique synagogale," 65. The reintroduction of instrumental music, excluded from the synagogue from the time of the Temple's destruction, also occurred in Reform synagogues outside France during the nineteenth

considers this musical reform an integral part of the evolution of French Jewish culture from emancipation to equality in the nineteenth century: with the gaining and strengthening of Jewish citizenship came a gradual alignment with French musical practice of church and conservatory. The use of orchestral instruments was one aspect of this gradual westernization of synagogue music in nineteenth-century Paris. Earlier than Halévy's psalm setting, for example, a performance by the singer Abrah Brandoni was accompanied by two harps and piano during the ceremony of 15 August 1809 for Napoleon's birthday.[76] The organ was later introduced into the service, in 1844.[77]

Along with the work of Lovy and Samuel Naumbourg (1815–80), the great *hazanim* (cantors) who each served as *Ministre officiant* of the Temple consistorial in different eras, Ganvert deems Halévy's contributions significant in this reform. Years after *De profundis*, Halévy set a series of psalms alluding to the style of traditional Hebraic chant for cantorial anthologies edited by Naumbourg.[78] Most are three- or four-voice responsorial settings for solo voices (either soprano, tenor, baritone, or bass) and chorus in standard early nineteenth-century harmonizations, with hints of "authentic" Judaic treatment (see Chapter 4, Examples 6 and 7). The publications, intended for use in synagogues throughout France, were dedicated to and approved by the Consistoire.

century. See A. Z. Idelsohn, *Jewish Music in its Historical Development* (New York: Henry Holt & Co., 1929), 232ff., for a discussion of attempts in Germany (primarily) to introduce European music into the synagogue. Idelsohn dates these efforts from the late eighteenth century and includes the introduction of hymns and Protestant chorales into Jewish services by Israel Jacobson (1768–1828) and Meyerbeer's father, Jakob Herz Beer (1769–1825).

[76] Ganvert, "La Musique synagogale," 62.

[77] *Ibid.*, 76. Ganvert discusses the debates surrounding synagogal use of the organ. See also *Recueil de chants religieux et populaires des israélites des temps les plus reculés jusqu'à nos jours*, ed. Samuel Naumbourg (Paris: Chez l'auteur, 1875), xl–xli. Naumbourg decried the introduction of the organ as "unfortunate" and not appropriate to the spirit of synagogue music.

[78] *Semiroth Israël: Chants religieux des israélites*, ed. Samuel Naumbourg (Paris: Chez l'auteur, 1847); *Nouveau Recueil de chants religieux*, ed. Samuel Naumbourg (Paris: Chez l'auteur, 1866); and *Recueil de chants*, ed. Naumbourg (1875). Ganvert cites Naumbourg collections published in 1857 and gives 1864 as the publication date of the *Nouveau Recueil*; he also lists other collections published by Emile Jonas (1854), Israël Lovy (1862), and Alphonse de Villers (1872).

As a member of this body, together with Maximilien Cerfberr (president), Marchand Ennery (rabbi), Adolphe Franck, Achille-Edmond Halphen, and five others, Halévy promoted the diffusion of these collections (and later became president of the Consistoire's Commission du chant synagogal).[79] In his endorsement printed in the 1847 edition, he writes of editor Samuel Naumbourg's collection of a "great number of traditional chants that are important to conserve in the liturgy" and expresses the hope that it "will exercise a positive influence on the performance of religious chants in our Temples, too often abandoned to a deplorable routine."[80] In Naumbourg's collection published in 1875 after Halévy's death, the editor reciprocates with an endorsement of the composer. In the preface, following remarks emphasizing the importance of preserving the quality of traditional songs, Naumbourg hails the composer's contributions to his collections, his zeal for promoting synagogue music, his knowledge of Hebrew, and his faith. He distinguishes him from Meyerbeer and Mendelssohn, who composed "nothing for our religion," and speaks of Halévy as "an Israelite in his heart" who "took a keen interest in all that he could contribute to the progress of our religious music."[81] Halévy also encouraged contributions to synagogal music among the Jewish students he taught at the Conservatoire.[82]

Besides his Temple affiliations, Halévy's composition of the opera *Le Juif errant*, produced at the Opéra in 1852, represents another public manifestation of his link with Jewish subjects. Halévy was undoubtedly prompted to write this opera in response to the popularity of Eugène

[79] *La Gerbe: Etudes, souvenirs, lettres, pensées*, supplement to *Les Archives israélites* (Paris: Au Bureau des Archives Israélites, 1890), 5.

[80] "Rapport," in *Chants religieux*, ed. Naumbourg (no page number): "un grand nombre de chants traditionnels qu'il importe de conserver dans la liturgie"; "qu'il exercera une heureuse influence sur l'exécution des chants religieux dans nos Temples, trop souvent abandonnés à une déplorable routine." Idelsohn, *Jewish Music*, 262, states that Naumbourg came to Paris in 1843, "warmly recommended" to Halévy.

[81] *Recueil de chants*, ed. Naumbourg, xlii.

[82] Ganvert, "La Musique synagogale," 107–8, 110. Among his students (during the 1840s) who wrote for the synagogue were Charles Le Bouc, Jules Erlanger, Jules Cohen, and Samuel David, who won the Prix de Rome for the cantata *Jephté*. Naumbourg also attended Halévy's Conservatoire classes.

Sue's novel (1845) and play (1849), which demonstrated a continued literary interest in the mythological wanderer Ahasvérus, and perhaps because of the success of *La Juive*.[83] Yet his involvement with a second opera centered on a Jewish theme or metaphor alludes to personal engagement. Moreover, Halévy began, but did not complete, a work with a biblical theme – the opera *Noé* (*Noah*).[84]

The extent to which Halévy maintained his associations with the Parisian Jewish community following his activities of the 1820s and prior to his Consistoire association of the 1840s – that is, during the years surrounding his work on *La Juive* – is difficult to assess. But his charity and Consistoire work, synagogue music, and knowledge of Hebrew (reputedly thorough by the end of his life, as claimed by Naumbourg) reveal a strong engagement with Judaic culture in adulthood, which likely represents a continuation of, or reconnection with, his early inculcation. Ruth Jordan believes that Halévy "had drifted away from religious observance in his early twenties, but like many of his emancipated co-religionists he retained an inalienable loyalty to his faith and his heritage."[85] Beyond the implications of the composer's early exposure to the Hebraic language, teachings, and ceremonies in the *heder*, synagogue, and home, there is the telling fact that the young composer had lived in the Jewish district in Paris before leaving for his Prix de Rome sojourn. From 1815, when his father began duties with the Paris Consistoire, Fromental lived on the same street on which the Temple Sainte-Avoye stood.[86] Despite the reform-minded stances of his father and the synagogue, it seems truly improbable that Halévy

[83] Earlier treatments of the myth were Edgar Quinet's prose work "Les Tablettes du Juif errant," *Revue des deux mondes* (January 1823), his epic poem "Ahasvérus," *Revue des deux mondes* (October 1833), and Pierre-François Camus Merville and Julian de Maillian's *Le Juif errant*, a five-act *drame fantastique* (Théâtre de l'Ambigu-Comique, 31 July 1834). Béatrice Prioron-Pinelli is completing a dissertation on Halévy's *Le Juif errant* (Montpellier III: Université Paul Valéry).

[84] See F-Pn, Mus., Ms. Vm² 1277. The opera was completed by his student and son-in-law, Georges Bizet. Jordan, *Fromental Halévy*, 1, also finds it noteworthy that Halévy's *Charles VI* (1843) centers on the same French king who expelled Jews from France in 1394, although the act of expulsion is not featured in the opera itself.

[85] Jordan, *Fromental Halévy*, 176.   [86] Léon Halévy, *Sa Vie*, 13.

would have been as distant from traditional Judaic rituals or from his Jewish identity as the ghetto account portrays.

If the account is read *with* the knowledge of his father's work and associations, as well as his own, a number of questions arise. Most importantly, why would the composer not allude to his identity, even if he were on the periphery of Judaism at this point in his life? When he spoke to the guard at the ghetto's entry, would he not have mentioned that he, too, was Jewish to ease his passage? When he asked the meaning of Hebrew words, of the tabernacle, of the Passover foods, would he not have pointed out that, while knowing something about these things, he wanted to discover more? Instead, he is "un étranger" without any awareness of what is being explained to him.

The non-Jewish face that the young composer presents to his host, to himself, and perhaps to future readers – in an account written shortly after his participation in at least two services at the Temple Sainte-Avoye – speaks to an equivocation about his Jewishness and about the strength of "disguise" that he had learned to wear in daily life. In light of the experiences of other first-generation emancipated Jews in France, the composer's suppression of his identity is not surprising. Blending into Christian society meant playing down, to some degree, one's Otherness, and the young composer had probably learned this art of camouflage to avoid estrangement or adolescent persecution. Gustave d'Eichthal, who associated with the Halévys in the Saint-Simonian circle, describes having been derisively taunted as "le juif" and "le juif errant" by his fellow *lycéens*.[87] Conversion was one avenue taken by European Jews, though undoubtedly some apostasies in France were superficial and opportunistic, coming as a means of breaking down social or employment barriers – as seems to have been the case with Heine in highly restrictive Prussia. Through baptism, what he sardonically called "the entrance ticket to European culture," he hoped for a professorship that would never come.[88]

---

[87] "Souvenirs d'enfance," F-Pa, Ms. 14717, fol. 40^r.

[88] Heine tried to pass off his baptism as a nominal, "indifferent affair," but as early as a year afterward he regretted the action, claiming to be hated by both Christian and Jew because of it. See Joseph Jacobs, "Heinrich Heine," in

Other entries in Halévy's journal speak of interactions with fellow Jews or point to the young composer's curiosity about Jewish interests. There are references to a visit to Uzielli, a rich Jewish merchant, to a traveling companion named Germain Mayer, and to a joke about Rothschild. On the last page of his travel entries, before the twenty-five pages of autograph musical sketches, he jots down the book title *Résumé de l'histoire juive depuis son origine, jusqu'à la prise de Jérusalem.*[89] Among the limited correspondence found before his work on *La Juive*, there is a colorful, jesting reference to his ancestry in a letter of 1829 to Salvador Cherubini, the son of his revered teacher, who was then traveling in Egypt. Halévy urges him to write

> to me who perhaps have Egyptian blood in my veins, given the long time that my ancestors stayed in that classic country. Because, after all, it's within the realm of possibility that one of my great-great-grandfathers offered sacrifices to Baal and fornicated with some beautiful Egyptian.[90]

Léon Halévy, like his older brother, also maintained contact with Parisian synagogues. He wrote an ode for the inauguration on 5 March 1822 of the Temple consistorial, which had superseded the Temple Sainte-Avoye as the official synagogue of Paris.[91] Twenty years later, his text *Chant funèbre*, commemorating the death of the duc d'Orléans, was performed on 26 July 1842 in the same synagogue.[92] But it is in Léon's early writings prior to the appearance of *La Juive* that a continuation of his father's concerns for the greater Jewish community and the promotion of a French–Jewish rapport are most strongly sensed. He wrote the *Résumé de l'histoire des juifs anciens* (1825) and its companion volume *Résumé de l'histoire des juifs modernes* (1828) to raise consciousness about Hebraic history, but also to discuss advancements made

The Jewish Encyclopedia, vol. VI, 328; Jeffrey L. Sammons, *Heinrich Heine: A Modern Biography* (Princeton: Princeton University Press, 1979), 107–9.

[89] Journal, fol. 35ʳ.

[90] Letter of 7 May 1829 (F-Pn, Mus., "Lettres autographes," vol. L); see *Fromental Halévy: Lettres*, ed. Galland, 3–4.

[91] Ganvert, "La Musique synagogale," 65–6, n. 2.

[92] *Chant funèbre, exécuté au Temple consistorial israélite de Paris le 26 juillet 1842, au service célébré pour le repos de l'âme de S. A. R. Ferdinand-Philippe, duc d'Orléans* (Paris: Imprimerie de Wittersheim, 1842).

by Jews and to condemn the perpetuation of restrictions and intolerance.[93] These objectives align with the ideals of *L'Israélite français*,
as well as those of other post-emancipation publications,[94] as Halévy
makes clear in his second *Résumé*. To the imperfectly integrated French
society and to other societies less integrated, he hopes to advance a
more positive Jewish identity, to prove "to Christian fanatics . . . or to
less-enlightened Christians . . . that the Jews are not only human beings,
but human beings who are useful, active, distinguished in organization, deserving of freedom, having done much for it; and to the Jews,
that while the times grant them new rights they also bring them new
responsibilities."[95] Pushing the ideas of reform and acculturation of
L'Israélite français even further, he calls for a "complete and permanent
fusion between the followers of Moses and other Frenchmen."[96]

In the second *Résumé*, Léon continues the survey of Jewish history
begun in the first, focusing on persecutions and inequities suffered at
the hands of Christian societies. Within the "Cinquième Epoque" of
his survey, covering a period from the end of the sixteenth century up
to the time of writing, the author notes the vast changes that had taken
place in the civil status of Jews following emancipation, the Sanhédrin
decisions that had "rehabilitated" the Jewish faith in the world's eyes,
the formation of Consistoires, and the role of Napoleon in the constitutional ruling that guaranteed freedom of worship for each religion.[97]
Among the Sanhédrin directives, some of those included in his father's
catechism, Léon discusses specific laws governing interactions between
Jews and Christians, conveying that restrictions and injustices had

---

[93] The first volume was published by Lecointe et Durey, the second by Lecointe.

[94] For example, *Des juifs au XIXe siècle ou considérations sur leur état civil et politique en
France* . . . by Bail (Paris, 1816) and *Considérations sur l'état des juifs dans la société
chrétienne, et particulièrement en Alsace* by Betting de Lancastel (Strasbourg, 1824),
reviewed by Cahen, "De la littérature hébraïque," 43, 45.

[95] *Résumé de l'histoire des juifs modernes*, vii: "aux Chrétiens fanatiques . . . ou aux
Chrétiens peu éclairés . . . que les Juifs sont non-seulement des hommes, mais
des hommes utiles, actifs, d'une organisation distinguée, dignes de la liberté, et
qui ont beaucoup fait pour elle, et aux Juifs, que si le temps leur assure de
nouveaux droits, il leur impose aussi de nouveaux devoirs."

[96] *Ibid.*, 325–6: "la fusion complète et définitive des sectateurs de Moïse et des
autres Français."

[97] *Ibid.*, 313–15. Note 1 refers to Articles 1 and 5 of the Charte.

continued to plague French Jews. He addresses the suspension of several rights during the period 1808–15, which represented a return to arbitrary and discriminatory treatment of French Jews. In 1818, an effort made by the marquis de Lattier to continue the "loi d'exception" represented, in the author's view, "the last direct and public attempt that had been made in France against the rights of Israelites."[98]

While his father had optimistically believed that cross-cultural struggles would gradually disappear as French society was exposed to the zeal, valor, intelligence, and patriotism of its "adopted children," Léon felt that only through Jewish acceptance of common customs and language would true tolerance and harmony be assured.[99] The more separate or "fanatical" Jews remained, he believed, the less accepted they would be as full citizens. Instead, he advocated that "the name Jew should become secondary, and the name French principal."[100] Only then would there be a future in which a true rapport of morality and doctrine and a consolidation of political and religious institutions could exist.[101]

As Halévy proposes in his first *Résumé* (1825), a key to this new future lay in religious reform, for Jews as well as Christians: in essence, a drawing together of the two religions along primitive lines. In his final chapter, Halévy aligns himself with *philosophe* views as he speaks of the resistance of modern-age Jews to further change, a resistance that hinders the practice of civil rights. Now that the Jews, especially the Jews of France, belong to a world delivered from the "grievous prejudices" that had prevented emancipation for so long, the need for religious reform is urgent, as "all the enlightened minds" recognize. As long as Jews hold onto superstitions and "barriers," their religion will remain *asiatique* (Asiatic, or oriental) and "an unfortunate line of demarcation" will separate them from their brothers of other faiths. Moreover, Christians will not offer peace and protection to a Judaism

---

[98] *Ibid.*, 317: "la dernière tentative publique et directe qui ait été faite en France contre les droits des Israélites."

[99] *Ibid.*, 325–7.

[100] *Ibid.*, 325: "le nom de Juif devienne l'accessoire, et le nom de Français le principal."

[101] *Ibid.*, 328–9.

full of "superstition." Halévy explains that a stronger rapport could be realized if Christians, particularly Catholics, recognized a truer form of Christianity, "le christianisme primitif," one closer to the religion of Moses as continued by Jesus and Rabbi Saul. Just as the Pharisees had distorted Mosaic law before Jesus, so had "the Pharisees of Catholicism" disfigured Christianity after Jesus. With recognition of the same religious foundation, Halévy sees hope for social change.

In later commentary, perhaps after the waning of youthful idealism (or of certain aspects of his Saint-Simonian beliefs), Léon appears to lean more toward religious separatism, although he continues to promote religious freedom, tolerance, and equality. In reaction to the Wormser affair in 1840 – the expulsion of the French Jew Abraham Wormser from Dresden after local French officials refused to intervene – Halévy became incensed that Wormser's French citizenship had not protected him in a foreign country. His response appears printed next to a letter Wormser wrote to *Les Archives israélites*:

> Religion or faith, on the one hand, and nationality or country, on the other, are two entirely different things; that is the fundamental principle that must govern the question. The French Catholic, the French Protestant, the French Israelite must be equal in the eyes of foreign governments, regardless of the restrictions imposed by these governments on the practice of religious freedom.[102]

Shortly after the Wormser incident, the even more incendiary Damascus affair (*l'affaire Damas*) exploded when French officials in Damascus accused Jews of the ritual murder of a Sardinian Capuchin friar who had disappeared, allegedly in the city's Jewish quarter; the impact of the accusation intensified in France as a number of leading newspapers assumed the Jews' guilt and called for condemnation.[103]

---

[102] *Les Archives israélites* 1 (1840): 147: "La religion, ou le culte, d'une part: de l'autre, la nationalité, la patrie, sont deux choses tout-à-fait distinctes; tel est le principe fondamental qui doit dominer la question. Le Français catholique, le Français protestant, le Français israélite doivent être égaux aux yeux des gouvernements étrangers, quelles que soient les restrictions apportées par ceux-ci à l'exercice de la liberté religieuse."

[103] In a reinterpretation of the ancient "blood libel," the accusation claimed that Jews had killed the *capucin* Father Thomas in order to use his blood for making

Despite the shock felt throughout Jewish communities at such responses, Halévy encouraged French Jews to continue as full participants in society, taking advantage of education in the *grandes écoles* to aid in their intellectual and moral progress. Such opportunities should be understood as *privileges* by Israelites, he writes, especially in light of the "heinous prejudices" during this period.[104] In two early plays, *L'Espion* (1828) and *Grillo; ou, Le Prince et le banquier* (1832), Léon dramatizes ideas about antisemitism and reformats a central objective of his historical writing: to prove the social and moral worth of Jews (see pp. 250–1).

Although Fromental and Léon appear to have been non-practicing Jews in a strict sense, their Jewish heritage served as a vigorous source in their lives and works. An attempt to understand their liberal, humanist ideologies and their devotion to *le pays* outside the context of this heritage would ultimately be misleading. Their ideas about socioreligious reform, political freedom, and universal tolerance – assimilationist and pluralistic attitudes that permeate *La Juive* – are deeply rooted in their eagerness to ameliorate the status of Jews and, on a personal level, to be accepted and lauded among the French cultural elite.[105] Though

unleavened bread. The indictment, and the ensuing arrest of notable Jews (some of whom died from torture), alarmed Jews throughout Europe and galvanized a solidarity among them. The French lawyer Adolphe Crémieux, along with a French delegation, eventually succeeded in freeing the accused. See Girard, *De l'émancipation à l'égalité*, 149–50, and the many articles and letters reacting to *l'affaire Damas* in the first year of *Les Archives israélites* (1840).

[104] "Instruction publique: Des améliorations introduites par M. Cousin dans l'instruction publique," *Les Archives israélites* 1 (1840): 467.

[105] The ideological legacy of the Halévys can be sensed in later generations of the family: the salon of Fromental's daughter, Geneviève, produced the manifesto of the Dreyfusards, while Léon's grandsons, Daniel and Elie Halévy (the latter named after his great-grandfather), were writers and historians whose interests and viewpoints in many ways represent a familial continuity of thought and purpose. In the 1890s, Elie Halévy, the younger, was one of the founders of a philosophical journal entitled *Revue de métaphysique et de morale*, which "aimed at nothing short of the moral reformation of France ... by providing a rationalist alternative to both positivism and to religiosity"; see Myrna Chase in *Elie Halévy: An Intellectual Biography* (New York: Columbia University Press, 1980), 20. Elie also published a study of Saint-Simon's *Doctrine* and, with Célestin Bouglé, a new edition of the work itself. Both Daniel and Elie joined the campaign to save Dreyfus: Chase notes that the Affair engaged Elie "uncharacteristically in furious political activism," for "[t]o save Dreyfus was to save republican justice" (14). Chase does not believe that there was any "racial

taking different paths in life, each brother keenly wanted to coordinate his role as *citoyen* and *israélite* – emancipated, reformed, educated, talented, with "much to offer."

Saint-Simonism, beyond advancing possibilities of more inclusive and prominent roles within a new social order, embraced pantheistic views and a heightened compromise with Christianity. At a meeting of the Saint-Simonians in 1832 (although years after Léon had formally broken with the movement), Olinde Rodrigues stated that when the Jew had met Saint-Simon, he discovered a new father and a new place as part of a universal family: "The feudal Christian gave a paternal kiss to the persecuted Jew who had crucified Jesus."[106] D'Eichthal, who joined the group in 1829 and remained through its mystical phase and retreat to Ménilmontant, wrote in October 1836 that Saint-Simonism represented "the pact of alliance between Jews and Christians."[107] He claimed to have been personally attached to the movement because of its belief in the "rehabilitation of Israel," illustrated by Saint-Simon's comments about "the people of God" in the introduction to *Le Nouveau Christianisme* (1825), and by those of Eugène Rodrigues concerning Jewish persecution in his *Lettres.*[108]

This Jewish–Christian alliance was widely recognized, for Saint-Simonians were often referred to as "new Jews," or sometimes as "new Christians." Szajkowski claims that the Jewish Saint-Simonians became more Christian than Jewish in their beliefs.[109] In the introduction to *Opinions littéraires* of 1825, Léon Halévy depicts Jesus as a positive social force, interpreting the French Revolution, which uprooted the old social order and built a base for a new structure, as a realization of "what Plato and Jesus Christ had begun."[110] Semi-Christian thoughts appear around the same time in Halévy's first Jewish history, in which he strongly emphasizes the historical connections between Judaism

---

consciousness" behind Elie's actions, but Alain Silvera, biographer of Daniel Halévy, believes that Daniel's choice was "dictated by a certain racial origin hitherto ignored" (Chase, *Elie Halévy*, 91).

[106] Quotation from *Le Globe* (16 January 1832), cited in Szajkowski, "Jewish Saint-Simonians," 38.

[107] F-Pa, Ms. 14393/20, letter to Adolphe d'Eichthal, 10 October 1836.

[108] *Ibid.*   [109] Szajkowski, "French Jews," 1023.

[110] Saint-Simon *et al.*, *Opinions littéraires*, 5.

and Christianity. In its penultimate chapter, Halévy views the teachings of Jesus not as a break from Judaism but as the beginning of its early reform.[111] Emphasizing his teachings as a continuation of the religious laws articulated by Moses and other Hebrew prophets, Halévy views Jesus as a necessary reformer of "superstitious practices" established in Judaic laws, which "set an insurmountable barrier against the free development of human abilities."[112] Halévy believed that, with Jesus' reforms and fulfillment of Jewish law, the "Jewish religion, by its dogma of the unity of God, by the excellence and the liberality of its morality, was destined to become the religion of modern civilization."[113] In his public violation of long-observed religious practice, Jesus becomes a "martyr of human passions" whom Halévy likens to Socrates.[114] Halévy reinforces the Judaic connection in the conversion of early Christians after Jesus' death. Referring to St. Paul as "Rabbi Saul," Halévy defines his Epistles as "the true canon of full-blown Mosaism."[115] Saul and other reformed Jews converted pagan Gentiles from idolatry to "the religion of Moses and Jesus" and therefore brought civilization to the world in a peaceful manner; but the majority of the Jewish nation remained "inaccessible to reform."[116]

After Halévy had officially broken off from the group over its increasing mysticism and moves away from liberal principles, the Saint-Simonians sought Judaic roots for what had become an almost cult-like semi-Christian religion under Enfantin's guidance.[117] In its most absurd phase, Enfantin, who proclaimed himself "Père" ("the Father"), spent

---

[111] This chapter (23) is titled "Successeurs d'Hérode; derniers rois des Juifs. Commencemens de la réforme du Judaïsme."

[112] *Résumé de l'histoire des juifs anciens*, 336: "opposaient une barrière insurmontable au libre développement des facultés humaines."

[113] *Ibid.*: "La religion juive, par son dogme de l'unité de Dieu, par l'excellence et la libéralité de sa morale, était destinée à devenir la religion de la civilisation moderne."

[114] *Ibid.*, 346.

[115] *Ibid.*, 351–2: "le véritable code du Mosaïsme développé."

[116] *Ibid.*, 352: "resta inaccessible à la réforme."

[117] Léon Halévy, "Souvenirs de Saint-Simon," 542, bitterly describes the suffocating of the "clear and positive ideas of Saint-Simon," his sharp ideological differences with Bazard and Enfantin after the failure of *Le Producteur* in 1826, and the movement's descent into foolish absurdities.

much time in search of "Mère" ("the Mother"), who was expected to appear in the form of a Jewish woman from the Orient.[118] After the group's public humiliation in 1832 and its subsequent disintegration,[119] d'Eichthal focused anew on his Jewish heritage, attending services at the Temple israélite and searching for ways to fuse his Jewish identity with Saint-Simonian and Christian beliefs and to highlight a new role for Jews in society. Some of d'Eichthal's ideas seem to parallel Léon Halévy's statements in the *Résumé* (1825), particularly his view of a reformed Judaism as "the religion of modern civilization."[120]

After Halévy's break, he very likely did not discard the semi-Christian views articulated in his *Résumé,* or at least not all of them. Jordan claims that Léon did in fact convert to Catholicism, but did so "discreetly" and, like Heine, with the sole motivation of breaking the social barrier that had held back his career; she does not give a precise date, or documentation, for this act, but implies that it came during Fromental's completion of Ferdinand Hérold's *Ludovic* in 1833.[121] Her dating seems insecure, however, for she also points out that this alleged apostasy made his appointment at the Ecole polytechnique possible, and that

[118] Szajkowski, "Jewish Saint-Simonians," 42.

[119] In the 1830–31 debates over the law of the *culte israélite,* concern was expressed that if the government gave subsidy to Jewish rabbis, then it would be forced to do likewise with other religions, including that of the Saint-Simonians; some comments about the group illicited laughter in the Chambre des députés; see *Archives parlementaires,* vol. LXV, 315.

[120] D'Eichthal began to characterize the Jew as an individual with a "dual character" and, therefore, "un homme *complet.*" As articulated in correspondence (for example, F-Pa, Ms. 14393/4; Ms. 14393/20) and in his book *Les Deux Mondes* (1835), d'Eichthal believed that, because Judaism was the source for both Christianity and Islam, the modern Jew had inherited the socioreligious role as mediator between the worlds of the Occident and Orient. He chose Austria as a locus of a new world order because of its inclusion of both oriental and occidental races within its borders, including a strong population of Jews. It was in this country that Jews were to act as religious and political mediators and bring about their full emancipation throughout Europe. D'Eichthal went to Austria in 1836 to advance his ideas, even presenting them to Metternich, who ignored them. Michael Graetz, "Une Initiative Saint-Simonienne pour l'émancipation des juifs," *Revue des études juives* 129 (1970): 67–84, views d'Eichthal's endeavor as one of the most significant, although failed, attempts to realize Saint-Simonian thought in public action.

[121] Jordan, *Fromental Halévy,* 43–4.

appointment came in 1831. While Léon's views imply Christian, especially Protestant, leanings, Fromental never converted, although he had clearly moved farther away from Orthodoxy than his father. A few years before his death, in a letter responding to queries of his nephew Ludovic Halévy about the function of Consistoires in France and Algeria (namely those of Oran and Alger), Fromental displays thorough knowledge of the subject as he advocates modification of Judaic practices under the umbrella of the French state. In referring to the plan to have these Consistoires operate under the Parisian Consistoire central, he reveals an admiration for traditional Jews, but also contempt for their "stubbornness" in not adapting to French law – echoing Léon's views of decades earlier and perhaps his own toward the "fanatique" Eléazar. He writes, "[L]et the devout, the pious, the pure, whom I respect, but who in general are stupid and stubborn, believe in the Rabbi of Jerusalem; no need to stop them, nor to restrain them from doing so."[122] During his mature years, a number of public statements (including his own) attest to the composer's loyalty, or perhaps facade of loyalty, to some form of Judaism. At his 1848 election as candidate to the Assemblée nationale (see p. 65 above and Appendix K), Halévy graciously thanked the abbé Deguerry for having praised him, which he attributed to the "grand *fraternité* proclaimed by the February Republic," since "we do not follow the same religion"; *La Revue et gazette musicale* reported that great enthusiasm broke out in the room at the cordial embrace of "the Christian priest and the son of Israel."[123] Halévy was venerated as Israelite at his 1862 funeral by Maximilien Cerfberr, president of the Consistoire central, as printed in *Les Archives israélites*: "We are happy to count him as one of us, not only because he brought honor to France, but because he held high the flag of his religion. In these sad times of religious indifference he had the good sense not to deny the faith of his fathers."[124]

---

[122] Letter dated 25 March [1859], *Fromental Halévy: Lettres*, ed. Galland, 164; Leich-Galland cites the letter in "Fromental Halévy et l'âge d'or de l'opéra français," in *La Famille Halévy*, ed. Loyrette, 75, 345, n. 30.

[123] *La Revue et gazette musicale* 15, no. 17 (23 April 1848): 126.

[124] *Les Archives israélites* 23, no. 4 (1 April 1862): 190; cited in translation in Jordan, *Fromental Halévy*, 200.

Seemingly, none of Fromental's or Léon's children was raised in the Jewish faith, at least not strictly: Fromental's oldest daughter, Geneviève (1849–1926) is said to have resisted a priest's attempt to convert her sometime after her marriage to the lawyer Emile Straus (her first husband was Georges Bizet), with the comment: "I have too little religion to change it."[125] The eminent politician Pierre Joxe, an Halévy descendant, acknowledged during a recent radio interview (accompanying a broadcast of a performance of *La Juive* at the Vienna Staatsoper on 23 October 1999) that Fromental's family was non-practicing.[126] But the children were clearly made aware of their heritage, and activism for Jewish causes continued through several generations of Halévys, with Geneviève playing a significant role in the support of Dreyfus, along with Léon's grandchildren Elie Halévy (1870–1937) and Daniel Halévy (1872–1962) (see n. 105).

The Halévys' own search for a strong, integral place as citizens and new Israelites in French society offers intimate perspectives on themes and allusions in *La Juive*: of persecution and freedom, of religious faith and ambiguity, and of concerns for *fraternité*, acculturation, and the social amelioration of Jews. The "faculty of strong emotion" that Wagner sensed in the opera may indeed have emanated from the wells of Halévy's own experience: behind Samuel's disguise in the opera's seder might be sensed the composer's own uncertainty; in the anguish of the persecuted Eléazar might be felt his own inner suffering, or that of his fellow Jews. While the opera, on a larger level, clearly pays homage to the governmental stances of the early July Monarchy, as well as to the collective liberal messages of its authors and collaborators, on a more personal level its subject raised questions that the composer and his brother confronted in different forms in their daily lives, continuing quests begun by Jewish liberals of earlier generations, not the least of all their father.

[125] *Ibid.*, 6ff.; Emanuel, "Léon Halévy," in *The Jewish Encyclopedia*, vol. VI, 169; Hansen, *Ludovic Halévy*, 31–2.
[126] Discussion with Pierre Joxe, France-Musique, 22 April 2000, 7:30–8:00 p.m.

The opera's setting at the 1414 opening of the Council of Constance (Konstanz), a historically pivotal convocation of Church authorities, offered an ideal backdrop for addressing the polemical themes of religious, political, and social intolerance, absolutist abrogation of religious freedom, and Jewish martyrdom. In some accounts of the opera's history, Scribe's initial choice was not Constance but Goa, once the capital of Portuguese India, a city in which the Inquisition was established in 1560.[1] (A Goa setting is not found in the earliest extant text sources, however; in the draft scenario in Scribe's hand, the setting is the one that remains.[2]) Convened to end the papal schism in the Western Church, the Council of Constance – officially, the Sixteenth Ecumenical Council – met from 5 November 1414 to 22 April 1418. Its determinations led to the abdications of the Roman Pope Gregory XII and John XXIII, the deposing of Benedict XIII, the pope in Avignon, and the election of a new pope, Martin V, three years after the Council began. In addition to church officials, the German king Sigismund (Siegmund) played a significant role as convener of the Council as well as its official protector.[3]

The historical setting also provided ample occasion for opulent staging, massed crowd scenes and processions, and intricate costuming, which enhanced, yet in one sense diverted attention from, the work's

---

[1] Léon Halévy (*Sa Vie*, 23), as quoted in Appendix E, and as corroborated by Monnais (*F. Halévy*, 14), states that Goa was the choice in "le plan primitif." Leich-Galland reiterates this claim in his introduction to Scribe, *La Juive*, ed. Marthe Galland, vi. A copy of the libretto's second edition (Paris: Jonas, Libraire de l'Opéra, 1835; F-Pan, AJ[13]202) contains handwritten editorial markings that change the setting to Goa as well as changing the names of the characters. This anonymous effort may have been an attempt to restore the original idea or, perhaps, to present this setting anew.

[2] F-Pn, Ms., n.a.fr. 22502, vol. xxiii, 1°:2°.

[3] Sigismund was king of Hungary from 1385 (crowned 1387) and German king from 1411 (crowned 1414).

deeper meanings. The *mise en scène* figured prominently in the immediate success of *La Juive*, with pre-première announcements of unprecedented expenditure fueling audience expectations and critics responding effusively to the opera's visual splendor.[4] Indeed, there is hardly one press report that does not devote a substantial amount of its space to detailed description of the decor and the sumptuously dressed king and cardinal, armored soldiers, and the multihued, insignia-laden tunics, leggings, and cloaks of banner carriers, trumpeters, peasants, and clerics.[5] A Hugoian depiction of a colorful scene in Constance, undoubtedly stimulated by the opera's staging, appeared in *Le Constitutionnel*, juxtaposed against a politically infused analysis of the historical event (see pp. 144–5 below):

> What a splendid medley of colors is this population of lords and priests arriving there from all countries, realms, abbeys, convents, and cathedrals: some mitred, others covered in crimson; some crowned in silver, others with a lavish shield and golden helmet sparkling in the sun! There the round, bare chin of the choirboys and the young priests, and the long and white beard of the old cardinals; foot soldiers and cavalry, cute pages, beautiful *châtelaines* and the black, filthy robes of mendicant friars; lances, military flags, crosses, candles, banners bearing the image of the Virgin and the saints, the gruff voices of soldiers handling their lances, and the clear and silvery voices [of the choristers] chanting litanies.[6]

[4] See, for example, "Nouvelles de Paris," *La Revue musicale* 8, no. 52 (28 December 1834): 413. Catherine Join-Diéterle, *Les Décors de scène de l'Opéra de Paris à l'époque romantique* (Paris: Picard, 1988), 281, gives the cost of the scenery as Fr 46,540 (compared to Fr 30,219 for *Gustave III* of 1833 and Fr 44,000 for *Les Huguenots* of 1836). An Opéra record, "Dépenses de matériel" (F-Po, Opéra Arch. 19/229), summarizes the cost of costumes at Fr 69,769 (compared to Fr 35,102 for those of *Les Huguenots*); according to Marie-Antoinette Allévy, *La Mise en scène en France dans la première moitié du dix-neuvième siècle* (Paris: Librairie E. Droz, 1938), 108, the armor alone cost Fr 30,000. Fulcher, *The Nation's Image*, 82, estimates the total production costs of *La Juive* at Fr 150,000. See Pendle and Wilkins, "Paradise Found," in *Opera in Context*, ed. Radice, 190–98, for significant details of the staging of *La Juive*.

[5] See Laurie C. Shulman's discussion of press reactions to the *mise en scène* of *La Juive* in "Music Criticism of the Paris Opera of the 1830s" (Ph.D. diss., Cornell University, 1985), 178–81.

[6] *Le Constitutionnel*, 25 February 1835; *Dossier de presse parisienne*, ed. Leich-Galland, 10.

Exceptions to the general clamor were reviews that criticized the *mise en scène* as excessive, and even oppressive. Berlioz, quipping that the opera was "a harsh nightmare" ("un rude cauchemar"), despaired that its extravagant staging threatened to overpower the music:

> Despite the efforts that were made to prevent hearing the score, despite the clanking of all that armor, the stamping of horses, the hubbub of the crowd, the peal of bells and firing of cannons, the dances, the laden tables, the fountains of wine, despite all the antimusical roar of the Académie royale de musique, we were able to catch some of the composer's inspirations.[7]

François Stoepel demanded: "Is there a single person who gave the slightest attention to the music during the long procession of the first act and the sumptuous festivity of the third?"[8] And Nourrit himself, in a letter of 27 March 1835, echoed these complaints but thankfully observed that, after the initial dazzling of the audience at the première, the music began to triumph over "the hardware" ("la ferblanterie").[9]

Notes in Scribe's travel journals (*carnets de voyage*) reveal that the visual images of Constance, as well as its historical associations with the Council, had been impressed on him as early as July 1826 during a vacation in Switzerland and Germany. It is possible that his visit to Constance inspired, or at least contributed to, the idea for the setting of *La Juive*.[10] Images described in terms of the stage permeate Scribe's journal commentary, suggesting a correlation between his observations about historical scenes and events and the historical realism attempted in some of his works.[11] That the librettist viewed his sightseeing as fact-gathering and atmosphere-absorbing experiences is

---

[7] *Le Rénovateur, courrier de l'Europe,* 1 March 1835; *Dossier de presse parisienne,* ed. Leich-Galland, 148, 151; Shulman, "Music Criticism," 170ff.

[8] *Journal de Paris et des départemens,* 28 February 1835; *Dossier de presse parisienne,* ed. Leich-Galland, 88.

[9] Quicherat, *Nourrit,* vol. III, 8–9.

[10] F-Pn, Ms., n.a.fr. 22584, vol. I, fols. 14^v–15^v.

[11] *Ibid.,* vol. 8, fol. 19^v. The interpenetration of art and reality is further demonstrated in Scribe's passage "après la description de Walter Scott, je m'y suis [en] transporté en regardant le lac de Wallenstatt," correlating with the incorporation of personal *scènes de voyage* into music and literature of the early nineteenth century.

evident in a number of passages. During a visit to Basel, for example, Scribe makes notes of paintings of Hans Holbein and selects one to serve as a model for a costume in *Ali-Baba*, the opera whose libretto he was preparing during the trip with his companion and collaborator Duveyrier-Mélesville.[12] There are also descriptions of grand scenic views, which he continually refers to as "spectacles" and experiences as if in the theatre. Scribe's imagined vantage point cannot be missed in his description of a waterfall on the Rhine that he and his party viewed from a small open door at the Imworth chateau: "[W]e also find ourselves suspended above the river, placed and seated as comfortably as in a loge at the opera, in order to enjoy one of the most beautiful and frightening spectacles that Europe can offer."[13]

No doubt Scribe was building on past opera experiences (having observed spectacular natural scenes depicted in French opera and melodrama during the 1820s), as well as projecting scenes in his mind's eye for future productions. It is impossible to know whether he was consciously thinking of the theatre as he made visual imprints of Constance, but his travel references to the cathedral, the "magnificent view" of the lake at Constance, and the town of St. Gall seem to correspond with his rough staging directions in the draft scenario (or prose draft) of *La Juive*, although with theatrical license, since St. Gall certainly would not have been visible from Constance. For Act I, Scene i, Scribe writes:

> The scene takes place in the town of Constance – on the lakeshore – a public square – a street to the right – a church at the back – in the distance the view of mountains conspicuously covered with snow – in the middle of which appears the episcopal city of St. Gall.[14]

The principal elements of the first set for the première, designed by Charles Séchan (1803–74), Léon Feuchère (1804–57), Edouard

---

[12] *Ibid.*, vol. 8, fol. 8. These were most likely the paintings of Hans Holbein the Younger (1497–1524), whose early career was centered in Basel, rather than Hans Holbein the Elder (1465–1524), a minor southern German painter.

[13] *Ibid.*, vol. 1, fol. 13^r.

[14] F-Pn, Ms., n.a.fr. 22502, vol. XXIII, 1°:2°, 2: "La scène se passe dans la ville de Constance – aux bords du lac – une place publique – une rue à droite – une église au fond – à l'horizon la vue des montagnes d'apparentes couvertes de neige – au milieu desquelles apparaît la ville épiscopale de St. Gall."

Despléchin (1806–70), and Jules Diéterle (1811–89), resemble the librettist's depiction: in the foreground is a crossroads in Constance with the entrance to a church at stage left and the turreted house (and / or shop) of Eléazar near the center of the stage,[15] in front of imposing Gothic structures; on a painted screen, the Alps appear in the distance (see Illustration 3).[16] Scribe may also have recalled his travel images when he placed, beyond the gardens of a palace at the beginning of Act III of the draft scenario, "the beautiful sights and fine countryside of the Canton of Thurgovie."[17] This early description was realized in the première, but shifted to appear at the beginning of Scene v of the third act; by the second performance on 25 February, with the omission of the first four scenes (three numbers) in Eudoxie's apartment, this scene opened Act III (see pp. 220 and 228–30 below).[18]

The draft scenario reveals that Scribe imagined the opulence of the Council setting at early conceptual stages. At the scenario's beginning (see Illustration 4), he writes:

> The Council of Constance, the largest ever assembled, was impressive and magnificent from the outset . . . illustrious princes with their brilliant retinues gathered together with innumerable ecclesiastics of all ranks, with countless numbers of senior and junior professors, the immense crowd of people and shopkeepers.[19]

---

[15] "La boutique" of Eléazar is designated in Schlesinger's printed libretto, 23 February 1835 (F-Po, Livr. 19[274]), while the Act I libretto refers to "ce logis" ("the home") of Eléazar. In Palianti's *mise en scène* sketch, the indication "maison d'Eléazar" appears; see H. Robert Cohen, *The Original Staging Manuals for Twelve Parisian Operatic Premières / Douze Livrets de mise en scène datant des créations parisiennes* (Stuyvesant, NY: Pendragon Press, 1991), 137.

[16] See also Join-Diéterle, *Les Décors de scène*, 37, no. 20. St. Gall does not appear to be shown in the distance in the set, although other buildings – seemingly the outskirts of Constance – can be seen in the middle distance; St. Gall goes unmentioned in the printed libretto and in Palianti's sketch.

[17] F-Pn, Ms., n.a.fr. 22502, vol. xxiii, 1°:2°, 11.

[18] F-Pan, AJ¹³202: "Mémoire des peintures faites pour l'opéra de la Juive."

[19] F-Pn, Ms., n.a.fr. 22502, 1°:2°, 1: "Le concile de Constance le plus nombreux qui ce soit jamais assemblé se montra de son origine plein d'éclat et de magnificence . . . des princes illustres avec des suites brillantes se joignirent aux innombrables écclésiastiques de tout rang, aux docteurs et aux maîtres en arts sans compte, la foule immense du peuple et de marchands."

3 *La Juive*, Act I, lithograph by Eugène Cicéri, Philippe Benoist, and Gaildrau of stage set designed by Séchan, Feuchère, Despléchin, and Diéterle, Paris Opéra, 1835

4 Draft scenario of *La Juive* by Eugène Scribe, title page

Even more trenchant than the visual images in Scribe's journal commentary are historical references to the Council. He says nothing of the papal schism, but instead focuses on the Council's heresy trial and execution of the Bohemian religious reformer Jan Hus (1372/3–1415). Hus,

a follower of John Wycliffe (1320?–84) and a writer of theological trea-
tises and scriptural commentary, whose challenges to Catholic views
of the Church anticipated Luther's by a century, voluntarily came to
the Council to defend his positions. He was given safe conduct by Sigismund, but after the Council condemned thirty propositions from his
works, he was arrested and burned at the stake as an obstinate heretic.
In Scribe's description, he gives details of the cathedral's "salle de concile," taking note of the thrones of Sigismund and Pope Martin V, the
bible of Jan Hus, and the chair that bore Hus to the stake.[20] Evocative
remnants of the trial and condemnation of the reformer stir deep emotion in the librettist, sending a wave of depression over him and his traveling companions. He points out the stone block on which Hus kneeled
when sentenced and the sites where he and his books were burned.[21]

Responses infused even more strongly with liberal sentiment appear in Scribe's travel journal of 1827 as he concentrates on themes
of religious oppression and immorality. On a visit to Avignon, another historic seat of Catholic power and judgment, he is accompanied by the writer Castil-Blaze (1784–1857), a native of the region who
acted as his local guide. Scribe's commentary is weighted with evidence of the Church's religious persecutions. He writes of the Inquisition tribunal that took place in the Papal Palace, describing the
proceedings room by room. In "la salle d'audience," the prisoners
were brought before the Inquisitors; in "la salle des tortures," they
were bound in iron chains and endured abuses by instruments so
barbaric that Scribe blushed when he viewed them.[22] As if to em-
phasize that the popes condoned the heinous proceedings with clear
consciences, he pointedly describes the proximity of the papal living quarters to the rooms and places of torture, condemnation, and
death. Scribe's aversion to these early Church actions becomes even
more pronounced as he speaks of "la salle préparatoire," where the

[20] F-Pn, Ms., n.a.fr. 22584, vol. 1, fols. 14ᵛ–15ʳ. Scribe spells the name "Hus" in this
source and in the draft scenario; it appears as "Huss" in early printed sources of
the opera.
[21] Ibid., fol. 15ᵛ.
[22] Ibid., vol. 2, "Voyage dans le Mydi de la France, 1ᵉʳ Avril-1827," fols. 19ᵛ–20ʳ.

Inquisitors went "to invoke the Holy Spirit or, rather, the devil who inspires them."[23]

The draft scenario and other sources documenting the libretto's development further point to Scribe's attraction to the subject of religious despotism and reveal his intent to illustrate the historical repressiveness of the Catholic Church. In the thumbnail sketch of his early ideas for *La Juive*, found in a pocket notebook marked "Quelques Idées des pièces," there is no mention of the Council in his outline of the love conflict between Jew and Christian and the malediction leading to their condemnation.[24] Yet the term *l'auto-da-fé*, entered for the fifth act, points to a line of thought beyond the love cliché (see pp. 214–15 below and Illustration 8). This term of Portuguese origin, well established as a standard term connoting the Inquisition of the Church and the burning of heretics, resonates with Scribe's travel descriptions of Constance and Avignon, as well as with Voltaire's use of religious metaphors and the anticlericalism prevalent in liberal rhetoric of the 1820s and early 1830s. In Scribe's draft scenario, the term *l'auto-da-fé* appears again as a subtitle (see Illustration 4), along with the introductory paragraph on the opera's prehistory, now fully related to the Council of Constance.[25] Scribe cites in this paragraph the resolution of the papal schism as the Council's main function, but – corresponding with the focus of his journal commentary – he also refers to the judgment of Hus as "a great object of interest."[26]

In Scribe's appropriation of the Council, he characteristically manipulates historical facts, compresses time and events, creates plot implausibilities, and interweaves fiction into the basically factual material to intensify dramatic effect and propulsion and highlight the intimate storyline. (See the synopsis of *La Juive* in Appendix B.) But he makes adaptations to obscure certain political associations while strengthening others. Besides his time limitation to 1414, Scribe presents Sigismund as emperor, although he did not become Holy Roman Emperor until

---

[23] *Ibid.*, fol. 20ʳ.   [24] F-Pn, Ms., n.a.fr. 22584, vol. VIII, fol. 66ʳ.

[25] Although Scribe crosses out "Rachel" in the draft scenario's title "Rachel ou L'auto-da-fe," replacing it at some point with "la juive" (see Illustration 4), he retains "Rachel" at the head of his draft verse (F-Pn, Ms., n.a.fr. 22562).

[26] F-Pn, Ms., n.a.fr. 22502, vol. XXIII, 1°:2°, 12.

1433; in actuality, he was newly crowned as German king in Aachen, or Aix-la-Chapelle, three days after the Council's opening. (Scribe's designation, however, corresponds with Voltaire's, as well as with references in early nineteenth-century historical accounts, including the excerpt from the *Biographie universelle* cited in the printed libretto; see p. 121 below.) His inclusion of Sigismund as a mute figurehead who does not take part in the action but whose presence is heralded by celebratory choruses, suggests self-censorship blatantly political in nature. A direct attack on a royal figure (even one drawn from history) was still questionable during this comparatively liberal period, as realized in the 1832 suppression of Hugo's *Le Roi s'amuse*.[27] The visual allusions to Sigismund's part in the Council were not lost on Parisian audiences, however, at least not on educated and politically sensitive individuals such as Alexandre Dumas *père*, who emphasized, like Voltaire, Sigismund's guilt and responsibility in the fate of Jan Hus in *La Gazette musicale de Paris* of April 1835.[28]

The princess Eudoxie (first named Theodora in the draft scenario) and the Catholic prince Léopold may be creative additions or possibly substitutes for historical figures.[29] Very clearly bending fact is the celebration of Léopold's victory over the Hussites at the time of the Council, since the Hussite wars began only after Bohemian nobles led conflicts to avenge the killing of the religious reformer. Not until Hus's death did the movement take on a revolutionary character, transforming him into a martyr and national hero for Bohemians seeking both religious and political reform.[30] In Scribe's most significant historical

---

27 Scribe initially included Catherine de Médicis in the action of *Les Huguenots*, before censors suppressed the role. See the letter of 2 March 1836 (F-Pan, AJ¹³183) from the duc de Choiseul, reassuring the Ministre de l'Intérieur that the queen who appears on the terrace is not Catherine de Médicis, but Marguerite de Valois.

28 Alexandre Dumas, "La Juive," *La Gazette musicale de Paris* 2, no. 17 (26 April 1835): 142, 144–5.

29 Hans Ulrich Becker believes Léopold to be a substitution for Archduke Frederick, as he noted in a conversation at the Colloque Halévy, Paris Conservatoire, 18 November 2000.

30 As cited in "Hussites," in *Encyclopaedia Britannica*, 32 vols. (New York: Encyclopaedia Britannica Inc., 1910), vol. XIV, 8. The majority of the battles

detour, he substitutes Jewish characters for the condemned Hus and for Jerome of Prague (1365–1416), a follower of Wycliffe and friend of Hus who was also put to death by the Council: in essence, Scribe replaces one type of "heretic" with another.[31]

Although Hus does not figure in the dramatic action (neither does Jerome), the reformer is referred to in the opera's libretto, as in the draft scenario and draft verse.[32] In a condensed passage of narrative by Albert, the emperor's *sergent d'armes*, in Act I, Scene i, No. 1, the connections between Hus, Sigismund, the Council, and the anachronistic victory over the Hussites are briefly made. Before the celebratory "Hosanna" chorus, Albert tells Léopold, seemingly uninformed, why a crowd has gathered:

Act I, Scene i, No. 1

Schlesinger-Garland[33]

Eh! ne savez vous pas	Ah! Don't you know
Qu'aujourd'hui Sigismond arrive dans Constance	That Sigismond arrives today in Constance
Pour ouvrir un concile où Princes et Prélats	To open a council in which Princes and Prelates
Vont de la Chrétienté terminer les débats,	Are going to finish the discussions about Christianity,

followed the papal bull issued by Martin V in 1420 which declared a crusade "for the destruction of the Wycliffites, Hussites and all other heretics in Bohemia."

[31] Jerome had to flee the Inquisition in Vienna in 1410; in 1415 he tried to defend Hus before the Council, but was arrested on the way home, returned, and coerced into retracting the articles of Wycliffe and Hus. When he later withdrew his retraction, the Council condemned him as a "relapsed heretic," and he was burned at the stake on 30 May 1416. See F. M. Bailey, "Jerome of Prague," in *Encyclopaedia Britannica*, 24 vols. (Chicago: Encyclopaedia Britannica, 1973), vol. XII, 1250. Scribe's substitution was noted by the *Constitutionnel* reviewer (25 February 1835).

[32] F-Pan, AJ[13]202; F-Pn, Ms., n.a.fr. 22502, vol. XXIII, 1°:2°; F-Pn, Ms., n.a.fr. 22562.

[33] This and most of the subsequent libretto excerpts are drawn from the orchestral score published by Maurice Schlesinger (Paris, 183[5], M.S. 2000) and reprinted in facsimile by Garland Publishing (New York, 1980) (hereafter, *Schlesinger-Garland*), which reflects changes made after the first three performances. The original publication date of this edition is not secure, but its advertisement in *La Gazette*

Décerner la thiare, éteindre l'hérésie,	Decide the [papal] tiara, extinguish heresy,
Et du fougueux Jean Hus juger le Dogme impie?	And judge the impious dogma of the tempestuous Jan Hus?
Déjà ses partisans, ces hussites fameux,	Already his partisans, these famous Hussites,

musicale de Paris on 9 August 1835 suggests that it was published by, or close to, this date; moreover, a letter written by Halévy on 16 January 1836 (Appendix I-1) speaks of sending sheets of the already engraved score. Anik Devries and François Lesure, *Dictionnaire des éditeurs de musique français*, 2 vols. (Geneva: Editions Minkoff, 1979), vol. II, 390, approximate its plate number as early 1836. Schlesinger's full score was based on the autograph (F-Po, A. 509a, vols. I–II), as revealed by printer's marks throughout the latter. It also corresponds to the archival score (F-Po, A.509b, vols. I–VI), a manuscript copy intended to represent the opera as performed at the Académie royale, typically the last musical material copied by the Leborne *atelier*. The archival score was prepared, or completed, sometime after the première (three numbers of Act III that were omitted by the second performance were never copied into the archival score, for example; see p. 229, n. 55, below). For music examples and references, I shall draw from both *Schlesinger-Garland* and the piano-vocal score published by Schlesinger, which was also based on the composer's autograph; it was edited by F. Hiller (Paris, 183[5], M.S. 2002) and reprinted by Henri Lemoine (4504 HL) (hereafter, *Schlesinger-Lemoine*); in some cases, particularly when discussing material excised from the full score, I will draw from *Schlesinger-Lemoine* only. (Leich-Galland, "*La Juive*: Commentaire musical et littéraire," 35, writes that the Lemoine editions were exact replicas of the Schlesinger editions; for a list of other editions of the piano-vocal score, see Elizabeth Giuliani, "Bibliographie," *L'Avant-scène opéra* 100 (1987): 128–9.) Other consulted sources include the first-production performing parts (F-Po, Mat. 19e[315, (1)–(183), (231)–(268), (479), (505)–(540), (547)–(548), (551)–(607)); score fragments (F-Po, Rés. 135, 1, and ♪4387); the printed libretti of 18 and 23 February 1835; a second-edition libretto dated 1835, published by Jonas (F-Pan, AJ^{13}202); a fair copy of the full libretto (F-Pan, AJ^{13}202); fair copies of libretto fragments, Acts IV and V (F-Pn, Ms., n.a.fr. 22502, vol. XXIII, 1°:4° and 1°:5°); draft verse (F-Pn, Ms., n.a.fr. 22502, vol. XXIII, 1°:3°, and n.a.fr. 22562, vol. II); and a draft scenario (F-Pn, Ms., n.a.fr. 22502, vol. XXIII, 1°:2°). Not fully used for this study is the orchestral score edited by Karl Leich-Galland, *La Juive: Opéra en cinq actes d'Eugène Scribe, musique de Fromental Halévy* (Saarbrücken: Musik-Edition Lucie Galland, 1985), which follows both the autograph and the Schlesinger piano-vocal score; as Leich-Galland notes in the preface, he is concerned with representing Halévy's (and Scribe's) conception of *La Juive*, and what he believes is closer to that presented at the première, rather than the Opéra's "arrangement" of it; to date, no critical apparatus has been supplied.

Sont tombés sous les coups d'un bras victorieux	Have fallen under the blows of victorious arms
Et l'Empereur au Ciel aujourd'hui même	And the Holy Emperor this very day
Rend grâce des exploits de ce héros qu'il aime![34]	Gives thanks to Heaven for the accomplishments of this hero whom he loves!

The recitative of the *crieur* that follows the "Hosanna" chorus makes clear Léopold's role as conqueror of the Hussites:

Act I, Scene ii, No. 1

Schlesinger-Garland

Monseigneur Léopold, avec l'aide de Dieu,	Monseigneur Léopold, with the help of God,
Des hussites ayant châtié l'insolence,	Having punished the Hussites for their insolence,
De par le saint concile assemblé dans Constance,	In the name of the holy council assembled in Constance,
De par notre Empereur, et Monseigneur Brogni,	In the name of our Emperor, and Monseigneur Brogni,
Largesse sera faite au peuple aujourd'hui!	Largesse will be given to the people today!

Enhancing the aura of historical authenticity lent by such textual references were the well-researched costumes designed by Paul Lormier and modeled after iconography of early fifteenth-century southern German soldiers and clerics.[35] Beneath many sketches, Lormier cites his source as "Maison de Bavière"; on others, he identifies the depicted historical personage. He notes, for example, Sigismund's name and title, when he became emperor, when he died, and whom he married,

---

[34] The punctuation of extracts from *Schlesinger-Garland* has been adapted in accordance with the punctuation found in *Schlesinger-Lemoine* and the 23 February libretto where the text in question also exists in those sources.

[35] Nicole Wild, *Décors et costumes du XIXe siècle*, vol. ii: *Théâtres et décorateurs* (Paris: Bibliothèque Nationale, 1987), 328. Wild refers to Lormier as the "champion of local color and historical exactitude"; see Lormier's watercolor and pencil sketches for *La Juive*, F-Po, [D. 216 (10)-ii, fols. 70–111.

and identifies the cardinal as "Jean francois de Brognye eveque de vivian/archeveque d'Arles" (see the sketches for Brogni and Sigismund, with Lormier's identifications, Illustration 5, and the renderings of costumes for Brogni, Léopold, and Eudoxie, Illustration 6).[36] One design of a male figure wearing a pointed hat on his bowed head is labeled "hérétique condamné à être brûlé."[37] Historical accuracy was also suggested by the inclusion of a biographical paragraph on Cardinal Brogni drawn from *Biographie universelle* that appeared in the printed libretto intended for audience members. It contains no overtly offensive or ideologically slanted language, but instead straightforwardly presents the cardinal's vital role in the Council and reveals his opposition to Hus and his followers:

> The ending of the schism and the maintenance of the authority of the Church threatened in Germany by the new opinions of the Hussites were what affected the cardinal the most. Despite his advanced age, he went to Constance in August of 1414 to discuss with the imperial magistrates and officers the advent of the Council which was to bring peace to the Church. He presided during forty sessions and had meetings day and night with Emperor Sigismund, with princes and prelates, etc.[38]

Although non-inflammatory, the passage clarifies the association of the cardinal with the Council and its decisions, as well as with Sigismund. In the opera's libretto and action, Brogni's direct responsibility for the executions is de-emphasized, but his role is understood. In Act V, for

---

[36] F-Po, [D. 216 (10)-II, fol. 105. As noted by Allévy, *Mise en scène*, 108, Lormier consulted the work of historiographer Pierre Palliot, *La Vraie et Parfaite Science des armoires*. On fol. 97, he refers to Palliot and copies a paragraph, seemingly from his work, on "*L'Ordre des Teutons*, dits de Prusse."

[37] F-Po, [D. 216 (10)-II, fol. 106.

[38] "L'extinction du schisme et le maintien de l'autorité de l'église menacée en allemagne par les nouvelles opinions des hussites, étaient ce qui affectait le plus le cardinal. Malgré son grand âge il se rendit à Constance au mois d'août de l'année 1414 pour s'y concerter avec les magistrats et les commissaires impériaux sur la venue du concile qui devait rendre la paix à l'église. Il se présida pendant quarante sessions et eut jour et nuit des conférences avec l'empereur Sigismond, avec les princes et les prélats, etc." The paragraph appears in the Schlesinger libretti of 18 and 23 February 1835 and subsequent libretti, with the citation "*Biographie Universelle*, tom. 6, pag. v."

5 Sketches for the costumes of Cardinal Brogni and Emperor Sigismund by Paul Lormier, 1834

6 Costumes for *La Juive*, Paris Opéra, 1835: Princess Eudoxie (Julie Dorus-Gras), Cardinal Brogni (Nicolas Levasseur), and Prince Léopold (Lafont), costume design by Paul Lormier

example, he does not speak any words as representative of the tribunal, but he does appear standing with the cardinals of the Council as the final death sentences are announced. As we shall see in Chapter 4, the cardinal is depicted as a just, compassionate Church father in much of the opera, particularly in his pivotal *air* of the first act, which diffuses the first attack on the Jews. With this attention on Brogni's compassion, Scribe may have wanted to obfuscate the attack on the Church as well as add moral complexity to his drama.

In perhaps another self-censoring gesture, Scribe may have chosen not to center his plot around the Council's persecution of Hus so as to diffuse the critique through historical allusion rather than re-enactment. Or he may have merely wanted to avoid repeating himself too obviously by adopting a conflict similar to the Catholic–Protestant pairing of *Les Huguenots*, which had been slated for performance before *La Juive*. But it seems highly plausible that Scribe chose Jewish protagonists not only because of the Jews' symbolic ties with the political liberation of the French Revolution, but, more specifically, in response to the July Monarchy's attempts to advance religious freedom and tolerance through passage of the 1831 law of the *culte israélite*. His substitution was also historically appropriate (if one does not think too literally), since Jews had frequently been Inquisition victims, particularly of the Spanish Inquisition. Liberal concern focused on this Jewish past of persecution and exclusion, as reflected in the statement of one discussant of the 1831 law, a M. Salverte, who reminded his colleagues: "[T]he Israelites were not only persecuted by governments; it wasn't only kings, princes, and heads of the priesthood who handed them over to the executioner; it was entire populations who enjoyed humiliating them, mistreating them, and who waited only for a signal to rush to assassinate them."[39] Besides acknowledging their unique historical position as a maligned minority, Scribe also connects with

---

[39] *Archives parlementaires*, vol. LXV, 315: "[L]es israélites n'étaient pas seulement persécutés par les gouvernements, ce n'étaient pas seulement les rois, les princes et les chefs du sacerdoce qui les livraient aux bourreaux, c'étaient des populations entières qui se plaisaient à les humilier, à les maltraiter, et qui n'attendaient qu'un signal pour courir les assassiner."

a literary tradition of using Jewish characters as symbols of social, political, and religious oppression. The substitution further touched on contemporary analogies made between Protestants and Jews, both positive and negative: liberals often viewed both groups as representatives of individual freedom and even emblems of an industrialized, modern society, while some conservative thinkers saw them as threats to traditional beliefs and culture (see pp. 266–8).

Intolerance toward and persecution of Jews figure strongly in the opera, beginning with three powerful scenes in the first act and culminating in Rachel's execution in Act V (Eléazar's is not depicted). Illuminated by Scribe's journal commentary, as well as by his other religious-political dramas, this highlighting of the abuse of power by the Church and by absolutist regimes and their partisans is central to the opera's messages, despite the benevolent gestures given to Cardinal Brogni. Scribe's appropriation of the Council of Constance and its burning of heretics, although with modifications, was both realistic and metaphorical. The actuality of these historical events reinforced the validity of his critique; as in other dramas and novels of the period, this setting of a historically distant past had incisive, contemporary applications: undoubtedly it was intended as a reminder of repressive actions of Church and State in the history of France, including those during the Restoration, particularly during the regime of Charles X. Despite the correspondence of this critique with the government's stance toward the protection of Jewish religious freedom, it may have also served as a warning to Louis-Philippe, a monarch who, in the minds of many liberals, had turned away from the principles and promises of 1830.

THE VOLTAIREAN CONTEXT

Scribe's accounts of Constance and Avignon, as well as the opera's setting and subject, correlate with Voltaire's use of the Council and the Inquisition as illustrations of the intolerance and barbarism of an absolutist Church and State; moreover, they resonate with sentiments expressed in contemporary debates that echo Voltairean rhetoric. In his *Essai sur les moeurs et l'esprit des nations*, Voltaire devotes two chapters to the Council, these following his discussion of the papal schism in the West.[40] In the first chapter he examines the Council's political objectives of dethroning a pontiff and reforming the Church's taxes and revenues, as well as such vices as simony; in the second, he focuses on the Council's religious zealotry, illustrated by the burning at the stake of Hus and Jerome of Prague. Voltaire sets the context by classifying Hus, Wycliffe, and Jerome as challengers to an ambitious, vice-ridden, and excessively rich clergy. Although Hus rejected much of Wycliffe's doctrine, Voltaire writes that he had adopted all the "bile" that the English reformer had launched against the scandals of popes and bishops, excommunications, and all forms of ecclesiastical power. Hus was killed, the philosopher emphatically concludes, for having attacked "the pretensions of priests."[41] Before the Council, Hus was defiant, adamantly believing in the truth of his writings and refusing to retract his statements. Although Voltaire clearly regards Hus as no less inflexible than the Council, he nevertheless portrays him as an unfairly condemned martyr, while emphasizing the complicity of governmental authorities:

> Jan Hus did not embrace any of Wycliffe's propositions that today separate the Protestants from the Roman Catholic Church; nevertheless, he was condemned to be burned at the stake . . . The Fathers of the Council absolutely wanted Jan Hus to retract; and Jan Hus, sure that he was right, did not want to admit that he was mistaken . . . Jan Hus was unyielding . . .
>
> The Council was as unyielding as he; but there was something heroic in his obstinate race toward death; the Council's obstinacy was indeed cruel. The emperor, despite his promise of safe conduct, ordered the Palatine Elector to drag him to the stake. He was burned alive in the presence of the Elector himself and he praised God until the flame smothered his voice.[42]

Jerome of Prague met with the same severe fate a few months later, despite his public retractions. Voltaire depicts him as more rational than

---

[40] *Oeuvres complètes*, vol. IV, part 1, 415–22.
[41] *Ibid.*, 418, n. 1.   [42] *Ibid.*, 421.

Hus and as eloquent as Socrates in his discourse before his judges. The comparative references to the condemned Greek thinker give Voltaire a point of departure for more politically emphatic statements. In a footnote he differentiates between the killing of Socrates and that of Hus, designating the former as an isolated example of injustice, unlike Hus's "legal murder," which was followed by "ten thousand murders of the same kind, of which not a single one was punished or rectified, even by a futile repentance."[43]

Voltaire scorns the cowardice of Sigismund with his betrayal of the promise of safe conduct in the face of the "treacherous and barbarous" Council, and notes that the king later met with fierce opposition to his succession to the throne in Bohemia, inducing him to fight sympathizers of the two martyrs with "the terror of the Crusades."[44] (Voltaire's account mentions Hus's disciples coming to the Council, but does not suggest they had already taken up arms for their leader's religious teachings.) In a footnote he condemns later apologists of the actions of Sigismund and the Council as he writes of the utter irony of granting to one such apologist "the first chair of moral doctrine" founded in France in the eighteenth century.[45]

In the chapter "De l'Inquisition" in the same *Essai sur les moeurs*, Voltaire describes Inquisition tribunals of various countries to illustrate how debased human nature can be "when superstitious ignorance is armed with power."[46] While distinguishing between the Inquisition and "public sacrifices" known as *autos-da-fé*, he pungently emphasizes the cruelty and violence of these sacrifices and the hypocrisy of Church figures and the collusion of kings behind them:

> It is a surpliced priest, a monk dedicated to gentleness, who delivers people in immense dungeons to the cruelest tortures. Afterward it is a stage set up in a public square, where all the condemned are led to the stake, at the end of a procession of monks and brotherhoods. They sing, they say mass, and they kill people. An Asian, arriving in Madrid on the day of one such execution, would not know if it is an entertainment, a religious festival, a sacrifice, or a slaughter; and it is all those things

---

[43] *Ibid.*, 421, n. 1.   [44] *Ibid.*, 420, 422.   [45] *Ibid.*, 420, n. 1.   [46] *Ibid.*, 682.

together. Kings, whose sole presence elsewhere suffices to pardon a criminal, witness this spectacle bare-headed, on a seat less elevated than that of the Inquisitor, and see their subjects expire in the flames. Montezuma was reproached for sacrificing prisoners to his gods; what would he have said if he had seen an *auto-da-fé*?[47]

Voltaire's account may not have been a direct source for the opera's subject, but the philosopher's historical interpretation appears to have provided at least a general subtext to Scribe's journal accounts and to the developing libretto. In one journal entry, the librettist alludes to the *philosophe*–Church opposition, when he reacts to the irony of the appearance of a verse of Voltaire beside a tomb in the cathedral at Avignon, with its legacy of the ill-treatment of those judged as heretics.[48] Scribe undoubtedly knew Voltaire's essays through his ed-ucation at Sainte-Barbe, and through his own extensive reading – he frequently jots down lists of newly published books in his journals. One list, compiled *circa* 1837 for the library at his new chateau outside Paris (headed "Bibliothèque pour Séricourt") itemizes fifty-six titles or authors, including Rousseau, Walter Scott, Mérimée, Balzac, Dumas, Hugo, Eugène Sue, and "Théâtre étranger–Shakspeare [*sic*]–Goethe–Schiller."[49] Although Voltaire's complete works are not included in this particular list, it is nonetheless likely that Scribe owned them, or at least the portions that were most frequently published in France. Voltaire's writings permeated early nineteenth-century French cul-ture: numerous editions of his complete works had appeared by 1830 (six editions were published in 1825 alone), along with approximately sixty-five editions of *La Henriade*, twenty of the *Poèmes*, twenty of the *Théâtre*, and ten of the *Contes*.[50] Between 1826 and 1831, according to Martyn Lyons, the complete works of Voltaire, as well as those of

---

[47] *Ibid.*, 682–3. Shortly before his description of the *auto-da-fé*, he discusses victimization of Jews and Muslims (681–2).

[48] F-Pn, Ms., n.a.fr. 22584, vol. II, fol. 19ᵛ.   [49] *Ibid.*, vol. XXXVII, fols. 26ᵛ–27ʳ.

[50] André Billaz, "Les Ecrivains romantiques et Voltaire: Essai sur Voltaire et le romantisme en France (1795–1830)," 2 vols. (Ph.D. diss., Université de Paris IV, 1974) (Université de Lille III: Service de Reproduction des Thèses, 1974), 8.

Rousseau, were among the best-selling publications in France.[51] More-over, as early as 1813, Scribe adapted the text of Voltaire's *Scythes* for his first melodrama, entitled *Koulikan* and written with Henri Dupin. Scribe's use of Voltaire's *Essai sur les moeurs* as a source for the libretto of *Le Prophète*, on which he began work in 1836, is well documented.[52] But the Voltairean foundation of Scribe's appropriation of the Council is perhaps most strongly implied by his parallel use in *Les Huguenots* of St. Bartholomew's Eve, examined by Voltaire in his *Essai sur les guerres civiles de France*.[53]

Contemporary references to the Council, St. Bartholomew's Eve, and other symbolic events and figures of religious history, as well as debates surrounding the theme of intolerance that raged among vary-ing factions of political conservatives and liberals, deepen the opera's Voltairean context. In 1828, a nine-volume publication, *Causes célèbres étrangères*, included a fourth volume on Hus and Jerome of Prague, "accused of heresy," as well as a ninth volume on Jean Coustos, tried by the Inquisition of Lisbon.[54] The historian Jules Michelet wrote about Hus and the Council of Constance in his *Histoire de France*, the first volumes of which appeared in 1833, and Etienne de Lamothe-Langon published his *Histoire de l'Inquisition* in 1829.[55] The Church reformer Martin Luther was also a popular subject.

[51] Martyn Lyons, *Le Triomphe du livre: Une Histoire sociologique de la lecture dans la France du XIXᵉ siècle* (Paris: Promodis, 1987), 86.

[52] Armstrong, *Le Prophète*, 8, refers to two letters from Scribe, dated 23 April and 2 May 1836, which relate the subject of "Les Anabaptistes" (later *Le Prophète*) to certain passages in Voltaire's essay. Armstrong also notes that a passage from the essay appears as a preface to the first and subsequent editions of the libretto.

[53] Pendle, *Eugène Scribe*, 472–3, discusses the possibility of Scribe's having borrowed from Prosper Mérimée's *Chronique du règne de Charles IX*, but Steven Huebner, "Les Huguenots," in *The New Grove Dictionary of Opera*, ed. Sadie, vol. II, 765, finds little evidence to support such a borrowing, pointing out that several plays of the late 1820s were built around this historical event.

[54] As advertised in *La Quotidienne*, 10 April 1828. In a book list (F-Pn, Ms., n.a.fr. 22584, vol. XIX, fol. 31ʳ), Scribe includes "cause celebre" – perhaps the same publication.

[55] Jules Michelet, *Histoire de France*, 6 vols. (Brussels: Louis Hauman et Cⁱᵉ, 1834), vol. VI, 214ff.; Etienne de Lamothe-Langon, *Histoire de l'Inquisition en France, depuis son établissement au XIIIᵉ siècle, à la suite de la croisade contre les Albigeois, jusqu'en 1772, époque définitive de sa suppression*, 3 vols. (Paris: J.-G. Dentu, 1829).

In the vortex of the ongoing political and religious battles of the Restoration, Voltaire appeared as both symbol and writer. Although the complexity and ambiguity of Voltaire's thought produced a myriad of often conflicting interpretations, ultraroyalists, legitimists, Romantics, and clerics generally echoed counterrevolutionary sentiments in their portrayal of the philosopher as an atheistic devil, an anti-Christ responsible for the bourgeois, secular trends of modern society. The abbé appointed to lead the University in 1822, for example, denigrated Voltaire's writings as impious and held him responsible for the French Revolution, the Terror, and even the 1820 assassination of the duc de Berry (a murder that took place at the Opéra). Liberals, republicans, and anticlericals saw Voltaire as an upholder of social justice and liberator of humanity and enlisted him in various political causes, frequently evoking his name to combat the gains of ultraroyalists and clerics. Hugo, after his youthful disdain for Voltaire as the inciter of "our cruel errors," cast him as "the apostle of humanity."[56] He served as inspiration to liberal factions alarmed by the strengthening alliance of throne and altar, the power of Church officials in public education, ultraroyalist efforts to increase press censorship and institute a sacrilege law, and actions of such extreme clerical groups as the proselytizing Société des missions de France, which engaged in book burnings and symbolic processions and denounced the Revolution and the Empire. Admiring of the philosopher's rationalism as well as the attacks on the abuses and intolerance of religious and political authority that culminated in his prescription "Ecrasez l'infâme," liberal writers echoed anti-authoritarian, anticlerical themes within a new political context. With the advent of the July Monarchy that marked a decline in clerical power, the ubiquity of Voltaire waned somewhat, but his symbolic presence nevertheless continued throughout the Orléanist regime.[57]

---

[56] Billaz, "Les Ecrivains," 37.

[57] In the early 1840s, when the Church attempted to regain control of education, Jules Michelet and Edgar Quinet called on Voltaire in their defense of the University and condemnation of the Church and the Jesuits. Reversing his early denigration of Voltaire, Michelet created a sentimental, Christ-like image of the philosopher in his *Histoire de la révolution française*, 7 vols. (Paris: Chamerot, 1847–53).

The Voltairean oeuvre attractive to reform-minded and anticlerical liberals, in addition to the *Essai sur les moeurs* and the *Essai sur les
guerres civiles*, ranged from the early "Epistle to Urania," which sharply
criticizes the vengeful biblical God, to late articles that attack the foun-
dations of the Christian religion. In the established Church Voltaire
saw a morality opposed to humanist reform, superstitions contrary to
reason, and a fanaticism that often led to repression and violence. In
his "Treatise on Toleration" (1763), he spoke of the religious fanaticism that resulted in the tortured death of Jean Calas of Toulouse, who
was accused of hanging his son to keep him from leaving the Protestant faith and, on judges' orders, was stretched on a wheel until he
confessed his alleged crime. Voltaire ended his treatise with a call for
brotherhood and universal tolerance, not only among Christians but
among all faiths and nationalities.

Voltaire's philosophically and politically imbued dramas were also
influential.[58] For its embodiment of the conflict between humanism
and barbarism, *La Juive* could be said to belong to the tradition of
Le Fanatisme; ou, Mahomet le prophète (1742), a play that features cultural
differences and emphasizes, as the title indicates, religious fanaticism.[59]
But for its use of Jews as symbols of persecution and freedom, the
opera connects more specifically with Voltaire's opera *Samson*, written
with Rameau in 1733–4, which censors found too incendiary to be
allowed on the stage of the Académie royale. Although Rameau's music
does not survive in its original form,[60] Voltaire's libretto, published in

[58] See Marie Wellington, *The Art of Voltaire's Theater: An Exploration of Possibility*
(New York: Peter Lang, 1987), 3–4, for a discussion of Voltaire's dramas as
skilled literary works and as "voice pieces for his philosophy."

[59] Through Mahomet's disciple Séide, who is ordered to kill in the name of
religion, Voltaire reveals the pull between religious duty and personal ethics:
"How horrible and powerful religion is! . . . I fear being barbaric or sacrilegious."

[60] Graham Sadler, "A Re-examination of Rameau's Self-Borrowings," in
*Jean-Baptiste Lully and the Music of the French Baroque: Essays in Honor of James R.
Anthony*, ed. John Hajdu Heyer (Cambridge: Cambridge University Press, 1989),
269–71, 287, suggests the probability that Rameau reused at least a portion of
the *air*, "Echo, voix errante," from *Samson* in an *air* of *La Princesse de Navarre*,
basing his conclusion on the fact that the first four lines of the text of each are
identical.

his collected works, clearly points to both a religious and a political captivity in its illustration of the Israelites' despair over their condition and Samson's attempts to arouse them to break the Philistine chains. Voltaire's theme is evident from the outset of Act I, Scene i, as a *coryphée* addresses the Hebrews:

Samson: Act I, Scene i

Voltaire, *Oeuvres complètes*, vol. II, part 2, 936

UN CORYPHEE	A LEADER
Race malheureuse et divine,	Divine and unfortunate race,
Tristes Hébreux, frémissez tous:	Sorrowful Hebrews, shudder all:
Voici le jour affreux qu'un roi puis-sant destine	The dreadful day has come when a mighty king has deemed
A placer ses dieux parmi nous.	To place his gods among us.
Des prêtres mensongers, pleins de zèle et de rage,	Deceitful priests, full of rage and zeal,
Vont nous forcer à plier les genoux	Will force us to bend our knees
Devant les dieux de ce climat sauvage.	Before the gods of that savage place.
Enfans du ciel, que ferez-vous?	Children of God, what say you to this?

An article by Edouard Monnais in *La Gazette musicale de Paris* entitled "Voltaire, la musique et les musiciens," which appeared several months after the première of *La Juive*, refers to both *Samson* and *Mahomet* and alludes to the controversial subjects that brought about their suppression as well as to the contemporary resonance with the opera.[61]

Voltaire's use of a biblical story as a tale of liberation, with Samson's appeals to crush the "tyrans" and his shouts of "Liberté! Liberté!," is not singular in French literature or theatre. Prior to this opera Racine's *Esther* (1689) carried similar overtones. Operas and dramas contemporary with *La Juive*, works with such titles as *Cain*, *Les Machabées*, and *Nabucodonosor* (the 1836 play that served as the basis

---

[61] *La Gazette musicale de Paris* 2, no. 43 (25 October 1835): 346. A review attacking *La Juive* in *La Gazette de France* (27 February 1835) compares its "pretense" of local color to that in Voltaire's *Mahomet* and *Alzire*.

for Verdi's 1842 opera *Nabucco*) may simply have expressed a natural focus for a Catholic society familiar with biblical stories. Many biblical operas produced by the Académie royale that belong in part to the oratorio tradition could be viewed as non-political, such as *Moïse et Pharaon* (1827) by Rossini and Jouy. Yet the text of this opera, among others, aligns with the ideas of political freedom and social change embedded in Voltaire's *Samson* as well as in the Restoration writings of Ballanche that compared the situation of post-revolutionary Frenchmen to that of the Hebrews in the desert, marching toward "la nouvelle terre sociale."[62]

Voltairean themes undergird religious-political arguments found in a wide range of periodicals, including the popular liberal newspaper *Le Constitutionnel* and the more extremely anticlerical *Le Courrier français*, with opposing viewpoints expressed in the legitimist, clerical organs *La Quotidienne* and *La Gazette de France*. The pro-Catholic periodical *L'Univers religieux, politique, scientifique et littéraire* recognized that liberal newspapers carried on the legacy of Voltaire, representing "a remnant of Voltaireanism."[63] One exchange in its columns with the short-lived, militantly republican paper of the July Monarchy, *Le Réformateur*, encapsulates many aspects of these polemical debates.[64] In the latter, the problems of social, political, and religious intolerance are specifically addressed in two unsigned articles, one of 12 October 1834 entitled "Tolérance" and another published 15 February 1835 entitled "Intolérance religieuse."[65] The October article is a plea for an open-minded acceptance of the social doctrines that its editors – "men of reform" – are putting forward. While admitting that the Enlightenment philosopher had himself become fanatic just as he had condemned the zealotry

---

[62] *Essai sur les institutions sociales*, cited in Billaz, "Les Ecrivains," 13.

[63] *L'Univers religieux* 3, no. 381 (29 January 1835). This paper was founded in 1833 by l'abbé Migne as successor to *La Tribune catholique*, which had replaced *L'Avenir*.

[64] *Le Réformateur: Journal des nouveaux intérêts matériels et moraux, industriels et politiques, littéraires et scientifiques* was founded in 1834 by François-Vincent Raspail and Théophile de Kersausie, but the censorship laws of September 1835 sealed its fate. After the infliction of penalties for articles deemed threatening to the monarchy and the imprisonment of its editors, the paper folded in November 1835.

[65] *Ibid.*, 1, no. 4 (12 October 1834): 1; 2, no. 129 (15 February 1835): 1.

of religious doctrine and faith, the author reminds his readers of "the continuous conspiracies of priests against the nation" during the 1789 Revolution and "the scandalous missions" of the Restoration.[66] In contrast with the priests' sectarian actions, he emphasizes the re-emergence of the principles of freedom and tolerance toward all men with the 1830 Revolution – he notes that "1830 inspired wiser ideas."[67]

In the 15 February article, a rebuttal to *L'Univers religieux* that appeared shortly before the première of *La Juive*, the author defends the enlightened views of *Le Réformateur*, which *L'Univers religieux* had attacked. In fact, the clerical paper had volleyed with its own accusation of intolerance, nearly shouting that "[t]he sciences, letters, philosophy, all doctrines, all systems, all religions, all beliefs, all opinions, including republican opinion itself, ARE GUILTY OF INTOLERANCE."[68] The *Réformateur* author again distinguishes the repressive intolerance of the Church, evidenced in part by the Inquisition and the *auto-da-fé*, from the open acceptance and rational thought of republican ideals:

> Intolerance is not satisfied to deny, it must persecute; it does not seek to convince, but to impose silence; it does not proffer reason, but punishment and torture. We alone, on the other hand, seek free discussion on each side, we alone profess respect and protection for all beliefs, we alone permit prayer in any language, allow the free development of doctrine; we alone wish to oppose error by reason, fault by forgiveness. Is the Church tolerant as we are? Is it satisfied with denying? The Church threatens and anathematizes, it dooms books to the Index and authors to the hell of excommunication; it opens the gates of hell to the souls of dissidents; it closes the doors of its temples to their mortal remains, it hoards overhead the arsenal of punishments its faith promises it in the other world, and when it can seize the scepter here below, it does not wait for the hereafter to take revenge on the recalcitrants; *the Inquisition becomes its tribunal, the* auto-da-fé *its scaffold* [my emphasis], enforced penitence the only recourse for those seeking to be brought back to grace.

[66] *Ibid.*, 1, no. 4: 1.   [67] *Ibid.*   [68] *Ibid.*, 2, no. 129: 1.

We ask you: if the Church were to ascend the throne again tomorrow, would it use other means of propaganda and repression? Well, republican opinion dares to flatter itself with a totally different kind of tolerance; it seeks liberty for itself *and* for you.[69]

The author's final question in this passage exposes a fear of a return to a Church-dominated government, possibly another restoration of the senior branch of the Bourbons, which was the legitimist hope.

In its responses (19 and 25 March 1835) to the indictments of *Le Réformateur*, *L'Univers religieux* defends the Church as non-persecuting, non-violent, and discouraging of "all ill-treatment of our wayward brothers." The writer repeatedly denies the Church's responsibility for violence that it insists is political or temporal, while acknowledging only its practice of "dogmatic or spiritual intolerance."[70] In the first response, the author emphasizes that the Church should not be blamed for the Inquisition and other violent endeavors commonly associated with it: "[Y]ou write: The Inquisition! The religious Wars! The Crusades! Was this not the work of the Church? But not really, for

---

[69] *Ibid.*: "L'intolérance ne se contente pas de nier, mais elle persécute; elle ne cherche pas à convaincre, mais à imposer silence; elle n'oppose pas des raisons, mais des châtimens et des tortures. Or, nous seuls nous demandons la libre discussion de part et d'autre, nous seuls nous professons respect et protection pour toutes les croyances, nous seuls nous permettons de prier dans toutes les langues; de formuler des doctrines de toutes les façons; nous seuls nous ne voulons opposer que des raisons à l'erreur, que le pardon aux fautes. L'église est elle tolérante à notre façon? se contente-t-elle de nier? Elle menace et elle maudit, elle jette les livres dans le tombeau de l'*index* et l'auteur dans l'enfer de l'excommunication majeure; elle ouvre l'enfer à l'âme des dissidens, elle ferme la porte de ses temples à ses dépouilles mortelles; elle accumule sur sa tête tous les châtimens dont sa foi lui promet un arsenal dans l'autre monde; et quand elle peut saisir le sceptre d'ici bas, elle n'attend pas une autre vie pour se venger des récalcitrans: l'inquisition devient son tribunal, l'*autodafé* son échafaud, la pénitence forcée le seul recours en grâce. [new paragraph] Nous vous le demandons: si demain l'église montait encore sur le trône, aurait-elle d'autres moyens de propagande et de répression? Eh bien! l'opinion républicaine ose se flatter d'une toute autre tolérance; elle veut la liberté pour elle comme pour vous."

[70] "De l'intolérance religieuse: Réponse au *Réformateur*," *L'Univers religieux* 3, no. 428 (25 March 1835): col. 1447–8.

the Inquisition was a political institution, born in certain countries, of certain political circumstances, for an essentially political goal."[71] To reinforce his argument, he attempts to deny that Jewish persecution was condoned by the Church, recalling Pope Gregory's reprimand to a bishop who had treated Jews severely: "It is with gentleness and exhortations that one must call the infidels to Christianity; one must not estrange them from it with threats and terror."[72] In the second part, the author defends the Church's authorization of attacks on the "heresies of the Middle Ages and Islam" with the reasoning that "[i]t was a question of overthrowing them or dying," but reiterates his denial of direct involvement: "The Church has neither soldiers nor executioners; the punishment it inflicts on criminals is purely spiritual; its ministers have never shed blood, all Christians are forbidden to shed blood, to take justice into their own hands. It nevertheless recognizes justice's need to punish crime with temporal sentences, to have jails, and torture."[73]

Analogous to these politically charged debates about Church intolerance, an active dialogue on Martin Luther enriches the political meanings behind the opera's setting. Luther, often linked with the martyred reformers Hus and Jerome, also figures in contemporary associations of Protestants with liberalism and democracy. Liberal thinkers upheld Luther as a revolutionary and humanitarian reformer, as did historian Jules Michelet in *Mémoires de Luther* (1835) and Léon Halévy in his hagiographical, five-part "poème dramatique" *Luther* (1834).[74]

---

[71] *Ibid.*, 3, no. 423 (19 March 1835): col. 1389: "[V]ous vous écriez: l'inquisition! les guerres de religion! les croisades! n'était-ce point l'oeuvre de l'Eglise? – Mais non vraiment, l'inquisition était une institution politique, née en certains pays, de certaines circonstances politiques, pour un but essentiellement politique."

[72] *Ibid.*, col. 1388: "C'est par la douceur et les exhortations qu'il faut appeler les infidèles au christianisme; il ne faut pas les en éloigner par les menaces et la terreur."

[73] *Ibid.*, 3, no. 428 (25 March 1835): col. 1447: "Il en est du soldat comme du bourreau; l'Eglise n'en a pas; les peines qu'elle prononce contre les criminels sont purement spirituelles; jamais ses ministres n'ont versé le sang, elle défend même aux chrétiens de le verser, de se faire justice à eux-mêmes, et pourtant elle reconnaît à la justice, de punir le crime par des peines temporelles, d'avoir des geôles, des supplices."

[74] See also Heinrich Heine, "De l'Allemagne depuis Luther," *Revue des deux mondes* 1 (1 March 1834): 473–505; 4 (15 November 1834): 373–408; 4 (15 December 1834): 633–78.

In his preface, after noting Luther's admiration for Hus, Michelet characterizes Luther as the "restorer of liberty in centuries past" as well as the "liberator of modern thought."[75] Halévy's poem, later submitted (but not performed) as a four-act play, also portrays Luther as a hero of liberation against a despotic Church, a depiction that resonates with Halévy's challenging of the dogmatic "Pharisees" of Catholicism in his second *Résumé*.[76] In language similar to Michelet's, Halévy identifies Luther as "the great Christian philosopher, the intrepid champion of political and religious freedom."[77] *Le Réformateur* speaks warmly of Luther, as well as Calvin, as "simple monks, with no power other than the influence of their eloquence and the noble effect of their new convictions."[78] These portrayals, along with the common recognition of Hus as a reformer whose defiance of the Church inspired Luther, connect with the setting and subject of *La Juive*; they also hint that Meyerbeer's use of the Lutheran chorale in *Les Huguenots* represents not so much a confusion over Protestant sects as an awareness of the strong philosophical and political symbolism attached to the Church reformer.[79]

Conservative, pro-Church writers, on the other hand, viewed Luther as an evil and corrupting force destructive to Catholic beliefs. In *L'Univers religieux*, a writer named Gorse condemns Michelet's portrayal of Luther as a "German god of the sixteenth century" and, in impassioned language, describes him as an ambitious man whose immorality and self-interests drove his attempts to supplant Church authority. He was "above all else, a man of flesh and blood, plagued by all the most miserable passions of our nature: debauchery, ambition,

---

[75] Jules Michelet, *Mémoires de Luther, écrits par lui-même*, 2 vols. (Brussels: Société Belge de Librairie, 1837).

[76] Léon Halévy, *Luther: Poème dramatique en cinq parties* (Paris: Dépot Central de la Librairie, 1834); *Martin Luther; ou, La Diète de Worms: Drame historique en quatre actes, en vers, imité de Zacharias Werner, reçu au Théâtre-Français, non-représenté* (Paris: A. Le Chevalier, 1866).

[77] *Ibid.*, preface, no page number.

[78] "Intolérance religieuse," *Le Réformateur* 2, no. 129 (15 February 1835): 1: "simples moines, sans autre force que l'ascendant de leur éloquence, et la haute influence de leurs nouvelles convictions."

[79] *Giacomo Meyerbeer: A Life in Letters*, ed. Becker and Becker, 62, notes that the chorale "was the equivalent of a Christian 'Marseillaise.'"

arrogance, anger, hatred, vengeance . . . crying at the top of his voice that the pope should be set upon like a *savage beast* . . . putting his authority over the authority of all the Church fathers and of tradition."[80]

This anti-Luther depiction corresponds with attacks upon anticlerical factions of the past and present, including Protestants, contemporary liberal thinkers, and the *philosophes*. *L'Univers religieux* railed against the fanaticism of Protestants, speaking of the actions of Anglican churchmen against non-Anglicans in Ireland and the King of Prussia's militaristic threats against Silesian pietists, and grouped anti-Catholic Protestants with *philosophes*: "Philosophers and Protestants have spoken a great deal about Catholic intolerance, but this has not prevented them from having themselves always been intolerant, from having themselves always persecuted."[81] Associations were also made between Protestants and sociopolitical disruptiveness and anarchy. An article entitled "Eglises protestantes de Paris" in the same paper, in speaking of Lutherans, Calvinists, and Methodists claims that: "Protestantism can sustain itself only by an *excessive and disorderly separatism, that is, by intellectual and moral anarchy, or by governmental action, that is, by tyranny."[82]

As *L'Univers religieux* claimed, the focus of French liberals on the barbarism of the Catholic Church and the characterization of Protestants as noble, beleaguered upholders of individual freedom do indeed echo

---

[80] Gorse, "Enseignement public, pensée philosophique: Cours de droit naturel par M. Jouffroy; Cours d'histoire du seizième siècle par M. Michelet," *L'Univers religieux* 3, no. 359 (3 January 1835): col. 616: "avant tout, homme de chair et de sang, tiraillé par toutes les passions les plus misérables de notre nature, la débauche, l'ambition, l'orgueil, la colère, la haine, la vengeance . . . criant de toute la force de ses poumons qu'il fallait courir sur le pape comme sur une *bête féroce* . . . plaçant son autorité au-dessus de l'autorité de tous les pères de l'Eglise et de la tradition."

[81] "Les Protestans persécutant les Protestans," *L'Univers religieux* 3, no. 379 (27 January 1835): col. 861: "Les philosophes et les protestans ont beaucoup parlé de l'intolérance catholique, ce qui ne les a pas empêchés dans tous les temps d'être eux-mêmes intolérans et persécuteurs."

[82] *L'Univers religieux* 3, no. 428 (25 March 1835): col. 1449: "[L]e protestantisme ne peut se soutenir que par un *séparatisme excessif et désordonné*, c'est-à-dire, par l'anarchie intellectuelle et morale, ou par *l'action gouvernementale*, c'est-à-dire, par la tyrannie."

Voltaire's views, including his deploring of Protestant persecution on St. Bartholomew's Eve and his portrayal of Protestants as victims of Catholic despotism in the *Essai sur les guerres civiles*. Voltaire attributes the growth of Protestant sects in part to "the superstition, the secret treacheries of priests, the immense power of Rome" and "the most violent persecutions" suffered at the hands of the Catholics.[83] The Protestant sects grew, he writes, "in the midst of scaffolds and tortures."[84] In his description of Luther and his followers, however, Voltaire did not refrain from pointing out fanaticism in their conduct (see, for example, "Suite du luthéranisme et de l'anabaptisme," in the *Essai sur les moeurs*). By comparison, the portraits of Luther by July Monarchy liberals more strongly emphasized the leader's enlightened spirit.

These blatant themes and symbols of differing religious and political ideologies – of Church oppression and hypocrisy, absolutism versus individual rights, the liberating reforms of Protestants, the persecutions of non-Catholic "heretics" by Catholic authorities, the separatism and fanaticism of non-Catholics – echo arguments of religious and political freedom that rang within governmental chambers in 1830–31 and that pervaded the intellectual world surrounding *La Juive*. Fusing with ideas present in the minds of Scribe and his collaborators, they came to life on the Opéra stage in 1835.

ADMINISTRATIVE AND JOURNALISTIC RESPONSES TO THE RELIGIOUS CONTENT OF *LA JUIVE*

The opera's religious content initially raised the eyebrows of administrative officials who attempted to oversee the developing work, but they would eventually view it as non-inflammatory. Journalists, on the other hand, clearly responded to *La Juive*'s politically infused Voltairean meanings after its première – some with frustration and ire. Despite the diminished power of the Church in the early July Monarchy, the sensitivity of presenting Catholic imagery on stage is clearly felt in

[83] *Oeuvres complètes*, vol. III, 147–8.   [84] *Ibid.*, 148.

administrative correspondence that refers to Scribe's early working title *L'Auto-da-fé*. In a letter of 21 May 1834, the duc de Choiseul, president of the Commission de Surveillance, the government-appointed, non-censorship body of Opéra administrators, complains to his superior, the comte de Montalivet, Ministre de l'Intérieur, of failed efforts to get information about the opera-in-progress.[85] Two days later, Choiseul writes again to the Ministre that he has finally learned the subject of *L'Auto-da-fé*: "it seems that this *inquisition* subject will bring to the stage a *cardinal*, the Grand Inquisitor and his retinue, etc."[86] Choiseul promises to report more details after Véron's explanation of the subject before a special session that the Commission president had called. The references to the Inquisition and the use of religious figures obviously made the Commission jittery; in fact, Choiseul's emphasis on *La Juive* as a possible title in this letter instead of *L'Auto-da-fé* may suggest that the final title choice was made to squelch the early fears of the Commission.[87] Later correspondence shows a continuing concern over the subject that persisted into the rehearsal period.

During February 1835, a number of letters were exchanged between Choiseul, the Ministre, and Véron before the première. A draft letter dated 3 February from the Ministre to Choiseul refers to the religious elements "in the developments of the subject and in the *mise en scène*" and demands that the libretto manuscript that reflected changes made in rehearsal be sent to him immediately.[88] Véron responded the following day, promising to obtain from Scribe within twenty-four hours "an accurate and true manuscript" that would reflect the many changes made in the previous six rehearsals.[89] Although the première was

---

[85] This letter was written two weeks before *matériel* for the *mise en scène* had begun to be ordered and two months before Halévy had signed a contract with Schlesinger for publication rights.

[86] F-Pan, F²¹960, Dossier v: "il paroit que ce sujet *d'inquisition* amènera sur la scène, *Cardinal*, Gd. [Grand] Inquisiteur et sa suite etc."

[87] The draft-scenario title, *Rachel; ou, L'Auto-da-fé*, corresponds with *Léonora; ou, St. Barthélemy*, the original title of *Les Huguenots*. Perhaps each of these subtitles was deemed too provocative.

[88] F-Pan, AJ¹³202.

[89] *Ibid.*, letter from Véron to the Ministre dated 4 February 1835.

delayed several times, as reported in the press, it appears that the expected date at this point may have been 16 February – thus, a little more than ten days after Véron promised to send the manuscript.[90] The review of the manuscript was not sufficient, however, to reassure the Ministre that the presentation of religious subject matter would not be "dangerous"; believing that a true assessment could not be made without seeing the *mise en scène*, he advised Choiseul that authorization of the work's performance should not be granted until the Commission had attended the last rehearsals.[91] Members should observe the first, third, and fifth acts in particular – that is, those acts that relate to the Catholic Church, including the singing of the *Te Deum*, the vitriolic attacks of Ruggiero and the Christian crowd, the cardinal's malediction, and the *auto-da-fé*. Choiseul then suggested that the Ministre himself attend the last full orchestral rehearsals "because there could be some opinions in the Commission dictated by insouciance or by some ideas on progress which perhaps might not conform with the sentiments and the good taste of Your Excellency."[92]

Choiseul's suggestion reveals that the mix of conservative and liberal ideologies among members of the Commission and the Ministre resulted in varied responses to the subject matter and demonstrates his attempts to guard against more lenient or progressive views.[93] Yet the conservative members apparently found nothing offensive when the Commission attended the dress rehearsal of the first and third acts on 12 February, as revealed in a formal report written the following day to the Ministre proposing authorization. Although the report notes

[90] *Ibid.* A letter from Choiseul to the Ministre dated 12 February 1835 relays Véron's request for authorization of a *relâche* on 16 February, postponing the first performance to 18 February.

[91] *Ibid.*, draft letter from the Ministre to Choiseul dated 12 February 1835.

[92] *Ibid.*, letter from Choiseul to the Ministre dated 12 February 1835: "car dans la Commission il y pourrait avoir des avis dictés par l'insouciance ou par des idées de progrès qui peut-être ne servient pas conformer aux sentimens et au bon goût de Votre Excellence."

[93] Fulcher, *The Nation's Image*, 58–9; Hallman, *"La Juive,"* vol. I, 39–40.

that the fifth act had yet to be seen, it approves of the respectful manner in which the Catholic ceremonies and church figures are depicted:

> In fact, one sees in them the most prominent members of the clergy, and notably cardinals, but in costumes that are no longer those of today; there are also crosses, banners; but in the drama all these emblems, as well as the clergy, are always the object of the people's veneration, and everything that happens is taken so seriously that it would be impossible for the most badly intentioned to turn anything into derision.[94]

It suggests that the Commission was not alarmed about the basic subject matter itself, the historical treatment of the Council and its tribunal, or about the portrayed animosity between Jews and Christians. Rather, its primary concern was that the Catholic ceremonies (nothing was mentioned about the Jewish service in the second act), religious figures, and emblems be presented with dignity and solemnity; secondarily, it was pleased that the costumes were historic, and not contemporary. Unlike *Robert le diable*, with its scene of the dancing nuns that the Commission found problematic, *La Juive* presented all its religious elements in a manner that suited the Commission, and, as it noted, the general morality. Following the 23 February première, the Commission again articulated its satisfaction with the religious treatment, adding the point that the luxurious *mise en scène* had not detracted from the religious ceremonies, but had enhanced them.[95] The unprecedented magnificence of costume and decor that elicited effusive commentary in the press pleased the Commission, meeting and reaching beyond its criteria for grandness.

Behind the Commission's initial concerns about the work's religious aspects, Fulcher contends, was a renewed "politically conciliatory attitude toward the church" that was emerging in the regime of Louis-Philippe as it became more authoritarian and less revolutionary in character.[96] The joining of religious ceremony with royal pomp is indicative of this ideological shift, Fulcher believes: because

---

[94] F-Pan, AJ[13]202. (See the transcription of the entire document and its translation in Appendix F.)
[95] F-Pan, AJ[13]202, *rapport* of 10 March 1835.   [96] Fulcher, *The Nation's Image*, 82.

the dignity of Christian ceremony was maintained, the work was not overtly anticlerical, nor overtly anti-authoritarian. In comparison with the presentation of priests, bishops, and popes as villains, murderers, and Lotharios in satirical works that appeared in other Parisian theatres as reactions against the previous regime shortly after the liberty of the theatre was declared by the Charte of 1830,[97] the anticlerical, anti-authoritarian elements of *La Juive* were indeed tepid and veiled.

Prior to this time, the presentation of religious ceremony and religious officials was highly scrutinized and usually censored. After the reinstitution of preventive censorship of the theatre in September 1835, censors again carefully examined references to and portrayals of the clergy or authoritarian Catholicism and often rejected provocative works or passages. Yet many works with religious subjects were allowed, including *Les Huguenots*, although passages were excised (particularly those surrounding the role of Catherine de Médicis in the massacre).[98] Censors suppressed *Impéria,* a work destined for the Vaudeville in 1841 that was reminiscent of anticlerical satires of the early July Monarchy;[99] however, they approved Donizetti's *Dom Sébastien, roi du Portugal* in 1843, despite the fact that the Grand Inquisitor was characterized as an embodiment of evil.[100] According to Odile Krakovitch, acceptance came because the Inquisition was a historical anachronism and therefore not politically harmful – perhaps a reasoning shared by the Commission overseeing *La Juive*.[101] In light of its symbolic importance in liberal rhetoric, however, it seems surprising that conservative voices of either body would have endorsed it. Shortly afterward, from 1843 to 1848, the presentation of religious figures was examined with a renewed severity.[102] (The aversion of Italian theatres to depictions of religious figures and symbols would keep *La Juive* out of the Italian repertoire for a number of years.)

---

[97] Odile Krakovitch, *Hugo censuré: La Liberté au théâtre au XIXe siècle* (Paris: Calmann-Levy, 1985), 157.
[98] Rehearsals for *Les Huguenots* had already begun by May 1835, several months before the September law.
[99] Krakovitch, *Hugo censuré*, 160.
[100] *Ibid*. Verdi's Inquisitor in *Don Carlos* (1867) is similarly malevolent.
[101] *Ibid*.   [102] *Ibid.*, 162–6.

The increasing conservativeness of the pre-censorship Commission of 1834–5, as reflected in its initial wariness about the religious-political aspects of *La Juive*, undoubtedly affected the libretto's development. Although the Commission was not a censorship body *per se*, Scribe and other creators certainly felt indirectly, or perhaps directly, the hesitation of at least some of its members and thus subdued or obscured potentially offensive aspects of plot and characterization. As several scholars have suggested, Scribe's long success as a playwright and librettist was partially dependent on his skills of self-censorship, of knowing the acceptable parameters within each political climate.[103] In this way, as in the controls suggested in the 1834–5 correspondence between the Commission and the Ministre, censorship, although "unofficial," certainly seemed to be at work. The potential threat of repressive censorship would also have been fresh in Scribe's mind as he worked on the libretto. The grandness and solemnity of Christian ceremony, as well as the sympathetic characterization of Cardinal Brogni, which to some degree acted as foils to the work's ideological agenda, may have been conscious attempts to make the opera palatable to the Commission, the Ministre, and conservative Catholics. From a philosophical vantage point, they might also be seen as appropriate to the liberalism of the *juste milieu* – to project basic liberal values while not offending tradition.

Despite the substitution of characters and equivocal treatment of the Council and the cardinal, the Parisian press did in fact respond to the historical significance and symbolism of the Council as represented in *La Juive*. The liberal *Constitutionnel* began its review of 25 February 1835 with an elaborate description of the Council full of acerbic allusions to its unjust actions, excessive wealth, and immorality:

> The Council of Constance is famous among the councils for the number
> of ecclesiastical and secular princes who converged there, for the
> importance of the questions that the religious passions provoked, and for
> the dreadful burnings at the stake that intolerance brought about. A vast,
> magnificent, and lugubrious arena that opened in solemn pomp and in

---

[103] See, for example, Fulcher, *The Nation's Image*, 24.

displays of extraordinary wealth, it persisted in subtle quibbles and in brilliant exercises of theological science and ended cruelly with two appalling executions ... The riches and the extravagances of the prelates reveal their greedy and corrupt morals, leprosy of the Church, against which Wycliffe and Jan Hus, these two precursors of Luther, were already advocating severe reforms ... Finally, to attest to the fanaticism of this curious and deplorable epoch, the cruel blindness and the cruel faith of persecutors and victims, consider Jan Hus and Jerome of Prague, attacked and condemned like two criminals, defending their doctrines and intrepidly walking to the stake like two martyrs.

... Constance, the imperial city, was thus, at one and the same time, a vast church, a tribunal, a Sorbonne, a camp, a bazaar, an immense hall of celebration and feasts, and a circus for martyrs.[104]

In pointing out the Church's hypocrisy evident at the Council, the reviewer is struck by the "strangest contrasts": "the pride and luxury of the Church next to the simplicity of its primitive institution, haughty and barbarous intolerance opposite the dogmas of charity and fraternity."[105] He refers to a host of courtesans among the gathering and notes ironically that their appearance gives "a good idea of the chastity of the Council."[106]

The Voltairean foundation of the *Constitutionnel* review is evident, suggesting further that the weighted symbolism of the Council influenced the reception of *La Juive*. One element linking Voltaire's account and the *Constitutionnel* review but seemingly missing from the opera is the allusion to the sexual immorality of Church figures. In the *Constitutionnel* description of the numerous participants that resembles Voltaire's narrative, the "almost 800 courtesans" servicing the Council nearly matches Voltaire's figure of 718 courtesans, which accompanies his sarcastic commentary about the many cabins built to house the "slaves of luxury and incontinence" who serviced the "Council fathers" as well as the lords.[107] Dumas also associates courtesans with the Church in his article of April 1835 for *La Gazette musicale de Paris*, a

---

[104] *Dossier de presse parisienne*, ed. Leich-Galland, 9–10. A fuller excerpt of the review may be found in Appendix H-1.

[105] *Ibid.*   [106] *Ibid.*

[107] Voltaire, *Essai sur les moeurs*, *Oeuvres complètes*, vol. IV, 415.

large portion of which is written as a travelogue of a visit to Constance (with more than a few similarities to Scribe's journal descriptions). In addition to his report of seeing wax figures of Hus and Jerome of Prague, he gives an even greater number of courtesans – 2,788 – who accommodated soldiers, priests, and cardinals. A review in the influential *Journal des débats* (25 February 1835), a paper catering to the liberal aristocracy and upper middle class of the July Monarchy, suggests that the stage action was in fact interpreted, at least by liberal newspapers, as an illustration of the sexual immorality of religious leaders. It refers to the "flock of young women" who dance before the Council, after commenting on "the number of courtesans" who were present.[108]

With a different political bias, a review of the première in the ultraroyalist, clerical paper *La Gazette de France* more explicitly reveals that the work was perceived as Voltairean-inspired. Besides labeling *La Juive* as a "truly little masterpiece of the Voltairean genre,"[109] the writer focuses on historical distortions in the opera's setting. He sees much of the treatment of the Council as "a great insult to religion" and a parody of the history of the Catholic Church. Taking issue with the opera's presentation of Jews, he sees the juxtaposition of Eléazar's residence with a church and his disruption of Christian worship historical impossibilities – such close contact between Jews and Christians did not occur in this early era, he adds, just as in the present day in many countries. In this vein, the reviewer continues to condemn the portrayed interactions, sarcastically pointing out the improbability of Léopold, conqueror of the Hussites, coming "to judaicize" (*judaïser*) or celebrate Passover in Constance.

Instead of condemning the Christians for attacking Eléazar for working on a Christian feast day, the reviewer admonishes him for not observing the Sabbath and states that the religion asks only "that one not disturb its ceremonies deliberately."[110] Reflecting similar views found in *L'Univers religieux*, the writer angrily rejects the opera's attack on Christian intolerance:

---

[108] *Dossier de presse parisienne,* ed. Leich-Galland, 106.   [109] *Ibid.,* 50.
[110] *Ibid.,* 51.

They speak of the barbarism, ignorance and fanaticism of another age and they treat you in the premier national theatre as the most stupid, credulous, and besotted people; they try to turn you into a fanatic against a religion whose first principle is tolerance.[111]

The reviewer scoffs at the Council's action of condemning the Jews to death: "Can you imagine the fathers of the Council of Constance having a good time making a great ceremony of boiling some Jews in a cauldron!"[112] With bitter sarcasm, he mocks the cauldron sitting on stage in the fifth act like "a big pot of stew" amidst joyful singing of the crowd; the only thing missing was an accompanying ballet, since the fifteenth-century Christians, "barbarous and savage like cannibals . . . danced and sang around stakes and cauldrons."[113] The reviewer refrains from making a direct parallel with the burning of Hus and Jerome, noted by the *Constitutionnel* writer, but he explicitly denies the responsibility of the Council (and of other Church Councils) in corporal punishment. In yet another argument analogous to that of *L'Univers religieux*, this author claims that the political state was alone responsible for the death of Hus.[114] The Council, in fact, made "unprecedented efforts to save Jan Hus, who was not only a heretic, but also a troublemaker, a ringleader."[115] The opera's treatment of the Council is particularly socially destructive, and he warns that "one does not lie with impunity in relation to the institution that is the most necessary to the social order."[116] While he denies taking Scribe's "historical frauds, anachronisms, and Voltairean philosophy too seriously," he insists that the librettist "has made a travesty of religious matters under the tinsels of the Opéra" with all his imaginings of "atrocious" and "distasteful" actions, rather than the "virtue" and "sublime charity" of Christianity. He concludes: "What is odious in all these Voltairean elaborations is the bad faith with which one attributes to religion that which belongs to the political powers, parties, and passions of the times."[117] (See Appendix H-2 for a fuller excerpt.)

---

[111] *Ibid.* [112] *Ibid.*, 50. [113] *Ibid.* [114] *Ibid.*, 58. [115] *Ibid.*
[116] *Ibid.* [117] *Ibid.*, 58–9.

In light of the philosopher's controversial image, the condemnation of the opera's Voltairean foundation by the *Gazette* reviewer is not surprising. He underscores this foundation by scoffing at Scribe's aping of Etienne de Jouy (1764–1846), a prominent Voltairean writer of the Restoration, demanding: "Has [Scribe] dressed himself up in M. Jouy's wig?"[118] The critic's association of Scribe with Jouy drives home his point, for the liberal image of this writer – before his work on the libretto for Rossini's *Guillaume Tell* (1829) – had been solidified through his struggles with Restoration censors over his Bonapartist historical dramas, *Belisaire* (1818) and *Sylla* (1822), as well as his imprisonment for articles condemning the trial and execution of Bonapartist officers following the Hundred Days.[119] With the *Gazette* writer's reference to donning a wig, however, he may have also implied that Scribe's Voltairean views were relics of an outdated, eighteenth-century past – or remnants of the vehement Restoration anticlericalism of the immediate past.[120]

This reviewer strongly reveals himself as an apologist for the Council, one whom Voltaire himself would certainly have chided. His reactions, reflecting the pro-Church bias of *La Gazette*, juxtaposed with the liberal views of Dumas and the *Constitutionnel* reviewer, exemplify the absolutist–liberal opposition that permeated French writing throughout the Restoration and July Monarchy. These accounts, while clearly serving as vehicles for political-philosophical views, point to the ambiguity of meaning that existed in the opera's subject, presentation, and reception. The extravagant staging of the processions and ceremony,

---

[118] *Ibid.*, 50.
[119] Alan Spitzer, *1820*, 120, notes that the Napoleon references in *Belisaire* and *Sylla* could not be missed since the actor Talma was dressed to look exactly like the fallen leader. The month-long imprisonment gave Jouy and his journalistic collaborator Antoine Jay (1770–1854) reputations as "martyrs of liberalism" and led to their writing of *Les Hermites en prison*, which capitalized on this "martyrdom."
[120] Gerhard, *The Urbanization of Opera*, 43, for example, notes that Jouy's tragedies "marked scarcely any advance on the dramas of Voltaire on which they were modeled." As M. Elizabeth C. Bartlet commented at the 1993 American Musicological Society meeting, Jouy was considered by many to be an obsolete voice by the 1830s.

for example, was accepted as an illustration of the lofty grandeur of the Church or, in another light, of its excesses and hypocrisy, as seen in the *Constitutionnel* review echoing Voltaire's account of the Council. For liberal thinkers who supported the law of the *culte israélite*, it undoubtedly referred to an unenlightened period and unenlightened views that Mérilhou warned were out of place in the nineteenth century, while the Jewish martyrs personified the liberal credo of religious freedom and equality. Whether supportive, indifferent, or condemning, the reception of *La Juive* illumines the Voltairean commentary on inhumane, intolerant institutions and groups signified by the Council of Constance and the political-religious messages it evoked.

Against the background of the Council setting and its weighted associations, the opposition of Jews and Christians intensifies the liberal
critique as it propels the drama. Symbolizing the struggle between
the individual and the dual forces of Church and State while resonat-
ing with religious-social conflicts of the nineteenth-century past and
present, this opposition permeates the text, music, characterization,
and staging of La Juive. Powerful large-scale choral scenes, vivid contrasts of emotion, striking *coups de théâtre*, and integrations of collective and intimate experience – elements essential to the *grand opéra*
aesthetic – heighten the portrayal of religious conflict in the outer,
public drama that predominates in Acts I, III, and V and in the inner
drama of the principal characters centered in Acts II and IV. The opera's
presentation of religious antagonism and identity will serve as the focus of the following selective analysis, which touches on elements that
are prominent in this portrayal and that would have been conspicuous
to contemporary audiences.[1]

Underscoring the import of this opposition and its ideological links
is evidence from the compositional history of La Juive: in addition to
minor textual changes, substantive alterations made throughout the
long rehearsal period (beginning in or, more likely, before July 1834)
and after the first three performances heighten the conflict or indirectly
sharpen the focus on it.[2] These modifications underline the authors'

[1] Also see Karl Leich-Galland's more traditional analysis of the opera, *"La Juive*:
Commentaire musical et littéraire"; Cormac Newark's "Ceremony, Celebration
and Spectacle"; and my chapter on Halévy's *grands opéras* in the forthcoming
Cambridge Companion to Grand Opera, ed. Charlton.

[2] The copying of the performing parts had begun by January 1834, according to
the *registre de copie* kept by Aimé-Simon Leborne, the head of the Opéra's *atelier*
of copyists (F-Po, RE 235); on 6 July 1834, *La Gazette musicale de Paris* announced
the rehearsing of the opera's first act. Rehearsals probably began earlier than July,

desire to place Christian oppression and antisemitism at the forefront of the drama, but also to highlight Eléazar's anti-Christian hatred and alienation from Christian society. Although the bigotry and exclusivity displayed by each side are mitigated by expressions of magnanimity, Catholic religious intolerance and institutional "fanaticism," in the Voltairean vocabulary of the day, are given far more emphasis than the actions of Eléazar, who responds as a representative of a minority group that has endured centuries of marginalization, and as an individual who has already suffered at the hands of Christians in the opera's prehistory. Yet while the drama highlights the victimization of both Eléazar and Rachel, there are implications that Eléazar's hate-inflected religiosity borders on the Voltairean idea of fanaticism.

Viewed within the liberal context, the Jew as an individual ostracized by the dominant group and denounced by the institution elicits compassion as he evokes the principle of individual freedom. As representative of a non-Catholic religion, he serves as a symbol of the July Monarchy's endorsement of religious freedom and its expansion of protection through the law of the *culte israélite* (see pp. 8–10). But the Jew's individuality borders on the separatism that both conservatives and liberals were wary of – as one governmental voice recalled, had not Jews themselves exacerbated their own past alienation? And as a conservative voice had protested, should the Jews of France be rewarded for being good citizens when they had made so little effort toward creating a true alliance with their Christian *concitoyens*? Taking the character of Eléazar further away from the role of oppressed minority are elements of Jewish stereotype (explored further in Chapter 5) that add to the inconsistencies of his character and deprive him of being fully sympathetic – although some passages blatantly suggesting Jewish greed and antisemitic contempt were deleted in early stages.

What might be interpreted as a theatrical parallel to the government's expanded support of Judaism, but also a poignant endorsement

particularly individual sessions with principal singers and composer. Leborne's "Fourniture de copie" (F-Pan, AJ¹³293), dated 8 April 1835, records the "successive cuts, restorations, and changes made after each of the 15 *répétitions générales*" and "after each of the first 3 performances" (23, 25, and 27 February). See Appendix D.

and others involved in judgments of plot and character. Nonetheless, most alterations, beginning with the reshaping of Act I, ultimately intensified the Jewish–Christian opposition – with its representations of and allusions to intolerance and hypocrisy, absolutism versus liberalism, and Jewish separatism and martyrdom – and situated it more strongly at the core of the opera.

THE MUSICO-DRAMATIC TREATMENT AND REWORKING OF ACT I

Religious conflict permeates Act I. The intense confrontations between Eléazar and Rachel and Catholic worshipers, clergy, and celebrants form the act's central dramatic thrust and anticipate the fate of the Jews that will unfold in the following four acts. After a brief orchestral introduction that segues to a twenty-seven-measure passage for solo organ,[4] the drama opens with a clash of Christian orthodoxy and hypocrisy, and accusations of Jewish "heresy": an offstage chorus representing worshipers in the cathedral of Constance sings the first verse of the Catholic *Te Deum*, followed by whispered disapproval of Eléazar by onstage celebrants gathered for the Council's opening. Enhanced by the stage set depicting a Gothic cathedral abutting the turreted house/shop of Eléazar (see Illustration 3), an oppositional tone is immediately set in the juxtaposition of the worshipers' placid praises and the celebrants' biting condemnation of the Jew, whom they resent for working on a Catholic feast day. The sharply etched intolerance of the Catholic crowd of this scene cannot be missed:[5]

[4] Mm. 38–76 preceding the organ entrance do not appear in the autograph, leading Karl Leich-Galland to conclude that they were not written by Halévy (private communication). But they were certainly approved by the composer, and may have been written at a late date without being reincorporated into the autograph. As confirmed by Leborne's copying records (F-Pan, AJ¹³293), the long overture was not performed until October 1835, eight months after the première; see my argument in *"La Juive,"* vol. 1, 86–7.

[5] Textual variants can be found in the pre-première printed libretto dated 18 February 1835 (F-Pan, AJ¹³202) and the printed libretto of 23 February 1835 (F-Po, Livr. 19[274]).

Act I, Scene i, No. 1

Schlesinger-Garland[6]

PLUSIEURS GENS DU PEUPLE	SEVERAL PEOPLE IN THE CROWD
En ce jour de fête publique	On this day of public celebration
Quel est donc ce logis où l'on travaille encor?	Whose house is this where people are still working?

D'AUTRES	OTHERS
C'est le logis d'un hérétique,	This is the house of a heretic,
Du Juif Eléazar	Of the Jew Eléazar
Qu'on dit tout cousu d'or!	Who is said to be rolling in riches!

Halévy heightens the emotions of public conflict and Catholic contradictions by setting an agitated triplet pattern in the strings immediately following the hymn-like chords of the church worshipers
(see Example 1). The repeated eighth-note rhythms and pitches of the
solo and ensemble voices who mutter about the Jew, some whispering
sotto voce, make their statements and questions pointed and excited.
At Rachel's warning to her father to seek refuge, the triplet figure
returns in the violas and lower strings, insistently stated three times.
The figure's rising line, ending a minor third higher (D, F, A♭) on each
varied restatement, builds in *crescendo* to a climax that elides with the
beginning of the second phrase of the *Te Deum* (*Schlesinger-Garland*,
No. 1, mm. 138–41; *Schlesinger-Lemoine*, No. 1, mm. 62–5).[7]

The tension eases during the Albert–Léopold recitative, the continuation of the *Te Deum*, and the chorus "Hosanna, plaisir ivresse,"
which marks the onset of public celebration. But the concord is short-
lived. Shortly after the inaugural announcements by the town *prévot*
Ruggiero, those of the *crieur*, and the choral response "Ah! pour notre
ville," the sound of anvils coming from Eléazar's shop (played offstage
and reinforced by two of the new *cors à piston*, or valve horns) brings

---

[6] For the sources of libretto excerpts and music examples in this chapter, see
chapter 3, note 33.

[7] The first verse of the *Te Deum* is *a cappella*, but the second is accompanied by the
organ, as is the return to the *Te Deum* at the end of Act I. Hugh Macdonald
describes this opening as a "thrilling effect which Wagner borrowed almost
unchanged in *Die Meistersinger*" ("Grandest of the Grand," 22).

Example 1 Act I, *Introduction*, *Schlesinger-Lemoine*, No. 1, mm. 36–48; *Schlesinger-Garland*, No. 1, mm. 112–24

on a direct attack on the rich jeweller by Ruggiero and the Catholic crowd.[8] Halévy emphasizes the anvils' obtrusiveness with G octave leaps sounding immediately after the A♭ cadence of the chorus, although he "prepares" the interruption with an augmented-sixth chord on F♯–A♭–C, the same harmony that supports Ruggiero's F♯ against the G octaves at his syllables "ce bruit é[trange]" ("this strange noise")

---

[8] See the editorial note, beginning at m. 358 of *Schlesinger-Garland*, printed to accommodate orchestras without *cors à piston*. The note corresponds with the discussion in Halévy's letter of 1836 to the conductor Charles Valter in Rouen (F-Pn, Ms., n.a.fr. 14346, fols. 352–3), in which the composer talks of adjusting parts for orchestras without the *cors à piston* (see Appendix I-1).

Example 2 Act I, *Schlesinger-Garland*, No. 1, mm. 366–7

(see Example 2).[9] The anvils/horns jar slightly when they shift to B♭ octaves, delineating the dissonance between the B♮ and B♭ of G major and E♭ major harmonies as Ruggiero begins his last accusatory phrase. Their harsh timbre and insistent repetition, atop Ruggiero's shouts as the orchestral texture and dynamic level change, add to their

[9] In the former, the harmonic clash is not starkly abrupt, however, since the octaves are prepared by the augmented-sixth chord and supported by G major and G⁷ chords (V⁷ of C minor) in the first two measures in which they sound, as well as by most harmonies in the following nine measures. At Ruggiero's words, the Gs sound immediately after the same augmented-sixth chord, which resolves quickly to G major.

intrusion.[10] Ruggiero forcefully condemns the disruptive behavior and calls for Eléazar: here Halévy makes the choral response more intense than in earlier whispered reproaches. The text phrases "C'est chez cet hérétique" and "C'est là dans la boutique" are sung in unison, as though voicing the like-minded conviction of the crowd, and are set to ascending lines that culminate on an emphatic, long-held eb^2 of the sopranos and altos against text repetition on eb^1 by tenors and basses. The rising lines and repeated eighth notes express the crowd's agitation, which Halévy makes even more incisive by bringing back variants of the previous triplet pattern in the unison strings. As the declaiming chorus acts as a collective character that emphatically points the finger at the "juif Eléazar, ce riche joaillier," leading to Ruggiero's order, the composer reiterates strongly accented arpeggiations in various harmonies in the lower strings against syncopated chords in the upper strings and winds. Rapid textural and dynamic changes, from the arpeggiated bass motive to triplet patterns and measured tremolos in the upper strings against a stepwise descent in the lower strings, nervously propel Ruggiero's phrase toward a climax on a fully diminished chord (F♯–A–C–Eb) on his last syllable. Immediately, Eléazar is dragged in by several male celebrants, with Rachel following.[11] With the resolution to G major (leading to C minor), tension is released only to build again in a triplet string motive of repeated notes beginning on g, moving first to ab and then rising through successive pitches to ab^1. Halévy continues the ascent up two octaves in the treble voices

[10] Halévy's use of the anvil was not unprecedented in French opera; as David Charlton notes in "Orchestration and Orchestral Practice in Paris, 1789–1810," 2 vols. (Ph.D. diss., Cambridge University, 1974), vol. 1, 259–60, Kreutzer's *Abel* of 1810 associated the anvil with demons and destruction in Act II and, in its use as a thematic reminiscence in Act III, with Cain's evil (the revised *La Mort d'Abel* of 1823 omitted the second act). Auber also incorporated it in *Le Maçon* of 1825. Wagner's later use of anvils to represent the Nibelungen workers as well as a force of greed and malevolence in *Der Ring des Nibelungen* may have a subtextual link to its association with Eléazar in *La Juive*, as Wagner's Nibelungen, as forgers of gold, are often interpreted as representing Jewish capitalists.

[11] In Palianti's *mise en scène* production manual, the guards, at Ruggiero's command, drag Rachel and Eléazar "brutally" from their house; see Cohen, *Staging Manuals*, 138.

(g^1–g^3) against a chromatically inflected descending bass to a climactic cadence on the dominant. At this moment Rachel bursts out in shock and fear, "Ah! mon père," and Ruggiero accuses Eléazar:

Act I, Scene iii, No. 1

Schlesinger-Garland

RUGGIERO, à Eléazar	RUGGIERO, to Eléazar
Juif!... ton audace impie	Jew!... your impious audacity
Mérite le trépas!	Deserves death!
Travailler dans un jour de fête!	To work on a festal day!
ELEAZAR	ELEAZAR
Et pourquoi pas?	And why not?
Ne suis-je point fils d'Israel	Am I not a son of Israel
Et le Dieu des chrétiens	And does the God of the Christians
m'ordonne-t'il à moi?	give me orders?
RUGGIERO	RUGGIERO
Tais-toi!	Quiet!
(au peuple)	(to the crowd)
Vous l'entendez, au ciel même il	You hear him, he is insulting heaven
insulte,	itself,
Il maudit notre sainte loi.	He curses our sacred law.
ELEAZAR	ELEAZAR
Et pourquoi l'aimerais-je?	And why would I love it?
Par vous sur le bûcher, et me	On your orders, I saw my sons
tendant les bras,	perish at the stake
J'ai vu périr mes fils!	While reaching out to me!
RUGGIERO	RUGGIERO
Eh bien, tu les suivras!	Well, you will follow them!
La mort au sacrilège	Death to the sacrilegious
Et ton juste supplice aux yeux de	And your just execution before the
l'Empereur	eyes of the Emperor
De ce jour solennel doublera la	Will double the splendor of this
splendeur!	solemn day!

In these exchanges (*Schlesinger-Garland*, No. 1, mm. 409–53, *Schlesinger-Lemoine*, No. 1, mm. 370–414), Halévy's music helps to set the expression and status of each: he reinforces Ruggiero's authority with echoes in the strings of his ascending and descending lines and intensifies the provost's threat of death ("La mort au sacrilège") with octaves in his vocal part against a unison chromatic line in the strings. (Later, he will reinforce with brass.) Halévy makes Eléazar's initial response to Ruggiero ("Et pourquoi pas?"), imitated in the strings, sound light and a bit flippant (in spite of the expression mark "Tranquillement" in the orchestral score); but beginning with the text "Et pourquoi l'aimerais-je?" he reveals Eléazar's increasing anger with vocal leaps to agogically accented, ascending pitches as the Jew recalls seeing his sons die at the stake. Eléazar's audacity incites Ruggiero to call for his death; this time the crowd responds only with the celebratory "Ah! pour notre ville," and Brogni's entrance further diffuses Ruggiero's intent. In recitative, the cardinal discovers that he knew Eléazar in Rome before his days of Church service, a realization that prompts his reconciliation aria, "Si la rigueur." Following the aria, the action pivots away from confrontation and fully toward celebration.

With the exception of Léopold's Italianate *sérénade* (No. 3), which introduces the romance between Rachel and the Christian prince disguised as the Jewish painter Samuel, the final three numbers of Act I are diversionary, building up to the spectacular Council procession.[12] These numbers include the light-hearted chorus "Hâtons-nous, car l'heure s'avance," the *choeur des buveurs*, "Ah! quel heureux destin," and the first *divertissement*, a waltz.[13] Shortly after the finale begins with expectant shouts of the Council's arrival, however, the most intense and prolonged confrontation of Act I is triggered by Ruggiero and halted by a second authority figure, Léopold, with the help of his aide, Albert (Leich-Galland attributes the crowd's hateful vehemence, more

---

[12] See a description of the cortège and other details of Act I stage action in Pendle and Wilkins, "Paradise Found," in *Opera in Context*, ed. Radice, 193–7.

[13] The text of "Hâtons-nous" does not appear in the draft verse or early printed libretti, suggesting a late addition or perhaps one that Scribe did not author. A manuscript note of the text written in a hand other than the librettist's is found among the Scribe papers, F-Pn, Ms., n.a.fr. 22502, vol. xxiii, 1°:1°. It is possible that the chorus's text originated from an unnamed collaborator, or from Léon or Fromental Halévy.

intense than in its sober moments prior to Brogni's appearance, partly to its drunkenness[14]):

Act I, Scene vi, *Final*
Schlesinger-Garland

RUGGIERO
Ah! grand Dieu! que vois-je!
Et quelle audace impie!
Aux portes de l'église un Juif se
réfugie!
Vous le voyez, Chrétiens, et vous
souffrez
L'empreinte de ses pas sur les
marbres sacrés!

RUGGIERO
Ah! Great God! What do I see!
And what impious audacity!
At the doors of the church a Jew
takes refuge!
You see him, Christians, and you
allow
The imprint of his steps on the
sacred marble!

TOUS
Il a raison!

EVERYONE
He's right!

RUGGIERO
Suivez l'exemple
Du Dieu saint qui chassa tous les
vendeurs du Temple!

RUGGIERO
Follow the example
Of the Holy Lord who chased all the
vendors from the Temple!

CHOEUR DU PEUPLE
Au lac!
Oui, plongeons dans le lac
Cette race rebelle et criminelle!
Oui, plongeons dans le lac
Ces Hébreux, ces maudits,
Ces enfans d'Isaac!

CHOIR OF PEOPLE
Into the lake!
Yes, let's plunge in the lake
This rebellious and criminal race
Yes, let's plunge in the lake
These Hebrews, these accursed ones,
These children of Isaac!

Halévy's music reaches a fevered pitch. As Ruggiero reminds the crowd of the imprint of the Jews' steps on the "sacred marble," Halévy maximizes Ruggiero's authoritative weight by doubling his descending line in the ophicleide and third trombone (*Schlesinger-Garland*, No. 7, *Final*, mm. 45–9, 52–8). At Ruggiero's emotionally packed reference to Jesus and the moneylenders, the drunken crowd unleashes its anger

[14] Leich-Galland, "*La Juive*: Commentaire musical et littéraire," 47.

and hatred. With rising fourths on "Au lac!" and detached, orchestrally reinforced choral syllables, which intensify in a Rossinian *crescendo*, Halévy admirably depicts the breathless anger of the enraged mob. After three distinct statements of "dans le lac," he separates each syllable in the second presentation of the entire phrase ("Oui, plongeons dans le lac / Ces Hébreux, ces maudits, ces enfans d'Isaac!"). Eléazar's mocking challenge reignites the crowd's anger in a section that rebuilds to a return of "Au lac!" (*Schlesinger-Garland* and *Schlesinger-Lemoine*, No. 7, mm. 112–25). Again its anger is diffused, this time by Léopold and Albert, stimulating mixed responses of surprise in ensemble and chorus: Rachel questions the power of Samuel / Léopold, Eléazar calls on God's power against the Christians, and Léopold and Albert pray that Rachel will not discover the prince's true identity.[15] As Pendle and Wilkins note, a "freeze-frame" *tableau* enhances the shock registered in music and libretto.[16] After the Council's procession begins, announced with brass fanfare, the finale ends with a celebratory chorus with integrated solo and ensemble material, leading to a final *Te Deum* phrase (in F major), followed by twelve measures of the "Hosanna" chorus, bringing symmetry and closure to the act.

Late in the compositional process, most likely during rehearsals close to the time of the première or even possibly during the early performances, the juxtaposition of worship, celebration, and confrontation had a different shape. As revealed in the autograph, performing parts, and late-stage archival score, the singing of the *Te Deum* was set immediately against the beginning of the "Hosanna" chorus and not the instigatory grumblings about Eléazar. Vestiges of the old placement of "Hosanna" at the opening, which can be seen in the early manuscript sources, reflect more closely the text ordering found in the printed libretti, including the pre-première 18 February libretto, the 23 February libretto intended to accompany the première, the 1835 second edition, and subsequent libretti included in numerous collected

---

[15] Thirty-two measures of the recitative preceding Léopold's crowd-stopping action appear in the autograph and piano-vocal score (*Schlesinger-Lemoine*, 105–6), but are omitted in the full score and crossed out and obscured in the archival score.

[16] "Paradise Found," in *Opera in Context*, ed. Radice, 196–7.

editions of Scribe's works.[17] In these, the "Hosanna" chorus is the first text to appear, adhering to the plan of an opening chorus commonly found in *grand opéra*; it reappears in Act I, Scene i, following the "En ce jour" recitative of the questioning crowd and at the end of the scene after the announcement of the Council's opening. (The *Te Deum* appears only in the stage directions preceding the chorus text.) In the manuscript performing parts, vestiges of this ordering can be found, partially obscured by revised sections that omitted the first presentation of the "Hosanna." Still visible in many of the chorus partbooks and the *partition de choeur*, the manuscript short score used by the assistant *chef de chant* Jean M. Schneitzhoeffer, is the overlapping of the last two syllables of "veneratur" of the *Te Deum* verse with the beginning of "Hosanna."[18] In others, the entirety of the original *Te Deum*–"Hosanna" combination can be clearly seen under *collettes*.[19] In this early version, Halévy further intersects the spiritual and secular when he elides another "Hosanna" phrase ending with the *Te Deum* phrase "tibi cherubini"; moreover, he sets up a counterpoint between the hymn phrase "Sanctus" and another "Hosanna" phrase (see Example 3).[20] As revealed in both the autograph and *partition de choeur*, the "En ce jour" recitative and the people's muttered reactions originally came after the initial presentation of the "Hosanna" chorus.[21]

[17] Very few changes were made to the printed libretto in publications subsequent to 1835, despite the discrepancies with the libretto as set in the musical scores. The only substantive change in the second libretto edition of 1835 was the omission of Act III, Scenes i–iv (see pp. 228–30 below). Among later printings, the libretto of the 1854 collected edition of Scribe's works, for example, corresponds to the second edition.

[18] See Schneitzhoeffer's score, F-Po, Mat. 19^e[315 (520), fol. 5^v. In partbooks for bass, Mat. 19^e[315 (52), and *second dessus*, Mat. 19^e[315 (39), for example, this version is obscured but still visible on the verso of the partially attached *collettes* (pasted-on paper strips) that contain replacement phrases.

[19] See, for example, the second tenor partbook, F-Po, Mat. 19^e[315 (46).

[20] These two older-layer combinations can be seen clearly in the autograph; in fact, a reconstruction of the "Hosanna" that follows and combines with the *Te Deum* could be made from phrases crossed out but still visible in the autograph, with a few exceptions.

[21] In the *partition de choeur*, a series of leaves stitched together, fols. 23^r–37^v, contain the old ordering; moreover, changes in paper and copyists in this source, in conjunction with clues found in the autograph, offer clear demarcations

Example 3 Early version of Act I, No. 1, *Introduction*, combination of *Te Deum* phrase with "Hosanna" phrase, transcribed from second tenor part, F-Po, Mat.19ᶜ[315 (46)

The repositioning of the crowd's whispered accusations about Eléazar *immediately* after the first *Te Deum* phrase sets the confrontational tone not only for the act but for the entire opera. The impact of this juxtaposition is more effective in underlining the theme of intolerance than in the original placement, when these exchanges followed the first "Hosanna" chorus. Although Halévy's first solution of combining the "Hosanna" phrases with those of the *Te Deum* exemplified more pointedly the coalescence of worshipers and celebrants, the separation of these phrases led to a greater musical and verbal intelligibility. This separation, in fact, made the sacred–secular connections of the scene more musically powerful through the greater clarity of this material. Among the changes made to Act I, the reworking of this opening most significantly intensified the opera's religious conflict.

Another alteration in the initial scene, the deletion of verse intended for Eléazar, resulted in a de-emphasis on Eléazar's stereotyped greed and, consequently, a re-emphasis on his victimization at the hands of Christians. The text, while not flagrantly antisemitic, takes on weighted meaning when coupled with the sounding of anvils, symbols of materialism and greed (see n. 10 above). With the combined stereotyped associations, the verse's placement at the drama's outset would have made Eléazar seem less a victim of the taunting crowd, particularly since he is not alone with his daughter, but overseeing

between earlier and later stages. The material on its obscured leaves corresponds to that in the autograph, pages 49 (120) up to the end of the chorus at the word "ciel." When Halévy moved "En ce jour" to its position following the *Te Deum*, he did not shift revised pages themselves; rather, he copied out the revised material, and recopied unaltered music, using paper unlike the predominant paper type found in the autograph. One layer of page numberings provides clues to these shifts of material (see pp. 15–17 that precede 4–14).

laborers whom he is insistently prodding to work. This four-line verse appears in Scribe's draft verse (F-Pn, Ms., n.a.fr. 22562, 32) as well as in the printed libretti:

Act I, Scene i, *Introduction*

23 February 1835 libretto (F-Po, Livr. 19[274][22]

ELEAZAR, à gauche, à ses ouvriers	ELEAZAR, stage right, to his workers
Amis, travaillez sans cesse.	Friends, work without ceasing.
C'est bien mériter du ciel!	It is to be worthy of heaven!
Fuir le vice et la paresse,	To flee vice and laziness,
C'est honorer l'Eternel!	Is to honor the Eternal Lord!

Scribe's intention to have this verse sung simultaneously with a verse of "Hosanna" is shown by his side-by-side placement of the verses in his *Vade mecum*, accompanied by a vertical stroke of the pen, as well as the "ensemble" indication in the printed libretti: Eléazar is to sing stage right while the chorus appears stage left. The matching rhyme scheme further underlines the intention that the verses are to be sung together. The "Amis, travaillez" verse does not appear in the music sources (one of several substantive discrepancies with libretto sources), suggesting that its combination with the "Hosanna" verse preceded the *Te Deum*–"Hosanna" combination described above. Although one reviewer's reference to Eléazar's verse and to the appearance of his workers implies that the verse was performed at the première, he likely wrote his review with libretto in hand.[23] Its deletion seems to correspond with the reduction in the Act II allusions to Eléazar's greed (see pp. 237–8 below).

Another libretto passage omitted in the early published scores removes one confrontational scene, one with more offensive condemnations of the Jews than the crowd's initial whisperings. The text, from the Act I finale, carries a strong trace of a scene in *Ivanhoe* (Chapter 7) in which Isaac and Rebecca, while searching for a seat at the martial

---

[22] In this source, the verse is repeated after the second presentation of the "Hosanna" chorus.

[23] *La Gazette de France*, 27 February 1835; *Dossier de presse parisienne*, ed. Leich-Galland, 51.

contests, are met with disparaging invectives, but in the libretto the reaction to the Jews is even harsher:[24]

Act I, Scene v

23 February 1835 libretto (omitted from *Schlesinger-Garland*)

ELEAZAR
Et comment dans cette foule
  immense
Trouver à se placer?

ELEAZAR
How is it possible in this immense
  crowd
To find a seat?

RACHEL
Mon père, suivez-moi!
Nous serons là très-bien, je crois.

RACHEL
Father, follow me!
We shall sit here very comfortably,
  I think.

(Elle lui montre une place vide sur
  un banc, Eléazar s'en approche,
  mais tous ses voisins le
  repoussent.)

(She shows him an empty place on a
  bench, Eléazar approaches it, but
  all his neighbors push him away.)

CHOEUR
C'est un Juif! c'est un Juif!
Redoute mon courroux!
Va-t'en! va-t'en! éloigne-toi de
  nous!
N'approche pas! ton souffle impur
Doit porter malheur, j'en suis sûr!
C'est un Juif! c'est un Juif!
Redoute mon courroux!
Va-t'en! va-t'en! éloigne-toi de
  nous!

CHOIR
He's a Jew! He's a Jew!
Beware of my anger!
Get away! Get away! move away from
  us!
Don't come near! Your unclean breath
Must carry misfortune, I am sure of it!
He's a Jew! He's a Jew!
Beware of my anger!
Get away! Get away! move away from
  us!

RACHEL
Hélas! hélas! ils nous méprisent
  tous!
Avec horreur ils s'éloignent de nous!

RACHEL
Alas! Alas! Everyone despises us!

They move away from us in horror!

[24] Sir Walter Scott, *Ivanhoe*, ed. A. N. Wilson (London: Penguin Books, 1984), 79–84. This Act I text, which corresponds with draft verse in F-Pn, Ms., n.a.fr. 22562, 46–7, is found in the copyist's libretto (F-Pan, AJ[13]202), 18 and 23 February libretti, but not in the second edition of the libretto.

ELEAZAR, à part
Ce Juif maudit, que vous méprisez
  tous,
J'en fais serment, se vengera de
  vous.

RACHEL, allant de l'autre côté, et
  s'adressant à des cavaliers
  richement habillés
Ah! nobles seigneurs que vous êtes,
Daignez nous souffrir près de vous.

PREMIER CAVALIER, à son voisin
Quel malheur d'être Juive, avec des
  yeux si doux!

DEUXIEME CAVALIER
Quelle pensée impie!
(à Rachel et à Eléazar les
  repoussant)
Ah! par les saints prophètes,
Plus loin!

ELEAZAR, à ceux qui sont devant
  sa porte
Je ne tiens pas à contempler vos
  fêtes,
Chrétiens! mais laissez-nous du
  moins rentrer chez nous.

TOUS, le repoussant
C'est un Juif! c'est un Juif!
[continues as above]

(Repoussés par la foule, Eléazar et
  Rachel se trouvent portés
  jusque sur les marches de pierre
  qui conduisent à l'église. Là, ils
  s'arrêtent adossés contre les
  murs du temple, et la foule ne
  peut pas les repousser plus loin.

ELEAZAR, aside
This cursed Jew that all of you
  despise,
I swear that he will take his revenge
  on you.

RACHEL, going to the other side
  and addressing some richly
  dressed gentlemen
Ah! Noble lords that you are,
Deign to allow us to sit near you.

FIRST GENTLEMAN, to his neighbor
What a misfortune to be a Jewess,
  with such sweet eyes!

SECOND GENTLEMAN
What an ungodly thought!
(to Rachel and Eléazar pushing
  them away)
Ah! By the holy prophets,
Go farther away!

ELEAZAR, to those who are before
  his door
I don't care about watching your
  celebrations,
Christians! But at least let us
  return to our house.

EVERYONE, pushing him away
He's a Jew! He's a Jew!
[continues as above]

(Pushed away by the crowd,
  Eléazar and Rachel find
  themselves swept toward the
  stone steps which lead to the
  church. There, they stop, their
  backs against the walls of the
  temple, and the crowd cannot

C'est elle, au contraire, qui alors s'éloigne d'eux, comme craignant de les toucher, et Eléazar et Rachel se trouvent isolés et en vue sur les marches de l'église.

push them any farther. It is now the crowd that moves away from them, as if fearing to touch them, and Eléazar and Rachel find themselves isolated and conspicuous on the steps of the church.

Dans le lointain, sur un air de marche majestueux et brillant, le cortège commence à défiler. Des soldats, conduits par Ruggiero, viennent faire ranger le peuple.)

In the distance, to a majestic and brilliant march tune, the procession begins to march by. Soldiers led by Ruggiero make the people stand back.)

A small vestige of this passage survives in the music sources. The initial exchange between Eléazar ("Et comment") and Rachel ("Mon père") appears verbatim in the piano-vocal score (*Schlesinger-Lemoine*, No. 7, mm. 14–20), but in the archival score and *Schlesinger-Garland* it is replaced by Rachel's commenting on the "immense crowd" in front of their house, with no mention of searching for a place to sit.[25] And instead of Rachel, Eléazar leads the way (*Schlesinger-Garland*, No. 7, mm. 14–21). Omitted are the crowd's verbal taunts and repulsion of the Jews, which Scribe undoubtedly conceived as a choral refrain. Stage directions reduced from Palianti's *mise en scène* manual indicate that the crowd's pushing away of the Jews remains in the stage action.[26] Corresponding to the stage direction, a small textual addition, Ruggiero's "Place rangez vous tous, vous manans et bourgeois" ("Make room, move over, you boorish bourgeois") appears in the music sources. A reviewer for *Le Temps* (26 February 1835) recognized the *Ivanhoe* basis of this scene, perhaps reminded by the libretto passage or simply cued by the staged rebuffing of Rachel and Eléazar, which he describes:

---

[25] In the archival score, this brief exchange, beginning with Eléazar's "Et comment," matches what appears in *Schlesinger-Lemoine*, but it is crossed out and replaced with the vocal lines of Rachel and Eléazar found in *Schlesinger-Garland*.

[26] See Cohen, *Staging Manuals*, 140. This source (141) further eliminates the Jews' seeming interest in the festivities in the omitted *Ivanhoe* scene, noting that Eléazar looks at the procession "with disdain" and drags his daughter from it.

One should note that not all of this is M. Scribe's. Remember the fine chapter in *Ivanhoe* on the tournament in which the Jew and his daughter cannot find a place to sit and are repulsed, sometimes by lords and sometimes by common people. In M. Scribe's opera, Eléazar goes in every direction: pushed, cursed, and swept with Rachel up to the steps of the church.[27]

Perhaps this passage was in the end deemed unpalatable or excessive in its close proximity to Ruggiero's venomous reaction to the Jews on the church steps and the ensuing choral furor. Indeed, it would not be surprising if the composer personally found the scene problematic: surely among those planned by Scribe, the odiousness of the crowd's verbal abuse, coupled with physical repulsion, would have triggered a sharp emotional response in Halévy.

Despite the implications of Christian hypocrisy suggested in the juxtaposition of worship and the attacks of Ruggiero and the crowd, the representation of Catholicism was otherwise dignified and respectful enough not to offend traditional mores, as the Commission *rapport* concluded. In addition to the *Te Deum*, the organ, and the emblems of Catholic ritual, the cardinal's clemency was a strong reminder of the beneficent aspects of Christian doctrine. The text of "Si la rigueur" encapsulates the Christian tenet of forgiveness and the music of calm dignity enhances its empathetic words. This aria's placement – after Ruggiero's reminder of Jesus' eviction of the moneylenders and the crowd's bloodthirsty shouts – offsets, for one very strong dramatic moment, the acidic intolerance of the Catholics.

As we shall explore below, Brogni's compassion is featured again in Act IV in his mournful lament of Rachel's imminent death. His more extended regrets in some sources were omitted or lessened, perhaps because it would have made him *overly* sympathetic, undermining the opera's basic critique, as well as the power of his Act III condemnation of Rachel, Eléazar, and Léopold. In other parts of the opera, as in Eléazar's recitative of Act IV, Scene iv, Brogni's castigating judgment is referred to, but cursorily and indirectly; in Act V, it is represented

[27] *Dossier de presse parisienne*, ed. Leich-Galland, 157–8 (article signed "L.-V.").

visually, as he stands in solidarity with Council members. With the exception of the forcefully delivered malediction of Act III, the single pointed realization of his doctrinal strictures (echoing Eléazar's own anathema of Act II), the opera avoids the blatant casting of Brogni as a thoroughly condemning Church leader.

ELEAZAR'S RELIGIOUS CHARACTERIZATION

The opera's commentary on Jews and Judaism centers on its portrayal of Eléazar as a pious, embittered figure guided by his devotion to God but also by his defiance and hatred of Christians. In the whole of his characterization, he is not solely presented as a victim of the cardinal, crowd, and Council, yet his antagonistic actions clearly derive from a sense of despair at his powerlessness and anger at his maltreatment. Like Brogni, he vacillates between forgiveness and hatred or condemnation of his social and doctrinal enemies. Corresponding to, while not comparable with, the split Christian image, Eléazar's intolerant stance – viewed as "fanaticism" in many contemporary minds – is countered by the sincere devotion expressed in the Act II Passover service and his pliability when his daughter's welfare is threatened. Brogni's banishment of Eléazar from Rome and the burning at the stake of the Jew's sons in the opera's prehistory give clear motivation for his defiance, which culminates in his Act V refusal to reveal Rachel's true identity to Brogni. In early libretto sources, Scribe depicted Eléazar as a rabbi, a symbol of religious ardor; while this identity as well as parts of the worship service were suppressed, the Jew's piety (together with the biblical significance of the name Eléazar) remains crucial to his portrayal.

In Act I, Eléazar's disruption of Christian worship and his challenging words to Ruggiero immediately demonstrate his unwillingness to cooperate with Christian society. The clerical *Gazette de France* reviewer, who did not want to accept any Christian transgression, was eager to point out Eléazar's intolerance, demanding: "où est ici le fanatique?" ("and, here, where is the fanatic?").[28] An unambiguous example of Eléazar's reluctance to make peace with Christians is his sharp refusal

---

[28] *Ibid.*, 51.

of Brogni's fraternal gesture of Act I.[29] Eléazar, undoubtedly pained by his maltreatment by Ruggiero and the crowd, is unaffected by Brogni's action: he can think only of the cardinal's previous act of banishment, an act representative of many historical expulsions of Jews over the centuries and one that adds weight to Eléazar's anger and hesitation. When Brogni asks forgiveness for having offended him, Eléazar shouts, "Jamais!":

Act I, Scene iv, No. 1

Schlesinger-Garland

ELEAZAR
Je n'ai point oublié que de Rome
   jadis,
Sévère magistrat, c'est toi qui me
   bannis!

ELEAZAR
I haven't forgotten that long ago,
   from Rome,
Harsh magistrate, you're the one
   who banished me!

RUGGIERO
Quelle audace!

RUGGIERO
What audacity!

BROGNI
Et cependant je lui fait grâce
   entière!
Sois libre, Eléazar,
Soyons amis, mon frère,
Et si je t'offensai pardonne moi!

BROGNI
And nevertheless I pardon him
   completely!
Be free, Eléazar,
Let us be friends, my brother,
And if I offended you, forgive me!

ELEAZAR
Jamais!

ELEAZAR
Never!

Late-stage textual changes in this passage (made after the archival score was copied) include an omission of several lines by Brogni which give Eléazar's usury as grounds for banishment – pointing to a softening of the depiction of a miserly Eléazar (see pp. 243–4 below and Illustration 11).[30] But other changes heighten the impact of the Jew's

---

[29] *Le Courrier français*, 27 February 1835 (*Dossier de presse parisienne*, ed. Leich-Galland, 25) reported that at the première Brogni (Levasseur) held out his hand to Eléazar (Nourrit) as he made his appeal.

[30] These changes, also found in the autograph and 1835 performing parts, represent discrepancies between the musical sources and the printed libretti.

obstinacy. One was merely a substitution of the words "Je n'ai point" for "As-tu donc" in the phrase "Je n'ai point oublié que de Rome jadis, / Sévère magistrat, c'est toi qui me bannis!" This small change shifts the focus to the first person, making Eléazar's reminder of the past seem more accusatory, less "diplomatic." The alteration with the greatest impact in this passage, however, is the omission of text that follows Eléazar's "Jamais!" in the 18 February and 23 February libretti. The omitted phrase, "Non jamais de pardon aux chrétiens que je hais!" ("No, never a pardon for Christians whom I hate!"), expresses in a verbally emphatic way how much Eléazar despises those he views as his persecutors. This phrase appears in the manuscript music sources in a number of musical variants (suggesting reworking in several stages), all of which are obscured through the stitching of pages or marks of red crayon (most likely Leborne's marks); two versions of the phrase can be seen in the autograph, but it does not appear in the published scores.[31] The 27 February review in *Le Courrier français* suggests that the phrase was sung at the première: "[T]he Jew, little moved by this excess of Christian humility, responds under his breath with a vow of eternal hatred."[32] While the alteration downplays the verbal intensity of Eléazar's enmity, the resulting dramatic intensity, with only the single-word shout, is far greater. The power of the ejaculatory retort is heightened by three measures of a conventional operatic flourish, a rising arpeggiation (on C^7, the dominant seventh) in the upper strings followed by punctuated chords in the full orchestra. These resolve, after a fermata, to F in the mood-changing transitional measures

---

[31] The earliest source that includes this phrase is Scribe's draft verse, F-Pn, Ms., n.a.fr. 22562, 40. The phrase belongs to a passage that went through several layers, corresponding to several transpositions of Brogni's *cavatine*: first written in A♭ major, it then appeared in G major, and finally F major, the key used in the Schlesinger scores. Evidence for this sequence of transpositions is found in many performing parts, including Brogni's partbook, F-Po, Mat. 19ᵉ[315 (26), fols. 11ᵛ–20ʳ. The G major version matches that in Halévy's hand in the autograph, with "en fa" written in ink above the top staff of the first page of the *air* (173); it also appears in F major in this source, in a copyist's hand on paper differing from the autograph's predominant paper types. One interesting passage of recitative, twenty-seven measures in F, which appears before the *cavatine* in Brogni's partbook, Mat. 19ᵉ[315 (26), fols. 7ᵛ–8ᵛ, cannot be found in the autograph.

[32] *Dossier de presse parisienne*, ed. Leich-Galland, 25.

to Brogni's aria (*Schlesinger-Garland*, No. 1, mm. 542–6; *Schlesinger-Lemoine*, No. 1, mm. 503–7). Following Eléazar's refusal, Brogni's compassionate "Si la rigueur" highlights, by dramatic contrast, the Jew's obstinacy.

Within Brogni's *cavatine*, when the choir and soloists respond to the cardinal's plea for forgiveness ("Tant de bonté, tant de clémence"), Eléazar continues to resist, unable to forget or forgive. Of the ensemble voices, Halévy sets Eléazar's line most distinctly from the others: his moving sixteenth notes and staggered entrances (with Ruggiero) isolate his voice and underscore the sense of separateness revealed in the text: "Sa vaine et tardive clémence,/Ne saurait ébranler ma foi,/Je garde en mon coeur la vengeance,/Point d'alliance entre eux et moi!" ("His hollow and belated clemency could not shake my faith; I hold vengeance in my heart, no alliance between them and me!") (see Example 4).

Example 4 Act I, "Si la rigueur," *Schlesinger-Lemoine*, and *Schlesinger-Garland*, No. 2, mm. 25–8

The poignant expression of Eléazar's religious devotion in the Passover seder that begins Act II is enhanced by the simplicity of the service, which sharply contrasts with the Council's ceremonial pomp. Its intimacy lends dramatic realism to the depiction of clandestine Jewish worship, but it also suggests a heartfelt conviction of the worshipers not conveyed by the extravagant Council processions. The service in the interior of Eléazar's house was conceived by Scribe, as documented by the draft scenario and draft verse, but Halévy helped to refine it through both his musical choices and the minor dramatic alterations that he (and perhaps his brother) likely effected. One such alteration was a clarification of the type of service being observed. The draft scenario reveals that Scribe originally intended it to be celebrated around the time of Christmas (see Illustration 4), perhaps because of its proximity to the date of the Council's opening.[33] In this source, Scribe does not designate the service as Passover. At first he notes that it is "le repas . . . et la prière du soir" and that the evening is "un samedi" (Saturday), but he then strikes out this time specification. Most likely, the designation of Christmas was omitted when the Passover service was decided upon – a choice clarified in the copyist's libretto in F-Pan, AJ^{13}202 in which "la pâque" is noted in stage directions at the beginning of Act II. The crowd's chant of "Noël" that announces the arrival of the cortège at the beginning of the Act I finale (No. 7), while seemingly a reference to Christmas, is a traditional French greeting of important personages, one also used to salute the king in the Act III finale of Halévy's *Charles VI*.[34] (A critic for *Le Moniteur universel*, however, noted that the emperor arrived in Constance on "la veille de

---

[33] F-Pn, Ms., n.a.fr. 22502, vol. XXIII, 1°:2°, 1–2. Scribe writes at the end of his introductory paragraph, "au moment où commence l'action – au mois de décembre 1414. le jour de Noël." But the words "au mois," "décembre," and "le jour de Noël" are crossed out and replaced with the more general dating "en 1414." Likewise, in his Scene v description, the phrase "fête de la nativité" is crossed out, but the subsequent phrase "vêpres de la nativité" is not, nor is "c'est le jour de Noël" in the draft Scene i – but scribbled in the opposite margin are the words "le jour de pâques et la victoire."

[34] Leich-Galland personally offered this clarification of the use of "Noël," a correction of my previous interpretation as presented in my dissertation, "*La Juive*," vol. II, 366–7.

Noël."[35]) A reference to Passover in recitative following Léopold's *sérénade*, when Rachel invites Léopold to join her family in the celebration of "la Pâque sainte," suggests that no lapse of time occurs between the first and second acts.

The basic elements of the scene as sketched in Scribe's draft scenario are maintained in later sources, although details other than the religious season were altered or omitted. One such detail is the explicit designation of Eléazar as "un des rabbins[,] un des prêtres de la loi juive" who says the evening prayer. In the early printed libretti, there is also a reference to Eléazar as rabbi, preparing to marry Rachel and Léopold at the end of Act II. Eléazar says to the couple in these sources: "A genoux! à genoux! . . . prêtre de notre loi, / Que je reçoive ici tes sermens et sa foi!" ("On your knees! On your knees! . . . priest of our law, I receive your vows and his faith!")[36] In the autograph, *Schlesinger-Garland*, and *Schlesinger-Lemoine*, he is identified only as "le juif Eléazar" and "un orfèvre joaillier" (a goldsmith-jeweller), without any designation of rabbinical ties. In these sources, he leads the prayer and distributes the unleavened bread, but these functions were traditionally carried out by the head of the family. Moreover, in the musical setting, the idea and action of Eléazar's marrying the couple are replaced by his simply accepting and blessing Léopold as Rachel's "époux." The 27 February review in *La Gazette de France* implies that the change was not made until after the première, although, again, the writer may have simply referred to the libretto at hand: in addition to identifying Eléazar as both "[o]rfèvre" and "rabbin," this report refers to the ceremony that he begins to conduct with the phrase "A genoux."[37] A 25 February

---

[35] *Le Moniteur universel*, 28 Februrary 1835; *Dossier de presse parisienne*, ed. Leich-Galland, 114.

[36] In the draft scenario (Scene ix in n.a.fr. 22502, vol. XXIII, 1°:2°, 11), Scribe has Eléazar refer to himself as "moi prêtre et pontif de notre loi – du dieu d'abraham et de jacob."

[37] *Dossier de presse parisienne*, ed. Leich-Galland, 55. As in other cases when the libretto is quoted in reviews, the writer was likely following the printed libretto and may not have recognized a discrepancy between it and the performed text. However, since this phrase would have been accompanied by a somewhat memorable action, it seems unlikely that it had already been omitted.

review in *Le Figaro*, however, speaks of Eléazar as "le père de la famille," but does not refer to him as a rabbi nor to marriage rites, merely to his granting permission for the marriage.[38]

This seeming suppression of Eléazar's rabbinical identity, along with the change to Passover, allows a more authentic treatment of characterization and ceremony. Although it is not known who determined these changes, it is likely, given the composer's heritage and his affiliations with the synagogue and the Jewish community, that he may have viewed Scribe's portrayal of Eléazar as rabbi as historically inaccurate. Scribe's concept of a rabbi was clearly a nineteenth-century one, closer to that of a Christian priest or minister than to the Talmudic rabbi, who was primarily an interpreter of the Bible and the Oral Law, or to the rabbi of the Middle Ages, who was spiritual head of a Jewish congregation or community as well as interpreter and expositor of the law.[39] Not until the beginning of the nineteenth century with the Reform movement did functions such as prayer leading and officiating in marriage and burial ceremonies become central to rabbinical office.[40] It seems probable that the composer would have pointed out the anachronism of such priest-like actions for a fifteenth-century rabbi, yet less probable when we consider that he incorporated his own anachronistic touches – or, one might argue, "reforms" of traditional music, as we shall explore below. Perhaps more likely, he may have objected to the incongruity of associating materialism and usury with a spiritual leader. Moreover, because Halévy had undoubtedly been a part of many traditional home services in which his own father led in prayer, as well as the Passover service led by Issakhar in his home in the Rome ghetto (described in the composer's Prix de Rome journal of 1821–2), he would have known that Eléazar's role as father was enough to meet the dramatic demands of the Act II service. Halévy certainly would have been sensitive to the common usage of unleavened bread in the Passover seder and perhaps suggested that Scribe's association in the draft scenario of the "pain

---

[38] *Ibid.*, 39, 41.
[39] See Godfrey Edmond Silverman, "Rabbi, Rabbinate," in *Encyclopaedia Judaica*, 18 vols. (Jerusalem: Macmillan, 1971), vol. XIII, 1445–8.
[40] *Ibid.*

sans levain" with the non-specified evening service be refined to that of Passover.[41]

The musical setting of the prayer, "O Dieu de nos pères" (identified as "Cantique" in the autograph), reflects an awareness of traditional Jewish practice and corresponds to aspects of Halévy's own works for the Parisian synagogue.[42] As in his later psalm settings, he uses *a cappella* in the opening phrases sung by Eléazar, as well as the responsorial treatment between Eléazar, as "precentor" (lay singer) or "cantor" (a *hazan* or professional singer), and Rachel and the small chorus of believers.[43] (As indicated in the printed libretti, there were seven men and five women, other than the two principals, who participated in the service.) That Eléazar is a tenor lends further credence to viewing him as cantor, as *hazanim* were traditionally tenors because of their greater vocal range and flexibility.[44] It is not known whether this aspect of Eléazar's role influenced Halévy's decision to reassign the role from bass to tenor (for Nourrit, who had first been given the traditional role of the lover, Léopold); the composer explained that the novelty of giving the central role of father to a tenor motivated the change.[45]

---

[41] Writing in his journal of his visit in spring 1821 to the Jewish home in the Rome ghetto, Halévy describes in detail the Passover seder in which he participated (F-Pn, Ms., n.a.fr. 14349, fols. 12ᵛ–13ʳ).

[42] Becker, "'Dieu de nos pères,'" grounds Halévy's treatment of the seder in the family's tradition in Fürth. Pendle and Wilkins, "Paradise Lost," in *Opera in Context*, ed. Radice, n. 59, suggest a link to Viennese synagogal music as described by Joseph Mainzer in "Vienne et la synagogue juive pendant les années 1826, 1827 et 1828," *La Gazette musicale de Paris* 1, no. 16 (20 April 1834): 125–8; no. 18 (4 May 1834): 143–6.

[43] Sacred Jewish music developed primarily into a vocal art following the destruction of the Temple in 70 CE, when the use of instruments was prohibited in synagogue worship. Moreover, the sung prayers in a home service would typically have been without accompaniment. Responsorial singing was common to Jewish psalmody and other types of synagogue song or prayer.

[44] *Recueil de chants*, ed. Naumbourg, xxxvi.

[45] Halévy, *Derniers Souvenirs*, 166: "[W]hen I began to work on the score, I was struck by the new inflections that the voice of a tenor, the voice of Nourrit, would give to the music in the role of a father. Thus I gained the voice and talent of M. Levasseur in the role of a cardinal, who is also a father." ("[L]orsque je commençai à m'occuper de la partition, je fus frappé des accents nouveaux que donnerait à la musique la voix de ténor, la voix de Nourrit, dans un rôle de père. Je gagnais ainsi dans le rôle de cardinal, qui est père aussi, la voix et le talent de M. Levasseur.")

Example 5 Act II, *Entr'acte et prière, Schlesinger-Lemoine,* and
Schlesinger-Garland, No. 8, mm. 30–45

Additionally, in Halévy's earlier associations with the synagogue, the
cantor for whom he had written his *De profundis,* Israël Lovy, was a
bass. But certainly making Eléazar a tenor role to be performed by
the star singer Nourrit was crucial in heightening its significance and
dramatic impact.

The responses to Eléazar's phrases, four-part choral harmonizations
moving in a simple progression beneath Rachel's echoes of Eléazar's
lines, are of a type that can be found in the Reform synagogue anthologies.[46] The responsorial part of the prayer consists of a series of
four-measure phrases, with the second phrase a slightly varied repetition of the first (see Example 5).[47] The bipartite subdivision of these

---

[46] In m. 42 the basses divide into two parts, but doublings among the parts
maintain the four-part harmony.

[47] In the prayer's longer version in *Schlesinger-Lemoine,* a three-measure phrase
sung by Eléazar and echoed by the worshipers, which offsets the regularity of
the square phrasing, is followed by a final four-measure phrase, in which Rachel

Example 6 Psalm 118, v. 25: *Chants religieux*, ed. Naumbourg, No. 77, 70

phrases, similar to the phrase structure of Halévy's psalm settings, is reflective of the subdivision of psalm verses into two equal parts, or hemistichs, by a caesura that was common to Jewish psalmody.[48] Each four-measure phrase is echoed by the chorus, recalling psalmodic practice; in some of Halévy's psalm settings, the solo and chorus alternate by hemistich, as in his setting of Psalm 118, v. 25 (see Example 6).

The narrow melodic span in "O Dieu de nos pères" is also suggestive of traditional melodies, which had to be easily remembered and easily expanded to fit texts of different lengths. The melody of the prayer, set

and the other celebrants join in the last two measures of the phrase, a common practice in responsorial psalmody. The omission of these ten measures (3+3+4) was likely one of the many small cuts made in the interest of performance time before publication of the full score.

[48] Concerning synagogue music, see, for example, Idelsohn's classic study, *Jewish Music*, and Aron Friedmann, *Der synagogale Gesang: Eine Studie* (Berlin: C. Boas Nacht, 1904). Reinhard Flender, *Hebrew Psalmody: A Structural Investigation* (Jerusalem: Magnes Press, Hebrew University, 1992), has also discovered tripartite verse structure in psalmody.

Example 7 Psalm 118, v. 5: *Chants religieux*, ed. Naumbourg, No. 76, 66

in the key of B♭, largely stays contained within B♭–F, with an occasional move one or two tones outside the fifth. In the first two measures, the melody outlines the tonic, in the second two, dominant and tonic; in phrases following the repeated A phrase (AAA'A'), the melody moves to an accented G on the second syllable of "mystères" (harmonized as G minor, the submediant, in the responsorial phrase, m. 59). There is no real suggestion of a psalmodic reciting tone, although one might imagine an expansion into recitation on the F in the initial hemistich of the first two phrases.

The slight hint of "oriental" color also alludes to traditional practice and corresponds to Halévy's psalm settings. The touch of oriental embellishment comes most strongly in A' (mm. 38, 42), with the E♮ (raised fourth) used as a passing tone to heighten the color of the accented E♭. (In the harmonized choral response, a fully diminished chord supports this E♮.) The raised or augmented fourth (C–F♯), with a suggestion of augmented second (E♭–F♯), also appears in the opening phrases of Halévy's setting of Psalm 118, v. 5 (see Example 7). Had Cicéri's arabesque-filled design for the interior of Eléazar's home been realized, the *asiatique* color would have been even stronger.[49]

---

[49] See this sketch in Join-Diéterle, *Les Décors de scène*, 191.

An additional synagogal association is his use of harp in the prayer: the serene orchestral introduction, or *entr'acte*, ends with a harp arpeggio that immediately precedes Eléazar's first phrase. The harp, although frequently appearing in contemporary opera, was traditionally linked to Jewish musical practice, a usage to which Halévy also referred in his later setting of Psalm 115.[50] After the responsorial section of the prayer, the harp returns, leading to and accompanying Eléazar's offering of the unleavened bread, as well as the choral response, "Partageons-nous ce pain." It also accompanies Eléazar's *cavatine*, which appears in *Schlesinger-Lemoine* but is omitted in *Schlesinger-Garland* (as discussed below).[51]

The labeling of the above elements as "Jewish" could easily be disputed: it could be argued that the responsory represents a quasi-church or generic religious style and that such elements as the raised fourth or use of the harp represent touches of local color not exclusively or even particularly "Hebraic." Ruth Jordan, while acknowledging that Halévy refers to Jewish practice in the "responsorial style of the psalmody," does not find a "recognisable Jewish element" in the musical setting and draws the conclusion that the composer consciously chose not to emulate the Ashkenazi or Sephardi liturgical music with which he was familiar.[52] Yet if Halévy's treatment is viewed with the knowledge of Reform synagogal music in the early nineteenth century and considered alongside his synagogue works in which he incorporated idioms of European art music while alluding to Jewish musical traditions, it is difficult to characterize his setting as completely "non-Jewish." The predominantly four-voice setting of the responses, for example, would not have been foreign to the Temple Sainte-Avoye, for which Halévy composed and where Israël Lovy established a four-part choir

---

[50] Halévy includes organ and then harp accompaniment in his setting of Psalm 115, v. 12 (No. 66 in *Nouveau Recueil*, ed. Naumbourg), written for the marriage of his nephew Edgard Rodrigues to Luise Mayer on 2 May 1858. A harp is featured on the cover of the 1847 Naumbourg collection; in the 1875 collection (xli), Naumbourg endorses the use of harp, rather than organ, because of the many biblical references to the *kinnor* and *nébel*; in 1846 he proposed to the Consistoire the adoption of the harp's use for ceremonies, particularly for marriages.

[51] Halévy also uses harp to accompany Brogni's *cavatine*, but less extensively than in Eléazar's sections.

[52] Jordan, *Fromental Halévy*, 204.

in 1822.[53] Indeed, the composer's connections to the synagogue, even if intermittent, make it highly probable that he was thinking beyond effects of local color in this scene.[54]

Following the reverent opening prayer, which cadences in B♭ major, an element of pious anger is introduced in a fourteen-measure section that begins in G minor with tremolos in the winds and an agitated bass sequence. In this section, Eléazar issues a fierce warning of God's wrath at ungodly and false-hearted individuals who may have dared "to slip among us":

Act II, Scene i, No. 8, *Entr'acte et prière*

Schlesinger-Garland

ELEAZAR	ELEAZAR
Si trahison ou perfidie	If treason or treachery
Osait se glisser parmi nous,	Dared to slip among us,
Sur le parjure ou sur l'impie,	On the disloyal or the blasphemer
Grand Dieu, que tombe ton courroux!	Let your wrath fall, great God!

In contrast with this stern warning, a thirty-measure section, beginning with the text "Et vous tous, enfans de Moïse," expands Eléazar's religious persona as he invites the small gathering of Jewish celebrants to honor the covenant by partaking of the unleavened bread. Halévy underscores Eléazar's devout expression with a change of texture and orchestration (the string tremolos are now legato arpeggiations, and

---

[53] Bathja Bachrach and Hanoch Avenary, "Music," in *Encyclopaedia Judaica* (Jerusalem: Macmillan, 1971), vol. xii, 645, note that Lovy composed music that incorporated the choral style of *opéra comique* into the *meshorerim* tradition (cantor and two assisting soloists). See also Idelsohn's discussion, *Jewish Music*, 235–41, on the introduction of the chorale into German synagogues during the early nineteenth century.

[54] Hugh Macdonald, "La Juive," in *The New Grove Dictionary of Opera*, ed. Sadie, vol. ii, 927, states, for example, that Halévy "treated the Jewish scenes as local colour, not in any way identifying with them as a Jew," and, in his entry on Halévy in the second edition of *The New Grove Dictionary of Music and Musicians*, ed. Stanley Sadie, 29 vols. (London: Macmillan; New York: Grove's Dictionaries, 2001), vol. x, 690, that the composer wrote "less as a Jew than a seeker of operatic effect."

the harp re-enters). In unison, the celebrants "recite" the text "Parta-geons le pain," largely on repeated B♭s, echoing the last two phrases sung by Eléazar in this section that cadences on E♭ major. In the au-tograph and piano-vocal score, this cadence leads to the A♭ major of Eléazar's *cavatine* (*Schlesinger-Lemoine*, Act II, No. 8, mm. 113–18). In *Schlesinger-Garland*, since the *cavatine* is omitted, the interruption to the service comes immediately after the six measures of cadential ex-tension that includes Rachel's reaction ("Que vois-je!") to Léopold's throwing down the unleavened bread (Act II, No. 8, mm. 103–8).

The omission of the entire *cavatine* significantly reduced the mu-sic of the service and the depiction of Eléazar's piety. (The autograph reflects the omission from *Schlesinger-Garland*: the red-crayon slash across its first measure, the last on fol. 399ʳ, and pin holes visible on successive pages suggest its at least temporary suppression.) Although the two-part *air* (AB A′C) is relatively short, it serves as a pointed illustration of Eléazar's devotion, as well as his personal angst over Jewish persecution and the degraded state of the Jewish nation.[55] Its text does not appear in libretto sources until the 18 February print-ing, a relatively late addition; as seen in the copyist's libretto (F-Pan, AJ¹³202), the *air* replaced a return to "O Dieu de nos pères" sung by the chorus:

Act II, Scene i, No. 8ʙ, *Cavatine*

Schlesinger-Lemoine (omitted from Schlesinger-Garland)

Dieu, que ma voix tremblante	God, may my trembling voice
S'élève jusqu'aux cieux,	Rise to the heavens,
Etends ta main puissante	Extend your powerful hand
Sur tes fils malheureux!	On your unfortunate sons!
Tout ton peuple succombe,	All your people succumb,
Et Sion, dans la tombe,	And Zion, in the tomb,
Implorant ta bonté,	Imploring your kindness,

---

[55] The two stanzas are built on two eight-measure phrases: the first is sixteen measures long, the second is seventeen, with a more emphatic elaboration of the final words, "A son père irrité!" With an introductory instrumental measure, as well as thirteen measures of cadential extension, the entire *cavatine* is forty-seven measures long.

Example 8 Act II, Eléazar's *cavatine, Schlesinger-Lemoine,* No. 8B, mm. 29–34

Vers toi se lève et crie,

Et demande la vie

A son père irrité!

Rises up to you and cries

And begs for life

From its angry father!

Halévy's musical setting augments the emotion built into the text through varied repetition, emphatic declamation, and long-held notes on the highest pitches that heighten key words, as in the g^1 on "crie" and the ab^1 on "vie" of the phrase "Vers toi se lève et crie / Et demande la vie" (see Example 8). In the second half, a nine-measure cadential extension containing minor- and major-sixth leaps (ab–fb^1, bb–g^1) and an embellished penultimate measure intensifies Eléazar's pleading (*Schlesinger-Lemoine,* Act II, No. 8B, mm. 35–42).[56]

Various accounts intimate that the *cavatine* was not restored until Gilbert Duprez (1806–96) first sang the role in 1837.[57] Duprez recalled that Halévy thanked him profusely for reintroducing the aria: "Halévy threw his arms around my neck the day that I proposed to him to re-establish the beautiful Passover *air* in the second act of *La Juive,* suppressed since its creation. One knows the powerful effect that this brilliant and inspired page always produces."[58] The singer's account seems to ring true as it hints of Halévy's attachment to the *air,* an anguished cry to God over Jewish misfortune.[59] Although the composer

---

[56] These nine measures appear crossed out in pencil and red and black crayon in the archival score, F-Po, A.509b, vol. II.

[57] Leich-Galland, *"La Juive:* Commentaire musical et littéraire," 52, 86, n. 16, citing Ernest-Marie-Edouard Deldevez, *Mes Mémoires* (Le Puy: Imprimerie de Marchessou fils, 1890), 191.

[58] G. Duprez, *Souvenirs d'un chanteur* (Paris: Calmann-Lévy, 1880), 150.

[59] But one should keep in mind that a number of scholars, including M. Elizabeth C. Bartlet, have found Duprez's claims to be unreliable. Bartlet has noted to me that she has discovered Duprez to be "more than an exaggerator." See her

understood well the mutable nature of opera in performance, he likely regretted the omission.

Following Rachel's response to Léopold's rejection of the Passover bread (or at the end of the *cavatine* if not suppressed), a knock on the door is heard, alarming the Jewish worshipers who are conducting their service secretly – and illegally. The lights are extinguished, the table preparations are hidden, and Eudoxie, the niece of Sigismund and the wife of Léopold (who attempts to hide himself), enters. With her interruption and the exchanges that follow, the Jewish service comes to an abrupt close.

Prior to the cuts reflected in *Schlesinger-Garland*, the Jews return to their worship following Eudoxie's departure. In the autograph, piano-vocal score, early libretti, and fragmented pages from the archival score, Eléazar brings back the aura of reverence by inviting Samuel/Léopold to join in a repetition of the prayer.[60] Although Eléazar's line is retained from its first presentation, the return to "O Dieu de nos pères" as a trio for Eléazar, Rachel, and Léopold (without chorus) is less worshipful and more "operatic" than before, with greater emphasis on character conflict than in the earlier verse and response. Reactions of guilt and fear from the disguised Léopold, for example, act as a counterpoint to Eléazar's and Rachel's prayer; moreover, Rachel's personal thoughts are woven into her discant above Eléazar's line. (See the beginning of the prayer's return, *Schlesinger-Lemoine*, Act II, No. 8, mm. 238–48.) In this trio version, following a varied repetition of "Si trahison" sung by Eléazar alone, Léopold and Rachel join him as he repeats his warning,

Guillaume Tell di Gioachino Rossini: Fonti iconografiche, with the editorial assistance of Mauro Bucarelli (Pesaro: Fondazione Rossini, 1996). I, too, found evidence of his false claims among the performing parts of *La Juive*: these contain several reminders made by orchestral players to transpose down a half-step for Duprez, thus casting some doubt on the singer's much-publicized statements about his "ut de poitrine." See, for example, the note "¹/₂ ton plus bas pour Duprez" in first and second violin parts for Acts IV and V, F-Po, Mat. 19ᵉ[315 (579) and (581).

60 In the eighteen-page score fragment (F-Po, 𝄞4387), the copyist's hand is the same as that which appears in the archival score; the paper type also appears to be the same: it is twenty-four-stave paper of similar measurement, color, texture, and watermarks. Red-crayon slashes on the first and last pages of this section in the autograph (A.509a, vol. I, 467–74) also reflect its suppression.

but Léopold breaks from them with the phrase "Je crains que sur ma tête impie,/Ne tonne leur Dieu jaloux!" ("I fear their jealous God will rage on my ungodly head!") This phrase, along with Léopold's previous reactions, refocuses attention on the exclusionary religious circle of the stage Jews as well as on his own deception. In this version, Eléazar then closes the worship service with a repetition of the prayer's first verse.

In Schlesinger's full score, in lieu of the invitation to pray and the ensuing trio section, Eléazar indicates in recitative that he is going to pray (*Schlesinger-Garland*, Act II, No. 9, mm. 220–38): this substitution cuts back on performance time as it emphasizes the sincerity of his individual faith, rather than that of the collective group. The character's turn to introspection appears more psychologically viable after Eudoxie's interruption, as it eases the sharp contrast between his religious persona and Jewish stereotype that emerges in the trio. Eléazar's words suggest the habitual observance of prayer:

Act II, Scene i, No. 9, Recitative following trio
Schlesinger-Garland

ELEAZAR	ELEAZAR
Quel trouble a mon aspect!	How troubled I seem!
D'où vient que vers la terre	Why is it that toward the earth
Leurs yeux restent baissés?	Their eyes remain lowered?
Il est tard; adieu, frère, retire toi!	It is late; goodbye, friend, go to bed!
Pour moi je vais prier,	I am going to pray,
Car les fils d'Israel	Because the sons of Israel
N'attendent pas le jour	Do not await the day
Pour louer l'Eternel.	To praise the Eternal.
Pendant cette nuit Sainte,	During this holy night,
Où Dieu qui nous contemple	When God who looks upon us
Ecoute nos pensées	Listens to my thoughts
Pour les inscrire aux Cieux,	And inscribes them in the heavens,
Pour toi, pour ton bonheur,	For you, for your happiness,
Il entendra mes voeux.	He will hear my vows.

In the whole of the seder scene, alterations notwithstanding, Halévy movingly pays homage to his heritage, and, undoubtedly, to his own father. An elegy other than Beulé's (see p. 21) later spoke of the composer's musical inspiration finding its source in "the remembrances of this domestic Israelite life."[61] The emotional sincerity emanating from Halévy's setting of the prayer sequence humanizes Eléazar, imbuing him and his fellow worshipers with a sense of deep morality that overrides other facets of his character soon to be revealed.

In the remainder of the opera, Eléazar's religiosity is tempered with anger and hatred, ambiguously suggesting his devotion or, in some contemporary minds, his fanaticism. At the end of Act II, his vengeful wrath is that of a father whose daughter has been wronged: when he surprises Rachel and Léopold, he warns of "la malédiction d'un père" and sings of "le bras vengeur." In the trio that follows, leading up to the moment when Léopold discloses that he is a Christian, Eléazar reacts as one whose religious principles have been breached:

Act II, Scene vii, No. 12, Trio
Schlesinger-Garland[62]

ELEAZAR

Et toi que j'accueillis, toi qui venais
    sans crainte
Outrager dans ces lieux l'hospitalité
    sainte,
Va-t'en! si tu n'étais un enfant
    d'Israël,
Si je ne respectais en toi notre
    croyance,
Mon bras t'aurait déjà frappé d'un
    coup mortel!

ELEAZAR

And you whom I welcomed, you
    who came without fear
To dishonor sacred hospitality here,

Leave! If you weren't a child of
    Israel,
If I didn't respect our faith in you,

My arm would have already struck
    you with a mortal blow!

LEOPOLD

Frappe! Je ne veux pas te ravir ta
    vengeance.
Je suis Chrétien!

LEOPOLD

Strike! I don't want to rob you of
    your vengeance.
I am a Christian!

ELEAZAR

Chrétien!

ELEAZAR

Christian!

---

[61] R., "Eloge de F. Halévy à l'Institut de France," *Les Archives israélites* 23, no. 2 (November 1862): 641.
[62] The text corresponds with that in the printed libretti.

Rachel fends off the threat of violence with an impassioned appeal that follows her own acceptance of blame, "Il n'est pas seul coupable."[63] In the text that Halévy sets, "Pour lui, pour moi, mon père," Rachel directly invokes Eléazar's love – "J'invoque votre amour" – as she tries to calm her father and ask for his blessing.[64] Her lyrical entreaty is enhanced by Halévy's setting in Db and an assuaging 6/8 *Andante espressivo*. Here, as later, Eléazar curbs his anger out of love for Rachel, but he fears God's punishment if he sets aside his convictions. As she continues her appeal, he yields to her pain and tears, revealing his conflict in the words "C'est Dieu qui l'inspire, / Sa douleur me déchire" ("God inspires her, her pain tears me apart"); in recitative, he not only pardons her but blesses the union: "Ma fureur vengeresse doit céder à tes pleurs, / Que le ciel en courroux comme moi te pardonne / Et qu'il soit ton époux!" ("My vengeful anger must cede to your tears, may Heaven, wrathful like me, pardon you and may he be your husband!") (Such a gesture of paternal malleability also displays an open-mindedness toward mixed marriage that was rare in the fifteenth century of the opera's setting, and still uncommon in the nineteenth.) Léopold's shocking refusal immediately sets off the malediction that Rachel had pacified. Augmenting a father's fury is Eléazar's distrust of Christians: "Trahison! anathème!/maudits soient les chrétiens et celui qui les aime!" ("Treason! Anathema! Cursed be Christians and he who loves them!")

In Acts IV and V, Eléazar holds onto his faith as well as his animosity toward Christians. In the Act IV duet, "Ta fille en ce moment," he refuses Brogni's impassioned appeal to save Rachel by renouncing his faith (*Schlesinger-Garland*, No. 18, mm. 40–66; *Schlesinger-Lemoine*, No. 21, 74–123). Brogni insists that Eléazar alone, through his conversion, can spare Rachel, a point Halévy makes emphatic through repetition and embellishment of his words "toi seul." After the cardinal's final elaboration of these words (*Schlesinger-Garland*, m. 34, *Schlesinger-Lemoine*, m. 68), Halévy suggests Eléazar's stunned disbelief at Brogni's

---

[63] The stage directions in the orchestral score indicate that Eléazar moves to strike Léopold but Rachel stops his arm and falls to her knees.

[64] The text appearing in the early printed libretti begins: "Oui, je l'aime! je l'aime!/Notre crime est le même." ("Yes, I love him! I love him! Our crime is the same.")

Example 9 Act IV, Brogni-Eléazar duet, *Schlesinger-Lemoine*, No. 21, mm. 69–79; *Schlesinger-Garland*, No. 18, 35–45

request through a tonally unstable passage of quickly changing chromatic harmonies and his monotone entry (see Example 9). Eléazar then breaks into upward leaps, exposing his increasing agitation and anger, mixed with religious fervor. He cannot worship "foreign idols" nor forsake the God of Jacob, "the only true God." But, as in Act II, thoughts of his daughter make him hesitate.

Permeating his famous *air* ending the fourth act, "Rachel, quand du Seigneur," is the acute emotional conflict driven by his desire to spare the daughter he had saved as a baby, loyalty to his faith, and vengeance. Although the text implies that vengeance is the most powerful emotion keeping him from accepting Brogni's jarring offer (and the Palianti *mise en scène livret* notes that he begins his recitative with a "cruel smile"[65]), the music speaks more strongly of the strength of his convictions. And in a harmonically transitional passage at the end of the return of A (of ABA), Eléazar relents with the words: "Ah! j'abjure à jamais ma vengeance, / Rachel, non, tu ne mourras pas!" ("Ah! I renounce my vengeance forever, / Rachel, no, you shall not die!") But his change of heart is short-lived. He hears distant shouts of death to the Jews – "Au bûcher, les Juifs! qu'ils périssent!" – in a *tempo di mezzo* that prompts an immediate return to his defiance against his Christian enemies and against conversion. After the retort, "Vous voulez notre sang,

[65] Cohen, *Staging Manuals*, 148.

Chrétiens, et moi j'allais / Vous rendre ma Rachel! non, non, jamais!"
("You want our blood, Christians, and I was going to give back my
Rachel! No, no, never!"), he bursts into a cabaletta in which he, enlightened by God ("Dieu m'éclaire"), exults in the fate of martyrdom
that he and Rachel will share.[66] As the death shouts continue and before he sings a final *couplet*, Eléazar repeats his vow not to give his
daughter (or himself) up to the Christians: "Israël la réclame, / c'est au
Dieu de Jacob que j'ai voué son âme!" ("Israel reclaims her, it is to the
God of Jacob that I have vowed her soul!")

This *air* represents the most powerful evocation of the Jew's raging
inner turmoil. As Eléazar contemplates his daughter's fate in the recitative, the delicate and carefully paced orchestral accompaniment underscores the progression of his self-confrontation, with pensive low
strings that begin a chromatic descent from D (*Schlesinger-Garland*, No.
19, m. 37; *Schlesinger-Lemoine*, No. 22, m. 15) to B♭ (*Schlesinger-Garland*,
m. 64; *Schlesinger-Lemoine*, m. 42). Immediately before Eléazar reminds
himself of the true horror of the situation, Halévy enunciates his mood
change to deep pathos with a late-resolving diminished-seventh chord
(B♯–D♯–F♯–A) softly repeated in the horns and mournfully outlined
in the low strings (*Schlesinger-Garland*, mm. 46–8; *Schlesinger-Lemoine*,
mm. 24–6). Through pauses and light touches of *pianissimo* accompaniment, Halévy reveals the shock of Eléazar's thoughts, which he
rapidly intensifies toward the culmination of his fierce self-accusation,
"C'est toi qu'immole ma fureur!" ("It is you whom my fury sacrifices!") After a short transition leading to the F minor tonic of the
aria, Halévy introduces Eléazar's haunting melody with two English
horns harmonized in thirds, whose expressivity Berlioz lauded in his
treatise on instrumentation.[67] Idelsohn claimed this melody to be the
only truly Jewish melody found in *La Juive*.[68] The prominent melodic
use of augmented seconds (D♭–E♮, A♭–B♮) and the inflection between B♭ and B♮ (creating an augmented fourth against the tonic

---

[66] Halévy uses this cabaletta tune in the long overture.
[67] Hector Berlioz, *Grand Traité d'instrumentation et d'orchestration* (Paris: Henri
Lemoine et Cie, 1843), 122.
[68] Idelsohn, *Jewish Music*, 473.

Example 10 Act IV, Eléazar's *air, Schlesinger-Lemoine*, No. 22, mm. 49–74;
Schlesinger-Garland, No. 19, mm. 65–96

root F) lends this *Andantino* an even stronger oriental color than in
the Jewish service and a poignancy that evokes the most profound
emotion from Eléazar – and perhaps from the composer himself (see
Example 10).

Eléazar's uncertainty and inner conflict re-emerge in Act V, as
Rachel's death becomes more imminent. Again he calls on God to
enlighten him – "Mon Dieu, que dois-je faire?/Hélas! éclaire-moi!" –
and reiterates doubts about Rachel's martyrdom as she voices her fear
of dying. Finally, when the execution signal is given, Eléazar's paternal
love once again breaks his anger, and he asks Rachel to convert, but
she chooses to die in the Jewish faith. Yet never does Eléazar retract his
malevolent feelings toward Brogni. When the cardinal begs to know

Example 11 Act V, *Final, Schlesinger-Lemoine,* No. 25, mm. 230–42;
Schlesinger-Garland, No. 22, mm. 241–53

his daughter's identity (entering over a G pedal, recalling the G–A♭ clash used at the anvils' entry in Act I), Eléazar answers only as two executioners hurl Rachel into the cauldron's boiling liquid. Eléazar's cruelly timed revelation, "La voilà!," which forces Brogni to pay bitterly for his actions against the Jews, seals his image as unforgiving and vengeful (see Example 11).

Eléazar's hatred of Christians, also linked with Shylockian allusions in his character, creates ambiguity in his religious persona and his symbolic role as oppressed individual, despite the historical justifications allowed in the text. It clouds the piety so evident in the Passover service, a scene that offers dramatic contrast on a larger scale in its counterpoising of religious groups. Halévy's setting lends the Jewish service a moral depth that makes the representations of Christian worship, so tightly bound to secular celebration, appear empty and ostentatious by comparison. Although Eléazar's religious sincerity does not wane, the opera refrains from making him a fully sympathetic character. In light of post-Enlightenment views about religious separatism that retained Voltairean distrust of the *fanatique*, he appears caught in the political-social paradox reflected in the 1830–31 debates about Judaism. He is given the voice of this religion more fully endorsed by the French state, yet his choice to hold onto his convictions leads to condemnation and death. It is a fate that evokes and warns against the severity of the Middle Ages, while speaking to fears of the *asiatique* Jew of the nineteenth century. Eléazar's hatred and vengeance undermine his essential morality and seemingly suggest – as even some liberal contemporary voices believed – that he himself exacerbated his position within Christian society. Although his anti-Christian sentiment is shown to have emerged from a history of persecution, its consequences are shown to be destructive: in Voltairean vocabulary, he is portrayed as separatist, and in the vocabulary of the Halévys and other reform-minded Jews, he appears as *juif* rather than *israélite*. Eléazar's vindictiveness, culminating in his final gesture of Act V, adds another dimension to the conflict and moves the opera from a completely one-sided opprobrium to a more complex critique of social, political, and religious intolerance.

RACHEL'S RELIGIOUS DUALITY AND THE CHANGE OF THE DENOUEMENT

The dual religious identity of Rachel underwent profound changes in relatively late stages of composition. Of the many reworkings of Acts IV and V, the most trenchant is the alteration of the opera's denouement that directly affected her characterization as well as the fundamental messages of the opera. As revealed in the draft scenario, Scribe initially planned the conversion to follow the discovery of her true identity as Brogni's daughter:

> [A]h, cries Rachel, overcome and falling to her knees, God of the Christians – receive your lost child who comes back to you again – soft, religious hymn. Solemn and heavenly song that ends the work. [T]he holy water of baptism purifies her brow.[69]

---

[69] F-Pn, Ms., n.a.fr. 22502, vol. XXIII, 1°:2°, 23: "[A]h, s'écrie Rachel éperdue et tombant à genoux, dieu des Chretiens – reçois l'enfant égaré qui revient dans ton sein – hymne doux et religieux. Cantique solennel et celeste qui termine la pièce. [E]au sainte du baptême reçu purifie son front."

Scribe's draft verse F-Pn, Ms., n.a.fr. 22562, 115–16, and the libretto fragments F-Pn, Ms., n.a.fr. 22502, vol. XXIII, 1°: 4°(a) and 1°: 4°(b), develop the conversion idea.[70] (Given that the *air* that began Act V in 1°: 4°(b) was composed and rehearsed – see pp. 226–7 below – Rachel's conversion may also have been set, but there is no extant musical evidence to support this possibility.) At the beginning of Act V in n.a.fr. 22502, vol. XXIII, 1°: 4°(a), Brogni himself tells Rachel that he is her true father. In this version, a less realistic one psychologically, Rachel immediately embraces Brogni and condemns Eléazar as her deceiver. Her identity is exposed in Act IV, Scene vi, in n.a.fr. 22502, vol. XXIII, 1°: 4°(b), but it is Eléazar who makes the revelation to Brogni, with Rachel overhearing. Despite these variant approaches, both sources end the opera similarly. As Eléazar and Rachel await their death in an amphitheatre filled with Council members, Church prelates, soldiers, spectators, and the executioner, Brogni recognizes the hypocrisy of executing the accused heretics on the "sacred day" of the Council's opening. He hopes instead to pardon them and win their conversion. (An incomplete sketch for an Act V set by Ciceri shows the beginnings of an expansive amphitheatre with hundreds of clerics seated in elevated galleries, perhaps corresponding with this early plan; see Illustration 7.) Rachel responds to his appeal but Eléazar refuses, even though he is freed from his chains; in the final scene, he looks at Rachel angrily as she is accepted into the Christian faith:[71]

Early version of Act V, Scene iii/iv (with conversion)

F-Pn, Ms., n.a.fr. 22502, vol. XXIII, 1°:4°(a) and (b)

BROGNI	BROGNI
Peuple! nous venons tous d'interroger le ciel!	People! We have all consulted heaven!
Prosterné, je priais, disant à l'éternel:	I prayed, prostrate, saying to the Lord:

---

[70] I designate the two partial versions of F-Pn, Ms., n.a.fr. 22502, vol. XXIII, 1°: 4°, as 4°(a) and 4°(b): the former's antecedence is suggested by its correspondence with the draft scenario's description of the beginning of Act V, as well as that of the draft verse (F-Pn, Ms., n.a.fr. 22562, 105).

[71] These verses correspond with those sketched in Act V, Scene v, of n.a.fr. 22562, 114–15.

7 *La Juive*, sketch of abandoned Act V set by Cicéri (1834?)

Mon Dieu! de ce concile ouvert sous
ton auspice,
Comment aux yeux de tous attester
la justice?
Comment reconquérir & ranger
sous ta loi
Le Juif & l'hérétique, ennemis de
la foi?
Comment les ramener à ta sainte
croyance?
Et Dieu m'a répondu: Chrétien! par
la clémence!

LEOPOLD ET SES AMIS
O doux espoir auquel je n'ose croire
encore!

BROGNI
Non, ce ne sera point par un arrêt
de mort
Que dans ce jour sacré s'ouvrira le
concile!
(s'adressant à Eléazar & à Rachel)
Et vous, fils d'Israél, vous dont
l'âme indocile
Repoussait notre Dieu
terrible & menaçant,
Peut-être désormais votre coeur
moins rebelle
S'ouvrira-t'il à la voix paternelle
De ce Dieu qui de vous se venge
en pardonnant!

ENSEMBLE
RACHEL
O céleste lumière!
Qui brille & qui m'éclaire
De ses feux radieux!
Bénissez moi, mon père,

My God! How may the justice of
this Council,
Opened under your auspices, be
proven in everyone's eyes?
How to recover and bring under
your law
The Jew and the heretic, enemies of
the faith?
How to restore them to your holy
truth?
And God answered me: Christian!
Through clemency!

LEOPOLD AND HIS FRIENDS
O sweet hope in which I don't yet
dare believe!

BROGNI
No, a judgment of death
Will not open the Council on this
sacred day!
(addressing Eléazar and Rachel)
And you, son of Israel, you whose
recalcitrant soul
Repulsed our fearsome and
threatening God,
Perhaps in future your less
rebellious heart
Will open to the paternal voice
Of this God who takes revenge on
you by forgiving you!

ENSEMBLE
RACHEL
O heavenly light!
That glows and shines on me
With its radiant flames!
Bless me, my father,

Et qu'à votre prière

Pour moi s'ouvrent les cieux!

And at your prayer

May the skies open for me!

BROGNI

O mon Dieu, je révère

Ta bonté tutélaire

Qui nous rend tous heureux!

Pour celle qui m'est chère

Qu'à la voix de son père

Enfin s'ouvrent les cieux!

BROGNI

O my God, I revere

Your protecting kindness

That makes us all happy!

For her who is dear to me

At the voice of her father

May the heavens finally open!

LEOPOLD

O bonté tutélaire!

Par qui mon coeur espère

Un destin plus heureux!

Près du Dieu qui l'éclaire

Son âme toute entière

S'élève vers les cieux!

LEOPOLD

O protecting kindness!

By whom my heart hopes for

A happier destiny!

Close to God who enlightens her

Her entire soul

Is raised to heaven!

CHOEUR

O bonté tutélaire!

O mon Dieu, je révère

Tes secrets glorieux!

Près du Dieu qui l'éclaire

Son âme toute entière

S'élève vers les cieux!

CHOIR

O protecting kindness!

O my God, I revere

Your glorious secrets!

Close to God who enlightens her

Her entire soul

Is raised to heaven!

ELEAZAR, regardant Rachel

Plus forte que la mort leur clémence cruelle

Triomphe de son coeur & me ravit mon bien!

ELEAZAR, looking at Rachel

Stronger than death, their cruel clemency

Overcomes her heart and takes away my wealth!

RACHEL, tendant vers lui les bras d'un air suppliant

Eleazar!

RACHEL, reaching out her arms to him in an imploring manner

Eléazar!

ELEAZAR

A leur dieu sois fidèle!

Moi je reste fidèle au mien!

ELEAZAR

Be faithful to their god!

I remain faithful to mine!

ENSEMBLE	ENSEMBLE
ELEAZAR	ELEAZAR
Dieu puissant de nos pères	Powerful God of our fathers
C'est toi seul qui m'éclaires	It is you alone who enlightens me
Et qui reçois mes voeux!	And receives my vows!
Et méprisant la terre,	And scorning the world,
Mon âme toute entière	My entire soul
S'élève vers les cieux!	Rises toward the heavens!
RACHEL	RACHEL
O céleste lumière!	O heavenly light!
[continues as above]	[continues as above]
BROGNI ET LE CHOEUR	BROGNI AND THE CHOIR
O bonté tutélaire	O protecting kindness!
[continues as choeur above]	[continues as choir above]
LEOPOLD	LEOPOLD
O bonté tutélaire	O protecting kindness!
[continues as Léopold above]	[continues as Léopold above]

(Rachel est à genoux devant Brogni qui la bénit. Le peuple se lève; toutes les bannières s'inclinent devant la nouvelle chrétienne. Une harmonie céleste se fait entendre. Léopold la regarde avec espérance & amour, & Eléazar dont on viens de détacher les fers, s'éloigne en jetant sur elle un regard de courroux. La toile tombe.)

(Rachel is kneeling before Brogni, who blesses her. The people get up; all the banners are lowered before the new Christian. A celestial harmony can be heard. Léopold looks at her with hope and love, and Eléazar, whose chains have just been removed, moves away as he gives her a look of anger. The curtain falls.)

Fin du 5ᵉ & dernier acte   End of the 5th and last act

Clearly, had Rachel's conversion and the expressions of clemency leading up to it been retained, *La Juive* would have been an entirely different opera. But a comparison of the early libretto manuscripts with later sources also reveals subtler transformations in her dual identity that led to a stronger Jewish persona: these transformations were tied to shifts in Rachel's relationship with Brogni and Eléazar. In the early stages, Rachel is overtly drawn to Brogni as both father and Christian leader, while she distances herself from Eléazar. In the final scene shown above, a noteworthy sign of Rachel's change of heart toward her adopted father occurs when she addresses him as "Eléazar" rather than "père," demonstrating that emotionally as well as spiritually she has pulled away. In n.a.fr. 22502, vol. xxiii, 1°: 4°(b), in which Rachel discovers her birth identity in Act IV, she is caught in the paternal struggle for her loyalty and, in essence, for her soul. Following an ensemble in which Brogni exclaims surprise and joy over his newfound daughter, Rachel passionately asks the cardinal, whom she addresses as "my father" (both spiritual and biological), to bless her:

Early version of Act IV, Scene vi

F-Pn, Ms., n.a.fr. 22502, 1°: 4°(b)

RACHEL

A vous que je retrouve à mon heure dernière,
Bénissez moi, mon père!
Bénissez moi! je vais mourir!

RACHEL

To you whom I find again in my last hour,
Bless me, my father!
Bless me! I am going to die!

After the ensemble is repeated, Brogni offers to save Rachel if she accepts the baptismal water, a gesture which sets off the fathers' struggle for control:

ELEAZAR

Prononce! à qui resteras tu fidèle?

ELEAZAR

Decide! To whom will you remain faithful?

BROGNI

Ton père te supplie!

BROGNI

Your father begs you!

ELEAZAR

Et notre Dieu t'appelle!

ELEAZAR

And our God calls you!

BROGNI

Avec moi le bonheur!

BROGNI

With me happiness!

ELEAZAR
Avec moi le martyre!

ELEAZAR
With me martyrdom!

BROGNI
Tu vivras!

BROGNI
You will live!

Rachel rejects Brogni's appeal at this point, but she seems to have immediately taken on a Christian point of view when she speaks angrily of Eléazar as an "infidel" who has tricked her:[72]

RACHEL
Oui c'est mon seul désir!
Cet infidèle à qui mon âme s'est
   donnée
Etait mon dieu, ma croyance & ma
   foi!
Il m'a trompée! il ne peut être à moi!

Sa vie est près d'une autre à jamais
   enchainée!
Je veux mourir & bénir mes
   bourreaux
(montrant Rannochia & les gardes
   qui entrent)
Dont l'arrêt va finir & ma vie & mes
   mains!

RACHEL
Yes, it is my sole desire!
This infidel to whom I gave my soul

Was my god, my belief, and my
   faith!
He has deceived me! He cannot
   belong to me!
His life is close to another forever
   chained!
I want to die and bless my
   executioners
(pointing to Rannochia and the
   guards who enter)
Whose sentence will end my life
   and my labors!

The fourth act in this version ends with Rachel momentarily remaining loyal to Eléazar (causing Brogni to fall to the stage, overcome with emotion), before her Act V conversion.

In the opera (première and post-première), a hint of Rachel's attraction to Brogni and to Christianity survives in his *air*, "Si la rigueur," when she responds to the cardinal's kindness. Joining the choral response, while Eléazar remains unmoved, Rachel sings: "Tant de bonté, tant de clémence / Désarment mon coeur malgré moi / Et les chrétiens

---

[72] "Rannochia," replaced by "Ruggiero" in later stages, appears in the draft scenario, draft verse, and autograph, where it is sometimes crossed through, with "Ruggiero" written above.

et leur croyance / Ne m'inspirent plus tant d'effroi!" ("So much kindness, so much clemency disarm my heart despite myself, and the Christians and their belief no longer inspire so much fear in me!") (see Example 4). In Act V, as she awaits execution, she sings with the Christian
women in the phrase, "Unissons nos prières / Vers le Dieu de nos pères"
("Let us join in prayer to the God of our fathers"). Although signaling
Rachel's religious charity (and willingness to die in her faith), these
phrases retain the stronger Christian affinity characterized by Scribe
in the developing libretto. Newark also suggests that Rachel's Christian identity is revealed to the audience in the cantabile of Eléazar's
Act IV *air*, when the father moves from his orientally embellished F
minor section to the diatonic A♭ major middle section as he sings in his
daughter's voice; in fact, the author interprets the *air* as "a testimony
to her non-Jewishness" and Eléazar's awareness of this identity as the
central source of his anguish.[73]

Other evidence reveals layers of transformations in the relationship
between Rachel and her two fathers. Draft verse of Act IV (F-Pn,
Ms., n.a.fr. 22502, vol. XXIII, 1°: 3°) includes the text of an *air* planned
for Eléazar.[74] Partbook *cahiers* copied by Leborne for Nourrit and his
"double" (understudy) Pierre-François Wartel contain an *Andantino*
with a lullaby-like text sung by Eléazar to a sleeping Rachel, beginning
with the words: "O fille chérie! / Ame de ma vie!" This *air* goes even
further than "Rachel, quand du Seigneur" in presenting the intimate
side of Eléazar's love for his adopted daughter.[75] Interpolated into his
Andantino (prior to B of an AABA structure) is a reminiscence of her
phrase "le jour du retour" from Léopold's Act I romance which she

---

[73] Newark, "Ceremony, Celebration and Spectacle," 163.
[74] The text for this planned *air*, with its reprise, is included in Act IV, Scene vi, of
this source, but the entire passage is crossed out, presumably by Scribe.
[75] The *air* is found in F-Po, Mat. 19ᶜ[315 (17) and (18), which are identical parts
copied by two different scribes, with similar alignment, suggesting that one part
was copied from the other. On the first page of both copies are the designations
"Eléazar" in the upper left-hand corner, "Acte 4ᵉ" in the top center, and "Andⁿᵒ"
above the first music stave; in the top right-hand corner of Mat. 19ᶜ[315 (17),
"Nourrit" is designated as the user of the part, and, likewise, in Mat. 19ᶜ[315
(18), "Vartel" (*sic*). (Wartel is shown to be Nourrit's understudy in Leborne's
records of copying, F-Po, RE 235, and F-Pan, AJ¹³289.)

undoubtedly intones in her sleep.[76] The aria's text gives Eléazar an image of protector similar to that embodied by Brogni in the Act IV *duettino*. In recitative that survives in *Schlesinger-Garland*, Brogni sings "Mourir, mourir si jeune!" before he sends for Eléazar and appeals to him to renounce his faith in order to save Rachel. In the printed libretti, manuscript performing parts, and the piano-vocal score (No. 20, mm. 74–137), a more elaborate version of Brogni's lament exposes a personal fear for her fate and an impulse to protect her. Using the same verb as Eléazar in his abandoned aria "O fille chérie," he reassures Rachel that he will watch over her. Eléazar tells her, "Je veille ici pour te bénir" ("I watch over you here to bless you"), and Brogni promises, "Je veillerai sur vous" ("I will watch over you"). This sixty-four-measure passage omitted from *Schlesinger-Garland* (which appears crossed out in red crayon in the autograph and which was not copied in the archival score[77]) reflects the early emphasis on him as the loving guardian father who offers life to Rachel, in lieu of a martyred death with Eléazar; in its opening words, which refer to "a secret voice" in Brogni's soul telling him to defend Rachel, there appears a Scribean foreshadowing of the mystery of her birth (unknown to him and to Rachel at this point).

Suppression of this material shifted the focus from paternal competition toward the opposition of Brogni and Eléazar as religious and historical symbols. In Act V, Rachel's choice of death and martyrdom over baptism represents a culmination of her devotion to her adopted father, expressed in her fear of abandoning him in Act II ("Lorsqu'à toi je me suis donnée"), and her loyalty to the Jewish faith she shares with him:

---

[76] See a transcription of the *Andantino* in Hallman, *"La Juive,"* vol. I, 228–30. Rachel sings a refrain of Léopold's romance in these early libretto versions; "Le jour du retour" is the final line of her text that appears in Act IV, Scene i, in F-Pn, Ms., n.a.fr. 22502, vol. xxiii, 1°:4°(b), and in Act V, Scene i, in F-Pn, Ms., n.a.fr. 22502, vol. xxiii, 1°:4°(a).

[77] As is evident in the *violon principal* short score, a number of cuts within this section preceded its entire omission prior to the copying of the archival score. There is no indication that these sixty-four measures were copied into the archival score since there is no evidence of a break in copying, change of paper, or crossing out of measures, and because the number of pages (thirty-six) corresponds to Leborne's indication of thirty-six copied pages in F-Po, RE 235.

Act V, Scene iv, *Final*

Schlesinger-Garland

ELEAZAR, comme à voix basse
Rachel, je vais mourir!
Veux-tu vivre?

ELEAZAR, in a low voice
Rachel, I am going to die!
Do you want to live?

RACHEL
Pourquoi? pour aimer? et souffrir?

RACHEL
Why? To love? And suffer?

ELEAZAR
Non! Pour briller au rang suprême!

ELEAZAR
No! To shine in the highest rank!

RACHEL, après un grand silence
Sans vous?

RACHEL, after a long silence
Without you?

ELEAZAR
Sans moi!

ELEAZAR
Without me!

RACHEL
Comment?

RACHEL
How?

ELEAZAR
Ils veulent sur ton front verser l'eau
du baptême,
Le veux-tu, mon enfant?

ELEAZAR
On your brow they want to pour
baptismal water,
Is that what you want, my child?

RACHEL
Qui? moi! chrétienne? moi!
La flamme étincelle,
Venez!

RACHEL
Who? Me! A Christian? Me!
The flames sparkle!
Come on!

ELEAZAR
Leur Dieu t'appelle!

ELEAZAR
Their God calls you!

RACHEL
Et le nôtre m'attend!
C'est le ciel qui m'inspire,
Je choisis le trépas!
Oui, courons au martyre,
Dieu nous ouvre ses bras!

RACHEL
And ours awaits me!
I am inspired by heaven,
I choose death!
Yes, let us hurry to our martyrdom,
God opens His arms to us!

ELEAZAR	ELEAZAR
Ah!	Ah!
C'est le ciel qui l'inspire,	She is inspired by heaven,
Je te rends au trépas!	I shall let you die!
Viens, courons au martyre,	Come, let us hurry to our martyrdom,
Dieu nous ouvre ses bras!	God opens His arms to us!

Palianti's *mise en scène* manual indicates that a frozen *tableau* and "profound silence" follow Eléazar's question, "Veux-tu vivre?"[78] With her response, Rachel seals her loyalty and her Jewish identity. The emphatic reinforcement of loyalty to the faith and father she has accepted, diametrically opposed to the pro-Brogni and conversion solutions, clearly makes her a Jewess in more than name only. The withholding of information about Rachel's Christian birth, while offering a penultimate shock to the audience as it illustrates Eléazar's vengeance, greatly lessens the religious duality so prominent in the even more conflicted persona of early libretto stages. But this last-minute revelation of Christian identity also diffused the opera's presentation of the Church's persecution of Jews, in allowing her "kinship" with the predominantly Christian audiences, although less so than in earlier stages.[79] Certainly a sentimentally happy ending of her conversion

---

[78] Cohen, *Staging Manuals*, 150. Compare the indication of dramatic silence in the excerpted text above.

[79] Pierrakos, "Chrétienté, judaïté et la musique," 23, writes that the revelation allowed the audience to have compassion for Rachel that would more naturally be given her as a Christian than as a Jew. The perception of Rachel's religious identity may have also been affected by a singer's ethnicity or physical appearance, although Newark, "Ceremony, Celebration and Spectacle," 156, suggests that her "physical traits could easily be mapped onto those of the singer who created the role." A few articles imply that successive interpreters were Jewish, including Nathan-Treillet (1815–73) and Catinka Heinefetter (1819–58) – and Falcon herself was identified as such in "F. Halévy," *Les Archives israélites* 23, no. 4 (1 April 1862): 188. Théophile Gautier, in a review of 1841 reprinted in *Histoire de l'art dramatique en France depuis vingt-cinq ans*, 6 vols. (Leipzig: Edition Hetzel, 1858–9), vol. II, 90, writes: "Since Mlle Falcon, no one had performed the beautiful Jewess Rachel with an appearance more pleasing and believable; there is an excellent reason for that, as Mlle Heinefetter is Jewish herself and very beautiful. And applause of the Israelites for her was not lacking. The twelve

would have given a decidedly more "Christian tone" to the opera.[80] Some critics, however, viewed the final twist of the plot as ridiculous and implausible (representing but one complaint among many about illogical aspects of Scribe's story).

It was Scribe, according to Véron, who created the final ending of Rachel's death in a cauldron of boiling oil (or water), one that he claims audiences found unappealing. In his memoirs, he makes no mention of the earlier ending:

> The staging of the denouement of *La Juive* scarcely pleased the public of the Opéra. M. Duponchel was the only one to admire this staging. "Why, you're the one," he said to Scribe, "who invented this denouement in a cauldron! Having the Jewess boiled in place of burning her at the stake as would be typical! The Classicists would never have had this stroke of genius! This denouement, M. Scribe, will give you the greatest honor all your life."[81]

In Véron's attribution, Duponchel was drawn to the theatricality of the ending, its shock value, and its supposed originality, at least for Inquisition scenes. In fact, the desire for a more tumultuous, melodramatic, tragic ending may have sealed the decision to rework the denouement. The cauldron (*chaudière*) as an instrument of death, rather than being original as Duponchel thought, may have been a literary borrowing or historical reminder, or both (see pp. 246–7 below).

Although audience members offended by the gruesome execution may have preferred Scribe's earlier concept, the authors of *La Juive*

tribes had their representatives there, but it is fair to say that the Christians brought out their bravos at several reprises." See also Philarète Chasles, "Notice sur *La Juive*," in *Les Beautés de l'Opéra; ou, Chefs-d'oeuvre lyriques* (Paris: Soulié, 1845), 5.

[80] A much altered *La Juive* given at Drury Lane in December 1835 ended with the saving of Rachel, as reported in *Le Ménestrel* 108 (27 December 1835): 4.

[81] Véron, *Mémoires*, vol. III, 181: "La mise en scène du dénoûment de *La Juive* ne plut guère au public de l'Opéra. Cette mise en scène n'excita l'admiration que de M. Duponchel. 'Comment, disait-il à M. Scribe, c'est vous qui avez inventé ce dénoûment dans chaudière! c'est vous qui avez imaginé de faire bouillir la juive au lieu de la faire brûler vulgairement sur un bûcher! Les classiques n'auraient jamais trouvé ce trait de génie! Ce dénoûment, monsieur Scribe, vous fera toute votre vie le plus grand honneur.' "

undoubtedly realized that the conversion ending weakened the opera's basic critique, and one would imagine that Halévy in particular endorsed the Jews' retention of their faith and their martyrdom. Previously, with Brogni's second powerful appeal for clemency, the weight of intolerance would have shifted more heavily away from the Christian Council and toward the Jew Eléazar, giving a stronger portrait of Christianity as the beneficent religion and Judaism as a morally depleted one. In addition to the omission of the Rachel–Brogni interactions outlined above, the alterations in Acts IV and V that accompanied the change of ending further point to a more pronounced focus on Christian intolerance and the despotism of Church and State. The decision to open Act V with a chorus rejoicing over the imminent death of the Jews, instead of Eudoxie's suicide *air* or other solutions which preceded it (see pp. 226–7 below), sealed the image of a Christian mass unwilling to be moved by clemency:

Act V, Scene i
23 February 1835 libretto[82]

CHOEUR DE GENS DU PEUPLE, se précipitant au milieu de la tente préparée pour recevoir les membres du concile, et contemplant les apprêts du supplice.	CHOIR OF THE PEOPLE, rushing forward to the middle of the tent prepared to receive the Council members and gazing at the preparations for the execution.
Plaisir, ivresse et joie! Contre eux que l'on déploie Et le fer et le feu! Gloire! Gloire! gloire à Dieu!	Pleasure, ecstasy and joy! Against them deploy Sword and fire! Glory! Glory! Glory to God!
PLUSIEURS GENS DU PEUPLE Plus de travaux et plus d'ouvrage,	SEVERAL PEOPLE No more toil or labor,

[82] The text also appears in the 18 February libretto and in the second edition of the libretto, and corresponds with that in the copyist's libretto, but as Scene iii (following Eudoxie's "Adieux terre chérie"); part of it can be seen as Act V, Scene i, on a loose-leaf sheet of draft verse, F-Pn, Ms., n.a.fr. 22543.

Jour de liesse et de plaisir!

Pour nous trouver sur leur passage,

Amis, hâtons-nous d'accourir!

Day of jubilation and pleasure!

To be there when they pass,

Friends, hurry, run!

D'AUTRES GENS DU PEUPLE

O spectacle qui nous enchante!

OTHER PEOPLE

O spectacle that enchants us!

D'AUTRES

Des juifs nous serons donc vengés.

OTHERS

On these Jews we will be avenged.

D'AUTRES

On dit que dans l'onde bouillante

Vivans ils seront tous plongés!

OTHERS

They say that into the boiling water

They will be plunged alive!

CHOEUR

Plaisir, ivresse et joie!

[continues as above]

CHOIR

Pleasure, ecstasy and joy!

[continues as above]

This version (to which the *Gazette de France* reviewer was undoubtedly referring when he complained about the ludicrousness of Christians boiling Jews in a "grand pot-au-feu") is slightly altered in specific wording in the published scores, but not in meaning. In the choral setting of the published scores, as well as the autograph and archival score, the opening phrase "Plaisir, ivresse et joie!" is replaced by "Quel plaisir, quelle joie," perhaps to accommodate Halévy's rhythmic ideas. Other minor changes include the substitution of the phrase "Voyez tout le monde accourir" for "Amis, hâtons-nous d'accourir!" and the addition of "Ah! tâchons, oui tâchons de bien nous placer." The length of this chorus attests to the intended weight of its message: although fast-clipped, 249 measures in *Schlesinger-Garland* (and 251 in *Schlesinger-Lemoine*) precede the number's final instrumental section introduced by the annunciatory phrase, "Voici l'heure." Within the B minor setting, Halévy's innocuous-sounding D major sections give an ironic twist to the crowd's sadistic intent, sharpened in the final, B major phrases about plunging the Jews into the boiling pot (*Schlesinger-Garland*, Act V, No. 20, mm. 233–49; *Schlesinger-Lemoine*, No. 23, mm. 231–47). The reviewer for the anticlerical *Le Temps* found the

chorus one "of powerful originality, in which the ferocious cries, dia-
bolical curiosity, and all the fanaticism of a population of the Middle
Ages is rendered."[83]

In the Act V finale, immediately following the funeral procession
of soldiers, monks, pages, cardinals, guards, and penitents, Ruggiero,
who enters with four men dressed in black, announces that Léopold
has escaped death for his role in the illegal liaison. This announcement, originally placed in Act IV in earlier versions,[84] adds weight to
Christian hypocrisy, particularly in its new position after the chorus
happily sings of executing the Jews. The irony does not escape Eléazar,
who sardonically comments on Christian justice before he discovers
that Léopold's freedom was won through Rachel's own declaration
of his innocence. (As interpreted by Leich-Galland, the orchestra's deceptive cadence on the word "innocent" suggests the falsity of her
statement.[85]) Ruggiero then proclaims that the Jews' guilt rests on
their accusation of a "Prince of the Empire" and their profanation
of the "holy majesty" of kings. Prayers of Brogni, who is flanked by
Council members, and the chorus ("Au pêcheur Dieu soyez propice"),
rather than dissipating the sense of Christian injustice, throw it into
sharp relief. The victimization of the "heretics" and their transformation into religious martyrs is further enhanced through the visual-
ization of a barefooted, white-robed Rachel moving in touching pan-
tomime, and through Halévy's scoring, from the doleful, bare sound
of the march to the haunting clarinet and horn accompaniment as the
Jewess sings of leaving a world of pain (*Schlesinger-Garland*, No. 22,
Schlesinger-Lemoine, No. 25, mm. 136–43). With the final jubilant cry of
the chorus, supported by the full orchestra, the opera's central message
becomes even more pronounced: rather than a return to the "Plaisir,
ivresse et joie" of the printed libretti, the phrase "Oui, c'en est fait et des
juifs nous sommes vengés" ("Yes, it is done and we are avenged on the

---

[83] L.V., *Le Temps*, 26 February 1835; *Dossier de presse parisienne*, ed. Leich-Galland,
161.

[84] It appears in Act IV, Scene vi, in F-Pn, Ms., n.a.fr. 22502, vol. xxiii, 1°:4°, and in
Act IV, Scene viii, in the F-Pan, AJ¹³202, copyist's libretto.

[85] Leich-Galland, "*La Juive*: Commentaire musical et littéraire," 83.

Jews") ends the opera as it began, with the juxtaposition of Christian piety, sadistic antisemitism, and institutional injustice (see Example 11). Its placement of the phrase immediately after Eléazar's own shout of vengeance reinforces the Voltairean-infused opprobrium of the destructiveness engendered by the hatred of both religious sides. Yet, as at the outset of *La Juive*, the weight of culpability is cast most vehemently on the authoritarian Church and State and its illiberal supporters.

The Jewish characters Eléazar and Rachel, humanized largely through the power and expressivity of Halévy's music, move well beyond convention, yet fundamental to their construction are stereotypes with numerous literary precedents. These stereotypes – the mercenary, recalcitrant Jew, epitomized by Shylock in Shakespeare's *The Merchant of Venice* (1598), and the kind, beautiful daughter who serves as his foil – belong to a literary tradition joining *The Merchant of Venice* and Christopher Marlowe's *The Jew of Malta* (1590) with works of later eras that feature Jewish characters, including Sir Walter Scott's *Ivanhoe* (1819).[1] In *The Jew of Malta*, Barabas is father of Abigail; in *The Merchant of Venice*, Shylock of Jessica; and in *Ivanhoe*, Isaac of York of the much-admired Rebecca. The pairing of a daughter with a wifeless Jew also appears in the influential German drama *Nathan der Weise* (1779) by the Enlightenment playwright Gotthold Ephraim Lessing (1729–81). Although Nathan, like Shylock, is a wealthy moneylender, his wisdom, honesty, and humaneness make him a more idealized character type than the Christian-hating, vengeful Shylock.[2] Shylock, and not Nathan, inspired the character of Eléazar, but Recha, Nathan's daughter, carries a double identity similar to Rachel's: both are adopted daughters whose Christian roots have been kept secret and are revealed to

---

[1] Edgar Rosenberg, *From Shylock to Svengali: Jewish Stereotypes in English Fiction* (Stanford: Stanford University Press, 1960), 34, believes Marlowe began the precedent of the old mercenary Jew with a beautiful daughter. Thomas Marc Parrott, in editorial notes to Shakespeare's *Twenty-three Plays and the Sonnets*, rev. ed. (New York: Charles Scribner's Sons, 1953), 210, adds that the playwright modeled Jessica after Marlowe's Abigail.

[2] Moses Debré, *The Image of the Jew in French Literature from 1800 to 1908*, trans. Gertrude Hirschler, with an introduction by Anna Krakowski (New York: Ktav, 1970), 21, discusses Shylock and Nathan the Wise as predominant types of Jewish characters in French literature. Lessing's character is viewed as a tribute to Moses Mendelssohn.

readers / audiences only after their identities as Jewesses have been established. The coupling of the daughter with a Christian lover also
appears in these sources – Abigail is wooed by Lodowick, Jessica
by Lorenzo, Recha by the Templier, and Rebecca by Brian de Bois-
Guilbert, the Templar (and admired by Ivanhoe himself). In her role
as a Jewess desired by a Christian lover, a stereotype sometimes identified as "la belle juive," Rachel exudes an aura of oriental exoticism
concordant with Scott's characterization of Rebecca.

Scribe, like others of his generation, admired Shakespeare and Scott
and clearly knew both *The Merchant of Venice* and *Ivanhoe*. From the
1820s, Shakespeare had captured the esteem of French Romantics
and had a certain popular vogue in France. In *Racine et Shakespeare*
(1823), Stendhal spoke of Shakespeare's plays as masterpieces and
models for the creation of insightful, topical tragedies.[3] Hugo, in his
famous preface to *Cromwell* (1827), declared Shakespeare the epitome
of "drame."[4] French translations of Shakespeare's works had been
available since the late eighteenth century, but the French public became re-engaged with his works in the 1820s and 1830s with the appearance of a number of new editions,[5] performances of Shakespeare's
dramas, and the endorsements of Romantic writers. A publication of
The Merchant of Venice appeared in France in 1827,[6] the year that a
troop of English actors scored brilliant successes in Shakespeare at

[3] Stendhal, *Racine et Shakespeare* (Paris: Bossange, 1823), 2–3; David-Owen Evans,
Le Drame moderne à l'époque romantique (Geneva: Slatkine Reprints, 1974), 13.
[4] Victor Hugo, *Cromwell* (Paris: A. Dupont, 1828), ii; Gary Taylor, *Reinventing
Shakespeare: A Cultural History from the Restoration to the Present* (New York: Oxford
University Press, 1989), 168.
[5] For example, *Oeuvres complètes de Shakspeare* [*sic*], *traduites de l'anglais par
Letourneur, nouvelle édition, revue et corrigée par F. Guizot et A. P.* [*Pichot*], *traducteur
de Lord Byron, précédée d'une notice biographique et littéraire, sur Shakspeare, par
F. Guizot*, 13 vols. (Paris: Ladvocat, 1821), and *Oeuvres dramatiques de Shakspeare*
[*sic*], *traduites de l'anglais par Letourneur, nouvelle édition, précédée d'une notice
biographique et littéraire par M. Horace Meyer*, 2 vols. (Paris: A. Saintin, 1835). An
edition overseen by Alexandre Dumas was published by Marchant in 1839–40.
[6] An English publication with French notes appears in *Bibliographie de la France*,
December 1827: *Merchant of Venice: A Comedy in 5 Acts, by W. Shakspeare* [*sic*], *as
Performed at the Theatres Royal in Drury-Lane and Covent-Garden, with Explanatory
French Notes* (Paris: Goetschy, 1827).

the Odéon, Théâtre-Français, and Théâtre-Italien.[7] Among many novels that captivated French readers, *Ivanhoe* ranked as one of the most widely read between 1826 and 1830, appearing in ten French editions.[8] The popularity of the novel inspired stage versions in Paris and elsewhere, including the pasticcio *Ivanhoé* based on music by Rossini arranged by Antonio Pacini (1778–1866), which had its première at the Odéon in Paris in 1826.[9] With the vogue of Scott and Shakespeare in French literary culture, it is not surprising to find among Scribe's many book lists the citation "Théâtre étranger–Shakspeare–Goethe– Schiller," as well as several references to Walter Scott.[10] Scribe could have known Lessing's play through the multivolume publication *Chefs-d'oeuvre des théâtres étrangers*, published in France in 1827, possibly the same series of foreign literature to which Scribe refers as "Théâtre étranger."[11] In the same list, Scribe includes "Mis Edgeworth" (Maria Edgeworth, 1767–1849), an Anglo-Irish writer who used a number of Jewish characters in her novels.[12] Like Scott, who heads chapters

---

7 Evans, *Le Drame moderne*, 62, notes that four years earlier the troop's Shakespeare performances in Paris had met with a comparatively cold reception.
8 Lyons, *Le Triomphe du livre*, 86–7. Lyons also lists the best-selling French translations of Scott's *L'Antiquaire*, *L'Abbé*, and *Quentin Durward* for 1826–30, and of *Woodstock* and *Château périlleux* for 1831–5.
9 A better-known stage work based on the novel is Heinrich Marschner's opera *Der Templer und die Jüdin*, first performed in 1829 in Leipzig.
10 Further pointing to a familiarity with the author, Scribe compares a scenic Swiss view to a Scott passage in his 1826 *carnet de voyage* (F-Pn, Ms., n.a.fr. 22584, vol. I, fol. 19^v), includes "Rebecca de Walter Scott" among his collection of dramatic ideas (F-Pn, Ms., n.a.fr. 22584, vol. VIII, fol. 14^r), and begins a poem draft, "Sir Walter Scott est bon anglais" (F-Pn, Ms., n.a.fr. 22584, vol. X, fol. 22^v).
11 *Chefs-d'oeuvre des théâtres étrangers . . . traduits en français. Lessing, Nathan le Sage, avec une notice signée P. B. Emilie Galotti, traduit par M. le c^{te} de Sainte-Aulaire. Minna de Barnhelm, avec une notice signée Merville* (Paris: Rapilly, 1827).
12 Frank Montagu Modder, *The Jew in the Literature of England to the End of the Nineteenth Century* (Cleveland and New York: The World Publishing Co., 1960), 131–7, discusses Edgeworth's Jewish characters, most of whom are based on "the old stock figure of the wicked Jew." These include three Jewish villains in *Moral Tales* (1801) and a Jewish moneylender named Solomon in *Belinda* (1801). In *Harrington* (1816), Edgeworth elaborates on the unjust treatment of Jacob, a poor honest Jewish peddler, and allows the protagonist Harrington to be attracted to a young Jewess, who is revealed as the christened daughter of a Christian mother.

of *Ivanhoe* with epigraphs from *The Merchant of Venice*, *The Jew of Malta*, and *The Jew*,[13] Scribe apparently familiarized himself with several works centered on Jewish characters and randomly blended elements of plot and characterization when they suited his dramatic purposes. Scribe's working *carnets* starkly reveal his habit of splicing together subjects and basic dramatic ideas from various sources: for example, Scribe reminds himself to "combine this subject with [Yermolof?] or Le Favori" and notes, "Les Patriciens and La Nonne sanglante / two ideas to combine for a grand opera."[14] As acknowledged in several Parisian reviews of the first performances of *La Juive*, and reiterated in standard literature on the opera, *The Merchant of Venice* and *Ivanhoe* served as literary sources for the opera's Jewish characterization, largely through indirect borrowing rather than direct quotation;[15] Scribe likely also drew from *Nathan der Weise* and *The Jew of Malta*.

LA BELLE JUIVE

Rachel, whose forbidden love affair sets off a chain of events in *La Juive*, belongs to a host of beautiful, desirable, and doomed heroines in nineteenth-century opera, although her portrayal as Jewess is more narrowly linked to the exotic "la belle juive." The sexual implications of this type merge with elements of the ambiguous religious identity discussed previously, touching her roles as love interest of a Christian prince and daughter of a Shylockian father. Scribe outlined the romance between Rachel and Léopold in what may be the earliest plot

---

[13] Richard Cumberland wrote *The Jew*, first performed at London's Drury Lane Theatre in the late eighteenth century, and the comic opera *The Jew of Mogadore* (published 1808).

[14] F-Pn, Ms., n.a.fr. 22584, vol. VIII, fol. 68^r; vol. IX, fol. 5^r.

[15] Among reviews noting Rachel's modeling on *Ivanhoe*'s Rebecca are those in *L'Entr'acte*, 26 February 1835, and *Le Ménestrel*, 1 March 1835; see *Dossier de presse parisienne*, ed. Leich-Galland, 36, 111. *The Merchant of Venice* and *Ivanhoe* are noted as principal sources in "(La) Juive," in Larousse, *Grand Dictionnaire*, vol. IX, part 2, 1090; see also Becker, "'Dieu de nos pères,'" 36–8.

8 Early sketch of "la belle juive," from the *carnet* of Eugène Scribe, 1812–33

sketch of the opera. In tiny, scrawled handwriting in a notebook labeled "Quelques idées des pièces" (see Illustration 8), he writes:[16]

La belle juive opera	The Beautiful Jewess opera
1er acte son epoux la quitte le soir	1st act her betrothed leaves her in the evening
2e – elle se presente comme femme de chambre chez sa rivale – apprend qu'elle est mariée	2nd – she presents herself as chambermaid at her rival's – learns that she is married
marie 3e – le voyant ~~pres à se marier~~ elle dicte qu'il a eu commerce avec une juive et que c'est elle – on les condamne tous les deux	3rd – seeing him married she says that he has had a liaison with a Jewess and that it is she – both are condemned

[16] F-Pn, Ms., n.a.fr. 22584, vol. VIII, fol. 66r. Scribe began this *carnet* in 1812, but the few dates scattered throughout point to his using it at least until the early 1830s to collect thoughts and rough scenario sketches. Given the occurrence of the entry "La belle juive" a few pages after the date 1832 in "La Marquise et le comedien/9-Xbr-1832–reviens de Paris," we can surmise that it was written no earlier than December 1832 and perhaps in the early part of 1833. This dating cannot be certain, however, as his *carnet* pages are not always written chronologically; in other *carnets* he demonstrates the habit of returning to pages partially used and writing in the remaining space.

4e – elle retraite ses aveux – s'avoue seule coupable	4th – she withdraws her confession – avows that she alone is guilty
5 – l'autodafe –	5 – *auto-da-fé* –

Scribe's thin sketch reveals his dramatic focus on the taboo affair between Jew and Christian – a redressing of operatic convention – as well as on other circumstances leading from it: the love triangle between wife, mistress, and lover; the condemnation of the two lovers after the Jewess's declaration; her subsequent disavowal, claiming guilt only for herself; and the death by "l'autodafé," apparently of the Jewess alone.[17] Curiously, Eléazar is missing in this rough outline. Perhaps Scribe was not yet thinking of his subject's deeper social implications, but concentration on romantic plotting would not necessarily preclude this possibility, for he characteristically made controversial subjects palatable to theatrical authorities and audiences by placing the love story strongly in the foreground. And he may not have begun to expand his preliminary structure with borrowed literary ideas.

An entry in the same *carnet* on earlier pages entitled "Rebecca de Walter Scott," however, shows that he had intentions of using this character as a model, although his specification "Bukingham [*sic*] de [Peveril?] 5 actes" below the title hints that he was considering Rebecca for another work.[18] As he does not check off this entry or designate "Traité" next to it (as with other subjects he goes on to realize – including "la belle juive"), Scribe may never have fleshed out the specific dramatic ideas included under this heading about "une jeune personne charmante" who is brought to court and with whom Buckingham falls in love. There is little in the sketch to point to Scribe's borrowings from *Ivanhoe* in *La Juive*. But the fact that he listed it as a potential source makes it conceivable that at some point between December 1832 and August 1833, the date of the contract for *La Juive*, he interpolated elements of the novel with dramatic ideas set aside for "la belle juive."

---

[17] A liaison between lovers from opposing sides has many operatic precedents, although Gerhard, *The Urbanization of Opera*, 76, credits Rossini and his librettists in *Le Siège de Corinthe* (1826) with the establishment of this plot convention – perhaps suggesting its use as particularly influential.

[18] F-Pn, Ms., n.a.fr. 22584, vol. VIII, fol. 14^r.

Scribe's first working title gives a clear signal that his *juive* is, like Rebecca and other contemporary Jewesses, an object of desire. Rosenberg designates "la belle juive" as a type that reached its apotheosis in Jessica but later evolved into an exotic prostitute in stories of Balzac, Maupassant, Zola, and Proust – for example, Esther in Balzac's *Splendeurs et misères des courtisanes*.[19] Lucette Czyba, in her examination of the nineteenth-century myth of "la femme orientale," including "l'esclave orientale," views the type as an object of fantasy.[20] Often she was a woman of extraordinary beauty, as in Hugo's 1835 poem "Sultane favorite" of *Les Orientales*.[21]

In one of many passages in *Ivanhoe* that elaborate on the appearance of Rebecca, Scott describes Ivanhoe's admiration of the "beautiful features, and fair form, and lustrous eyes of the lovely Rebecca – eyes whose brilliancy was shaded, and, as it were, mellowed, by the fringe of her long silken eyelashes, and which a minstrel would have compared to the evening star darting its rays through a bower of jessamine" (Chapter 27). In *La Juive*, the most direct textual reference to Rachel's beauty comes not from a male admirer but from her rival Eudoxie. In

[19] Rosenberg, *From Shylock to Svengali*, 34; Maurice Bloch, "La Femme juive dans le roman et au théâtre," *Conférence faite à la Société des études juives le 23 janvier 1892, extrait de la Revue des études juives XXIII* (Paris: Librairie A. Durlacher, 1892), 9. Marie Lathers refers to the image and the popularity of the Jewish model from the 1820s to 1850s in "Posing the 'Belle Juive': Jewish Models in Nineteenth-Century Paris," *Woman's Art Journal* 21, no. 1 (spring–summer 2000): 27–32. Cormac Newark links Rachel and her creator Cornélie Falcon to Balzac's Coralie of *Illusions perdues* in "Ceremony, Celebration and Spectacle," 158–9.

[20] See Czyba's "Misogynie et gynophobie dans *La Fille aux yeux d'or*," *La Femme au XIXᵉ siècle: Littérature et idéologie*, ed. Jean-François Tetu *et al.* (Lyon: Presses Universitaires de Lyon, 1978), 141, and *Mythes et idéologie de la femme dans les romans de Flaubert* (Lyon: Presses Universitaires de Lyon, 1983). Likewise, Pierrakos, "Chrétienté, judaïté et la musique," 23, defines the exotic Jewess as "un fantasme" ("a fantasy") in nineteenth-century literature.

[21] Victor Hugo, *Théâtre complet* (Paris: Gallimard, 1963–4).

Que m'importe, juive adorée,	Adored Jewess, who brings
Un sein d'ébène, un front vermeil.	A breast of ebony, cheeks of ruby.
Tu n'es point blanche ni cuivrée,	You are neither white nor copper,
Mais il semble qu'on t'a dorée,	But it seems that you have been gilded
Avec un rayon de soleil.	With a ray of sun.

the Act III duet, although omitted after the première, Eudoxie sings of Rachel:

Act III, Scene iii, No. 14

Schlesinger-Lemoine (omitted from *Schlesinger-Garland*)

Que d'attraits! qu'elle est belle!	What charms! How beautiful she is!
Son oeil noir étincelle	Her black eye sparkles
D'un sombre désespoir,	With dark despair,
Oui, je vois dans ses yeux	Yes, I see in her eyes
Un sombre désespoir!	A dark despair!

Rachel remarks equally on Eudoxie's beauty by repeating her first line as she looks at her "with jealousy." In a developing stage represented by the manuscript libretto F-Pn, Ms., n.a.fr. 22502, vol. XXIII, 1°:4°(b), when Brogni regrets Rachel's impending death, he, too, is moved by her beauty: "Hélas! qu'elle était belle." With greater impact than these references (abandoned at different stages) is the conveyance of Rachel's attractiveness through costuming and through her seduction of a prince who disguises himself to be near her, serenades her, and almost elopes with her.

Rachel's feminine persona blends innocence with eroticism. She appears young and naive, and in love with a man she assumes to be a simple Jewish painter; she does not discover his true identity until the shocking revelations of Act II, that he is Christian, and of Act III, that he is married. A review in *Le Journal de Paris et des départemens* (28 February 1835) spoke of her as "this poor little Rachel, who has succumbed like the Hussites" to the attentions of Léopold.[22] In Scribe's early ideas for the draft scenario, there was an even greater focus on Rachel's innocence and on the background of her romance with Samuel/Léopold. In the sketched paragraph of Act I, Scene ii, later suppressed with a single vertical pen stroke, Rachel has an exchange with Samuel about his work that reveals her belief that he has been away painting the cardinal's portrait, not fighting a battle.[23] Even more dramatically extraneous is

[22] *Dossier de presse parisienne*, ed. Leich-Galland, 90.
[23] F-Pn, Ms., n.a.fr. 22502, vol. XXIII, 1°:2°, 3.

the excised paragraph's suggestion that Rachel is Samuel's painting student. In the opera, references to Samuel as painter do not come until the seder scene.

Allusions to Rachel's licentiousness seem equally strong. Despite her lack of awareness of Léopold's status, her liaison with a married man hints at a non-conventional sexuality, which is intimated but not realized in *Ivanhoe*: Rebecca, who is "not without a touch of female weakness," loves the affianced Ivanhoe and he admires her, but he is "too good a Catholic to retain the same class of feelings towards a Jewess" (Chapter 28). Unlike Rebecca's "purity" depicted in much of the novel, Rachel's is somewhat tainted. The conservative reviewer for *La Gazette de France* (27 February 1835), who viewed *La Juive* as Voltairean blasphemy, referred to Rachel as a "woman without morals" and a "licentious woman" whose depravity defiled marital bonds and degraded a royal personage.[24] Extending his ideological spin to his judgment of her night rendezvous with Léopold, he writes of "Mlle Rachel who, all Jewess that she is, has received an extremely philosophical and liberal education, as one can see."[25]

Her sexuality is partially implied through hints of oriental exoticism, enhanced through costuming, music, and elements of text and plot. Rachel's Act I costume, a tight-bodiced dress somewhat reminiscent of a Swiss folk outfit (without décolletage and at a maidenly length above her ankles in one artist's rendering), gives a simple, somewhat demure effect, but the Asiatic turban and scarves seem to belie this innocence; in du Faget's watercolor, the costume is blue and white, atop pale yellow fabric trimmed in black; the exposed sleeve linings are yellow, and gold tassles ornament the sash hanging from her waist (see Illustration 9).[26] A portrait of Falcon by Grévedon (1837) shows the same costume in a mustard gold fabric under the bodice lacing, gold tassles on the sleeves,

---

[24] *Dossier de presse parisienne*, ed. Leich-Galland, 56.   [25] *Ibid.*, 54.
[26] Watercolor by du Faget, F-Po, [D. 216 (O²), fol. 82. A lithograph by Devéria (F-Po) shows a floor-length skirt. Another watercolor for the first production, F-Po, [D. 216 (O²), fol. 84, shows the same costume, but without the blue and white overdress; without a turban, her hair hangs down in youthful braids from the back of her head.

9 Costumes for *La Juive*, Paris Opéra, 1835: Rachel (Cornélie Falcon), Eléazar (Adolphe Nourrit), and Princess Eudoxie (Julie Dorus-Gras); watercolor by Eugène du Faget, costume design by Paul Lormier

and gold accents on the headpiece close to the face; in other portraits, the sensuality of Rachel, or of Falcon as Rachel, is made more explicit.[27] Rachel's second-act costume, introduced for the private Jewish service, had a decidedly more Eastern flavor; it was a flowing sky blue silk caftan ornamented with purple velvet and touches of gold.[28] Although the turban and scarves of Rachel's first-production costumes may have been modeled on a variety of sources, they bear an affinity with Scott's description of the "turbaned and caftaned" Rebecca – whom Ivanhoe at first mistakes for an Arabian woman – featuring the symbolic yellow fabric also chosen by Delacroix in his 1832 watercolor of a Jewess.[29] Rebecca first appears in "a sort of Eastern dress, which she wore according to the fashion of the females of her nation," a turban of yellow silk decorated with an ostrich feather, a vest with "golden and pearl-studded clasps," and jewels "of inestimable value" (Chapter 7).

At the première, and perhaps in successive early performances, Rachel's appearance in Act III disguised as a slave carried allusions to an oriental harem. Among the act's initial scenes abandoned shortly after the première, Rachel, who has been brought before Eudoxie as "une pauvre fille inconnue, étrangère" ("a poor unknown, foreign girl"), asks the princess if she can be admitted as one of her slaves: "Parmi vos nombreuses esclaves / Daignez pour aujourd'hui m'admettre!" ("As one of your many slaves, deign to accept me for today!")[30] In the 1835 libretto, she takes on this persona during a celebration of Léopold's

---

[27] Grevedon's portrait appears on the cover of *L'Avant-scène opéra* 100 (1987). See also the Falcon portrait in "L'Oeuvre à l'affiche," *ibid.*, 111.

[28] Another portrait of Falcon, seemingly in Rachel's second-act costume, appears in Philip Robinson, "(Marie) Cornélie Falcon," in *The New Grove Dictionary of Opera*, ed. Sadie, vol. II, 110. Also see F-Pan, AJ[13]202, costume inventories.

[29] Eugène Delacroix, *Jeune Femme juive assise* (Musée du Louvre, Cliché RMN-Gérard Blot). The turbaned Oriental permeated French Romantic art, literature, and ballet, as described by Marie-Jacques Hoog in "Ces Femmes en turban," in *Women in French Literature*, ed. Michel Guggenheim (Saratoga, CA: ANMA Libri, 1988), 117–23; see also Marian E. Smith, "Music for the Ballet-Pantomime at the Paris Opéra, 1825–1850" (Ph.D. diss., Yale University, 1988), 38ff.

[30] Act III, Scenes ii and iii, 23 February 1835 libretto; *Schlesinger-Lemoine*, No. 14, Duo, mm. 11–13, 132–4; F-Po, A.509a, vol. II, 39, 52. See the abandoned material in F-Po, Mat. 19[e][315 (7), "retiré de la juive."

victory in a canopy or tent set among the "magnificent gardens" of the emperor's palace. Following the chorus "O jour mémorable!" a ballet *divertissement* extraneous to the opera's storyline enhanced the atmosphere with its mock battle between *chevaliers* and a Moor who holds women captive in an enchanted castle. A review in *Le Figaro* (25 February 1835), which refers to the castle's guards as turbaned "infidels," points to an Orientalist display thought appropriate for an opera set in an early historic period and one that featured Jewish characters:

> [B]y means of a machine hidden inside, there appears a fortress decorated with towers and battlements; guarded by infidels in turbans, it is called upon to surrender: at the refusal of the infidels, the men-at-arms get ready to attack it, when all of a sudden it is transformed into a graceful gothic edifice, from which gracious hostesses emerge who execute a ballet before the emperor.[31]

After the ballet, the chorus "Sonnez, clairons!," and Eudoxie's tribute to her husband-hero, a prince of the Empire toasts Léopold, who then calls for a drink; he is served by Rachel in her slave costume:

Act III, Scene v
(23 February 1835 libretto)

LEOPOLD, voulant rendre raison au prince, tend sa coupe à une des servantes qui sont près de lui.

LEOPOLD, wanting to give an explanation to the prince, holds out his cup to one of the servants near him.

Esclave! à boire!!

Slave! Bring me a drink!!

(Du groupe des femmes s'élance vivement Rachel, habillée comme ses compagnes, et tenant un vase de vin. Elle en verse dans la coupe de Léopold qui, en ce moment, se retourne, l'aperçoit et reste immobile de surprise. La coupe s'échappe de sa main tremblante.)

(From the group of women, Rachel quickly rushes forward, dressed like her companions and holding a pitcher of wine. She pours it into the cup of Léopold, who, at this moment, returns, sees her, and is paralyzed by surprise. The cup falls from his trembling hand.)

---

[31] *Dossier de presse parisienne*, ed. Leich-Galland, 46. See a basic description and diagram of the Act III ballet in Smith, "Ballet-Pantomime," 91–3.

LEOPOLD

O surprise! ô terreur! C'est elle!
Un Dieu vengeur l'offre à mes yeux!

LEOPOLD

O surprise! O horrors! It is she!
A vengeful God puts her before
my eyes!

Le Corsaire confirms that Rachel appeared at the première "en habits d'esclave."[32] A later review in *Le Journal de Paris et des départemens* (22 March 1835) implies that Rachel continued to appear as a slave in the celebrations of Act III, even after the suppression of scenes in Eudoxie's apartment: the writer describes Rachel arriving with the slaves and holding a "costly ewer full of the wine of Constance."[33] But other reviews suggest the abandonment of Rachel's disguise as early as the second (25 February) or third (27 February) performance, since the opera's first review in *Le Journal de Paris* (28 February) recalls Rachel entering the emperor's tent with Eléazar rather than the slaves.[34] In the Palianti manual, which corresponds to Schlesinger's full score, Rachel enters with Eléazar after the *divertissement*, and no mention is made of her appearance as a slave or of her pouring drinks.[35]

In the first musical expression of the Rachel–Léopold romance, the Act I serenade of seduction by the disguised Léopold, Halévy adds touches of oriental color in the A minor *couplets* (that move to E minor in the B phrases of AA'BB'): he uses augmented seconds, raised fourths, grace notes, and turns in Léopold/Samuel's vocal line and the oboe's embellishing cadential motive (see Example 12); he also creates a modal feel with the use of G♮ (alternating with G♯) and D♮ (alternating with D♯).[36] Through these evocative touches the composer very likely

---

[32] *Le Corsaire*, 23 February 1835; *Dossier de presse parisienne*, ed. Leich-Galland, 21. Among costume inventories (F-Pan, AJ[13]202) I did not find a listing for a separate third-act costume for Rachel/Falcon.

[33] *Dossier de presse parisienne*, ed. Leich-Galland, 107.

[34] *Ibid.*, 92. The author, "Z. Z.," speaks of the omission at the second performance of the opening scene of Act III, in which Rachel asks Eudoxie if she can be her servant.

[35] Cohen, *Staging Manuals*, 146.

[36] Leich-Galland, "*La Juive*: Commentaire musical et littéraire," 43, finds this number reminiscent of Don Giovanni's balcony seduction. (Mozart's opera had been produced at the Paris Opéra in 1834, translated and altered by Castil-Blaze.) Halévy originally scored the accompaniment simulating Léopold's mandolin with two guitars, but these were replaced by violins in the autograph (the guitar

Example 12   Act I, Léopold's *sérénade*, *Schlesinger-Lemoine*, No. 3, mm. 36–47; *Schlesinger-Garland*, No. 3, mm. 28–39

wanted to give Léopold a musical disguise to match his dramatic mask (while perhaps covertly alluding to his own straddling of Jewish and non-Jewish worlds).[37] The contrasting sixteen-measure C major sections dividing and ending the two A minor *couplets*, together with the subsequent Rachel–Léopold duet included in *Schlesinger-Lemoine*, mm. 123–69,[38] contain a few chromatic inflections and an augmented second, but without a sense of oriental color. One might argue that these sections allude to the two characters' occidental identities.

In the final three numbers of Act II centering on the romance, the aria "Il va venir" (No. 10), the duet "Lorsqu'à toi je me suis donnée" (No. 11), and the trio "Je vois son front coupable" (No. 12), Rachel gradually loses

---

lines are crossed out in ink), performing parts, and *Schlesinger-Garland*. As suggested by the appearance of the guitar parts in the archival score, along with the new violin parts copied by a Leborne copyist on *collettes* obscuring the guitars, the change was probably made after the première, but it could have occurred relatively soon afterward, since Act I would have been the first act to be copied. (Records of extra musicians hired for the 1834/5 season indicate that guitars were not used in *La Juive* by June 1835.) In his 1989 edition, Leich-Galland restores the guitars; the 1999/2000 production of the opera at the Vienna Staatsoper, which followed this edition, also reinstated them, with amplification.

[37] Following Newark's suggestion that the audience's position as secretly observing outsiders to the seder corresponds to that of Léopold ("Ceremony, Celebration and Spectacle," 171), one might assume that Halévy also allows the audience to join in Léopold's pretense as lover.

[38] This material is also suppressed in the performing parts by red crayon cross-outs, *collettes*, and stitching.

her "innocence" as she reveals her suspicion and subsequently discovers Léopold's Christian identity. Her own identity as Jewess is strengthened as their opposition is underscored. In aria and duet, Rachel emerges as a full-blooded, passionate woman who expresses excitement, frustration, fear, and rage: poignant wind motives and shifting textures of rhythmic ostinati, syncopated figures, and rising sequences mark her changing emotions. Having seen Léopold's action in quelling the crowd in Act I and his rejection of the unleavened bread in Act II, she begins to sense betrayal. When Léopold enters, greeting her "ma bien aimée," she backs away, trembling (according to Palianti's manual); she then angrily confronts him, and Léopold acknowledges that he has indeed deceived her: his God is not hers. To his stunned lover, he reiterates remorsefully, "Je suis chrétien," his penitent tone suggested by the falling third at the end of the statement. Halévy heightens the inevitable reaction of shock and the frozen, awkward moment between the lovers with two tonic chords (ff) on downbeats followed by an extended alternation between full-measure pauses and chords (p) under long-held clarinet tones. Rachel recovers and launches into an enraged attack in the duet, marked "avec force," which begins with an octave leap from g^1 to g^2. She is an "infortunée" to have given herself to one outside her religion, she says to her lover against a syncopated pattern in C minor, and then in a vocal line intensified with agogic accents on ascending pitches (rising chromatically in mm. 16–19), wide leaps (eb^1 to ab^2 in m. 20), and insistent declamation (see Example 13). Rachel shrieks her complete dishonor before her father and "un Dieu vengeur," moving from Eb minor to Eb major and ending with a cadential flourish peaking on c^3. When Léopold attempts to soothe her (in the major key she has prepared for him) and explain his deception, Rachel reminds him that their forbidden relations will inevitably bring death. He implores her to escape with him, to put aside "gloire, amis, parens"; Rachel, although despairing at the thought of abandoning her father, responds to his visceral persuasion and sets off with him, only to be stopped cold by Eléazar. As pointed out by a critic in *La Quotidienne* (27 February 1835), Rachel's choice to flee with her Christian lover is reminiscent of Jessica's decision to follow Lorenzo in *The Merchant of Venice*.[39]

[39] *Dossier de presse parisienne*, ed. Leich-Galland, 141.

Example 13 Act II, Rachel–Léopold duet, *Schlesinger-Lemoine,*
Schlesinger-Garland, No. 11, mm. 16–23

Eléazar's interruption stimulates responses of shock and fear in the
trio; with gasping rests and jagged rhythms in the vocal lines, Halévy
captures the sense of the text "glacé par la terreur" ("frozen with
terror"), and builds the emotional tension up to the moment Eléazar
is told of Léopold's true identity.[40] Predictably, Eléazar spews out his
wrath, only to be calmed by Rachel, whose poignant appeal wins her
father's acceptance of her betrothal to this non-Jew.[41] But when the
married Léopold hears the word "époux," he shouts "Jamais!" and
sets off Eléazar's *anathème*, later joined by the spurned Rachel and a
despairing Léopold in a stirring end to Act II.

The romance so integral to Scribe's particular mix of historical-
political topic and operatic convention was more extensively featured
in earlier stages, primarily through stronger emphasis on the resulting
love triangle and Eudoxie's role in it. Omissions in Act V late in the
rehearsal period and in Act III after the première greatly reduced the
conventionally treated role for coloratura soprano, removing a romantic subplot and refocusing on the central problematic liaison. External considerations may have affected the changes. One possibility is

---

[40] Hugh Macdonald, "Grandest of the Grand," 21, refers to this number as a
"frozen" trio.

[41] *Le Figaro,* 25 February 1835, described this appeal as "a seduction so profound"
that her father was willing to grant her permission to marry a Christian.

that material slated to showcase the florid voice of the popular, well-established soprano Laure Cinti-Damoreau was diminished when the role was given to Julie Dorus-Gras (by July 1834, according to Opéra accounts of costume materials), most likely because of vocal troubles that were plaguing Damoreau around this time.[42] It may have been decided that Eudoxie, at least as sung by Dorus-Gras, should not have more arias than Rachel, the more dramatic soprano and "title" role, who is given only the brief Act II *romance* (although she sings throughout a good portion of the opera).[43] It is also possible that the material was deemed lacking in strength, Dorus-Gras did not like it, or her performance was found ineffectual.

An early version of the opening, as represented in libretto fair copies, includes a farewell *air* for Eudoxie rather than the chorus "Quel plaisir." In the *air*, Eudoxie prepares to drink a cup of poison in an act of suicidal despair over her husband's betrayal. In one libretto fragment of Act V, F-Pn, Ms., n.a.fr. 22502, vol. XXIII, 1°:4°(b), Eudoxie actually drinks the poison and dies shortly after Léopold discovers her and is forgiven by her in the second scene. In the same scene of the F-Pan, AJ[13]202 libretto manuscript, which most likely succeeds the material in n.a.fr. 22502, Léopold interrupts her *before* the poison touches her lips. He admits his guilt and begs that she offer a pardon – not for himself, but for Rachel. After Léopold admits that he has ridded his heart of "une flamme adultère," Eudoxie gives him the document authorizing her release and, when a signal from the emperor is heard, hurries him on to save Rachel.

While there is no evidence among the music manuscripts to indicate that Halévy set this version to music, Eudoxie's suicidal *air* "Adieu terre

---

[42] Damoreau's name appears in Leborne's *registre de copie*, with Dorus-Gras as her understudy ("double"), under the first four acts designated for the copying of the roles. Her name is crossed out, however, and replaced by that of "Me Jawureck"; under Leborne's notes for the copying of Eudoxie's Act V part, he writes only the names of Dorus-Gras and Jawureck, undoubtedly underscoring the fact that by the time this last act was copied Dorus-Gras had been assigned the role and Jawureck the understudy. Damoreau, the highest-paid singer at the Opéra after beginning a career there in 1827, left the institution sometime in 1835; Dorus-Gras made her debut at the Opéra in 1831 in *Le Comte Ory*.

[43] See documents related to costumes and *mise en scène* in F-Pan, AJ[13]202.

chérie," AJ^{13}202 and n.a.fr. 22502, vol. xxiii, 1°:4°(b), was composed, the performing parts were copied, and the set was designed. In G major and ABA form, the *air*'s first verse is: "Adieu terre chérie!/Adieu riant séjour!/J'ai perdu son amour,/Je dois perdre la vie!" ("Goodbye dear earth! Goodbye happy sojourn! I have lost his love, I must lose my life!")[44] It does not appear in the autograph, although its original placement is implied by the renumbering of the chorus "Quel plaisir."[45] The omission of the *air* and Léopold's responses appears to have come late in the rehearsal period, but probably not at the very last minute before the première: a *mise en scène* record dated February 1835 indicates that the Act V *décoration* for Eudoxie's room was only sketched, and not fully realized, before its suppression.[46] The cut possibly came as late as 1 February, when Acts IV and V were overhauled and when *La Gazette musicale de Paris* reported that "*La Juive* attend ses décors."[47]

[44] See the full transcription of the libretto text from F-Pan, AJ^{13}202, of these early Scenes i and ii in Hallman, *"La Juive,"* vol. ii, 412–14, and a transcription of Eudoxie's vocal line drawn from F-Po, Mat. 19e[315 (269), in *ibid.*, 418–19. The *air*, followed by Eudoxie's dialogue with Léopold, appears in partbooks copied by the Leborne *atelier* for Eudoxie, F-Po, Mat. 19e[315 (7bis), and Léopold, F-Po, Mat. 19e[315 (508) and (510), along with a full set of orchestral parts, F-Po, Mat. 19e[315 (269)–(306).

[45] Halévy designates this chorus in A.509a, vol. ii, as "5eme acte grand choeur N° 2," suggesting that No. 1 may have been Eudoxie's *air* (which may also have supplanted Rachel's repetition of the refrain from Léopold's romance).

[46] The relatively late omission is documented by its existence in three variant fair copies of the Act V libretto – the latest of which reveals the major dramatic change in the opera's ending – but more particularly its existence in orchestral parts, the fourth and fifth acts of which were the last copied and last rehearsed with orchestra. See the first entry for Act V in "Mémoire des décorations composées et exécutées pour Monsr Véron, directeur de l'Académie royale de musique, par MM Séchan Feuchères et Cie" (F-Pan, AJ^{13}202).

[47] *Gazette musicale de Paris* 2, no. 5 (1 February 1835), 43; it also reported that the first four acts were almost ready as rehearsals continued and predicted that the première would take place between 15 and 20 February. The *Revue musicale* of the same date (9, no. 5) announced that the opera was being delayed until at least mid-February, since the fourth act had been reworked and rehearsed again *en quatuor*. Although these sources do not say anything about the fifth act, manuscript sources show that parts of Act IV were being integrated into Act V, and so it might follow that the suppression of the first two scenes of Act V was made in conjunction with these other reworkings.

The post-première abandonment of three numbers at the beginning of Act III further reduced the role of Eudoxie. These numbers appear in the autograph and in *Schlesinger-Lemoine* (Nos. 13–15) but not in *Schlesinger-Garland* or the archival score: the first, "Tandis qu'il sommeille," and the third, the *Boléro*, "Mon doux seigneur et maître," are sung by Eudoxie, and the second, "Que d'attraits! qu'elle est belle," is the duet for Eudoxie and Rachel referred to above. Undoubtedly the cuts were made partially in the interest of performing time, as *La Juive* at its première lasted well over five hours, from 7 p.m. to 12:30 a.m.[48] The omissions stimulated mixed responses. *Le Figaro* welcomed them, since a "mediocre effect" was produced by Dorus-Gras's *air* (whether the first or third is not clear); the writer instead preferred the intense drama leading to Brogni's malediction in the finale.[49] A critic for the *Journal de Paris et des départemens* felt the reductions were healthy on the whole, but sardonically regretted that the Opéra had not finished its "*toilette* backstage": "We announced that some cuts had been made for the second performance; others have been made since. We believe that from now on works should be subject to this sad operation behind closed doors, and that the audience should not be given a *répétition générale* in the guise of a première performance, at the risk of compromising the success of a work."[50] On the other hand, *La Gazette musicale de Paris* praised the opening *air*, which allowed Dorus-Gras to expose "all the richness of her beautiful voice and the flawlessness of her technique," and concluded that the cuts came because the character was not appreciated.[51]

---

[48] *Le Constitutionnel*, 25 February 1835; *Dossier de presse parisienne*, ed. Leich-Galland, 11. A reviewer for *Le Ménestrel*, 1 March 1835 (*Dossier de presse parisienne*, ed. Leich-Galland, 112) remarked that the reductions made the work's proportions "more rational."

[49] *Le Figaro*, 3 March 1835; *Dossier de presse parisienne*, ed. Leich-Galland, 49. The critic for *Le Temps*, 26 February 1835 (*Dossier de presse parisienne*, ed. Leich-Galland, 159), who thought both Eudoxie's *air* and the duet too long, advised omitting one and reducing the other.

[50] *Journal de Paris et des départemens*, 22 March 1835; *Dossier de presse parisienne*, ed. Leich-Galland, 101.

[51] *La Gazette musicale de Paris*, 1 March 1835; *Dossier de presse parisienne*, ed. Leich-Galland, 73. "J. J." (Jules Janin?) echoes this view in a reference to

Given the general practice at the Opéra that called for a composer's approval, Halévy undoubtedly condoned these cuts, at least
formally.[52] Because these numbers appeared among the eighteen
morceaux détachés (Nos. 10–12) published by Schlesinger for "dilettanti"
(advertised for sale in April 1835), in the Schlesinger piano-vocal score
(advertised in August 1835), and in arrangements, they continued at
least as salon tropes to the staged *La Juive*.[53] But Opéra sources, including the early performing parts and archival score, make it clear they
were not part of the post-première opera.[54] Perhaps the strongest indication of their "official" exclusion is their omission from the archival
score: in fact, they were never copied for it.[55]

Although the drama does not deviate in these three numbers
into a subplot as extrinsic as Eudoxie's suicide or suicide threat that

Dorus-Gras's talent in singing "le rôle ingrat de la princesse Eudoxie" in the
Journal des débats, 25 February 1835, 109.

[52] Leich-Galland believes Halévy did not condone them; see *"La Juive*:
Commentaire musicale et littéraire," 61. See also his analysis of the Act III arias
and duet, which he advocates reincorporating, since "the listener needs the
calm and charm of these three pieces after the ordeal of the second act."

[53] Leich-Galland notes the prevalent use of the first theme of Eudoxie's *Boléro* in
Liszt's *Réminiscences de la Juive*, for example. *Ibid.*, 65.

[54] Among the performing materials for the duet are the orchestral parts, F-Po, Mat.
19[e][315 (583)–(605); written across the cover page of the first violin part (583), for
example, is the phrase, "Coupures de la Juive." Eudoxie's partbook, F-Po, Mat.
19[e][315 (7), contains the duet and the *Boléro*; written on the first page of (7) is
"retiré de la juive." The first *air* can be found in orchestral parts F-Po, Mat.
19[e][315 (231)–(268). Many variants appear among the performing parts, the
autograph, and piano-vocal score in these numbers, and all sources should be
consulted if the numbers are to be reinstated in performance.

[55] In Leborne's copy records for *La Juive*, F-Po, RE 235, in the space reserved for his
delegation of copying of the archival score, he first lists Nos. 1–6 under "Acte 3,"
but then crosses these out, renumbering 5 and 6 as 1 and 2. The old Nos. 1–3 are
the two Eudoxie arias and Eudoxie–Rachel duet; No. 4, as numbered in
Eudoxie's partbook, F-Po, Mat. 19[e][315 (7), is the recitative, "Ah! c'est trop
supporter," which precedes the chorus "O jour mémorable." No page counts or
copyists' names appear next to these numbers, as they do next to the new
Nos. 1–4. In the archival score, "No. 1" is the chorus "O jour mémorable" and the
number of pages equals forty, the number cited in RE 235; the page counts of the
following numbers of Act III similarly match the RE 235 notations. (As further
clarification, Leborne's early designation "No. 5" can be seen on the first page of
the chorus in the autograph, before being crossed out.)

accompanied the rejected "Adieu terre chérie," there is a similar focus on Eudoxie's personal feelings. The *airs* are light and charming love songs to her husband (the first a so-called *air de sommeil*) full of coloratura flourishes. Despite their musical appeal, particularly Eudoxie's *Boléro*, they are dramatically inessential, and easily omitted. The critic for *La Quotidienne* implied that the cuts sharpened the drama, resolving "all that had seemed vague and diffuse," and made "the progress of the libretto swifter and more satisfying."[56]

Without these numbers, Act III centers more solidly on the revelation of Léopold's full identity, made evident through Eudoxie's presentation of the necklace bought from Eléazar. Rachel's discovery that Léopold is Eudoxie's husband incites her to expose, and denounce, their liaison publicly, distinguishing her role as a Jewess coupled with a Christian, more than Léopold's adultery, as a crime deserving of death.[57] The non-acceptance of a Christian–Jewish pairing is realized most vehemently in the stern malediction of the cardinal, who is joined by principals and chorus in another intense finale.[58] As noted above (see p. 169), Brogni condemns the lovers together with Eléazar, but the Council pardons Léopold in Act V after Rachel proclaims his innocence in a compassionate response to Eudoxie's appeal. Despite her proclamation, the Council's pardoning of Léopold seems reminiscent of the exemption of *Ivanhoe's* Bois-Guilbert from responsibility in his affair with Rebecca, whom the Grand Master of the Temple accuses of having cast a witch-like spell "whereby she hath maddened the blood, and besotted the brain" of a knight of the Holy Temple (Chapter 37).

---

[56] J. T., *La Quotidienne*, 27 February 1835; *Dossier de presse parisienne*, ed. Leich-Galland, 146.

[57] Halévy's chromatic writing in the six orchestral measures following Rachel's last word strongly prefigures Wagner's fire music in *Der Ring des Nibelungen*.

[58] Julian Budden, "Gaetano Donizetti," in *The New Grove Dictionary of Music*, ed. Sadie (1980), vol. v, 559, believes that Brogni's malediction influenced the setting of Baldassare's denunciation in Donizetti's *La Favorite* (1840). A review in *Le Temps*, 26 February 1835 (*Dossier de presse parisienne*, ed. Leich-Galland, 160), signed "L. V.," complained of too many maledictions in *La Juive*, of the redundancy of the dramatic situation following Eléazar's Act II *anathème*.

Although one reviewer objected to the force and anger of Rachel's earlier pronouncement of Léopold's guilt as "trop en opposition avec la délicatesse de son sexe" ("too much in conflict with the delicacy of her sex"),[59] many of her reactions fit the almost saintly demeanor that dominates the characterization of Rebecca and other literary Jewesses. Both Rachel and Rebecca are shown to act differently from their fathers; neither is depicted as avaricious and both are forgiving. There are implications of greed in Eléazar's character, but not in Rachel's; in *Ivanhoe*, while Isaac is reluctant to part with his money, Rebecca is explicitly shown to be generous with it.[60] Moreover, while Eléazar never relents in his hatred of Brogni, Rachel responds to Eudoxie's plea and selflessly saves Léopold from death. Her protectiveness of her father at Ruggiero's first attack in Act I and, even more emphatically, her intercession for Léopold in Act II embody the sacrificial ideal belonging to nineteenth-century heroines, as well as the stereotype of the beautiful Jewess. In Chapter 39 of *Ivanhoe*, Rebecca forgives Bois-Guilbert in the same way that Rachel pardons Léopold: "But I do forgive thee, Bois-Guilbert, though the author of my early death." Like her counterpart Rebecca, Rachel is a noble, courageous, compassionate, and consoling woman who cares for both Jews and Christians.

The emphasis on the virtues and morality of the Jewish heroine was in part a literary device for contrasting her with a comparatively unsympathetic or immoral father. A more concrete way of distinguishing the Jewess was to make her Christian by blood, as Scribe chose, or through conversion, as implied by Abigail's entry into a nunnery in *The Jew of Malta*.[61] Rachel's portrayal as adopted daughter may follow from allusions in *The Merchant of Venice* that Jessica is not Shylock's true daughter. In Act III, Scene i, lines 34–6, Salerio challenges Shylock's

---

[59] *Dossier de presse parisienne*, ed. Leich-Galland, 81.
[60] In Chapter 10, when Gurth pays Isaac eighty zecchins for a horse and armor for his master, the Disinherited Knight, Rebecca returns a hundred zecchins, without her father's knowledge, causing Gurth to say, "[T]his is no Jewess, but an angel from heaven!"
[61] In Act III, Scene iv, lines 1–6, Barabas reacts to news from his daughter: "What, Abigail become a nun again! / False and unkind! what, hast thou lost thy father?"

assertion that she is: "'There is more difference between thy flesh and hers than between jet and ivory; more between your bloods than there is between red wine and Rhenish.'"[62] A remark by the clown Launcelot to Jessica again opens the question in Act III, Scene v, lines 9–10: "'Marry, you may partly hope that your father got you not – that you are not the Jew's daughter.'"

In *Nathan der Weise*, instead of implication there is the revelation of Recha's Christian birth. This basic fact, and elements surrounding the disclosure, corresponds with Scribe's treatment. Recha's identity as a Jewess is also clear, and the full exposure of her birth identity, like Rachel's, is not made until the end of the drama, although there are foreshadowings of it. In Lessing's drama, however, the moral behind this identity switch is sharper; the discovery of Recha's true identity, which accompanies the exposure of the Christian character as part Muslim, clearly stems from the author's intent to show the fallacy of religious and ethnic prejudices.[63] Lessing's identity twists may have inspired Scribe to create the split persona of Rachel (and perhaps of Samuel/Léopold as well), and he may have similarly intended to expose religious and social intolerance through the fact of Rachel's Christian birth, but the impact of its disclosure as the final *coup de théâtre* may have been more evanescent than in Lessing's drama.

As noted above, this plot idea was not exclusive to *Nathan*: in another work that Scribe may have known, Maria Edgeworth's novel *Harrington* of 1816, the Jewess discovers that she was born of a Christian mother in time to marry her Christian lover (see n. 12 above). Of course, disguise and identity change were common theatrical devices favored by Scribe and may not have come from a specific source, and not necessarily one with Jewish characters. But correspondences between the opera's text and Lessing's narrative about Recha's rescue and adoption underscore a possible relationship with the play. One example is Nathan's exchange with a monk in Act IV, Scene vii, in which he tells of losing his wife

---

62 Quotations from *The Merchant of Venice* are taken from the edition by Louis B. Wright (New York: Washington Square Press, 1957).

63 It is only one of several mistaken identities that Lessing uses in *Nathan* to expose the wrongheadedness of bigoted statements and misjudgments previously made.

and seven sons in the midst of violence – losses that produce in him an uncontrollable anger and "irreconcilable hatred against Christians" – and of God giving him the baby Recha to take the place of his lost children. Nathan's recounting of losing his family to violence at the hands of Christians and of adopting a Christian child in the midst of more violence parallels Eléazar's recollection in Acts I and IV of his sons dying at the stake, a brutal act that triggers a similar hatred of Christians. In the Act IV passage (Scene v, "Quand les Napolitains dans Rome"; *Schlesinger-Garland*, No. 18, mm. 139–75; *Schlesinger-Lemoine*, No. 21, mm. 173–209), previous events that Eléazar narrates contain a similar juxtaposition of family members dying in a burning home and the protection of a Christian baby, although in this instance it is Brogni's family that has burned rather than his own. Moreover, unlike Nathan, Eléazar himself saves Rachel from the flames rather than being given the child by another individual. The act of saving the Christian/Jewess from a burning house is, in fact, part of the plot of *Nathan* and is similarly incorporated in a narrated passage (by Daya, Nathan's servant, at the beginning of Act I), although the circumstances differ: Recha is not rescued as a baby by the Templier, but as a young woman. Despite the obvious plot discrepancies, and Scribe's incorporation of a historic event relevant to Brogni, the similarities are notable.[64]

The possibility of a literary basis to both the original and the retained denouements of *La Juive* exists, although Scribe could have relied on generalized precedents rather than exact literary models. Tragedies with Jewish characters often ended with the death of one – usually the Jewish usurer – and comedies typically culminated in a conversion. As previously hypothesized, Halévy most likely preferred the idea of Rachel's martyrdom. But since *Ivanhoe* inspired other elements, the ending may also have been cued by Rebecca's tenacity in holding onto her faith and her father in the final pages of *Ivanhoe*. After Rebecca has revealed that she and her father will leave England, a place unfavorable for "the children of my people," Rowena tries to convince

---

[64] Becker, "'Dieu de nos pères,'" 37–8, connects the chorus's phrase "Au bûcher, les Juifs!" (Act IV, Scene v) to "Tut nichts. Der Jude wird verbrannt" in *Nathan* (Act IV, Scene ii).

her to stay and be counseled in the Christian faith, but the Jewess refuses:

> "O, remain with us; the counsel of holy men will wean you from your erring law, and I will be a sister to you."
>
> "No, lady," answered Rebecca, the same calm melancholy reigning in her soft voice and beautiful features; "that may not be. I may not change the faith of my fathers like a garment unsuited to the climate in which I seek to dwell; and unhappy, lady, I will not be. He to whom I dedicate my future life will be my comforter, if I do His will."

ELEAZAR AS SHYLOCK

Several reviews of the first performances of *La Juive* relate the characterizations of Eléazar and Shylock. *L'Entr'acte* (26 February 1835) and *Le Ménestrel* (1 March 1835) speak generally of this modeling; other accounts draw specific critical comparisons, particularly to Eléazar's greed and his deep-seated hatred of his Christian persecutors.[65] *Le Courrier français* (27 February 1835) finds a common character trait of stubbornness and links Shylock's insistence on the inhuman terms of default on his loan (the infamous "pound of flesh") to Eléazar's refusal to reveal the secret of Rachel's birth to Cardinal Brogni: "[H]e persists in keeping quiet with the obstinacy of Shylock asking the Venetian magistrates for a pound of human flesh."[66] This same Shylockian emblem appears in the *Journal des débats* as an illustration of Eléazar's subversiveness, along with comments about his wealth and usury:

> Eléazar is modeled somewhat on the Jew of Shakespeare, that singularly energetic model of the rebellious Jew. Eléazar would himself also eat an ounce of Christian flesh with pleasure, meat and blood. He was in Rome, rich, and as honored as a Jew can be ... Chased from Rome, Eléazar settled in Constance. There, he deals in gold and silver and he lends at usurious rates of interest, as is the right and freedom of his nation.[67]

[65] *Dossier de presse parisienne*, ed. Leich-Galland, 36, 111.
[66] *Ibid.*, 28.   [67] *Ibid.*, 103.

Berlioz, in his review in *Le Rénovateur* (1 March 1835), implies similar traits in his reference to "an old usurer named Eléazar."[68] Such references, along with the critics' assumption that readers would understand them, highlight Shylock's secure place in the popular consciousness.

The interpretation of Shylock varied through the ages, including eighteenth-century British performances in which a popular clown named Doggett created Shylock as a comic role, adhering to a tradition of playing Jewish characters and costuming them in red wigs.[69] But early nineteenth-century portrayals, in both England and France, presented Shylock as a tragic figure belonging to a martyred race rather than a repulsive, dehumanized creature.[70] In its essence, the role of Eléazar belongs to this interpretation. Like Shakespeare's character, Eléazar is despised and treated poorly, fomenting a hatred for his persecutors and an overpowering thirst for revenge. The humanity of Shylock was more clearly defined than the inhumanity of the evil, murderous Jew of Marlowe's play, but Eléazar has virtues that are even more prominent. Whereas Shylock displays a loyalty to his own people, Eléazar's religious devotion counterbalances his hatred as it creates a jarring contrast to his stereotyped greed;[71] moreover, his paternal love appears deeper than Shylock's.

The spurning of the Jew as social and religious pariah permeates *The Merchant of Venice*, although Shylock has no real religious persona to match that of Eléazar. Eléazar's recognition of his persecution and his reproaching of Christians bring to mind Shylock's angry retorts to those who seek his help without disguising their loathing. Although Eléazar's statements relate to persecution and not directly to financial dealings – as Shylock's blatantly do – the anger of both characters

---

[68] *Ibid.*, 148.

[69] Shakespeare, *Twenty-three Plays*, ed. Parrott, 211. According to Rosenberg, *From Shylock to Svengali*, 11, the stereotype of comic miser was also represented in Scott's Jew.

[70] Shakespeare, *Twenty-three Plays*, ed. Parrott, 211.

[71] As Newark also suggests in "Ceremony, Celebration and Spectacle," 167, such disparate elements give the audience an "unstable, or at least incongruous" idea of Eléazar's characterization.

is equally strong and justified. Illustrative of Shylock's embitterment about Christian abuse and hypocrisy is his response to Antonio in Act I, Scene iii, lines 106–29:

> Signior Antonio, many a time and oft
> In the Rialto you have rated me
> About my moneys and my usances:
> Still have I borne it with a patient shrug,
> For suff'rance is the badge of all our tribe.
> You call me misbeliever, cutthroat dog,
> And spet upon my Jewish gaberdine,
> And all for use of that which is mine own.
> Well then, it now appears you need my help:
> Go to then, you come to me and you say,
> "Shylock, we would have moneys." You say so –
> You that did void your rheum upon my beard
> And foot me as you spurn a stranger cur
> Over your threshold. Moneys is your suit.
> What should I say to you? Should I not say,
> "Hath a dog money? Is it possible
> A cur can lend three thousand ducats?" or
> Shall I bend low, and in a bondman's key,
> With bated breath and whisp'ring humbleness,
> Say this:
> "Fair sir, you spet on me on Wednesday last;
> You spurned me such a day; another time
> You called me dog; and for these courtesies
> I'll lend you thus much moneys?"

A more famous passage that similarly resonates with pain and bitterness is the celebrated revelation of Shylock's humanity, "Hath not a Jew eyes?," of Act III, Scene i, lines 45–65.

The acts of contempt that Shylock describes reverberate in the crowd's treatment of Eléazar, particularly in Act I. Christian derision is perhaps uglier in *Ivanhoe*, as in the scene in which Isaac and Rebecca are cursed and refused seats, the model for the abandoned Act I scene.[72]

---

[72] See pp. 166–8 above. The cursing of Isaac as "the dog Jew" in this scene is reminiscent of the language used to attack Shylock.

Eléazar's refusal to forgive his persecutors, as recognized by the critic of *Le Courrier français*, echoes Shylock's resistance.

The partially compassionate characterization of Eléazar also reflects the sympathetic aspects of Scott's Isaac. The novelist modified but did not dispense with the stereotype of Jewish usurer: Isaac is indeed a wealthy miser who hoards gold, counts it with relish, and is reluctant to part with it (except when his daughter's safety is threatened). But he is less hate-filled and avaricious than Shylock and other moneylenders of the stage. Although Scott is thought to have modeled Isaac after Aaron of York from the chronicles of Matthew Paris, the novelist clearly drew ideas from *The Merchant of Venice* and *The Jew of Malta*, as accentuated in chapter epigraphs excerpted from these plays.[73]

Shylock's avarice touches Eléazar's characterization, although less strongly than in Scribe's draft scenario. In the librettist's early ideas for Act II, Scene ii, immediately after the Jewish prayers, Eléazar brings out a cash box and contemplates the sale of his necklace, thinking of all the rich princes and lords attending the Council. He is also anxious about his bag of gold on the table when he hears a knock at the door. In this part of the scene, subtly reminiscent of an exchange between Barabas and his daughter Abigail in *The Jew of Malta*, he orders Rachel to put away the gold and an account register. Together with his cash box, both are conspicuous symbols of an acquisitive Eléazar. Scribe writes:

> Now, my friends, says Eléazar, withdraw and go and eat – before going to bed I am going to count the day's profits and balance my accounts . . .
> What a shame, says Eléazar, that I cannot sell my beautiful ruby necklace, a necklace worth 30,000 silver florins which should be in the coffers – I was hoping that of all the princes and great lords who are now in this city . . . there is another knock at the door – who is there, says Eléazar, holding in his purse the gold that he had already put on the

[73] These epigraphs help to delineate Scott's meaning in the narrative proper of *Ivanhoe*: several concentrate on the sympathetic aspects of Shylock's characterization, particularly the quotation from "Hath not a Jew eyes?" placed at the beginning of Chapter 5; a quotation from *The Jew of Malta* focusing on the Jew's persecution heads Chapter 10.

table – go and see, daughter – she half-opens a small window in the door and looks out – a stranger – a woman – followed by two valets . . . the stranger can enter – but alone – here, daughter – here, take away the purse of gold and this account book and wait for me in my room – yes, father.[74]

With the omission of the scene (Scribe crosses it out in the draft scenario) went overt, textual references to the miser stereotype. What remains is a comparatively less conspicuous depiction of Eléazar's love of money in his exchange with Eudoxie about the necklace, sketched in the following scene of the scenario ("Scène 3ème"). This sketch gives the basic structure and details for the dramatic action leading to and entailing the Act II trio in which Eudoxie sings of her desire to honor her husband, Léopold shudders at being discovered, and Eléazar revels in his prospective sale. But one symbol from the previous crossed-out scene was retained in the *mise en scène*, as documented in Palianti's stage manual: a box that Eléazar retrieves offstage (through a door at stage left) and holds tightly. It is a jewelry box (*coffret*) rather than a cash box: "In both hands and against his chest, he holds a rich jewelry box in which the gold chain decorated with precious stones is locked up."[75]

In the published musical scores and *mise en scène* directions, this Act II trio (No. 9), "Tu possèdes, dit-on," contains the most pointed indications of Eléazar's greed after the textual and dramatic allusions of Act I. In this number, following the interruption of the Jewish service, Eléazar is transformed into an avaricious Jew whose thoughts

---

[74] F-Pn, Ms., n.a.fr. 22502, vol. XXIII, 1°:2°, 7: "Maintenant, mes amis, dit Eléazar, retirez vous et livrez vous au repas – je vais compter avant de me coucher mes bénéfices de la journée et régler ma caisse . . . quel dommage, dit Eléazar, que je ne puisse vendre mon beau collier de rubis, un collier de trente mille florins de l'argent qui doit en caisse – j'esperais que parmi tous les princes et grands seigneurs qui sont en ce moment dans cette ville . . . on frappe encore à la porte – qui est là dit Eléazar en tenant dans son sac son or qu'il avait déjà mis sur la table – vois, ma fille – elle entrouve un petit guichet qui est à la porte et regarde – une étrangère – une femme – suivie de deux valets . . . l'étrangère peut entrer – mais seule – tiens ma fille – tiens emporte le sac d'or et ce registre et attends moi dans ma chambre – oui, mon père."

[75] Cohen, *Staging Manuals*, 143.

of "bons écus d'or" override his fears at being discovered at worship. After Eudoxie sings of honoring her husband with the jewel (and the disguised Léopold, hearing her praises, sings his regrets), Eléazar speaks of his love for gold in the same breath as his hatred for Christians:

Act II, Scene ii, No. 9

Schlesinger-Garland

Je tremblais que cette femme	I trembled that this woman
Ne surprît tous nos* secrets	Might discover all our* secrets
Et je maudissais dans l'âme	And I cursed in my soul
Tous ces Chrétiens que je hais,	All these Christians whom I hate,
Mais pour moi plaisir extrême	But what true pleasure
Et quel heureux avenir,	And a happy future for me:
Ces bons écus d'or que j'aime	These good crowns of gold that I love
Chez moi vont donc revenir!	Are going to return home!

*"mes" ("my") in *Schlesinger-Lemoine*

According to the Palianti manual, Eléazar sings this solo in a room ("Pièce B," stage left) separated by a wall from the central room where the service has been held (see Illustration 10).[76] After going offstage during Eudoxie's solo, "Ah! dans mon âme" (*Schlesinger-Garland*, *Schlesinger-Lemoine*, mm. 36ff.), Eléazar returns to this separate room during Léopold's repetition of Eudoxie's phrases and remains there clutching the box – with both hands against his chest, according to the Palianti manual – as he sings "Je tremblais" (*Schlesinger-Garland*, *Schlesinger-Lemoine*, mm. 52ff.). After showing Eudoxie the necklace, he places it in the box and leaves to put it away, returning to the adjoining room as he repeats his words (*Schlesinger-Garland*, *Schlesinger-Lemoine*, mm. 147ff.) in the reprise of "Ah! dans mon âme." This image strikes a clear portrait of the stereotyped miser, supported by the text and enhanced by Eléazar's costume and gestures. The costume of the first production (and subsequent ones in Paris) served as another strong

---

[76] In French *mise en scène* directions, the standard designation "droite" is equivalent to "stage left" and, conversely, "gauche" is "stage right."

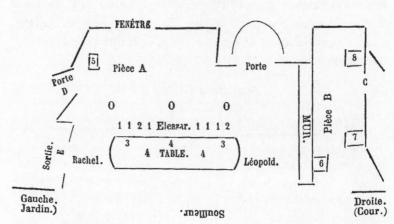

ACTE DEUXIÈME.

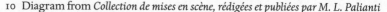

10 Diagram from *Collection de mises en scène, rédigées et publiées par M. L. Palianti*

visual cue for the stereotype: atop his flowing robes a money bag is prominently placed (see Illustration 9 above).[77]

Halévy's setting strengthens this portrait. He creates the feeling of nervous excitement, shifting accentuation from the duple division of Eudoxie's "Ah! dans mon âme" (and Léopold's repetition of it) to quadruple as Eléazar begins to fret about her interruption. Quick dotted notes, rising lines, and repetition of text phrases (mostly syllabic) express an anxiety that merges with titillation at his thoughts of gold.

---

[77] A lithograph by Alexandre-Désiré Collette of the actor Chilly as Shylock in *Le Juif de Venise* at the Ambigu-Comique shows a money bag attached to the side of a buckled belt, with tassles hanging from the bottom of the purse, quite similar to Eléazar's. He also wears a similar long tunic, but with an overcoat; his longish beard divides into two points. *Galérie illustrée des célébrités contemporaines: Les Théâtres de Paris. Texte par une société de gens de lettres, dessins par Eustache Lorsay. Lithographiés par Collette*, 4 vols. (Paris: Administration/Martinon, Libraire, 1854), vol. I, 1–4. A photograph of Léonce Escalaïs as Eléazar in 1883 at the Paris Opéra (Bibliothèque de l'Opéra) shows him in the costume of the production of 1835, but with a two-pointed beard like Chilly's; the singer poses clutching the jewel box to his chest with both hands, with a rather gleeful look on his face. One must note, however, that other male costumes of early periods include a purse hanging from a belt, though perhaps not as large: in fact, a small purse is sketched for one of Léopold's costumes (F-Po, [D. 216 (O^2), fol. 81).

Example 14 Act II, trio of Eléazar, Eudoxie, and Léopold, *Schlesinger-Lemoine, Schlesinger-Garland*, No. 9, mm. 151–5

The composer gives special emphasis to the phrase "Ces bons écus d'or que j'aime/Chez moi vont donc revenir!" in m. 55 by reducing the accompaniment to a staccato viola line in unison with Eléazar's ascending vocal line. Halévy continues to highlight bits of the text phrase by staggering Eléazar's entrances, separating them from Eudoxie's optimistic exclamations and Léopold's anxieties about the prospect of seeing each other – just as he remains physically isolated during their ensemble (such a physical separation was a common operatic staging device used to delineate multiple statements occurring simultaneously). Eléazar's agitation intensifies with quick octave leaps, triplets, and sixteenth notes in mm. 58–63. But he becomes most overwrought in the reprise that follows an exchange with Eudoxie concerning the sale price, when he emits a flustered stream of triplets, a comic patter, on various types of currency (see Example 14).[78] In this patter, Halévy

---

[78] The types of currency referred to are various gold coins used in earlier centuries in France and other European countries (for example, the florin originated in

may have been alluding to the comic tradition of playing Jewish characters. Théophile Gautier comments in a review of 1837 that Duprez emphasized the *buffa* qualities of this section more than Nourrit: "Before him, hadn't there been a neglecting of the entire *buffa* [*bouffe*] part in the trio of the same act, where the Jew commends himself for fooling the Christians, and which Duprez expressed in such a comic and witty way?"[79] In the trio's final phrases, Eléazar intones the words "Ah! quel plaisir de tromper ces chrétiens!" ("Oh, what a pleasure to fool these Christians!") on repeated B$^\flat$s for four measures (mm. 165–9), with rhythmic stress on the mid-bar repetition of the word "tromper" (on the offbeat and beat 3). Immediately afterward comes the phrase "je les hais tous, ces ennemis de mon Dieu de ma foi" ("I hate them all, these enemies of my God and my faith"). A phrase similar in meaning, "Oui – oui vengeons nous sur eux tous" ("Yes – yes, let's avenge ourselves on them all"), followed by the indication "Stretta du trio," appears in Scribe's draft scenario but is not set musically; however, Scribe's early Shylockian combination of the Jew's vengefulness with usurious dealings is retained. Curiously, the extended text phrases about "ces bons écus" and duping the Christians that are sketched in the draft scenario and included in the score do not appear in the copyist's libretto or the early printed libretti. Perhaps the discrepancy resulted from additions, or reinstatements, late in the compositional process, but it also seems feasible that Scribe may have considered them too insulting to Jewish readers of the libretto – a supposition

---

Florence in 1252, the ducat in Venice in 1284). The decision to refer to these coins in the text was undoubtedly an attempt at historical authenticity, as in the novels of Balzac and Hugo. The term "écu," another old type of gold (and sometimes silver) coin, was commonly used in French literature of the nineteenth century, with a variety of connotations. The phrase "avoir des écus à remuer à la pelle," for example, meant to be very rich, perhaps a connotation pertinent to its use in *La Juive*; see "Ecu," *Grand Larousse de la langue française*, 6 vols. (Paris: Librairie Larousse, 1971–8), vol. II, 1484. Also noteworthy is Balzac's use of *écu* in *La Maison Nucingen* (1838), cited in *Trésor de la langue française: Dictionnaire de la langue du XIXe siècle (1789–1860)*, 15 vols. (Paris: Gallimard, 1973–92), vol. VII, 720–21; see also vol. VII, 532, vol. VIII, 993, and vol. XV, 375.

[79] *Histoire*, vol. I, 21: "N'avait-on pas négligé avant lui toute la partie bouffe, dans le trio du même acte, où le juif s'applaudit de tromper les chrétiens, et que Duprez a fait ressortir d'une façon si comique et si spirituelle?"

that is nevertheless weakened by the inclusion of other inflammatory passages.

One textual variant among the sources – a difference in Eléazar's price for the necklace offered to Eudoxie – also hints of stereotype. In Scene iii of the draft scenario, he offers the price "quarante mille florins," ten thousand more than the price he quotes to himself in the previous scene (Scene ii, which was crossed out, but presumably not until after Scene iii was already sketched). Here it seems likely that Scribe intended the higher price to illustrate usurious practices. In the copyist's libretto and printed libretti, the sale price was "trente mille florins," altered to "trente mille ducats" in the published music scores.[80] Whether florins or ducats, the price is noteworthy in its biblical symbolism and its similarity to the form of Shylock's loan in *The Merchant of Venice*. Surely the choice of a multiple of thirty carries a symbolic reference to Judas's thirty pieces of silver. Moreover, a multiple of three undergirds Shylock's loan of "three thousand ducats" to be repaid by the merchant Antonio ("in three months") on threat of losing a pound of flesh. The modification to ducats, using the same form of currency as in the play, may indeed have been made to strengthen the Shylock impression.

Halévy's musical treatment in the trio and the visual clues of costume and staging clearly define the image of the Jewish miser, but the reduction of certain allusions to Eléazar's greed and love of deception in Scribe's draft scenario points to a softening of the image during the compositional process. In addition to the excision of the references to the cash box, sack of gold, and account book, one notable change reveals still more cutting back on overt stereotyping.[81] In the Act I

---

[80] The reference to "trente mille florins" in *La Gazette musicale de Paris*, 15 March 1835, hints that the critic used the printed libretto as a guide.

[81] Also undeveloped from Scribe's scenario is the allusion to the historical practice of levying fines against Jews that appeared in literature, including the governor's demand of a tribute from Barabas and other Jews in *The Jew of Malta*. In Scribe's sketch of Act I, Scene iv (F-Pn, Ms., n.a.fr. 22502, vol. XXIII, 1°:2°, 4), when the crowd stops Eléazar and Rachel for having dishonored a sacred day, a fine of one thousand gold pieces is imposed by Ruggiero (Rannochia in the scenario) or another authority figure – the speaker's identity is unclear. Eléazar protests, but Rachel, sensing the danger of his situation, advises compliance. Immediately

exchange between Brogni and Eléazar in the printed libretti, when the Jew accuses the cardinal of having banished him from Rome, Brogni gives usury as the reason for his past action: "Est-ce à tort? Convaincu d'une usure coupable,/On demandait ta mort, j'ordonnai ton exil!" ("Is this wrong? Convicted of culpable usury, your death was called for, I ordained your exile!") Halévy set this response, but its eight measures appear crossed out in the autograph, as well as in other manuscript music sources, corresponding with its omission from published scores (see Illustration 11).[82] The review in *La Quotidienne* (27 February 1835) includes the text, suggesting reference to the printed libretto but also the possibility of post-première omission.[83]

Not adopted in Eléazar's characterization is the Shylockian conflict between materialism and familial love. As father, Eléazar appears more closely modeled on Isaac of *Ivanhoe*, whose deep love for his daughter outweighs his materialism; by contrast, Shylock's paternal feelings seem superficial. When Jessica runs off with her Christian lover (as Rachel almost does in Act II) and takes her father's money and jewels, Shylock's concern for his material loss matches and at times dominates his feelings of parental love or betrayal. His patter overheard in Act II, Scene viii, begins: "My daughter! O my ducats! O my daughter!/Fled with a Christian! O my Christian ducats!/Justice! the law! My ducats, and my daughter!"[84] In Act III, Scene i, Shylock wishes his "daughter were dead at my foot" and, at the news of her spending money in Genoa, moans, "I shall never see my gold again." Scott hints of clashes between love and money in *Ivanhoe*, but in many passages seems to

---

after the exchange comes the cardinal's questioning of Eléazar, similar to what remains in *La Juive*.

[82] In Eléazar's partbook, F-Po, Mat. 19ᵉ[315 (13), fol. 6ᵛ, the passage is blocked out in red crayon, corresponding to the same inked-out measures in the autograph. The measures precede Brogni's appeal, "Sois libre, Eléazar," and Eléazar's "Jamais!" (see p. 171 above).

[83] *Dossier de presse parisienne*, ed. Leich-Galland, 140.

[84] Barabas, the more thoroughly nefarious Jewish father in *The Jew of Malta*, involves his unwitting daughter in a plot that leads to the death of two of her suitors, one of whom she loves. After discovering the deed, she joins a nunnery to escape her father, who then poisons her (along with all the nuns) without remorse or regret.

11 *La Juive*, Act I, No. 1, omission of text phrase "Est-ce à tort? Convaincu d'une usure coupable,/On demandait ta mort, j'ordonnai ton exil!" ("Is this wrong? Convicted of culpable usury, your death was called for, I ordained your exile!") from the autograph

challenge the stereotype. In Chapter 22 he pointedly distinguishes Isaac from Shylock, heading the chapter with the passage quoted above but emphasizing Isaac's passion for his daughter's wellbeing in his narrative:

> "Take all that you have asked," said he [Isaac], "Sir Knight; take ten times more – reduce me to ruin and to beggary, if thou wilt, – nay, pierce me with thy poniard, broil me on that furnace; but spare my daughter, deliver her in safety and honour. As thou art born of woman, spare the honour of a helpless maiden. She is the image of my deceased Rachael – she is the last of six pledges of her love. Will you deprive a widowed husband of his sole remaining comfort? Will you reduce a father to wish that his only living child were laid beside her dead mother, in the tomb of our fathers?"
>
> "I would," said the Norman, somewhat relenting, "that I had known of this before. I thought your race had loved nothing save their money-bags."
>
> "Think not so vilely of us, Jews though we be," said Isaac, eager to improve the moment of apparent sympathy; "the hunted fox, the tortured wild-cat loves its young – the despised and persecuted race of Abraham love their children!"[85]

The author's ambivalence comes through in the implication that Isaac is slightly feigning in the final paragraph of the above passage, as it does in allusions to the conventional familial–materialistic conflict later in the novel, as in a reference to Isaac's love of his worldly goods, "which, by dint of inveterate habit, contended even with his parental affection."[86] As in Isaac's characterization, Eléazar's paternal feelings mitigate less virtuous traits, but unlike Isaac to some degree, and completely unlike Shylock, Eléazar is torn between the love for his daughter, his faith, and his hatred for Christians – not between his daughter and his ducats.

La Juive also carries traces of Marlowe's *The Jew of Malta*.[87] Death by immersion in a cauldron is the method used to kill Barabas in

---

[85] Scott, *Ivanhoe*, Chapter 22, 233. [86] *Ibid.*, Chapter 33, 368.
[87] Scribe makes no mention of Marlowe's play in the previously cited book lists, but he could have easily obtained a copy through English publications; the play had also been revived in 1818 by Edmund Kean at London's Drury Lane Theatre.

Marlowe's play, albeit brought about by very different circumstances. Whether Scribe used this or another literary source is uncertain, and the idea may have come from history rather than literature, as Scribe made a note that one method used in Avignon to kill heretics was to plunge them into a vat of boiling water. (He wrote about this method on his visit in 1846, but he may have made a similar observation during his travels of 1827.)[88] Yet Scribe's other literary borrowings point to a connection between the opera's ending and a literary convention in which a Jewish usurer meets with a gruesome death – even though only Rachel's death, and not Eléazar's, is shown in stage action. The early conversion denouement and the unheeded attempts to convert Eléazar relate to the usurer's apostasy in *The Merchant of Venice* and other comedies with Jewish characters.

Some journalists attempted to go beyond the literary associations in the early reception of *La Juive* by presenting historical contexts for their interpretations of Eléazar. A reviewer in *La Quotidienne* (27 February 1835), for example, related Jewish wealth and commerce to their historical treatment as oppressed pariahs, explaining that restrictions and the levying of fines – brought on by public animus or governmental voracity – justified their concern and need for money:

> In order to understand the subject's interest, we have to refer back to the
> religious ideas that preoccupied Christianity at the beginning of the
> fifteenth century and to the social loathing of which the Jews were then
> the object and the victims in all European countries. Placed outside
> civilized society by their customs as much as by laws, this nation, in order
> to live, was reduced to having to create industries that were often very
> reprehensible: without political existence, it restricted its ambition to a
> financial existence, and it prospered and enriched itself by clandestine
> negotiations and by shameful trafficking in currency, precious stones, and
> gold and silver objects. By these means, Jews amassed immense treasures
> that they removed from circulation and enjoyed in secret, until they were
> violently stripped of them through the anger of the people or the greed
> of sovereigns: then persecutions would rise against them, confiscations
> seized their gold, and stakes suppressed their complaints. It is one of

---

[88] F-Pn, Ms., n.a.fr. 22584, vol. v, fol. 7^r.

these Jews, enriched by his work as goldsmith and jeweller, whom the author has made the hero of his work.[89]

Jordan characterizes this passage as a "pseudo-analysis of Jewish history" that revives "old prejudices and innuendos."[90] Yet its main points, and links between Jewish political restrictions and usury, parallel those made in a number of forums beyond music criticism – although with greater refinement – from essays in *L'Israélite français* and Léon Halévy's writings to discussions surrounding the 1831 law of the *culte israélite*.

French literature and drama contemporary with *La Juive* that feature or allude to the stereotype (in addition to the Wandering Jew or the wise Nathan[91]) underscore its familiarity among the French public. The rather sympathetic Nucingen of Balzac's *La Maison Nucingen* (1838) – generally thought to be modeled on James Rothschild – is a financial genius who generously comes to the aid of a former employer who has met with financial ruin. But Balzac's Jewish capitalist Gobseck (*Gobseck*, 1842) reverberates with Shylockian avarice more intense than Eléazar's. Although he is a complex figure who is also portrayed as a magnanimous philosopher, he persists in collecting debts even when his clients are on the brink of disaster. In later decades, the Jewish banker and other Jewish characters in the works of René Maizeroy (1856–1918) and Paul Bourget (1852–1935), for example, were grotesque, unscrupulous usurers and parvenus.[92]

A number of French dramas capitalized on audience expectations of the stereotype by modifying or challenging it, while others presented Jewish characters in new, idealized lights. Among the plays preceding *La Juive* that re-examined the stereotype of the Jewish miser with a beautiful daughter was a two-act *comédie anecdotique* of 1823 entitled *Le Juif*.[93] In this *comédie*, rather than a father, Isaac Samuel is first

---

[89] *Dossier de presse parisienne*, ed. Leich-Galland, 138–9.

[90] Jordan, *Fromental Halévy*, 63.

[91] The French dramatist Baron Isidore-Justin-Séverin Taylor (1789–1879) borrowed from *Nathan* in his three-act play of 182[3], "La Fille de l'Hébreu et le chevalier du temple" (F-Pan, AJ[13] 1033).

[92] See Anna Krakowski's introduction to Debré, *The Image of the Jew*, 6–7.

[93] Auguste Rousseau, Marc-Antoine-Madeleine Désaugiers, and Jean-Baptiste Mesnard, *Le Juif: Comédie anecdotique en deux actes, mêlée de vaudevilles, par MM. A.*

shown as befriender and protector of Lucette, a young, naive woman; both are among a group of travelers on their way to Orléans by stage-coach. Toward the end of Act I, however, Isaac quickly becomes treacherous, beginning with his exposure of Lucette's hidden money to robbers in exchange for a cut of it.[94] This and other apparently deceptive and self-serving actions induce his fellow voyagers to label his conduct "odious" and to speak of him as a "dishonest man" and "damned Israelite."[95] In the end, however, Isaac emerges as a clever, brave mastermind who outwitted the thieves by using Lucette's money as decoy to hide the much larger sum that he carries as a gift for Lucette and her fiancé. He is in fact unmasked as the Paris banker who had anonymously sent her money and as the "intimate friend and associate" of her father, who is away fighting in the American Revolutionary War.

This comedy obviously attempts to expose the hollowness of the stereotype and the pitfalls of prejudgment. With an exploitative gloss, it presents Isaac as a German Jew with heavily accented French (undoubtedly a reference to the predominance of German Jews in France, particularly in Alsace, and perhaps an even more specific allusion to the heavy German accent of James Rothschild).[96] The play was controversial, however. Despite the fact that it had been reviewed by censors, the *comédie* was suppressed by theatrical authorities sometime after its première at the Théâtre de la Porte Saint-Martin in May 1823, but reappeared in 1825 "without controversy," according to a report in *L'Opinion*.[97]

Rousseau, Désaugiers et Mesnard, *représentée, pour la première fois, sur le théâtre de la porte Saint-Martin, le 14 mai 1823,* in *Fin du répertoire du théâtre français* (Paris: Mme veuve Dabo, 1824).

[94] The authors ensure that the audience will view Isaac as an unethical man through his effusive reactions to receiving the money (Act I, Scene xv).

[95] The invectives are spoken in Act II by Madame Simonne, the mother of Lucette's fiancé, Charles.

[96] Isaac's accented French was indicated by a consistent use of "f" for "v", "p" for "b", "t" for "d", and "ch" for "j" or "g," as in the lines spoken to Lucette in Act I, Scene vii, beginning: "Chenti Temoiselle, fous li être pien cheune, c'était peut-être la première fois que fous foyachez."

[97] See the censors' libretto, F-Pan, F^18 644. "Echo," *L'Opinion: Journal des moeurs, de la littérature, des arts, des théâtres et de l'industrie* 1, no. 5 (5 December 1825): 4.

A work co-written by Léon Halévy, *Grillo; ou, Le Prince et le banquier*, a two-act *comédie-vaudeville* (Théâtre des Variétés, 22 December 1832), resembles *Le Juif* in genre and approach to Jewish characterization.[98] Like the authors of *Le Juif,* Halévy played with audience assumptions about the Jewish moneylender – again, a rich banker. (Léon undoubtedly knew *Le Juif* since he was an editor of and writer of literary pieces for *L'Opinion.*) At the outset, he presents the international banker Grillo Cataneo – whose Jewish identity is suggested by his occupation – as an individual whose only concerns are material and whose usefulness is seen in terms of those who need his money, including the irresponsible marquis d'Albano. A description of Grillo in Act I by the marquis's companion portrays a cosmopolitan, globetrotting banker, perhaps in the image of the Rothschilds, the Pereires, and other successful bankers:

> [H]e has offices in all the capitals of Europe, and when one thinks he is in Rome or Genoa he is in London or Paris; traveling incessantly, he stops in a town only for the time necessary to verify the accounts of his associates and to share their profits.[99]

Like Isaac, Grillo moves beyond a purely materialistic image: he is ultimately revealed as a wise, honorable, and altruistic man who saves the marquis from financial ruin, prevents the duke from disowning the marquis, his nephew, and restores the defamed name of comte Sestini, whose daughter he had adopted after her father's death.

Grillo, like Isaac, sympathetically spins off from the Shylock stereotype.[100] He has an adopted daughter and good intentions behind

---

[98] Paris: J. N. Barba, 1833.

[99] *Grillo*, Act I, Scene v: "[I]l a des comptoirs dans toutes les capitales de l'Europe, et quand on le croit à Rome ou à Gênes il est à Londres ou à Paris; voyageant sans cesse, il ne s'arrête dans une ville que juste le temps qu'il lui faut pour vérifier les comptes de ses associés et partager leurs bénéfices." So mysterious is this "nomadic speculator" that Montforte, the marquis's companion, would doubt his existence were it not for the assurances of "the honest Jewish financiers" whom he knows.

[100] Léon Halévy collaborated on another work with a central Jewish character, a *colporteur: L'Espion*, a five-act play which had its première at the Théâtre de l'Odéon on 6 December 1828 (Paris: Riga et Jeannin Editeurs, 1828). Here

his machinations. Through this portrayal, Halévy seemingly defends against common diatribes leveled at prosperous Jews, perhaps alluding to the much-derided ostentatious lifestyle of the Parisian Rothschild, and to his reputedly ignoble manner. When the marquis registers surprise over the renovations that Grillo has made to the chateau that he had bought from him, Grillo replies: "[Y]ou princes, you don't need extravagant luxury . . . I need all that; I have a mien so base, because I am taken for a beggar, a vagabond" (Act II, Scene v).[101]

These plays, which in a sense turn the Shylock stereotype on its head while simultaneously reinforcing it, underline its viability in France during the decade leading up to *La Juive*. The harsh portrayals of the miserly Jew illustrate even more pointedly the continuity of the Shylock characterization in the nineteenth century. The stereotype was not merely a literary habit, as the late nineteenth-century author Abraham Dreyfus concludes in his essay "Le Juif au théâtre,"[102] nor was it a literary throwback without contemporary social relevance. In the context of the view that literary expressions cast light on social truths and values, the reinterpretation of Shylock in *La Juive* as well as in contemporary dramas and novels testifies to a perpetuation of encrusted notions. Yet increasing humanization of the character, along with the depiction of idealized Jews in French literature, reflects

Léon does not reinterpret the Shylock stereotype, but presents another idealized Jew, Harvey Birch, who is initially misjudged an untrustworthy character suspected of British espionage in the American Revolutionary War, but is in fact a spy for the American forces who follows the commands of Harper, alias George Washington, who later eulogizes him as "a great citizen." (The American War of Independence was a favored setting for French dramas of the later 1820s and 1830s.)

[101] Act II, Scene v: "[V]ous autres princes, vous n'avez pas besoin d'un luxe bien positif . . . j'ai besoin de tout cela; j'ai l'air si peu noble, car on me prend pour un mendiant, un vagabond." While Léon may have been commenting on the less-than-noble manner of Baron James Rothschild or others of the Jewish nouveaux riches, he may also have been alluding to the awkward position of the Rothschilds, whose wealth brought them social and political power as well as accusations of greed and usury. Derek Wilson, in *Rothschild: The Wealth and Power of a Dynasty* (New York: Charles Scribner's Sons, 1988), 86, writes that the Rothschilds discovered that no matter how they lived, political antisemites would pillory them as usurers.

[102] *Revue des études juives*, 1886: 62, cited in Debré, *The Image of the Jew*, 4.

attitudinal changes, or, at least, the utopian desires of authors to create new images. The Shylockian elements of Eléazar's character, set against a sympathetic and emotionally powerful religious persona and coupled with the portrayal of a compassionate, desirable Rachel, add dimension to the conflicting and ambivalent attitudes surrounding the fifteenth-century Jews of *La Juive*, as well as French Jews of the early nineteeth century, as we explore in a wider context below.

Several years after the première of *La Juive*, the writer Ben-Lévi spoke mockingly of the ubiquity of Jewish images in France:

> Do you like the Jew? He is everywhere. In the theatre, from Shakespeare to Scribe; in novels, from *Ivanhoe* to Paul de Kock; in newspapers, now that we have writers who produce serials for a public inclined to gobble them up daily like a slice of buttered bread. In short, in this world of printed paper and cardboard decorations we are surrounded by conventional Jews: grimacing, usurious, shamming, speaking jargon, and more or less manufactured of mist.[1]

Nothing more than false stereotyping could be found in any of these forms, Ben-Lévi accused – not even in the opera of his co-religionist Halévy (whom he, in this context, chooses not to mention). His anger at these conventional images burst forth shortly after the appalling *affaire Damas* of 1840, when *La Gazette de France*, *La Quotidienne*, and other French papers openly voiced medieval beliefs about Jews. Ben-Lévi and other Jewish writers in the new journal *Les Archives israélites* registered both shock and exasperation that these distortions would not go away, despite the changes in political climate during the previous decade.

As Ben-Lévi accuses and as we have seen, *La Juive* was not isolated in literature and drama in its recasting of conventional Jewish images. But these images also appeared in mild to offensive forms in various types

---

[1] Ben-Lévi, "Les Complices d'un adjectif," *Les Archives israélites* 2 (1841): 151, cited in Girard, *De l'émancipation à l'égalité*, 141: "Aimez-vous le juif? On en a mis partout. Au théâtre, depuis Shakespeare [*sic*] jusqu'à Scribe; dans les romans, depuis Ivanhoé jusqu'à Paul de Kock; dans les journaux, depuis qu'il y a des écrivains qui commettent des feuilletons et un public qui consent à en avaler quotidiennement une tartine, partout enfin dans ce monde de papier imprimé et de décorations de carton, on nous donne des juifs de convention, grimaçant, usurant, feignant, jargonnant et plus ou moins fabriqués à la vapeur."

of public discourse, signifying a mixture of fear, fascination, and antisemitism and raising questions about discrepancies between legal and social equality within the post-emancipation milieu. In its social and political dimensions, the prominent stereotype of the usurious Jew expresses the Jew's historical experience as a pariah in Christian societies, while also touching on contemporary French wariness about this relatively new group of citizens. Shylock variants, including Eléazar, seem particularly relevant to complaints about Jewish usury and economic power during the July Monarchy, appearing nearly simultaneously with the government's deeper symbolic embrace of Judaism and Jews through its passage of the *culte israélite* law, and with Louis-Philippe's endorsement of the law. As the king assured the Consistoire israélite in January 1831, he continued to support both the religious freedom of the Jews and their reclaiming of civil rights, commended them for being good citizens, and noted "[w]e shall always welcome you among us with pleasure."[2]

Despite these assurances, with the economic and political shifts of power and the growth of industry during this era – one that historians have commonly labeled a "Bourgeois Monarchy" in which France was run "like a joint-stock company by a narrow oligarchy"[3] – fears about capitalistic expansion fueled concerns and obsessions about Jewish wealth and added to a growing Rothschild mythology. Despite the fact that Jews represented a small portion of the French populace (approximately 70,000, with slightly over 12,000 of the nearly 775,000 Parisians in the early 1830s), and that the majority lived in poor to modest conditions, the image of the Jewish usurer took on renewed power as a symbol of materialism during this period. By the 1840s, an "anti-capitalist antisemitism," grafted onto Christian antisemitism, appeared in public forums.[4]

Contemporary non-Jewish writers, although seemingly a vocal minority, demonstrated a hardened belief in the old stereotype and

---

[2] *Le Constitutionnel*, 4 January 1831: 1: "Nous vous verrons toujours au milieu de nous avec plaisir."

[3] Roger Magraw, *France, 1815–1914: The Bourgeois Century* (New York: Oxford University Press, 1986), 51.

[4] Berg, *Histoire des juifs*, 155–6.

a hatred of Jews who supposedly embodied it. Underlying their ran-
corous convictions was a fear of Jewish domination, at times made
obvious through inflammatory language. The image emerged in condemnations of capitalism, as well as of other developments considered
foreign and detrimental to French traditions by some citizens, including the rise of philosophical influence at the expense of religious faith
(that is, Christianity) and the shift of power from a refined and deserving aristocracy to an immoral, money-hungry bourgeoisie, which was
characterized as caring little for established authority or honest working classes. Conservative Catholic writers who viewed the *philosophe*
legacy as atheistic and immoral, for example, at times emphasized the
relationship between capitalistic Jews and philosophical movements
and groups. Some writers who bemoaned the increase of industrialization for its threat to agrarian France placed the "cosmopolitan Jew"
at the center of their discussions. Moreover, many Jews who were eager
to strike a rapport with French Christian society acknowledged the past
practices of usury within economically restricted Jewish communities,
but warned that its continuation would hinder the progress of Jewish
citizens toward social equality. At the same time, they regretted the
exaggerated associations between Jews and usury.

Along with the conventional image of the miser, the narrow-minded
Jewish fanatic was recognized by a number of contemporary
Frenchmen as representative of Judaic practices. In this era of reform,
Jews who were resistant to modifying their religious traditions to fit
the mores of the dominant culture attracted the label "fanatique" or
"séparatiste." (Léon Halévy's attack on Jewish fanaticism is a case in
point.) In some discussions and representations, the images of separatist and miser, who were both viewed as alien to modern society, are
merged. Conservative voices who debated the *culte israélite* law spoke of
Judaism as an "anti-Christian religion" and of Jews in France as "a nation
apart." One liberal voice of the Chambre des députés noted that Jews
of the past might be reproached for arousing medieval hatreds against
them through the conservation of their language, writing, and part of
their "oriental dress," as well as their "immense wealth" – with the likely
implication that those who continued to separate themselves in these

ways would further engender hatred. Others spoke of the progress French Jews had made toward "civilization" – with the exception of two Rhine departments.[5]

Liberal encouragement of a new, less "oriental" Jewish identity, *israélite* rather than *juif*, was partially grounded in Enlightenment ideals. But with this encouragement came a certain Enlightenment wariness toward Jews and Judaism. Eléazar's depiction as a victim of obviously unjust treatment by the Christian majority illustrates well the Voltairean theme of intolerance recurring in contemporary writings and governmental debates in the July Monarchy. Yet his portrayal as a vengeful hater of Christians and Christianity sends mixed messages that are rooted in the paradoxical views of the *philosophes*, who expressed sympathy for Jewish persecution while condemning rabbinical Judaism as evil and unassimilable. The ambiguity in Rachel's religious characterization also touches on unresolved questions concerning the social integration of Jews.

Bound to issues of Jewish acculturation and fears of Jewish economic power was the Orientalist fascination with Semitic characters. Rachel's romantic/sexual image, while bearing on social views of women in the nineteenth century, illustrates the attraction to oriental exoticism that was often embodied as a feminine or domesticated character. It is the more pleasant and seemingly innocuous view of the Oriental Other: Rachel is a pariah, but an acceptable one because she is an object of desire and sexual fantasy who can be controlled. Eléazar, as the unassimilable Jew whose actions foment disharmony and destruction, arouses fear because he cannot be dominated. Such Orientalist expressions entail what Edward Said describes as "a kind of free-floating mythology of the Orient" that emerged from a Western consciousness of dominance and authority over the East. Many of these relish the Orient as exotic and mysterious; its differences, in opposition to the Occident, are intriguing, but, at times, fear-inducing. As Said writes, the Orient "vacillates between the West's contempt for what is familiar and its shivers of delight in – or fear of – novelty."[6] Because

---

[5] *Archives parlementaires*, vol. LXV, 312, 316; vol. LXVI, 459.
[6] Said, *Orientalism*, 59.

of these apprehensions, and the assumption of cultural superiority, European portrayals of Muslims, Ottomans, Arabs – or Semites – acted as a way of controlling the mysterious and relatively unknown Orient.[7] In this dynamic of fear and fascination and vantage point of domination, Orientalism explicitly resembles Western antisemitism.[8]

La Juive resonates with these eclectic but related views and relationships. In its vivid portrayal of stereotypes blended with elements of Judaism and clerical history, the opera gains in power and complexity if considered alongside social imagery and identity that suggest a keen interest in Jewish issues as they point to a latent and possibly rising antisemitism during the July Monarchy. Although the opera's 1835 première predates the explosion of antisemitic pamphlets and essays of the 1840s, its Jewish elements bear upon currents of thought that ran through both decades of this political era. With the use of Eléazar and Rachel as symbols of religious and political persecution along with allusions to the images of the Jewish miser and embittered fanatic, the opera touched on a contemporary social paradox: the vacillation between the embracing and rejection of Jews in the land that promised *fraternité* to all its citizens. Moreover, in its characterizations and its presentation of a Passover seder, the ambiguities surrounding issues of Judaic religious identity in the July Monarchy are evoked, adding to the vibrancy and controversy of the opera's subject.

JEWISH ECONOMIC AND POLITICAL STATUS

French anxiety about the economic power of the Jewish minority did not emerge for the first time in the 1830s and 1840s. As revealed in a number of official actions and debates about Jewish practices in earlier decades, this anxiety had frequently taken form in accusations of usury, at times to justify general restrictions against Jewish communities. During the Empire, Napoleon drew political attention to the accumulation of wealth among Jews, specifically to practices among Jewish

---

[7] *Ibid.*, 60.
[8] *Ibid.*, 28. Although Said treats Orientalism primarily in its Islamic branch, he stresses the "historical, cultural, and political truth" of this resemblance.

creditors in Alsace.[9] With his 1807 convocation of the group of Jewish savants known as the Sanhédrin, he made aggressive efforts to address these practices and to oversee the reinterpretation of Jewish laws in closer alignment with French civil law. On the question of loans ("prêts"), the Sanhédrin declared that the making of "excessive or ruinous profit" went against the dictates of the Holy Scripture.[10] As a result of the group's doctrinal guidelines, however, Napoleon issued an imperial decree on 17 March 1808, transforming them into restrictive regulations of Jewish civil rights.

The decisions of this body were promoted by the French Consistoires and by individual Jews who supported reform and improved relations with French Christians and the French government. Elie Halévy's Consistoire-endorsed catechism reflects Sanhédrin directives (see pp. 80–1 above), including its condemnation of the practice of usury. In Halévy's journal *L'Israélite français*, an article entitled "Le Mot juif" discusses historical associations of the term "usury," beginning with an exploration and denunciation of the erroneous equivalence between "juif" and "usurier" in French and other languages.[11] The article reiterates the Sanhédrin's definition of usury as "illicit interest" only, including interest exceeding the legal rate.[12] While the author emphasizes that usury in this sense was a vice contrary to Jewish law, he justifies its practice during the "centuries of barbarism" because of

---

[9] According to Heinrich Graetz, *History of the Jews*, 6 vols. (Philadelphia: The Jewish Publication Society of America, 1895), vol. v, 476, Napoleon's concerns had been triggered in 1806: while in Alsace after the campaign of a hundred days against Austria, he had been besieged by complaints by local officials and a deputation of residents that Jewish creditors had taken possession of entire villages and that a large number of estates were mortgaged to them.

[10] Léon Halévy, *Résumé de l'histoire des juifs modernes*, 307, 342.

[11] *L'Israélite français* 1 (1817): 239: "The word 'juif' is used in French in the same way that *Giudeo, Judio, Jew* and *Jude* are used in Italian, Spanish, English and German with the same meaning, to which dictionaries add that of *usurer*, because Jews, it is said, are in the habit of practicing usury. Nevertheless, not all Israelites are usurers, and not all usurers are Israelites." ("Le mot Juif est employé en français comme *Giudeo, Judio, Jew* et *Jude* en italien, en espagnol, en anglais et en allemand dans la même signification, à laquelle les dictionnaires ajoutent celle d'*usurier*, parce que les Juifs ont l'habitude, dit-on, de faire l'usure; cependant tous les Israélites ne sont pas usuriers, et tous les usuriers ne sont pas Israélites.")

[12] The author ("E. F.") refers to Articles VIII and IX of the Sanhédrin decisions.

restrictions from sanctioned methods of commerce, as well as governmental taxes and tributes imposed on Jews. But, he went on to stress,
for the emancipated, legally protected French Jew, the practice was
loathsome and even criminal:

> But the nineteenth-century Jew who practices usury becomes *guilty* in
> the eyes of the society of which he is a part, and which can reward him
> for his industriousness and his talents, and pay the cost of his work.
> Finally, the French Israelite who decided to engage in usury would be
> looked upon as a *criminal*, because he lives in one of the most beautiful
> countries of the world, where national agriculture and industry, the
> [Atlantic] Ocean, and the Mediterranean offer immense resources for
> commerce and navigation; because the law empowers the monarch, and
> the monarch upholds the law; in a word, because in a country such as
> France, he cannot become a usurer without appearing to be an ingrate
> toward the country, without violating the tutelary laws which protect
> him and make him equal to the other subjects of the wisest, the most
> just, and the best of all kings.[13]

The successive generation of Jewish writers examined the same
subject, most pertinently Léon Halévy in his 1828 history of modern
Jews. As in his father's catechism, Léon incorporated the Sanhédrin
decision on "Loans between Israelites and non-Israelites" in the volume's appendices. In his most extensive discussion, he defends the
practice along similar historical lines to those given in "Le Mot juif"
(and, in a diluted version, in the review of *La Juive* in *La Quotidienne*;
see p. 247 above). Under the subheading "Usure," in a section on
the seventeenth and eighteenth centuries, Léon explains that French

---

[13] *L'Israélite français* 1 (1817): 241–2: "Mais le Juif du XIXᵉ siècle qui fait l'usure, se
rend *coupable* envers la société dont il fait partie, et dont il peut obtenir la
récompense réclamée par son industrie, le tribut dû à ses talens, ou le prix de
son travail. Enfin, l'Israélite français qui se livrerait à l'usure, deviendrait
criminel, parce qu'il habite un des plus beaux pays de l'univers, où l'agriculture
et l'industrie nationale, l'Océan et la Méditerranée offrent des ressources
immenses au commerce et à la navigation; parce que le monarque y règne par la
loi, et la loi par le monarque; en un mot, parce que dans un pays tel que la
France, il ne peut devenir usurier sans encourir la tache d'ingrat à la patrie, sans
enfreindre les lois tutélaires qui le protègent et qui l'égalent aux autres sujets du
plus sage, du plus juste et du meilleur des rois."

Jews were restricted from all modes of commerce and industry except trade in livestock, gold, or silver, but that when these legal means of subsistence were successively proscribed, Jews were "reduced" to the practice of usury.[14] Despite recognition of the practice, however, he heatedly points out how many Jews of Alsace-Lorraine were falsely accused, arrested, and convicted under its pretext through the illegal actions of judges, ministers, and police superintendents.[15] Léon does not condone usury, but stresses that other, more just methods of control could have been followed rather than subjecting Alsatian Jews to the whims of a single official and to "irregular, persecutory procedures."[16]

Unlike the writer in "Le Mot juif," Léon did not overtly attack the practice in the nineteenth century, nor did he mention it among his admonitions about Jewish *régénération*. But his inclusion of the Sanhédrin decision suggests that, like his father and other reform-minded Jews, he viewed the practice as antithetical to the Jewish religious heritage and the values of good citizenship. His seeming restraint from open criticism appears linked to his awareness that attacks on usury, particularly official attempts to control it, were often stratagems for a more diffuse oppression of Jews. He cites the restrictive Napoleonic decree that violated the principle of legal equality and "brought such a great joy to the persecutors of the Jews";[17] moreover, he passionately describes the marquis de Lattier's 1818 proposal to renew Napoleon's decree against Jewish usury (the so-called "loi d'exception") as a generalized attack on Jewish rights, emphasizing that this petition before the governmental houses contained "vague

[14] Léon Halévy, *Résumé de l'histoire des juifs modernes*, 283–6. With no other alternatives, usury "became the source of their misfortunes, if, that is, one can accuse of a crime men who are deprived of means that are legal and common to everyone else for making a living" ("est devenu la source de leurs malheurs, si toutefois l'on peut accuser de crime des hommes privés des moyens licites et communs à tous les autres pour soutenir une vie").

[15] *Ibid.*

[16] *Ibid.*, 286. One wonders if some of Léon's "proof" of official misconduct toward Alsatian Jews came from first-hand accounts by his father, who lived in Metz shortly before the Revolution.

[17] *Ibid.*, 309–11.

denunciations" common to ignorance and prejudice rather than facts.[18] The proposal failed, much to the relief of French Jews.

Indirect antisemitic actions and accusations of usury persisted during the Restoration and even into the July Monarchy. Despite increased institutional support of French Jews, attacks on Jewish usury and avarice were rife in contemporary writings and iconography, contradicting the one-dimensional portrayals of this era as a fully tolerant period. Although these did not represent a formalized, systematic antisemitism or a majority view, they reveal that age-old stereotypes remained valid for an outspoken minority at least. The 1833 terracotta sculpture of Nathan Rothschild by the French caricaturist Jean-Pierre Dantan *jeune* (1800–69), for example, embodies overtly and vehemently the old image of the miserly Jew: Rothschild's face is grotesquely distorted, with a thickly lipped, fish-like mouth; he tightly clutches purses and bags, with coins spilling down around his feet (see Illustration 12).[19]

Interspersed among published complaints about the increasing materialism of the Monarchy's bourgeois society were similar images and references to Rothschild, many of them from the pens of Catholic adherents and socialists. In 1835, for example, the pro-Catholic journal *L'Univers religieux* despaired of "this epoch of money," Jewish usury, and "the authority of the name Rothschild."[20] Among authors who combined the charges of materialism with issues and events of a larger scope included such Catholic writers as Renault Bécourt: in

[18] Léon Halévy, *Résumé de l'histoire des juifs modernes*, 317. See the discussion of the "décret contre l'usure" and Lattier's proposal to renew it in Bernhard Blumenkranz, *Histoire des juifs en France* (Paris: Edouard Privat, 1972), 306.

[19] According to Jean-Pierre Dantan's *Dantan jeune: Caricatures et portraits de la société romantiques* (Paris: Paris-Musées, 1989), 80, the caricature appeared in London in June 1833. Although the sculpture is of James Rothschild's brother Nathan, whose office was in London while James's was in Paris, Dantan undoubtedly aimed his harsh ridicule at the entire banking family. According to Anka Muhlstein, *Baron James: The Rise of the French Rothschilds* (New York and Paris: Vendome Press, 1987), 73, James was extremely sensitive to the many caricatures that appeared, whereas "his brothers pinned them to the wall, as signs of Rothschild success."

[20] *L'Univers religieux* 3, no. 416 (11 March 1835): col. 1309; 3, no. 368 (14 January 1835): col. 730.

12 Terracotta sculpture of Nathan Rothschild by Dantan *jeune* (1833) (Cliché Musée de Carnavalet: © PMVP/Andréani)

his *Conspiration universelle du judaïsme* (1835), he held Jews responsible for the French Revolution and claimed them to be intent on world domination.[21] The socialist philosopher Charles Fourier integrated familiar antisemitic notions with attacks on capitalism and philosophical

[21] Szajkowski, "Jewish Saint-Simonians," 48.

movements in his critical writings on French social institutions, including *La Fausse Industrie* (1835–6).[22] In the second decade of the July Monarchy, publications by the Catholic leader Louis Veuillot, Fourier disciple Alphonse Toussenel, historian Théophile Hallez, and pamphleteer Mathieu Georges Dairnvaell, often using incendiary language, articulated irrational fears of Jewish power and blamed Jews for the social ills of modern French society.

The image of the usurious Jew recurs throughout the often extreme, anti-capitalist arguments of these writers. In *La Fausse Industrie*, Fourier, whom some considered a demented crank,[23] speaks of dishonest, villainous Jews, whom he accuses of having brought about the poverty and ruination of honest, productive members of society. He targets both small- and large-scale capitalists, using such biblical and literary images as "the Jew Iscariot" and "Scapin the small shopkeeper" to make his points, while aiming directly at Rothschild.[24] In Fourier's mind, Jews embodied the "false industry" that had moved France away from all that was "natural" and beneficial.

Toussenel intensified the anti-capitalist antisemitism of his mentor in *Les Juifs, rois de l'époque: Histoire de la féodalité financière* (1847).[25] In an acidic introductory diatribe, Toussenel reiterates the associations of "juif" with usury that contemporary Jewish writers were fighting to dissolve.[26] Throughout his essay, Toussenel attempted to prove his central thesis that Jews had become the virtual kings of France and,

---

[22] *La Fausse Industrie morcelée, répugnante, mensongère, et l'antidote, l'industrie naturelle, combinée, attrayante, véridique, donnant quadruple produit*, 2 vols. (Paris: Bossange Père; L'auteur, 1835–6). See Jonathan Beecher, *Charles Fourier: The Visionary and His World* (Berkeley, Los Angeles, and London: University of California Press, 1986), 416ff.

[23] *Government and Society in France, 1814–1848*, ed. Irene Collins (London: Edward Arnold, 1970), 77.

[24] Beecher, *Fourier*, 201; Fourier, *La Fausse Industrie*, vol. II, M8.

[25] 2 vols., Paris: Gabriel de Gonet, 1847.

[26] Toussenel, *Les Juifs*, vol. I, i: "Like all Frenchmen, I use the despised name of Jew to describe anyone who traffics in money, any unproductive parasite living off the work of others. As far as I am concerned, Jew, usurer, trafficker are synonyms." ("J'appelle, comme le peuple, de ce nom méprisé de juif tout trafiquant d'espèces, tout parasite improductif, vivant de la substance et du travail d'autrui. Juif, usurier, trafiquant, sont pour moi synonymes.")

in their powerful position, were destroying the country. He claimed that from 1830 real sovereignty had been vested not in the king but in merchants, manufacturers, and bankers. Through the government's imprudent and overly generous granting of *droit de cité* (citizenship) to Jews, France had become "slave" to Jewish masters.[27] Proof of its enslavement was the Jewish monopoly of banks, mining, and the new railroad.[28] Further evidence lay in the failure of the press, particularly the *Journal des débats*, to criticize this "true royalty," while it openly attacked the "official royalty."[29]

The metaphor of a Jewish capitalistic monarchy, centralized in the Rothschild banking family, was more elaborately portrayed in several cheaply printed pamphlets written by journalist Georges Dairnvaell under the pseudonym "Satan." In one such pamphlet, *Histoire édifiante et curieuse de Rothschild Ier, roi des juifs*, which went through eighteen editions, Dairnvaell writes in mock historical style of the Rothschild dynasty and of the reign of James Rothschild in France, referring variously to the "royalty of Rothschild I" and "royalty of money and speculation," and ending with a kingly salute that echoes his title: "Vive Rothschild Ier, roi des Juifs!"[30] In this satiric chronicle, Dairnvaell narrates Mayer Anselm Rothschild's founding of the dynasty, its continuation through Nathan, James, and three other sons, its superseding of the European Jewish dynasty of Cohen, and its coexistence with that of "Fould I" (Benoit Fould), deputy under Louis-Philippe. The author concentrates on Rothschild affiliations with European rulers, the loans and war subsidies that made them "maîtres de la banque" after 1815, and their triumph and enrichment at the expense of France's impoverishment and defeats, including Napoleon's failure

---

[27] *Ibid.*, ix.   [28] *Ibid.*, 115.   [29] *Ibid.*, 140.

[30] Georges Dairnvaell, *Histoire édifiante et curieuse de Rothschild Ier, roi des juifs, par Satan*, 2nd ed. (Paris: L'Editeur, 1846), 5, 12, 32. (The size of this pamphlet, approximately 4" × 6", and its price, 30 centimes, suggest a "street" circulation.) Dairnvaell's other pamphlets include *Rothschild Ier, ses valets et son peuple* (Paris, 1845) (five editions) and *Histoire édifiante et curieuse de Rothschild Ier, roi des Juifs, suivie du récit de la catastrophe du 8 juillet, par un témoin oculaire* (Paris, 1846) (fifteen editions). For a discussion of these and other pamphlets, as well as pro-Rothschild rejoinders, see Szajkowski, "Jewish Saint-Simonians," 51–2.

at Waterloo.[31] (At this point Dairnvaell's rhetoric becomes particularly inflammatory as he remarks that the Rothschilds remained in France as "a leech remains on the vein of humanity."[32]) Enumerating the millions of francs loaned to the French government by the Rothschilds during the July Monarchy, the author attributes to them a powerful political leverage, suggesting that they "imposed peace on the French government" for their own ends.[33] The dynasty's power reached its peak in the 1840s, according to Dairnvaell: with the borrowing of 200 million francs by the French government in 1844 and the inauguration of the railroad, Chemin de fer du Nord, James Rothschild was crowned "Rothschild I."[34] Like Toussenel, Dairnvaell credits the *Journal des débats*, among other periodicals, with advancing this Rothschild "royalty."

The usurious practices that Dairnvaell places at the foundation of Rothschild loans, and thus of Rothschild power, are attributed to the majority of French Jews in Théophile Hallez's *Des Juifs en France: De leur état moral et politique depuis les premiers temps de la monarchie jusqu'à nos jours*.[35] Like Toussenel, he accuses French Jews of participating in dishonest professions, with the exception of Jews who worked in the "liberal professions" and others he considered "useful"; only these few understood modern society. Addressing his imagined majority directly, Hallez declares usury as "the most common profession among you," and speaks of lucrative transactions and deals that ruined others, buying land for profit rather than cultivation, and selling mercenaries. Claiming that many French Jews had replaced the selling of slaves with the selling of soldiers, he links these types of "trafficking of human beings" that motivate "the harsh and all too merited name of *merchant of human flesh!*" By continuing such practices, simply by "remaining Jews" in Hallez's mind, these new citizens showed how little they deserved citizenship:

> These are the services you render to the homeland in return for the right of citizenship which she granted you.

[31] *Ibid.*, 12.   [32] *Ibid.*   [33] *Ibid.*, 15.   [34] *Ibid.*, 20.
[35] Paris: G.-A. Dentu, 1845.

You ask us to treat you like our brothers; we want to, and we have proved it. But isn't it time you began to treat us the same way? . . . You don't lend your brothers money at usurious rates; perhaps you don't even require legal interest on the sums you lend them: why do you inflict the most sordid, the most ruthless usury on us? . . . Why, in a word, can you not stop being Jews?[36]

Brimming with hatred, Hallez created a portrait of French Jews that makes the Shylock vestiges in Eléazar pale by comparison. The author's reference to Shakespeare's Jew is clear in his accusation of Jews trading in human flesh. Beyond this allusion, an epigraph from *The Merchant of Venice*, which opens the book, illustrates the merging of literary and social images and, as in the early reception of *La Juive*, the penetration of Shylock into the public mind. The quotation, Shylock's famous declaration of social separateness, save for business dealings with Christians – "I will buy with you, sell with you, talk with you, . . . but I will not eat with you, drink with you nor pray with you" – underlines much of Hallez's discussion. Hallez casts the Jews of France as pariahs, whose "shameful dealing" has brought about a "plague on the nation."[37] Similar castigations emerged in the self-contradictory Heine, who lashed out at the capitalistic "Jewish poison" and "Herr von Shylock," his moniker for Rothschild.[38]

Associations between these stereotyped attacks and regrets about basic changes in traditional French values appear in the writings of Fourier and Toussenel. According to both mentor and disciple, Jews figured prominently in philosophical groups who, in affiliation with capitalists, were leading French society in errant directions. Fourier

---

[36] Hallez, *Des Juifs*, ix–xi: "Voilà les services que vous rendez à la patrie, en retour du droit de cité qu'elle vous a octroyé! [new paragraph] Vous demandez que nous vous traitions comme nos frères; nous le voulons, et nous l'avons prouvé. Mais vous-mêmes, n'est-il pas temps que vous commenciez à nous traiter ainsi? . . . Envers vos frères, vous n'exercez pas l'usure; peut-être même n'en exigez-vous pas l'intérêt légal des sommes que vous leur prêtez: pourquoi exercez-vous l'usure la plus sordide, la plus impitoyable envers nous? . . . Pourquoi, en un mot, voulez-vous pas cesser d'être des Juifs?"

[37] *Ibid.*, xviii.

[38] Sammons, *Heinrich Heine*, 250, cited in William G. Atwood, *The Parisian Worlds of Frédéric Chopin* (New Haven and London: Yale University Press, 1999), 381, n. 48.

speaks of a "philosophical cabal," which he defines as a "vast collection of conspiracies against authority, propriety ... the educated and artistic classes, cultivators and workers, that philosophy pretends to protect."[39] Among this cabal, Fourier focuses his attack on the Saint-Simonians, alluding to the largely Jewish makeup of the movement's leaders by labeling them "apostates."[40] He condemns their stances as moralists who wanted to change human nature, their attacks on "property, religion, and power," and their respect for the entrepreneurship and skills of successful bankers and industrialists.[41]

Like Fourier, Toussenel links Saint-Simonians and French Jews in their joint path to domination and their disregard for French traditions. In a section of his *Les Juifs* entitled "Saint-Simon et Juda," Toussenel stresses the large percentage of Saint-Simonians who were Jewish and the alignment of Saint-Simonian social and economic credos with what he views as innate Jewish greed. The alliance between "the dispersed remnants" ("les débris dispersés") of the Saint-Simonian and Jewish tribes indulged in the spoils of France, taking for themselves *"the cream of the milk cows,* as the Jews say."[42] Toussenel points out that the advancement of this alliance was built on the Saint-Simonian principle, "to each according to his ability, to each ability according to his works" ("à chacun selon sa capacité, à chaque capacité selon ses oeuvres"). Rather than viewing this as a positive principle of individual merit and accomplishment, he deems it selfish, and "revolutionary and subversive" in its opposition to hereditary rights.[43] In its push to power, the Saint-Simonian alliance had built an "industrial, financial, or commercial feudalism" ("la féodalité industrielle ou financière, ou commerciale") that was characterized by Jewish avarice and treachery and, moreover, "personified by the city-dwelling Jew."[44] This commercial

---

[39] Fourier, *La Fausse Industrie*, vol. I, 2.   [40] *Ibid.*, 8.

[41] Beecher, *Fourier*, 415–16. According to Beecher, Fourier became increasingly hostile because of his jealousy of the success of the Saint-Simonians in attracting disciples and his anger that they had ignored his doctrinal critique.

[42] Toussenel, *Les Juifs*, vol. I, 123: *"la crème des vaches à lait,* comme dit le juif."

[43] *Ibid.*

[44] *Ibid.*, 132–3. Toussenel, like Fourier, refers to Judas Iscariot to drive home his point about Jewish treachery.

system had grown through an eschewing of the pure traditions and morality of French society, Toussenel argues: "The words *homeland, religion* and *faith* have no meaning for those men whose hearts have been replaced by an *écu*."[45] (The *écu* in Toussenel's caricature of the Jewish capitalist is the same gold coin that Eléazar sings of in the Act II trio in *La Juive*.)

Toussenel and other antisemitic writers lamented the loss of power of the hereditary aristocracy to "feudalistic" capitalism. Aligning with Hallez's depicted Rothschild royalty, Toussenel speaks of this alleged Judaic power base as "l'aristocratie des écus," "l'aristocratie financière," or "l'aristocratie d'argent." This elite, he insists, was characterized not by a generous-spirited *noblesse oblige*, like the traditional nobility, but rather by the comparatively self-serving "chacun pour soi" (each for himself). True aristocrats "left the lucrative professions of commerce, usury, and chicanery to villains," while the cosmopolitan "aristocratie des écus" preferred inferior, deceitful professions, especially law, and disdained such "honorable" professions as farming.[46] Furthermore, unlike the traditional aristocracy, this privileged group proved neither chivalrous, philanthrophic, or poetic, as demonstrated by its lack of concern for the impoverished and by its attacks on Lamartine in the Saint-Simonian paper *Le Globe* – that "*Catholic* paper maintained by *Protestant* bankers and edited by *Jews*" – and in the *Journal des débats*, that "friend of the *haute banque*" (that is, the Rothschilds).[47] More "insatiable" than the old nobility, this new, judaicized aristocracy

---

[45] *Ibid.*, 134: "Les mots de *patrie*, de *religion*, de *foi*, n'ont pas de sens pour ces hommes qui ont un écu à la place du coeur." Toussenel ran down a list of wealthy and influential Jews and Saint-Simonians (chiefly former Saint-Simonians) who belonged to this alliance; other than the non-Saint-Simonian Rothschild, he included Emile Pereire, director (and co-founder with Rothschild) of the Chemin de fer du Nord, Père Enfantin, Advisory Secretary of Administration of the Chemin de fer de Lyon, Alfred d'Eichthal, brother of the Saint-Simonian Gustave d'Eichthal, who earned huge sums in the Bourse's "roulette," Michel Chevalier, the writer and editor who became Advisor of State and professor of political economy, Charles Duveyrier, who "monopolized" the commercial press, and Olinde Rodrigues, who advised the Rothschilds (*ibid.*, 130).

[46] *Ibid.*

[47] *Ibid.*, 136: "feuille *catholique* entretenue par des banquiers *protestants* et rédigée par des *juifs*"; "ami de la *haute banque*."

"bleeds a nation white, turns it into an idiot, debases it, and kills it morally and physically in the same blow."[48] With the incendiary exclamations that permeate his text, Toussenel clearly intended his critique as a call to arms to break the exploitative "financial feudalism" and to denigrate Jews, his primary enemies, and, secondarily, Saint-Simonians, Protestants, and others who cooperated with them in capitalistic endeavors. In the book's preface, he does not obscure his belligerent summons: "merciless war on parasites of all religions and nationalities, war on cosmopolitan bankers, war on Jewish monopolizers!!"[49]

More directly suggestive of antisemitism within the milieu of *La Juive* and its reception is a parody of the opera that appeared a year after its première, not in Paris, but in Lyon. This work, *La Juive de Pantin; ou, La Friture manquée*, described as a *"folie* [folly] in three acts and in verse, mixed with *couplets,"* and "imitating a very serious opera," was performed at the Théâtre du Gymnase on 25 April 1836. This parody answered Eléazar's Shylock with yet another variation of the stereotype of the Jewish miser. While the name of the title character (Rachel) is retained, Eléazar becomes "Balthazard" and is identified in the list of personages as *"juif"* and *"marchand-fripier,"* an old-clothes dealer. Although an allusion to a common occupation among the poorer Jews of Europe, it is undoubtedly a denigrating one. With overt references to Balthazard's usury, and the transformation of Rachel's early rescue into a kidnapping, the parody's bias is clear.[50]

---

[48] *Ibid.,* 138: "saigne une nation à blanc, la crétinise et l'abâtardit, la tue du même coup au physique et au moral."

[49] *Ibid.,* xviii: "guerre impitoyable aux parasites de toutes les religions et de tous les drapeaux, guerre aux banquiers cosmopolites, guerre aux Juifs monopoleurs!!"

[50] The comedy also satirizes the dual identity of Rachel, but avoids her death – "la friture manquée." In one final scene, Rachel says to Balthazard and Dugrognon, her Christian father, that she will be daughter to both; however, she will also marry her Christian lover Popold and become Christian. (The changes in plot are remarked on in Act II by Popold, who says, "c'est mieux qu'à l'Opéra" – "it's better than at the Opéra".) At the end of the parody, Rachel says to the audience ("au public") that, like another *juive* "not far from you," she does not want to "fry."

The tenacious stereotyping and often vicious antisemitism represented in these accounts disturbed many Jews, shocking particularly those who, in the 1830s, had been given positions of honor in public arenas that had been off limits in earlier regimes. Ben-Lévi's reaction to the alarming frequency of conventional Jewish imagery was not singular, neither were his complaints about the ingrained associations of the term "juif" with usury. Writing in *Les Archives israélites* in 1842, Ben-Lévi reiterated the protest of *L'Israélite français* more than two decades earlier, but emphasized the sanctioning of this association by French authorities (not merely by isolated bigots) in his quotation from the *Dictionnaire de l'Académie*: "A Jew is a man who lends at usurious rates of interest, sells at exorbitant prices, and seeks to earn money by unjust and sordid means."[51] He also commented on a type of finger-pointing he observed, seemingly in casual conversation, that did not jibe with the religious and civil liberty enjoyed under Louis-Philippe's regime:

> What is the meaning of this senseless phrase "He's a Jew"? I hear it said: "M. Crémieux is a very distinguished lawyer, *he's a Jew*. M. Azévédo, the new prefect of the Pyrenees, is an eminent administrator, *he's a Jew*. Who wrote the admirable music for *La Reine de Chypre*? Halévy, *he's a Jew*" ... When you tell me that M. Delessert is the father of the French savings bank, do you add that he is a Protestant? When you talk to me about M. Guizot, do you tell me that he belongs to the Reform Church? ... For if it is in an attempt to praise that one expresses oneself in this way, it is on the contrary an insult that implies that the words *Jew* and *eminent* are somehow contradictory; if it is due to persistent ill will, why should we put up with it in a country where we are all equal under the law, where the monarchy is free of religious prejudice and the judiciary has only one religion: that of impartiality?[52]

---

[51] Ben-Lévi, "Les Complices d'un adjectif," *Les Archives israélites* 3 (1842): 147, cited in Girard, *De l'émancipation à l'égalité*, 128, n. 1: "On appelle juif un homme qui prête à usure, qui vend exorbitamment cher et qui cherche à gagner de l'argent par des moyens injustes et sordides."

[52] Ben-Lévi, "Les Complices d'un adjectif," *Les Archives israélites* 3 (1842), cited in Girard, *De l'émancipation à l'égalité*, 128: "Que signifie cette phrase vide de sens: *C'est un juif* ? J'entends dire: M. Crémieux est un avocat très distingué, *c'est un*

As Ben-Lévi acknowledges, discrepancies between political recognition and social tolerance of Jewish citizens had become glaringly apparent by the 1840s. The adaptation of old stereotypes, the "singling out" of Jews in a variety of venues, and the public (and undoubtedly private) efforts of Jewish and tolerant Christian citizens to fight against old distortions cast light on the contradictions and controversies surrounding the Jewish minority in France. Despite the positions of Louis-Philippe's regime and the outwardly liberal atmosphere of this era, outdated attitudes – throwbacks to the Middle Ages, as the politician Mérilhou accused – held on tenaciously. As reflected in the accounts of Fourier and other antisemitic writers, opposition to the social advancement and acceptance of Jewish citizens, especially in positions of power and prestige, ran parallel with opposition to political factions that encouraged individual rights over hereditary rights and religious tradition. Although Fourier represents an extremist voice, it seems that a portion of conservative Frenchmen (how large a portion is impossible to determine) shared his discomfort with Jewish acculturation and social equality, associating them with a range of threats to old ways of life, including an agriculturally based economy, the cultural dominance of the aristocracy, and the authority of the Catholic Church and faith.

ANTISEMITISM WITHIN THEATRICAL AND MUSICAL CIRCLES

It is clear that antisemitic attitudes existing to some degree within the French populace contributed to the topicality of La Juive. But did such views belong to the theatrical, musical, and literary milieu of Scribe

juif. M. Azévédo, le nouveau préfet des Pyrénées, est un administrateur éminent, c'est un juif. De qui est l'admirable musique de la reine de Chypre? De Halévy, c'est un juif... Quand vous me dites que M. Delessert est en France le père des caisses d'épargne, ajoutez-vous 'c'est un protestant'? Lorsque vous me parlez de M. Guizot, me dites-vous qu'il appartient au culte réformé?... Car enfin si c'est à titre de louange qu'on s'exprime ainsi, on nous insulte en donnant à entendre que les mots juif et éminent sont étonnés de se confondre; si c'est par suite d'une malveillance continue, pourquoi le souffririons-nous dans un pays où nous sommes tous égaux devant la loi, où la royauté est exempte de préjugés de croyance, où la magistrature n'a qu'une religion, celle de l'impartialité?"

and Halévy? Among friends and acquaintances, in the rarefied worlds of the salon and the Académie royale, and in the musical press, open-minded attitudes appear to have coexisted with hidden and overt expressions of antisemitism suggestive of social ostracism and Jewish stereotyping. Although we can skew our interpretations from our own ethnically sensitized vantage point, period writings suggest that polarized images at times mingled within the mind of one individual. Frédéric Chopin, for example, reveals contradictory attitudes toward Jews in his correspondence. In a letter written in 1830, before his arrival in Paris, the young composer speaks in a positive light of a pianist he has heard, a M. Woerlitzer, whom he notes to be "a Jew and, consequently, has an open mind."[53] Yet in another letter to a friend, Chopin, who corresponded and dined with Halévy and other Jewish musicians and artists after his move to Paris in 1831, felt no hesitation to speak of his discomfort in having to share a carriage ride with "un juif." When Chopin speaks of finances or business dealings, he angrily implies that Jews put profits before artistry. This attitude comes through in a letter to his parents of 1830 in which he writes of having sought artistic subsidy, unsuccessfully, from a M. Geymüller; as he ends his report, he lashes out with the phrase: "Attendez un peu, coquins, juifs!"[54] Such a view is reinforced in his later complaints of negotiations with Maurice Schlesinger. In correspondence of March 1839, Chopin refers frequently to the publisher as "le Juif" and to Schlesinger's underhanded ways: he remarks that "Schlesinger has always duped me" and advises his friend that "as long as one has dealings with Jews, at least it should be with Orthodox Jews."[55] He alludes to Schlesinger having used him to make unreasonable profits, while slightly conceding the expenses that publishing entails. In discussing a work that he recommended

---

[53] Letter from Chopin (Warsaw) to Titus Woyciechowski (Poturzyn), 15 May 1830, *Correspondance de Frédéric Chopin*, ed. and trans. Bronislas Edouard Sydow, with Suzanne and Denise Chainaye, 3 vols. (Paris: Richard-Masse, 1981), vol. I, No. 55, 164.

[54] Letter from Chopin (Vienna) to his family (Warsaw), 1 December 1830, *ibid.*, vol. I, No. 70, 227.

[55] Letter from Chopin (Marseille) to Julien Fontana (Paris), [12 March 1839], *ibid.*, vol. II, No. 297, 307–9.

to Schlesinger, an *Oratorium* by Joseph Elsner, he writes that he must "defend [the publisher] a little" since a large work is costly and rarely sold except to the Conservatoire; however, this remark comes after a note that he will refrain from giving "philosophical comments about *juiverie*."[56]

Chopin's companion George Sand, the progressive novelist who advocated social equality for women and supported the Saint-Simonians, appears to have had even coarser views against Jews – it is possible that Chopin's own negative attitudes may have intensified during their association in the last years of his short life. Her deprecations of Halévy's music take on a biting, and sometimes antisemitic, edge. In December 1841, she told the painter Eugène Delacroix, her friend as well as Halévy's, that he had been wise to stay home instead of attending the première of the composer's latest creation, remarking: "I trust your truffles gave you more musical inspiration than *La Reine de Chypre* had given to Monsieur Halévy."[57] She writes with a conspicuous antisemitism ten years later, when she endorses the decision of soprano Pauline Viardot to turn down an offer to sing the lead in Halévy's *La Dame de pique*, and possibly another opera by the same composer:

> You are quite right to take a rest, you have been overdoing it far too long. You will be ten thousand times better off not exhausting your voice and soul singing any Halévy, the ugliest, most hook-nosed and most stupid music there ever was, so say I.[58]

Allusions to Jewish greed and chicanery also crop up in the recollections of individuals in the Opéra world. Véron, writing about his experiences leading up to his directorial stint, spoke disparagingly of bankers who hampered his early entrepreneurial endeavors. Although he did not identify these as Jewish bankers, the implication is likely:

---

[56] Letter from Chopin (Paris) to Joseph Elsner (Warsaw), 24 July 1840, *ibid.*, vol. III, No. 370, 26–7.

[57] George Sand, *Correspondance*, ed. Georges Lubin, 25 vols. (Paris: Garnier frères, 1964–91), vol. V, 25 December 1841, 529–30, cited in translation in Jordan, *Fromental Halévy*, 92.

[58] *Ibid.*, vol. X, 16 October 1851, 496, cited in translation in Jordan, *Fromental Halévy*, 155.

"I often came across some of the bankers I knew in my youth who, now grown rich through usury, carved a niche for themselves in philanthropic organizations, became knights of the Legion of Honor or passed as local luminaries."[59] Charles de Boigne's memoir (although published two decades after *La Juive*) gives a portrait of James Rothschild that subtly corresponds to the Rothschild depictions by Dantan and Dairnvaell. Yet by speaking of others who sought his money, the author obscured any accusation of "usurious Jew" that might underlie his description of the banker's never-ending money deals:

> M. de Rothschild has his box at the Opéra as well. He goes there to try to forget for the evening the millions he manipulated during the day, but often the business-beggars and the advantage-seekers force him to flee from his box. The solicitors imagine that they can get more out of him at the Opéra, to the strains of music, than in his office to the tinkle of coins.[60]

Numerous remarks about the wealth of Rothschild, particularly his influential loans to the Paris Opéra, appear in the 1836–48 *Les Cancans de l'Opéra* of Jean-Pierre-Louis Gentil, *contrôleur du matériel* at the Paris Opéra, who chronicles and criticizes behind-the-scenes life and events at the Opéra with heavy sarcasm and disgruntlement (see pp. 85–7 above). Because the author disguises himself in both title and manuscript as "une habilleuse" (a female dresser) at the Opéra, his true identity as inspector/controller of the theatre's immense *matériel* (including costumes and stage sets) was unknown to scholars until the recent discovery by Jean-Louis Tamvaco. Prior to his hiring by Edmond Cavé in 1831, Gentil held a variety of posts, but failed in each, as Tamvaco suggests: he was a high-ranking civil servant in the Empire's financial administration, co-founder of *Le Constitutionnel* in 1815, founder of the literary journal *Le Mercure* in 1829, and administrative secretary of the Théâtre de l'Odéon.[61] Through the eyes and ears

---

[59] Véron, *Mémoires*, vol. III, 39.
[60] Charles de Boigne, *Petits Mémoires de l'Opéra* (Paris: Librairie nouvelle, 1857), 157. Again, the use of the term "écu" appears significant.
[61] Tamvaco, *Cancans*, vol. I, 19–31. Tamvaco also notes (p. 19) that Gentil further disguises himself in these journals through the "vocabulary of a seamstress in the costume workshop (*atelier*)."

of this middle-aged administrative figure emerges a vivid description of the workings of the vast Opéra enterprise, attitudes of employees toward those who wield power, personalities of star singers, dancers, and administrators, ego conflicts, and a host of romantic intrigues. Coursing through the journals, in addition to the Rothschild references, are antisemitic themes that obviously color his depictions of Halévy and Meyerbeer, especially the former. While his commentary certainly reflects his own biases (his Catholic faith and mores are evident, for example), and perhaps the "unstable and difficult" personality ascribed him by Tamvaco, Gentil's entries may also represent a distillation of views and comments floating through Opéra *coulisses* or within certain administrative divisions, although Tamvaco paints him as a figure who was "generally hated" by administrative colleagues.[62]

Gentil begins his journals in the year following *La Juive*, but he frequently reflects on the Véron years, and even on previous decades, as he tries to convey his belief in the moral decline at the Opéra since the July Revolution and especially since Duponchel's succession in 1835. References to undignified, immoral capitalists (including Jewish bankers), Duponchel's misguided leadership, and the degeneration of the Opéra's ambiance are commingled in Gentil's often passionate descriptions of the ill-treatment of the *demoiselles* of the dance by the men of the new era. In 1838, he writes:

> It should be proclaimed and repeated constantly: one of the disgraceful consequences of our political revolutions was to affect the morale of our Opéra in relation to what was once a characteristic elegance. Never have the race of merchants, the *incroyables* under the management, the general officers of the Empire, the dandies of the Restoration, the *Lions*, the journalists, the stockbrokers, and the Jewish bankers of our time replaced properly vis-à-vis our ladies of the dance the great financiers and great English "milords," the gallant abbots and great lords of the *ancien régime* who knew how to give special value to these near-beauties.[63]

---

[62] *Ibid.*, 10.
[63] "La Fête d'une danseuse," in Tamvaco, *Cancans*, vol. I, 475.

His disparagement of Halévy often merges with his ridicule of Duponchel's leadership, or lack thereof, and his suggestions of Rothschild's unfortunate influence. Unlike Véron, whom he portrays as a true director who earned the respect of his employees, he claims that Duponchel, who rose from head of set design to director, never showed himself capable of his expanded responsibilities. He complains that he occupies a "false position," one granted him largely because he had curried favor with Rothschild through the decorating of his apartment. (It is the loans and financial support of Rothschild and the marquis Aguado, Gentil reminds his future readers, that enable Duponchel to keep the Opéra aloft.) Halévy, appointed by Duponchel as "acting director" when he is away on *congés*, is condemned for a number of offenses. Gentil finds that the composer spends far too much time in this role and not enough time composing, spreading himself too thinly among his various occupations. He implies that Halévy's aid to Duponchel does not compensate for the director's lack of true authority, but exacerbates it: the composer acts "comme chien" in protecting Duponchel's interests, including the concealment – from Madame Duponchel and others – of the director's licentious affairs with dancers and singers.[64]

The composer himself, as Gentil notes on a number of occasions, participates in similar escapades with young female choristers, whom he oversees as *maître* or *chef de chant*. Although Halévy was unmarried at the time of Gentil's writing, he views his behavior as immoral and unprofessional, and even responsible for the declining state of the chorus. Because of the "seductive thoughts and libertine desires" of Halévy and other "*maîtres* of the Conservatoire and Opéra," Gentil claims that the chorus is filled with women with mediocre voices, making it one of the weakest parts of the Opéra.[65] (A complaint about the weak chorus also appears a few years later in *Le Ménestrel*, but the author, Julien Martin, believes lack of proper conservatory training

---

[64] "Les Deux Entrepreneurs de l'Opéra," in Tamvaco, *Cancans*, vol. 1, 204–5; "Les Quadrilles de M͏ʳ Duponchel," in Tamvaco, *Cancans*, vol. 1, 392–3; "L'Alter-Ego de M. Duponchel," in Tamvaco, *Cancans*, vol. 1, 293–5.
[65] "Les Choeurs," in Tamvaco, *Cancans*, vol. 1, 360–61.

and low pay to be the chief causes.[66]) Gentil particularly frowns upon Halévy's relationship with chorus soprano Catherine-Clothilde-Aimée Proche (see pp. 86–7 above).

In his professional involvement with the Opéra, Halévy is not only too involved in life in the *coulisses*, he is lazy and procrastinating in composition, Gentil complains.[67] He accuses the composer of finding pretexts for delaying the *mise en scène* to hide the fact that he was still composing a work. He also depicts him as taking advantage of the affection of Duponchel and others at the Opéra who were caught up in his "dealings." The image of the calculating Jew emerges sharply in one angry passage:

> Let us hope all the same that the guiding spirit of our first lyric theatre intervenes in this case. It will enlighten MM. Duponchel and Aguado as to the disruptive and shady dealings of the likes of Halévy and his Judaic race. Let us hope as well that, having been taught higher sentiments, more in conformity with his education than with his birth, the scheming Jew will disappear altogether and leave the way free for the artist worthy of the applause of persons of quality. Amen!!![68]

Even more discomforting to the author was the decision-making power that he believed Halévy exerted. In his description of Monday committee meetings of the director, administrator, and division heads in which works in progress and future repertoire concerns were discussed, he writes:

> It is to this Sanhédrin (because Halévy himself controls completely) that important questions relating to pantomime and music are submitted. Habeneck only rarely brings the benefits of his experience and the clarity of his Breton candor. Apart from the situations concerning the service of the orchestra, this leader always speaks his mind with diplomacy and reserve. The other members of this committee usually discuss things off the top of their heads and without considering the extraordinary situations in which one must deal ruthlessly with an important matter for

---

[66] Julien Martin, "Les Choeurs de l'Opéra," *Le Ménestrel* 9, no. 47 (24 October 1841): [2].

[67] "L'Alter-Ego de M. Duponchel," in Tamvaco, *Cancans*, vol. I, 294.

[68] *Ibid.*, 295.

the company. The director is very pleased to have his authority reinforced by a reasoned decision which is recorded in the register and for which those present at the deliberations may be held responsible.[69]

Gentil's allusion to a Sanhédrin – a meeting of Judaic religious leaders as in the Napoleonic era – blatantly exposes his resentment of Jewish empowerment. In this entry, he may reflect opinions other than his alone, perhaps echoing the grumblings of committee members.

Similar complaints about Halévy's control at the Opéra surfaced in *Le Figaro* on 8 March 1838.[70] Central to its castigation was the charge of conflict of interest: in his roles as composer and *chef de chant*, he bore too much influence in the choice of repertoire (namely, his own) and in the casting of singers and dancers. The Opéra, *Le Figaro* claimed, existed as a company for the performance of Halévy's works (despite the fact that only two *grands opéras* by Halévy had been produced by that time) and the prevention of others from coming to the stage. It noted his salary as *chef* and the benefits of Opéra lodging (with his entire family, it stressed), blamed him for the increase in annual expenditure (140,000 francs), and called for his resignation. Shortly after this article, a series of imaginary, punning exchanges between Duponchel and Halévy appeared daily in the same paper (11 March to 13 April). All cast the composer as straight-man to Duponchel's witticisms, most of which are cryptically or innocuously bland, while a few are more obviously suggestive. The "conversation" of 22 March, for example, puns with Hebrew names (including Assuérus, or Ahasvérus, the Wandering Jew), seemingly alluding to the composer's alleged indiscretions: "M. Duponchel demandait hier à M. Halévy:– Sais-tu quel est l'amant le plus discret? – Je ne sais pas, répondit M. Halévy. – Eh bien! reprit M. Duponchel, c'est *Assuérus*, parce qu'il sut aimer *et se taire* (Esther)." ("M. Duponchel asked M. Halévy yesterday:– Do you know who is the most discreet lover? – I don't know, M. Halévy replied. – Well!

---

[69] "Composition du spectacle," in Tamvaco, *Cancans*, vol. 1, 357–8.

[70] In "Lettres sur les musiciens français," part 1: "M. Halévy: Guido et Ginevra," *Revue des deux mondes* 13 (15 March 1838): 777, Henri Blaze de Bury also emphasized that Halévy's personal influence in the administration placed the Opéra's vast resources at his disposal.

M. Duponchel resumed, it is Ahasvérus, because he knew how to love and keep quiet.") Taken in their entirety, the puns characterize a rather feckless duo and a sycophantic Halévy.

Some of the accusations of *Le Figaro* almost directly parallel those of Gentil, who was offended that the composer lived in a sixteen-room apartment at the Opéra with his family (including sisters Flore and Mélanie, brother Léon, sister-in-law Alexandrine, and nephew Ludovic).[71] In one passage he rattles on about the way Halévy heartlessly clipped the tree branches outside his balcony (which he and "other" *couturières* can see from their workshop windows), thus displacing sparrows that had found refuge there. Triggered by this imagery, he repeats the accusations of *Le Figaro* concerning the composer's monopoly at the Opéra, with added contempt:

> Since he's been *maître de chant* and established fabricator of scores at the Académie royale de musique, it is claimed that this damned Halévy is also trying to keep at bay those composers who might offend him, just as he chased from the neighborhood of his home these poor birds whose innocent chirping was less inconvenient than the sounds of his lousy piano that afflict your ears morning and night.[72]

On several occasions, Gentil recognizes Halévy's significance as a composer, but attributes his advancement and status largely to the help of Cherubini. A few other positive statements filter through: in comparing him to his brother Léon, for example, the journal writer describes Fromental as a "robust" and sociable man.[73] And among the predominantly unflattering images, Gentil surprisingly does not depict Halévy as an avaricious Jew. (Others did, however, particularly after his success with *La Juive*. His brother felt compelled to discuss Halévy's nominal Conservatoire salary, from 300 to 2,500 francs over forty-three years of service, perhaps to put right the accusations that his position there was too lucrative to give up, as well as to show how inadequate the remunerations had been at such an honorable

---

[71] "Etat des personnes logées à l'Opéra," in Tamvaco, *Cancans*, vol. 1, 364.
[72] "La Grande Cour de l'Opéra," in Tamvaco, *Cancans*, vol. 1, 434. (Here Gentil seems to contradict his other claims of Halévy's compositional laziness!)
[73] "L'Alter-Ego de M. Duponchel," in Tamvaco, *Cancans*, vol. 1, 293–4.

institution.[74]) In contrast, he frequently refers to Meyerbeer's large fortune and enumerates his propensity for giving boxes and tickets as gifts, seemingly as bribes.[75] In one entry he labels Meyerbeer as "the villain Jew" for not delivering music for a *divertissement* of *Les Huguenots* to the choreographer Taglioni, thus angering the dancers who would have shared his ample profits.[76] Like "ce diable Halévy," this term of disapprobation corresponds to references to Jewish villainy that recur throughout contemporary antisemitic writings.[77]

One wonders how many others at the Opéra may have held similar thoughts. If so, were they kept close to the chest, whispered only to those of like mind, or were they expressed somewhat openly? Moreover, to what degree did such biases directly affect Halévy and Meyerbeer behind the scenes? These questions can never be answered fully, as they probably could not have been during the composers' own lifetimes. The extent of antisemitism should not be exaggerated: it is likely that such views were in the minority, for the presence of Jewish composers at the Opéra speaks to a basic acceptance by administration and directors if not a general spirit of openness. The maliciousness of Véron and the animosity of Duponchel sensed by Meyerbeer may have been based on personality differences, basic power struggles, or perhaps the impatience or disregard of the composer himself (he wrote to his wife Minna of Duponchel's "indescribable stupidity and carelessness").[78] Yet, bigoted views may have coexisted beneath the surface of antagonistic behavior as well as tolerant actions. As Meyerbeer recognized, "richesse" (antisemitism) could easily

---

[74] Léon Halévy, *Sa Vie*, 33–4.

[75] "Le Bailleur de fonds n'est qu'un bailleur d'avis," in Tamvaco, *Cancans*, vol. I, 135.

[76] "Musique de danse pour Les Huguenots," in Tamvaco, *Cancans*, vol. I, 108.

[77] It also relates to a caricature of a horned Meyerbeer found in a collection of iconography on the composer held at the Bibliothèque de l'Opéra, as reported in Joan Lewis Thomson, "Meyerbeer and His Contemporaries" (Ph.D. diss., Columbia University, 1972), 245–6, n. 1.

[78] *Giacomo Meyerbeer: A Life in Letters*, ed. Becker and Becker, 56, 67, 73–4. In a letter to Minna (10 October 1832) concerning the contract for *Les Huguenots*, Meyerbeer wrote: "Both Véron and I dread the moment when two people who do not trust one another but need one another, as is the case with us, propose their contract conditions."

be triggered: he remarked – perhaps thinking of both the Germans and the French – that "individuals can forget this word for a certain period of time (but not forever), but an assembled public can never forget it, for it takes only one to remember and all revert to their prejudices."[79]

Halévy's status as a leading musician at the Opéra, Conservatoire, and among the cultural elite of Paris rose dramatically after the brilliant success of *La Juive*. His election to the Institut and the Légion d'honneur signals this new eminence, along with the many laudatory appraisals of the opera and of Halévy's compositional skills. Leading his partisans in the musical press was *La Revue et gazette musicale*, a source of musical news and critique as well as a promotional organ for the publications of its editor Maurice Schlesinger – including the scores of Halévy, Meyerbeer, and other composers for the Paris Opéra.[80] Seemingly as numerous as his champions were his detractors, some of whose aesthetic judgments may have been affected by professional jealousy as well as antisemitism. On 30 May 1835, Meyerbeer wrote to his wife that the *Messager* had cited Halévy's Jewish identity as the reason for his initial rejection by the Académie des beaux-arts in favor of Anton Reicha: "they say that religious considerations, which people thought were banned in the epoch in which we live, caused several members of the Institute to vote against Halévy."[81] The harsh criticism of writers for *La France musicale* and the *Revue des deux mondes*, particularly the father and son critics, Castil-Blaze and Henri Blaze, most apparently stemmed from a strong preference for *bel canto* composers, but it also seems tinged with personal animosity and, perhaps, antisemitic attitudes.

In a discussion of Halévy's compositional merit and operatic works in the *Revue des deux mondes* in 1838 (focusing particularly on *Guido et Ginevra*, which had just appeared), Henri Blaze hammers away on

---

[79] *Ibid.*, 60.
[80] See a thorough study of this journal in Ellis, *Music Criticism in Nineteenth-Century France*.
[81] *Giacomo Meyerbeer: Briefwechsel*, ed. Becker, Becker, and Henze-Dohring, vol. II, 459.

themes that would become familiar in Halévy criticism. Bolstering his attack – described by Leich-Galland as an attempt at a "real demolition" of Halévy's renown – with philosophical discussions about true genius and divine inspiration, he emphasizes that Halévy is not a natural, original, or inspired composer, but one of those who had become "lost in the abysses of science where the torch of thought does not shine on them."[82] Without a natural gift for melody like the Italian composers, but rather a focus on the "correct and regular style" of harmony and counterpoint absorbed from his master Cherubini and a concentration on his skills of instrumentation, Halévy lacked the true inspiration that can be obtained only from the "sky of Italy," not from the Conservatoire. He reiterates the idea that "science cannot, under any pretext, take the place of inspiration," and that what inspiration Halévy does exhibit is not his own, but borrowed. This portrayal of the "false," the "unnatural," and the "calculated" in Halévy's art resonates with Fourier's vocabulary and links with Blaze's accusations that the Opéra of the July Monarchy had become too much of a capitalistic venture. Castil-Blaze's commentary in *La France musicale* of 1841 is also weighted in anti-capitalist imagery, including his comparison of the directors of "spectacles lyriques" to gamblers whose "sack of *livrets*" represents the "sack of the lottery," and his reference to "Rothschild's treasures" behind the theatre's gaming tables.[83] His words prefigure those of composer Vincent d'Indy (1851–1931), who would later define the era of French grand opera as "la période judaïque" – not only for the Jewish composers who dominated it but for what he viewed as the era's aberrational and excessive concern for profits over art.[84]

Clearly, then, the Jewish–Christian conflict of *La Juive* and the partial modeling of Eléazar after Shylock reverberated with contemporary attitudes and imagery. Indeed, it seems impossible that the authors of *La Juive*, as well as the director who accepted the work, were unaware

---

[82] "Lettres sur les musiciens français," part I: "M. Halévy: Guido et Ginevra," *Revue des deux mondes* 13 (15 March 1838): 770: "perdus dans les abîmes d'une science où le flambeau de la pensée ne les éclaire pas."

[83] *La France musicale* 4, no. 52 (26 December 1841): 465–6.

[84] Vincent d'Indy, *Cours de composition musicale*, 3 vols. (Paris: Durand & Cie, 1903–1950), vol. III, 104.

of the pertinent social implications of subject and characterization. Scribe, so astute in creating topical comedies, consciously or subconsciously sensed the appropriateness of evoking liberal sympathies for his Jewish characters, while assigning them traits that audiences would recognize from literary tradition, but that also symbolized what was assumed and feared about Jews in French society. For some Frenchmen, Rothschild and other successful Jewish capitalists "proved" that the stereotype of the Jewish miser was a valid depiction – hence, Heine's labeling of Rothschild as "Herr von Shylock"; within this milieu, it is possible that Scribe himself found the Shylock stereotype valid on a personal level, despite his obvious concern for social injustice and his warm associations with many individuals from the Jewish community.[85]

Since Halévy shared responsibility for dramatic development, we must question the composer's attitudes toward Eléazar's characterization. As hypothesized above, it is probable that the composer, with the aid of his brother, pushed to cut back the allusions to Eléazar's avarice. Yet despite these alterations, vestiges of the Shylock image remain, and were in fact enhanced through Halévy's setting in the Act II trio. Léon Halévy's statements about Jewish identity and his apparent sensitivity about stereotyped associations may offer some insight. Through his attacks on unjust indictments of usury and abuses of French Jews leading from them, as well as the portrayals of noble, altruistic Jewish characters in his plays *Grillo* and *L'Espion,* Léon consciously worked to counteract the negative stereotyping. Although Léon's recorded views seem more extremely assimilationist than those suggested in his brother's statements and life choices, the friction that existed between their fraternal respect for Judaic devotion and their simultaneous disdain for "fanatical" Jews as barriers to social progress corresponds to the

[85] In a journal reference to *Ali-baba* (1827), the opera that he was writing with Mélesville and Cherubini, Scribe notes, undoubtedly referring to the "oriental" main character who hoards gold and jewels in a cave: "Madame Duveyrier copied the costume of a Jew robbed of his money-bag by death. We will use this costume for the Jew of *Ali-baba* – we want the actor who will play him to wear a similar one." ("Madame Duveyrier a copié le costume d'un juif à qui la mort enleve [*sic*] sa bourse et ce costume nous servira pour le juif d'*ali-baba* – nous voulons que l'acteur qui le jouera en porte un pareil." F-Pn, Ms., n.a.fr. 22584, vol. i, fol. 7ᵛ.)

conflict between Léon's distress over conventional images and his own discussions of usury as an outworn, immoral practice. The Halévys' views about good citizenship point to their own condemnation of Eléazar's anti-Christian stance as well as to the touches of Shylockian behavior. But one also wonders whether (and, if so, to what degree) the composer struggled against the "prescription" laid out by Scribe, and whether, in certain cases (especially if one recalls his junior status), he was simply unable to overturn the stereotype and convention built into the libretto. In the curious "splicing" of Eléazar's character, most roughly exposed in the juxtaposition between the seder and the necklace sale in Act II, it is Halévy's music (particularly in the seder and in Act IV) that enriches the character beyond stereotype and conveys a depth of morality and humanity not evident in the libretto.

The occupation of Eléazar and his dealings with a royal figure undoubtedly brought to the minds of some audience members the inevitable association with James Rothschild, or the Rothschild family, already the epitome of the avaricious Jew in many circles, as articulated above. Whether the authors themselves made such an association is unknown, although a number of Saint-Simonians deplored his connections with royalty and aristocracy and believed his banking methods represented anachronistic practices that were out of touch with their progressive economic ideas. There were in fact professional ties between the Saint-Simonian bankers, the Pereires, and Rothschild in the 1830s, but divisions were beginning to develop that would later turn into a fierce rivalry between Rothschild's "haute banque" and the Pereires' "banque nouvelle." Moreover, Rothschild's image as a foreigner, who remained unnaturalized, spoke French with a heavy German Jewish accent, and relied on a secretary for all his French correspondence, did not fit Léon Halévy's depiction of a good Jewish citizen of France.[86]

---

[86] Other liberal voices spoke harshly of Rothschild, particularly after his role in bringing down the Thiers ministry of 1840. Michelet, disdainful of Rothschild's distance from the 1830 Revolution and its ideals, reverted to an odious caricature when he described a fleeting encounter with the banker in his journal in 1842: "[H]is profile of an intelligent monkey struck me like a Rembrandt sketch, a pencil stroke that says everything." Cited in Jean Bouvier, *Les Rothschild*, 2d ed. (Paris: Fayard, 1967), 114.

A Rothschild innuendo would not be without irony, of course, since the banker was a central contributor to the Opéra. It is difficult to assess whether Scribe, the Halévys, Nourrit, or other collaborators believed that the Shylockian traits of this fifteenth-century Jew of the stage reflected social realities outside the theatre, whether they themselves (like Heine) saw them in Rothschild or other Jews of capitalism and commerce, but they certainly recognized that a portion of Frenchmen believed in their validity within the historic past, and, to some degree, within the French present.

THE PLACE OF JUDAISM WITHIN THE JULY MONARCHY

Informing the opera's presentation of Judaism and Jewish religious-political identity are contradictory actions and views within the July Monarchy. Three events, each of which occurred within several years of the opera's première, signal the sharp divergences in the acceptance of the Jewish religion and populace within Catholic France. The first is the law of the *culte israélite* of 1831 (see pp. 9–10, 124 above), which broadened the Charte's stipulation of religious freedom to the specific recognition of Judaism as a state religion through its allocation of government stipends to Jewish rabbis; its supporters intended it both to protect Judaism and to combat prejudice. Yet only a year later, a sensational *affaire* and anti-Jewish campaign exploded at the arrest of the duchesse de Berry that was prompted by the revelation of her Legitimist conspiracies against Louis-Philippe by the Jew Simon Deutz. Even though the Orléanist papers *Le Constitutionnel* and *Le National* supported Deutz as a French patriot who had saved the country from civil war, many individual liberals attacked him as a traitor, heightening their charges with stereotyped rhetoric.[87] In a poetic diatribe, Victor Hugo accused Deutz of "selling his soul" through impure deeds, intensifying his indictment with the weighted image of the legendary Jew

---

[87] Zosa Szajkowski, "Simon Deutz: Traitor or French Patriot? The Jewish Aspect of the Arrest of the Duchesse de Berry," in *Jews and the French Revolutions of 1789, 1830 and 1848* (New York: Ktav Publishing House, 1970), 1047–9.

divinely cursed for his refusal to allow Christ a resting place on the path to Calvary: "March, you other Wandering Jew! March with the gold that may be seen glistening through the fingers of your barely closed hands!"[88] Condemnations of Deutz, who had converted to Christianity a few years before the *affaire*, also emanated from Jewish communities themselves, even extending to the denigration of his father, Emmanuel Deutz, the Chief Rabbi of France: the Consistoire central exploited the event to complain of the Rabbi's practice of conducting services in Yiddish, which it believed went against the idea of *régénération*, and began to press for the abolition of his office.[89] Then, in 1840, *l'affaire Damas* sparked the nation: when French officials in Damascus accused a group of Jews of killing a Catholic cleric to use his blood for making unleavened bread, a number of French newspapers assumed the guilt of the indicted Jews and passionately called for their condemnation (see p. 101). These stances revealed, as many contributors to *Les Archives israélites* would bemoan, that a portion of the French populace maintained not only narrow-minded beliefs about Judaism, but medieval ones, for the accusation was clearly a reinterpretation of the ancient "blood libel." Between the extremes of tolerance and ignorant bigotry represented by these contentious events lay a range of conflicting ideas about the respect of Judaism by the largely Catholic majority, as well as by French Jews themselves.

Christian beliefs often lay at the basis of the non-acceptance of Jewish citizenry and religion: the basic conviction that Christianity was the one true religion and the belief in Judas's betrayal of Jesus. Heulard de Montigny, a member of the Chambre des députés who opposed the 1831 law, felt that the government should protect and favor only Christianity because its "evangelical doctrine ... is the most admirable and perfect."[90] Running through the most emotionally

---

[88] Hugo, "A l'homme qui a livré une femme," cited in *ibid.*, 1043: "Marche, autre Juif errant! Marche avec l'or qu'on voit/Luire à travers les doigts de tes mains mal fermées!"

[89] Szajkowski, "Simon Deutz," 1050.

[90] *Archives parlementaires*, vol. LXV, 314. In addition to the minority who voted against the law (71 out of 282 in the Chambre des députés, a quarter of the voters), such papers as *La Gazette de France* (1 January 1831) protested against it largely out of support for Catholicism as the religion of state.

charged antisemitic views were allusions to the "stain" of Judas that made it impossible for Jews to be trusted compatriots in a Christian nation. In one of Dairnvaell's slanderous pamphlets, for example, he charges that the "New Judas would sell all of humanity for a few pieces of silver."[91] Among the Catholic clergy, Judaism continued to be viewed as heretical. Ironically, a distrust of Judaism also existed among French citizens who believed passionately in religious and political tolerance, as suggested above. Contrary to their notions of tolerance and social equality, this skepticism among Christian and Jewish liberals stemmed from the same Enlightenment thought that had inspired France's granting of civil rights to its Jewish populace.

The French *philosophes*, themselves influenced by the English Deists' depiction of Jews as superstitious, barbaric, and fanatical, reproached the Talmud as a source of Jewish superstition and immorality and the rabbinic tradition as a hindrance to a much-needed intellectual, religious, or social reform of Jews.[92] Montesquieu, for example, criticized rabbinic Judaism as detrimental to Jewish character, despite his acceptance of biblical Judaism and condemnation of religious bigotry.[93] Influenced by Montesquieu, the liberal Catholic Abbé Grégoire, an important voice in late eighteenth-century appeals for Jewish civil rights, argued in his *Essai sur la régénération physique, morale et politique des juifs* (1789) that Judaism was "morally deficient" and that its reform was crucial to the "regeneration" of Jews.

The harsh attacks on Jews and Judaism by Enlightenment thinkers have been deemed antisemitic by several scholars. Arthur Hertzberg interprets them as "essentially a secularization of the theological contempt without any modification of the basic hatred," thus representing "the transition from medieval to modern anti-Semitism."[94] A different

---

[91] Georges Dairnvaell, *Guerre aux fripons: Chronique secrète de la Bourse et des chemins de fer. Par l'auteur de Rothschild Ier, roi des Juifs* (Paris: L'Editeur, 1846). In this pocket-sized booklet, Dairnvaell uses similar vocabulary and ideas to those found in Toussenel's 1847 publication.

[92] Berkovitz, *Jewish Identity*, 34.

[93] *Ibid.*, 35–6, 255, n. 36; see Auberry, "Montesquieu et les Juifs."

[94] Berkovitz, *Jewish Identity*, 34–5. Like Hertzberg, Jacob Katz recognizes the antisemitism among certain *philosophes*, particularly Voltaire, that was inconsistent with their liberal philosophy. Berkovitz cites Katz's *From Prejudice to*

line of thinking is represented in Peter Gay's discussion of Voltaire's attacks on Judaism as a mask for his true target: Christianity.[95] Gay suggests that because Christianity could not be attacked directly and openly, attacks on Judaism, which many *philosophes* viewed as the antithesis of tolerance, served as a different means to essentially the same end. As Jay Berkovitz notes, the paradox in the treatment of Jewish questions among Enlightenment thinkers lay in the fact that the same philosophical stance that helped to break down religious prejudice and discrimination "lent credence to the notion that Judaism was morally and intellectually bankrupt."[96] He reiterates:

> The philosophes' conception of toleration could not coexist with anything that might be perceived to be antithetical to the aims of the Enlightenment. According to the philosophes, Judaism represented the moral and intellectual antithesis of enlightenment and toleration and therefore was a deserving target of extensive vilification. Paradoxically, the negative attitude toward the Jews and their religion was logically derived from the same philosophical position that enabled Enlightenment thinkers to address the Jewish problem sympathetically.[97]

The contradictions in Voltaire's thinking even extended to the type of antisemitic bias linked to the stereotype of the usurious Jew: throughout his writings are comments about Jews as materialist, calculating, and rootless.[98]

Ironically, such Enlightenment mixtures do not seem too far removed from Toussenel's flagrantly antisemitic melding of anticapitalist sentiments with attacks on the Jewish religion and anti-Jewish references from the New Testament. Toussenel mocked the Bible as a history of immoral behavior and labeled it "the catechism and the code of murderous people" who were "the enemy of humanity."[99] Repeating the familiar condemnation of Jews as murderers of Jesus, he

Destruction: Anti-Semitism, 1700–1933 (Cambridge, MA: Harvard University Press, 1980) and "Judaism and the Jews in the Eyes of Voltaire," *Molad* 5 (1973), 614–25.

[95] Peter Gay, *Voltaire's Politics: The Poet as Realist* (New Haven and London: Yale University Press, 1988), as discussed by Berkovitz, *Jewish Identity*, 35.

[96] Berkovitz, *Jewish Identity*, 35.   [97] *Ibid.*   [98] Gay, *Voltaire's Politics*, 351.

[99] Toussenel, *Les Juifs*, vol. 1, ix.

went so far as to identify Jews as "the people of Satan."[100] In his biting castigation of Jews as "usurers" and "parasites," Toussenel referred to the same act that Ruggiero uses to incite the crowd against Eléazar and Rachel in *La Juive*: Jesus' act of chasing the merchants from the temple. This reference is a key point for the author, as he placed it as an epigraph on the book's title page and alludes to it frequently.[101]

Enlightenment beliefs that traditional Judaism was antithetical to a tolerant, rational, and progressive society figured strongly in post-emancipation debates among Jewish scholars and leaders centered in religious and national identity. Many of those who called for reform in the early decades of the nineteenth century reiterated the arguments of French *philosophes* and advocates of Jewish reform and emancipation. A key figure in winning emancipation, Berr-Isaac Berr, for example, reflected the vocabulary and reasoning of Abbé Grégoire when he called for a moral regeneration of Jews in *Réflexions sur la régénération complète des juifs en France* (circa 1806). Reform-minded French Jews were also influenced by Moses Mendelssohn, leader of the Jewish Enlightenment in Germany and writer of *La Délivrance des juifs* (1782). Elie Halévy, who was friendly with Mendelssohn in Germany, had been among a circle of Jews in the Haskalah movement in Metz, the leading Jewish community in northeastern France, before moving to Paris.[102]

The suggested replacement of "juif" and "juive" with "israélite" figured significantly in this *régénération*. Following the early efforts of Berr-Isaac Berr, journals founded more than two decades apart, *L'Israélite français* and *Les Archives israélites*, promoted the new term, acknowledging in their titles and text new roles and identities and signaling a break from the negative connotations of *juif*. For the most part, governmental representatives adopted the term *israélite*, as reflected in the 1830–31 discussions about the law of the *culte israélite*.

[100] *Ibid.*, iii.
[101] *Ibid.*, title page: "The house of my father is a house of prayer, and you have made it a den of thieves." ("La maison de mon père est une maison de prière, et vous en avez fait une caverne de voleurs.")
[102] Berkovitz, *Jewish Identity*, 60, notes that the Jewish intellectuals of Metz, encouraged by liberal voices such as Pierre-Louis Lacretelle and the Société des arts et sciences, translated works of the Berlin Haskalah and adapted its ideology to the French context.

Opposing the calls for *régénération* were many Orthodox Jews, who warned against the decline of Judaism and the loss of communal autonomy in the wake of the Enlightenment and emancipation.[103] Baron Silvestre de Sacy, the renowned Orientalist who endorsed Elie Halévy's poem *Ha-Shalom* of 1802 (see p. 76 above), believed that the adoption of Enlightenment values was tantamount to apostasy; in his mind, an enlightened Jew ceased to be a Jew.[104]

Key points in the post-emancipation debates were the manner and degree to which Jews, as citizens, should adapt to the dominant values and mores of French society, and whether the practice of Judaism should be modified to coordinate with them. Varying levels of social integration were advocated. Many Jewish leaders believed Judaism to be complementary to French culture, and that it could be retained while enjoying the full benefits of French citizenship. Some supporters of reform, including Elie Halévy, belonged to the Consistoires: among Consistoire rabbis and lay members, it was often the latter who were most concerned with Jewish *régénération* and social change.

Whereas many leaders supported acculturation – that is, the adoption of French cultural behavior – most did not encourage assimilation, which would threaten the retention of Jewish customs and Jewish loyalties.[105] Elie Halévy, who fought to dispel the notion that Judaism was incompatible with modern society, leaned toward acculturation. "Tiens au pays, et conserve la foi," the directive that headed his journal *L'Israélite français* (see p. 74 above), corresponds to the Consistoire logo, "Patrie et Religion."[106] The belief in this dual commitment was echoed in the 1830s by Abraham Créhange, the leader of Parisian Orthodox Jews, who supported "a perfect union with our Christian co-citizens," with mutual respect for the king and Charter and cooperation in all civil and military matters, including elections, the judicial system, the army, and the National Guard. But, he emphasized, there must be "total separation" in religious matters, for

---

[103] *Ibid.*, 15. See also Girard, *De l'émancipation à l'égalité*, 93.
[104] As noted by Cahen, "De la littérature hébraïque," 43.
[105] Berkovitz, *Jewish Identity*, 111–12.
[106] Béatrice Philippe, "Elie Halévy," in *La Famille Halévy*, ed. Loyrette, 63.

he believed this to be the only condition on which to base *israélite* identity.[107]

Many of the more liberal *réformateurs* who pushed for greater degrees of integration, including Léon Halévy, were Jewish intellectuals who had been educated in French schools and who desired futures unhampered by discrimination. They were undoubtedly affected by the resurgence of Catholic power during the Restoration, which corresponded with an intensification of anti-Jewish sentiments and restrictions. In addition to the Lattier proposal, other actions resulted in the turning away of Jews from the universities and liberal professions. Before 1830, for example, Olinde Rodrigues was denied admission to the higher teachers' school because of his Jewish heritage.[108] For the same reason it appears that Léon Halévy was hindered from obtaining a post in public education, despite the honors he had accumulated at the lycée Charlemagne.[109] According to Ruth Jordan, Léon Halévy "discreetly converted to Catholicism" because he knew an academic career would be thwarted by his Jewish religion; she offers no evidence to support this statement, however.[110] Halévy's references to the antisemitic machinations of a "parti-prêtre" in his second *Résumé*, as well as the anti-Catholic slant of his 1829 poem "L'Extradition" (see p. 45 above), may have been stimulated by his own experience, as well as that of his friends, during these years. As suggested by the prefatory remarks to the *Résumé*, Léon's aim of proving the merit of Jewish citizens to "Christian fanatics . . . or less enlightened Christians" was, like his belief in the social and religious reform of Jews, tied to his ultimate goal of ameliorating the status of French Jews.

---

[107] *La Sentinelle juive: Réponse à la dix-septième lettre de la correspondance dite israélite de Tsarphati* (Paris: Chez l'auteur, 1839), 10.

[108] When the geologist and mathematician Abelard Servedier was refused a professorship in France in 1816, he left for England; he was finally given one in France after 1830. See Zosa Szajkowski, *Jewish Education in France, 1789–1939*, ed. Tobey B. Gitelle (New York: Columbia University Press, 1980), 28.

[109] Pierre Guiral cites Vapereau's dictionary as the source of this information in *La Famille Halévy*, ed. Loyrette, 82.

[110] Jordan, *Fromental Halévy*, 43.

Léon Halévy's advocacy of a full social assimilation is demonstrated in his own life through his participation in the Saint-Simonian movement, his attempts to bring Christian and Jewish theology closer together, his marriage to a Catholic, his alleged apostasy, and his appeal for a "complete fusion" between Jews and other French citizens. Unlike the balanced allegiance to faith and country that his father and the Consistoire advocated, Halévy emphasized that the loyalty of a French Jew should be to his country first. In choosing the term "fusion," he aligns himself with "gentile discussants of the Jewish question" during the Restoration, according to Berkovitz.[111] His ideas on Judaism and the reform of Jewish customs also correlate with Enlightenment thought: his commentary concerning the distortions of Pharisees in his first *Résumé* finds kinship with *philosophe* attacks on rabbinic Judaism; in his second history, his aggressive call for the discarding of "Asiatic superstitions" reveals even more strongly the roots of his language (see pp. 98–101 above). Fromental Halévy's later comment about "stubborn" Jewish beliefs brings to mind his brother's views. In a disturbing proximity of viewpoints, Léon Halévy's assimilationist arguments intersect with some of the venomous antisemitic themes represented in Toussenel's and Hallez's writings; Hallez, in fact, quotes liberally from Halévy's Jewish histories, although using his ideas for completely different ends.

Liberal Jews spoke of the fanaticism and separatism of French Jews who opposed reform, particularly religious reform. Michel Berr, in his essay on Jewish traditions *Du rabbinisme et des traditions juives* of 1832, writes of several members of the Consistoire central "who want the Israelite religion to remain rigidly stationary."[112] It is they who do not recognize that modifications to "forms and expressions of beliefs" had been made necessary by "the progress of *lumières* and of morality."[113]

---

[111] Berkovitz, *Jewish Identity*, 113.

[112] Michel Berr, *Du rabbinisme et des traditions juives* (Paris: Sétier, 1832), xiii: "qui veulent que le culte israélite reste inflexiblement stationnaire."

[113] *Ibid.*: "des formes et des expressions de croyances qui ont fait leurs temps et l'ont fait d'une manière utile et salutaire, mais dont les progrès et les modifications sont devenus nécessaires par les progrès des lumières et de la morale." It was also these same members who rejected Berr's candidacy for the Consistoire central.

Like-minded men of an earlier generation had, by their "fanaticism and hypocrisy," persecuted Moses Mendelssohn, whose "new religiosity" had shown the way to progressive Judaism.[114]

Many of the so-called *séparatistes* were disturbed by what they interpreted as assaults on Judaism by *réformateurs*. Although Créhange modified the more stringent Orthodox views of the late eighteenth century in his support of acculturation, he voiced strong opposition to religious reforms that were being debated in the 1830s, including the supplanting of Hebrew with French in the synagogue and the shift to the Sunday worship of Christian tradition. In a series of letters published under the title *La Sentinelle juive*, Créhange responds to a Sephardic Jewish *réformateur*, whom he chastises for attacking the Consistoire and "our institutions" and for "getting on your hobbyhorse, reform."[115] He rebukes the *réformateur* for calling for change without truly knowing the "religion of your fathers" or having any theological credentials or spiritual inspiration. He mocks his opponent's hypocritical demands for "liberty for everyone," while wanting to take away the "liberty of conscience" from faithful followers of Judaism, to divorce them from Hebrew, "the sacred language" responsible for the centuries-long unity among Israelites, and to force Sunday worship on them.[116] He concedes that moral reform is an honorable goal, but warns the *réformateur*, in vocabulary borrowed from liberal rhetoric, that "you regenerate the Jewish people not by lighting the torch that is to give them light at the stake [au bûcher] of the Institutions of Moses, but by setting them an example of respect for these Institutions."[117] Créhange accepted the separatist label, although not in the condemnatory way it was intended: he notes that Jews should not be cursed for wanting to "live and die in the religion in which they were born."[118] Moreover, he reminds the *réformateur* that the government, through the Charte's designation of Judaism as a

---

[114] *Ibid.*, 33.   [115] Créhange, *La Sentinelle juive*, 5.   [116] *Ibid.*, 6.

[117] *Ibid.*, 14: "vous ne régénérez pas le peuple juif en allumant le flambeau qui doit l'éclairer au bûcher des Institutions de Moïse, mais en lui donnant l'exemple du respect pour ces Institutions."

[118] *Ibid.*, 9–10: "vivre et mourir dans la religion où ils sont nés."

state-subsidized religion, had honored the right of French Jews to be *séparatistes!*[119]

Despite the views of religious conservatives, the progression of Jewish assimilation in France gradually resulted in "a certain de-Judaization," according to Bernhard Blumenkranz, particularly with the changes encouraged and effected by the French Consistoires.[120] Many young Parisian Jews of the Restoration, faced with a society that did not fully embrace them and sharply curtailed their ambitions, had moved away from traditional Judaism. Some even became apostate, although conversions never reached epidemic proportions as in Germany from 1820 to 1848, even with the Church's active promotion.[121] The Saint-Simonian Gustave d'Eichthal converted to Christianity in 1817, an action that coordinated with the family's name change from Seligmann to d'Eichthal. Yet, in a letter written *circa* 1836, d'Eichthal insisted that he never stopped thinking of himself as Jewish:

> [Y]ou know that I was born a Jew and that the memories of my
> childhood, especially of the family of my grandparents, inspired in me a
> deep attachment to the race of my fathers, an attachment that not only
> persisted but also continued to grow alongside my Christian faith.[122]

Sammons writes that Heine, who moved to Paris in 1831, "suffered a self-inflicted wound to his own integrity" by converting, and that he grew to realize that "his Jewishness remained a significant fraction of his cultural consciousness and poetic imagination, and he could not . . . cast it off like an old coat" although he tried.[123] This biographer, among many others, stresses the identity conflict that Heine exhibited through his behavior and in his writings, noting that especially in Paris

---

[119] *Ibid.*

[120] Blumenkranz, *Histoire des juifs*, 305.

[121] Girard, *De l'émancipation à l'égalité*, 156. *L'Univers religieux* celebrated in its pages the conversion of Jews, as well as Protestants, to the Catholic faith. See, for example, "Nouvelles religieuses," *L'Univers religieux* 3, no. 358 (1 January 1835); "Nouvelles religieuses," *L'Univers religieux* 3, no. 368 (14 January 1835).

[122] F-Pa, Ms. 14393/5, fol. 1: "[V]ous savez que je suis né Juif et les souvenirs de mon enfance, surtout de la famille de mes grands parents, m'ont inspiré un attachement profond à la Race de mes pères, attachement qui non seulement s'est concilié, mais n'a pas cessé de croître avec ma foi chrétienne."

[123] Sammons, *Heinrich Heine*, 110.

Heine tried to obscure his Jewish identity, claiming he had never been to a synagogue (untrue, says Sammons) and becoming enraged at public depictions of him as a Jew.[124]

Intermarriage with Christians (as Léon Halévy chose) represented one non-traditional route, although Jewish–Christian unions were relatively rare in nineteenth-century France, suggesting that the Rachel–Léopold romance may have indeed carried more than the taboo of the opera's time. But it undoubtedly retained some element of its revolutionary value as a symbol of a new age of brotherhood and equality: during the 1789 Revolution, for the first time, a Jew was not required to convert in order to marry a Christian.[125] According to Szajkowski, both supporters and opponents of Jewish emancipation had promoted intermarriage; missionaries saw it as one means of obtaining conversions.[126] In addition to voluntary conversions, some as a result of missionary appeals, conversion was often imposed on Jewish children.[127] Intermarriage remained a complex issue in both Jewish and Christian communities following emancipation. The Sanhédrin of 1807, in response to Napoleon's demand for a ruling on intermarriage, declared that the Jewish partner of a mixed marriage would remain Jewish, but refused to encourage such a union.[128] The rabbis stated somewhat evasively that "they were not more disposed to bless the marriage of a Christian woman with a Jew or of a Jewess with a Christian man than the Catholic priests would be disposed to bless such unions."[129] The majority of French Jews avoided the practice; in Paris, from 1808 to 1860, mixed marriages represented only six percent of Jewish alliances.[130] Among the many plays about marriage and divorce on the French stage of the 1820s and 1830s, one *vaudeville* of 1838, *Sara la Juive*, ends with the title character deciding against marrying her Christian lover, after dreaming that her father was damning her; she instead

---

[124] *Ibid.*
[125] Zosa Szajkowski, "Marriages, Mixed Marriages and Conversions among French Jews during the Revolution of 1789," in his *Jews and the French Revolutions*, 834.
[126] *Ibid.*   [127] *Ibid.*, 840.   [128] Girard, *De l'émancipation à l'égalité*, 135.
[129] *Ibid.*: "ils ne seraient pas plus disposés à bénir le mariage d'une Chrétienne avec un Juif ou d'une Juive avec un Chrétien que les prêtres catholiques ne seraient disposés à bénir de telles unions."
[130] *Ibid.*, 104.

marries her Jewish cousin.[131] This conclusion parallels that of *La Juive* in social terms, since both move the Jewish character away from this manner of assimilation.

The ambiguities in Rachel's religious characterization, the tug between her Christian and Jewish sides, undoubtedly struck at the uncertainties and ambivalence surrounding issues of Jewish reform in both the Christian and Jewish communities. Represented in Eléazar was a religious faith that the government honored as a renewed symbol of religious tolerance, but also a social and religious separation that enlightened Jews and Christians condemned – even though it had been imposed by European Christian society, as Créhange pointed out to his *réformateur*. In Rachel might be seen the new, reformed Jew, an *israélite*, who accepts or adopts semi-Christian, occidental ways, without giving up the faith in which she was raised.

Issues of Jewish identity, which persisted in the July Monarchy as the Jewish minority continued to adapt to a society that promised *liberté*, *fraternité*, and *égalité* while struggling with prejudices handed down from many years of Christian ostracism, clearly offer a subtext to the Jewish–Christian world of *La Juive*. Set within this political-religious milieu, the opera's controversial messages become more apparent, and more paradoxical. Undoubtedly, the characterizations of Rachel and Eléazar, especially, revealed the contradictions involving the simultaneous acceptance and rejection of Jews in French society. They underscored particularly the discrepancies in the liberal ideology that inspired the work. As in Enlightenment thought, the opera's sympathy for the persecution of Jews as individuals and for Jewish martyrdom, its concern for the abrogation of their civil rights by an absolutist Church and State, and its message of religious freedom vie with its critique of "unenlightened," separatist Jewish practices and attitudes. As Voltairean themes resounded in *La Juive*, reminding its audiences that through intolerance and despotism lay a continuation of the follies of the past, the opera concurrently reinforced ideas about the Jewish Other already present in the minds of its audiences.

---

[131] Evans, *Le Drame moderne*, 113.

Epilogue

A vibrant subject and an intensely dramatic plot – this was what Véron regarded as the essential core of *grand opéra*: a subject and plot that would engage "the grand passions of the human heart and powerful historical interests."[1] *La Juive*, the last work he was to oversee at the Paris Opéra, certainly met these criteria. With its Voltairean commentary on the abuse of power by Church and State and the oppression of individuals and minority groups outside the dominant culture, with its endorsement of the government's protection of religious freedom and its mixed commentary on Jews and Judaism, the opera realized the desires of both the Opéra administration and the authors for a controversial subject that would captivate the public. The opera's ideology also aligned with, even though it may not have realized, the utopian Saint-Simonian hopes for theatrical works articulated by Léon Halévy and seemingly shared by the composer and Nourrit: to address the "imagination and emotions" of man and to have – at least potentially – "an electric and victorious effect" on the education and moral uplift of society.

In the opera's reflection of the liberalism of the early July Monarchy and its authors, and its capturing of a complex of social attitudes, fears, and biases, it leaned toward disproving Scribe's 1836 assessments before the Académie and proving Villemain's proposition that Scribe was indeed a historian in spite of himself. In the sense that its conscience-raising topic was directed at symbols of institutions debilitated under the July Monarchy – the Church and the senior-branch Bourbon regime – Scribe's comments about the theatre representing the inverse of the reigning political reality bears some truth. Yet with the threatening and even reversing of no-censorship promises of the 1830 Charte,

[1] Véron, *Mémoires*, vol. III, 181.

the autocratic repression of republican uprisings, and a strengthening reconciliation with the Church, its authors may in fact have viewed the anti-authoritarian commentary as a critique of the present regime as well. The softening or masking of the opera's anticlericalism through the cardinal's beneficent gestures and the dignified though extravagant processions presumably assuaged and impressed the largely Catholic audiences. But the balanced presentation may also have been motivated by a desire to strike a *juste milieu* tone and to represent multiple points of view coexisting in the government and among the public.

La Juive marked a turning point in the composer's career, moving him into pre-eminent arenas as Opéra composer and artistic leader, and undoubtedly fulfilling personal aims. His colleague at the Conservatoire, composer Henri-Montan Berton (1770–1844), alluded to his ambitions, but perhaps also to a higher goal, in a note of tribute to commemorate Halévy's success with his first work at the Opéra:[2]

Cher Halévy! Marche à ton noble But!	Dear Halévy! March to your noble Goal!
Le Pont des Arts conduit à l'Institut!	The Bridge of Arts leads to the Institute!
Viens t'asseoir près de nous, et si l'on dit *qui vive?*	Come sit near us, and if anyone says, *who lives**?
Nous répondrons, *La Juive*!!!	We will answer, *La Juive*!!!

* [or, "who's there"]

Clearly an important part of the "goal" or "mission" of *La Juive* for Halévy and his fraternal "coopérateur" was the vivid representation of the historical persecution of Jews with the assumed allusions to contemporary prejudices and social shunning. Although this study has not offered definitive conclusions about individual authorial responsibility in many aspects of the developing work, the composer indisputably played a large role in shaping the story and characterization, particularly through his musical choices. As we have noted, his evocation of the painful experiences of Eléazar and Rachel, the intense Christian hatred

[2] F-Pn, Mus., "Lettres autographes," vol. IX, No. 53.

for the Jews, and the embittered anger of Eléazar seem weighted with "subjectivity" in musical expression that parallels his brother's literary accusations against "Christian fanatics," or, at least, "less enlightened Christians," as well as against intolerant Jews. In a likely homage to his devout father, and to the traditions that he respected even though he partially rejected them, Halévy infused his prayerful settings and Eléazar's religious persona with sincerity and solemnity. The dilemma and split portrayal of Eléazar, whose devotion contrasts sharply with his anti-Christian antagonism and the allusions to stereotyped greed, appear touched with both personal and generational ambivalence toward Jews and their place and identity in Christian society. The pain and melancholia fueling Eléazar's bitter recalcitrance may indeed have emerged from the composer's own experience, while Samuel's deceptiveness, though linked to his conventional disguise, may have reminded Halévy of his own pretenses. As suggested by the "distance" Halévy assumed in his description of the Jewish ghetto, instead of being a Christian disguised as a Jew, he probably felt at times the Jew posing as a Christian or non-Jew.

Viewed against the larger social and political backdrop, both Léopold and Christian-born Rachel appear as metaphorical representations of post-emancipation Jews whose alignment with Christian society had moved them away from traditional beliefs and practices; neither is "fully Jewish." Léopold "plays" Jewish and wavers between observation of and participation in Jewish life; Rachel, who martyrs herself as a Jew, is nonetheless linked to the Catholic world by blood and is drawn to it at key moments. Symbolically, she belongs to both Christian and Jewish societies, on the one hand representing the pull of assimilation into a Christian world and the temptation and advantages of conversion and, on the other, the moral "rightness" of the individual's choice to hold onto religious convictions in the face of social and political castigations and circumscriptions.

With this placement of *La Juive* within multiple contemporary contexts, today's interpreters gain insights into the interrelationships between the developing genre of *grand opéra* and the world of the July Monarchy. A cultural artifact of the Monarchy and its generation, the opera is equally an artifact of the early era of modern Jewish history, as it embodies views and sentiments about Jews held by the dominant culture while simultaneously touching the conflicted identities within Jewish communities and individuals themselves. The social and political ramifications of *La Juive* suggest points of departure for contextualizations of other *grands opéras* that could enrich generally recognized notions about the genre's melding of art and politics, and perhaps balance the interpretations and reinterpretations of these works as primarily commercial endeavors.

As scholarship of *grand opéra* continues, questions need to be raised about the manner in which the historiography of the genre as a whole has been encumbered with capitalistic symbolism and constructions of the Monarchy as an era devoid of ideological depth and characterized by capitalistic greed. The extravagance of the spectacle of *grand opéra*, the entrepreneurship of Véron, and the royalties that librettists and composers enjoyed from the performance of their works, for example, have reinforced the capitalistic metaphors of many interpreters. Despite the validity of many of these past and present explications, scholars should further ponder whether the concentration on the genre's commercialization has not also been touched by an antisemitism hidden within capitalistic depictions since the nineteenth century. One wonders about the extent to which twentieth-century assessments of *grand opéra* carry vestiges of earlier criticisms, from Castil-Blaze's diatribes to Wagner's anti-Meyerbeer maledictions (in curious contrast to his lauding of Halévy and *La Juive*) or even d'Indy's unfortunate characterization of the *grand opéra* era as "la période judaïque," in which the ideal of "profits over art" reigned supreme.[3] Is it conceivable that allusions to the genre's tawdry commercialism and artificiality that seemingly persisted throughout many decades of the twentieth century are tied to nineteenth-century strands of an "anti-capitalist

---

[3] *Cours de composition musicale*, vol. III, 104. In *French Cultural Politics and Music: From the Dreyfus Affair to the First World War* (New York and Oxford: Oxford University Press, 1999), 24–35, Jane Fulcher offers insights into the meshing of d'Indy's political ideology and Wagnerian antisemitism with his artistic agenda, which included the founding of the Schola Cantorum in opposition to the Conservatoire and the "Italo-judaïque" legacy.

antisemitism" (or, rather, an antisemitic anti-capitalism)? D'Indy's construct of an "artistic Dreyfusism," bound up with his attacks on Jewish "métèques" and "cosmopolites,"[4] is likely only one of a complex web of related cultural views affecting assessments of the genre. The musicological disregard of *grand opéra* for many decades was certainly touched by the anti-Meyerbeer sentiments of Wagner and Wagnerites, but endeavors of the last twenty years have begun to redress the years of inattention and even disdain: German scholarship surrounding the work of Meyerbeer, including that behind the collected edition of his works, for example, might be viewed as a musicological "apologia" for previous attitudes or disregard.

Although this examination of *La Juive* has not extended beyond the contexts of the July Monarchy, the opera's presence in the later nineteenth century, not only as a work featured at the inauguration of the Palais Garnier in 1875 but as one that formed part of the repertoire of European and American musical capitals, raises questions for future research about its relevance and reinterpretation within different political environments, such as the pre- and post-Dreyfus years. One writer in *Les Archives israélites* of 1890, on the fiftieth anniversary of the journal's founding, implies that the central meanings and symbols of *La Juive* of 1835 could still be appreciated in the late nineteenth century. In his reflection on the junctures between the periodical's history and French Jewish history (recalling its proximity to the incendiary days of *l'affaire Damas*) he restates important goals of the *Archives*: to keep alive the principles of 1789 that were inscribed in the Constitution but not absorbed into French customs (he pauses to ask whether they are fully absorbed in 1890) and to modify "dispositions" that retain the "idea of persecution" and the "idea of exclusion."[5] Echoing debaters of the 1830–31 *loi du culte israélite*, he characterizes "the persecution and scorn of the Jew" as "the last vestiges of the Middle Ages and the *ancien régime*."[6] He reminds his readers how important the Jew had

[4] Fulcher, *French Cultural Politics*, 31–3.
[5] *La Gerbe*, supplement to *Les Archives israélites* (Paris: Au Bureau des Archives Israélites, 1890), 6.
[6] *Ibid.*, 23.

been in the great shift in the social order from the eighteenth to the nineteenth century: it was the Jew who had been "the most character-istic personification of the revolutionary movement" and of the great "revolt of modern democracy against ancient theocracy" – and there-fore the bane of the "fanatics of the *ancien régime*." "Jew and liberal, Jew and democrat," he writes, "are essentially synonymous."[7] In the mind of this late nineteenth-century Jew, the basic symbolism of *La Juive's* Jews as individuals oppressed by "ancient theocracy" and autocratic regimes would have been clear.

For others in the 1890s, at a time when constructions of the Jew had become increasingly racialized and antisemitism had intensified sharply as a result of the Dreyfus Affair, this symbolic value most likely lost its original power as the opera's meanings were inevitably reshaped. Marcel Proust signifies the work's place in late nineteenth-century popular consciousness in his naming of a character "Rachel, quand du Seigneur" in the novel *A la recherche du temps perdu*: by giv-ing this name to a prostitute whose identity is suggested rather than secure, Proust alludes both to the opera's ambiguous Jewish repre-sentation and to its own orientalized and sexualized Rachel.[8] Recent scholarship of the opera's reinterpretation outside France points to a fractious and varied performance history. Frank Heidlberger, who has begun to research the opera's reception in Vienna, has discovered the suppression of aspects of its religious subject in the 1836 Viennese pro-duction, as well as antisemitically tinged reviews of early twentieth-century performances, including one in 1903 under Mahler.[9] In her tracing of performances of the opera in Russia and the Ukraine, Marina

---

[7] *Ibid.*, 25: "dans le Juif la personnification la plus caractérisée du mouvement révolutionnaire"; "la révolte de la démocratie moderne contre la théocratie antique"; "ces fanatiques de l'ancien régime"; "juif et libéral, juif et démocrate, sont essentiellement synonymes."

[8] See Lawrence R. Schehr, "Rachel, quand du Seigneur," *Esprit créateur* 37, no. 4 (winter 1997): 83–93. Proust's choice of name may also bear a hidden allusion to his close personal connection with Halévy's descendants, Daniel, Elie, and Geneviève Halévy.

[9] Colloque Fromental Halévy, Conservatoire de Paris, 17 November 2000. Papers given at this colloque will be published under the auspices of the universities Paris III and Paris XII.

Tcherkashina has found that *La Juive* held too much political actuality to be allowed on the stage in St. Petersburg during years in which Jews were brutally tyrannized; in Odessa in the 1920s, its Jewish identity was clearly altered under the title "The Cardinal's Daughter," yet a 1925/6 production in Yiddish in the Ukraine was viewed as an "exceptional folk event," one "enriching of Jewish national culture."[10] By the 1930s, when *La Juive* disappeared from the stages of the Paris Opéra as well as from many European and American theatres, its Jewish characterization, and perhaps its partial identity as a "Jewish opera," had made it increasingly controversial; surely in the immediate post-Holocaust context, the persecution and fate of these operatic Jews bore a painful proximity to reality.

From our own post-Holocaust vantage point, when demonstrations of antisemitism electrify and anger, and "fanatic," or "fanatique," carries a range of heavy, slanderous connotations, we strain to peel away the layers of accumulated meanings as we consider the pre-Holocaust *La Juive*. Yet in the mediation between our own present and that of the 1830s, we inevitably question the viability of this opera today. Several recent productions of *La Juive* have exploited the ripe memory of the Holocaust and have enhanced the opera's portrayed victimization and martyrdom of the Jews through twentieth-century settings and recastings. Performances in the late 1980s and early 1990s in Bielefeld, Ludwigshafen, and Nuremberg featured Nazi costumes and symbols in stark, somber sets, while the production of the 1999/2000 season at the Vienna Staatsoper (a production directed by Günter Krämer in cooperation with the New Israeli Opera) depicted the opera's royal figures as decadent Austrian nobility who were set in clear opposition to the stoic, morally superior Rachel and Eléazar – signified through the use of white versus black costuming and spatial contrasts in upper and lower regions of the stage. The Staatsoper's *Chef-Dramaturg*, Christopher Wagner-Trenkwitz, unconsciously tapped into the embedded ideology of *La Juive* as he recently discussed his role (and that of tenor Neil Shicoff) in bringing the opera to

[10] *Ibid.*, 18 November 2000.

Vienna.[11] He spoke excitedly of discovering in the opera the power "to make people think" and the relevance of its attack on religious and political intolerance in the face of the ascendancy of the alleged Nazi apologist Jörg Haider and right-wing extremists in Austria. In the mind of this *Dramaturg*, *La Juive's* potency as a topical work of social, political, and moral import had not died in the 165 years since its première, but through its reinterpretation within one post-Holocaust milieu had found renewed power to touch human passions, interests, and consciences.

It is to be hoped that through the present study of *La Juive* the opera's deeper meanings within the early nineteenth-century past will have found equal resonance with readers of the early twenty-first century. Although the power of the anticlerical and anti-authoritarian symbols of French liberalism of a former age is undoubtedly diminished and the import of its Jewish characterizations is obscured by the anachronism of their stereotypes as well as the elusiveness of past antisemitism, the opera's central messages remain vibrant in a world filled with the ongoing struggles of political, religious, and ethnic antagonisms, disenfranchised minorities, and questions and conflicts of Jewish identity.

[11] Private conversation with Wagner-Trenkwitz, Vienna, 26 June 2000.

Appendix A
Personnel, *La Juive*, Paris Opéra, 1835

Commission de Surveillance
(functioned under le comte de Montalivet, le Ministre de l'Intérieur)
PRESIDENT Antoine-Gabriel de Choiseul

Entrepreneur-Directeur Louis Véron
Librettist Eugène Scribe
Composer Fromental Halévy
Mise en scène Adolphe Nourrit
Divertissements Philippe Taglioni
Directeur de la scène Edmond Duponchel
Décorateurs

Acts I, II, IV, and V	Act III
Charles Séchan	René Philastre
Léon Feuchère	Charles Cambon
Edouard Despléchin	
Jules Diéterle	

Peintre en chef Pierre-Luc-Charles Cicéri
Dessinateur de costumes Paul Lormier
Premier chef de chant Fromental Halévy
Deuxième chef de chant Jean M. Schneitzhoeffer
Premier maître de ballet Philippe Taglioni
Machiniste en chef Contant
Chef d'orchestre/violon principal François-Antoine Habeneck
Chef de la copie Aimé-Simon Leborne

PRINCIPAL CAST

ROLES	CREATORS
Eléazar, goldsmith-jeweller	Adolphe Nourrit
Rachel, adopted daughter of Eléazar	Cornélie Falcon
Cardinal Jean-François de Brogni	Nicolas Levasseur
Princess Eudoxie, niece of the emperor	Julie Dorus-Gras

Léopold, prince of the Empire	Lafont
Ruggiero, *Grand Prévôt* of Constance	Henri-Bernard Dabadie
Albert, *Sergent d'armes* of the emperor's archers	F. Prévost
Herald of the emperor	Dérivis
Officer of the emperor	Prévost
Men of the People	Massol
	F. Prévost
	Alexis Dupont
Regular of the *Saint-Office*	Pouillet
Butler of the emperor	Hens
Sigismund, emperor [mute]	[?]

CHORUS (as listed in the Schlesinger *livret* of 23 February 1835; variant spellings of performers' names have been preserved)

ACT I

Bourgeois and artisans
MM. Gufon, Godefroy, Berdoulet, Ducauroy, César, Begrez, Emery 1er, Emery 2e, Doutreleau, Vaillant, Bouchet, Goyon, Guignot, Georget, Damoreau *père*, Piccardat, Colona, Alizard, Dauger, Cognet, Bouvenne, Popé, Bernoux, Tardif, Forgues, Laty, Heins, Clavé, Charpentier, Damoreau *jeune*, Saint-Denis, Gontier, Robin, Douvry, Olen, Laissement, Ménard, Laussel, Delaforge, Monneron

Bourgeoises and artisans' wives
Mesd. Sèvres, Laurent, Augusta, Blangi, Prévost, Dussard, Lorotte, Bataillard, Proche, Othman, Bouvenne, Ingrand, Boilard, Riquiener, Bournay, Gilles, Mathilde, Villiers, Céleste, Tuillard, Fitzjames, Barbier

ACT II

Jews
MM. Piccardat, Laissement, Charpentier, Guignot, Popée, Guyon, Bouvenne

Jewesses
Mesd. Lorotte, Proche, Grosneau, Bouvenne, Ingrand

ACT III

Princes of the Empire
MM. Alexis Dupont, Massol, Wartel, Ferdinand Prévot, Trevaux, Pouillet,
Charpentier, Poppée

Cardinals
MM. Guyon, Georget, Goyon

Gentlemen
MM. Bouvenne, Bernoux, Tardif, Forgues, Laty, Clavé, Damoreau *jeune*,
Saint-Denis, Gontier, Robin, Douvry, Olen, Laissement, Mesnard, Laussel,
Delaforgue, Monneron

Ladies of the emperor's court
Mesd. Sèvres, Augusta, Prévost, Dussard, Bataillard, Proche, Othman,
Riquiener, Bournay, Gilles, Mathilde, Villers

Ladies of the princess
Mesd. Laurent, Lorotte, Céleste

ACT V

Penitents
MM. Clavé, Bernoux, Dauger, Delaforgue, Piccardat, Monneron,
Charpentier, Mesnard, Olen, Bégrez, Tardif, Saint-Denis, Emery 1er,
Emery 2e, Bouvenue, Ducauroy, Hens, Doutreleau, Godefroy, Douvry,
Halizard, Berdoulez, Boucher, Guignot, Forgues

Mesd. Sèvres, Lorotte, Othman, Proche, Laurent, Blangi, Bouvenne,
Grosneau, Ingrand, Baron, Bataillard, Villers

DANCE (as listed in the Schlesinger *livret* of 23 February 1835; variant
spellings of performers' names have been preserved)

Pages of the emperor, cardinal, and various seigniorial houses
Mesd. Petit, Angélina, Pujol, Ragaine, Coupotte, Florentine, Welch,
Delucenay 1re, Delucenay 2e, Lemousse, Ligny, Roussel, Jomard,
Célarius, Jouve, Martial, Clément, Cottiau, Marin, Popelin, Euphrasie,
Julia, Debroux, Célestine, Dumilâtre 2e, Baptiste, Lechêne, Guillemain,
Courtois

Artisans
MM. Mazillier, Simon
MM. Lenfant, L. Petit, Coraly, Josset, Keffer, Mignot, Alexandre, Ch. Petit,
Adrien, Millot, Guiffard, Grosneau

Artisans' wives
Mesd. Montessu, Elie
Mesd. Pérès, Marivin, Guichard, Pierson, Fitz-James 2e, Beaupré, Caré,
Forster, Fitz-James 3e, Mélanie, Albertine, Larchet

ACT III

Characters of the intermède
Mesd. Noblet, Julia, Dupont, Leroux, Duvernay, Fitz-James

Knight-Errants
M. Mazillier
MM. Lenfant, H. Petit, Coraly, Josset, Kaiter, Mignot, Alexandre, Ch. Petit,
Adrien, Milot, Guiffard, Grosneau

Enchanted princesses
Mesd. Pérès, Marivin, Guichard, Pierson, Fitz-James, Beaupré, Caré, Forster,
Mélanie, Albertine, Larchet, Fitz-James

A Saracen enchanter
M. Cazzo

A dwarf
Mlle Elise

Dukes and princes in the service of the emperor
MM. Clemet, Prevost, Isambert, Cornet

Cardinals and archbishops in the retinue of the Council president
MM. Desplaces, Grenier, Ragaine, Lefèvre, Begrand, Monnet

Appendix B
Synopsis of *La Juive*

A crossroads in Constance in 1414: on the right facing the audience, the door of a church; to the left, at the street corner, the shop and home of a goldsmith-jeweller. Many fountains.

The townspeople of Constance (Konstanz), Switzerland, are celebrating the opening of the Council of Constance in 1414, the ecumenical convocation that promises to mend the rift in the Catholic Church. On this Christian feast day declared by Emperor Sigismund, they also honor the victory of Prince Léopold over the Hussites, followers of the religious reformer Jan Hus (No. 1: *Introduction*, "Te deum laudamus"). As worshipers sing the *Te deum* in the cathedral, a crowd outside whispers accusingly about Eléazar, the Jewish goldsmith who continues to work, ignoring the feast day. Ruggiero, the town provost, hears the sounds of Eléazar's labor and orders the offender to be brought before him. After Eléazar and Rachel are dragged out of their house, Ruggiero incites the crowd further against the Jews and orders their execution for desecrating the feast day. The crowd's anger is diffused and the Jews' death is averted by Cardinal Brogni, who arrives on the scene and discovers that he knows Eléazar. Eléazar reminds the cardinal that in his earlier days as magistrate in Rome, he had banished him and other Jews from the city. Although Eléazar vehemently rejects Brogni's plea for forgiveness and his offer of a brotherly hand, the cardinal prays for clemency and tolerance (No. 2: *Cavatine*, "Si la rigueur").

Eléazar and Rachel have returned home and Léopold, disguised as the Jew Samuel, approaches Rachel's window and serenades her (No. 3: *Sérénade*, "Loin de son amie"). When Léopold asks to see her, Rachel invites him to a Passover service that evening. Their conversation is cut short by the crowd gathering for the continuing festivities (No. 4: *Choeur*, "Hâtons-nous"; No. 5: *Choeur des buveurs*, "Ah! quel heureux destin"; No. 6: *Valse*). The crowd shouts the arrival of the victors of the Hussite battles (No. 7: *Final*, "Noël, Noël, Noël"). As Eléazar and Rachel situate themselves on the church steps for a view of the procession, Ruggiero incites the crowd anew against them, recalling the famous biblical passage about Jesus chasing the moneylenders from the temple. The crowd virulently responds, threatening to throw the Jews into Lake Constance. For a second time, their death is averted by an official, this time by Léopold, who (although disguised) instructs his aide, Albert, to hold back the mob. Rachel is puzzled by this action; she continues to be confused by this suggestion of Léopold's power. As the crowd turns its attention to the emperor's arrival, Eléazar prays, and Léopold hopes Rachel will not discover his true identity.

ACT II

The interior of Eléazar's home.

Eléazar leads Rachel, other members of his family, a few other Jews, and the disguised Léopold in a prayer as part of a celebration of the Passover seder (No. 8: *Entr'acte et prière*, "O Dieu de nos pères"). As the unleavened bread is distributed, Léopold throws his to the floor, an action that Rachel sees and questions. A loud knock at the door startles the celebrants; when Eléazar hears that it is a party of the emperor, he orders all religious items hidden and asks Léopold/Samuel to remain. Princess Eudoxie, the niece of Sigismund and the wife of Léopold, enters. Léopold exclaims his dismay in an aside; in the muted light, Eudoxie does not recognize her husband. She asks Eléazar who Léopold is, and is told he is a painter. Eudoxie then tells the purpose of her visit: to purchase a rare jewel from Eléazar to honor her husband's victory (No. 9: *Trio*, "Tu possèdes, dit-on"). In his dealing with Eudoxie, Eléazar reveals his eagerness to profit from the transaction, as Léopold frets about his deception and fears. After Eudoxie leaves, Rachel tells Léopold that she wants to see him later.

As she awaits her lover's arrival, her conflicting emotions and doubts about him emerge (No. 10: "Il va venir"). When he comes, she confronts him with her suspicions and he reveals that he is a Christian, but, quelling her with soothing words, begs her to leave all behind and run away with him (No. 11: *Duo*, "Lorsqu'à-toi"). Rachel is on the verge of responding when her father interrupts them. Eléazar, furious at Léopold's betrayal, tells the young lover that he would kill him were he not Jewish (No. 12: *Trio*, "Je vois son front coupable"). Léopold again reveals that he is Christian and awaits Eléazar's blows, but Rachel averts violence as she coaxes her father into forgiving him. Eléazar's love for his daughter is so strong that he is willing to bless their marriage, but Léopold refuses, inciting Eléazar's curses and Rachel's bewildered cries.

ACT III

[In Scenes i–iv omitted after the première, Eudoxie sings joyfully of her husband's return in her apartment. She is approached by Rachel, who has followed Léopold to the royal palace; Rachel asks to be her servant (or slave, "esclave") for a day and Eudoxie, though puzzled, grants her request.]

Magnificent gardens. In the distance the rich countryside of the canton of Thurgovie. To the left, under a velvet dais, the emperor's table, higher than all the others, with velvet-covered steps leading up to it. The emperor is seated; to his right is Cardinal Brogni; a little below them are Eudoxie and Léopold; to the left seated at smaller tables are princes, dukes, and electors of the Empire. At stage left, dressers of wine and crockery, laden with rich vases of beautiful goldplate, appear at intervals. At the raising of the curtain, four men on horseback appear with the plates of honor. Pages take them and place them on the emperor's table; other pages come and go, carrying the various dishes, pouring wine, and attending to the service of the imperial table. Above buffets of silverware, lords and ladies are seated on amphitheatre-style steps. At the back, soldiers prevent the crowd from approaching.

In the gardens of the royal palace, the festivities continue (No. 13: *Choeur,* "O jour mémorable"; No. 14: *Pantomine et ballets*). At the end of the *divertissements,* the emperor descends from his throne; he thanks his niece, Eudoxie, and Léopold, and leaves, followed by court officers and servants. After his departure, all the lords and prelates surround Léopold and congratulate him on the honor he is going to receive. A victory chorus is sung (No. 15: *Final,* "Sonnez, clairons") and Eudoxie calls attention to her husband's heroism ("Pour fêter un héros"). [In an early version, and likely at the première, Rachel, disguised as a slave, pours Léopold a celebratory drink; he recognizes her and drops the cup, stimulating surprise in those who observe him; Rachel reacts sharply as she realizes who he is and then disappears into the crowd.] Eléazar enters with the jewel-encrusted chain he has made for Eudoxie ("A vos ordres sommis"). Just as the princess presents it to her husband, Rachel steps forward and rips it from Léopold's hands. Having recognized Léopold as her lover, Samuel, she angrily denounces him, admitting their love and pointing out the laws against their liaison.

Begun by Léopold, the sextet of principals responds with the chorus in fear and consternation ("Je frissonne et succombe"). Brogni pronounces a stern malediction on Rachel, Léopold, and Eléazar for breaking God's laws ("Vous, qui du Dieu vivant"), and the crowd, singing against varied responses of the ensemble, intensifies the cardinal's condemnation with their own ("Sur eux anathème!").

ACT IV

A Gothic apartment before the Council chamber.

Rachel, Léopold, and Eléazar have been given death sentences. Eudoxie, desperate to save the husband she still loves, begs Rachel to retract her accusations against Léopold (No. 16: *Scène et duo*, "Du Cardinal voici l'ordre suprême"). Initially reluctant to be lenient with the lover who has wronged her, Rachel finally agrees to speak on his behalf. An officer announces the entrance of the cardinal; after Eudoxie leaves, Brogni enters and speaks to Rachel of his regrets that she should die so young (No. 17: *Scène*, "Le Cardinal, madame"). He calls for Eléazar, whom he confronts with an appeal to save Rachel and himself by renouncing his faith and adopting Christianity (No. 18: *Duo*, "Ta fille en ce moment"). Eléazar adamantly refuses; he then sings a tribute to the God of Jacob, as Brogni sings of the Christian God. Embittered toward Brogni, Eléazar reminds him of the loss of his daughter during the pillaging of Rome; he discloses that she did not die, but was saved by a Jew. Despite Brogni's moving appeals, Eléazar does not divulge the name of this Jew (his own), vowing to keep the secret until death. The cardinal is then summoned to the Council by Ruggiero.

In solitude, Eléazar becomes racked with pain and self-doubt as he thinks of his beloved daughter's approaching death (No. 19: *Air*, "Rachel, quand du Seigneur"). Affected by his deep paternal love, he decides to renounce his vengeance and save her; but, just as he declares his intent, the crowd (offstage) calls out once again for the demise of the Jews. His anger renewed, Eléazar vows that Rachel will die a martyr, "reclaimed by Israel."

ACT V

An immense tent, supported by Gothic columns with gilded capitals, overlooks the village of Constance, whose grand square and principle buildings are visible. At the edge of the square sits an enormous bronze vat heated by a blazing furnace; around the square, people are massed on tiered steps.

The large crowd gathered for the *auto-da-fé* celebrates the imminent death of the Jews (No. 20: *Choeur,* "Quel plaisir"). To the sounds of an orchestral march, the Council and court enter (No. 21: *Marche*). Ruggiero announces the condemnation of the Jews and the commuting of Léopold's sentence to banishment (No. 22: *Final,* "Le Concile prononce"). Shocked at the injustice of the sentence, Eléazar reacts harshly, but is told that someone has declared Léopold innocent. To her father's dismay, Rachel steps forward and renounces her former accusations, shocking those who hear her and moving Ruggiero to reconfirm the Jews' guilt. As the cardinal and the people repeat a prayer, Rachel and Eléazar are led to the scaffold that stands over the cauldron of boiling liquid. When Ruggiero announces "it is time" for the execution, Eléazar cries out for a delay, again wanting to prevent his daughter's death. He asks Rachel if she wants to convert and thus save herself, but she adamantly refuses, preferring to die with Eléazar. At this final moment, Brogni pleads for Eléazar to tell him where his daughter is. As executioners hurl Rachel into the cauldron, Eléazar points toward her with the shocking words, "La voilà!" Before a stunned cardinal, to the last vengeful cries of the celebrants, Eléazar climbs the scaffold to meet his fate.

Appendix C
Contract between Louis Véron and Eugène Scribe
for the libretto of *La Juive*, 25 August 1833

F-Pn, Ms., n.a.fr. 22839, vol. 1, fol. 276

25 août 1833
Académie Royale de Musique

Entre les soussignés.

Louis, Désiré, Véron, Directeur et entrepreneur de l'Académie royale de musique, demeurant à Paris, rue Pinon, N°8, d'une part;

Et M. Eugène, Scribe, homme de lettres, demeurant à Paris, rue Olivier S^t. Georges, N°8, d'autre part;

A été convenu ce qui suit:

Article 1er.

M. Scribe s'engage à composer* les paroles d'un opéra en cinq actes intitulé *La Juive*, dont il a soumis le plan à M. Véron qui l'adopte et le reçoit. M. Scribe lira le premier acte le premier Septembre, le second, le quinze du même mois, et les trois derniers actes le quinze Octobre prochain.

Art^e. 2.

M. Véron s'engage à payer à M. Scribe à titre de prime, et en outre des droits d'auteur fixés par les règlements ordinaires, une somme de *cinq mille francs* payable, savoir: *Deux mille cinq cents francs* au moment où M. Scribe lui remettra les cinq actes du dit opéra, et *deux mille cinq cents francs* le premier mars mil huit cent trente quatre, que le dit opéra ait été représenté ou non à cette époque; vû que M. Véron est le maître de faire jouer le dit ouvrage quand bon lui semblera.

Art^e. 3.

En outre, et à chaque représentation du dit opéra, M. Scribe jouira d'une loge de *troisième de face de six places* et il aura le droit de donner sur sa

---

*crossed-through phrase follows in original: "dans l'espace de deux mois à dater de ce jour"

signature *deux billets* de *deux places chacun* où bon lui semblera excepté dans les places louées d'avance.

Art^e. 4.

Dans le cas, de la part de M. Véron, d'une cession ou renonciation à son bail ou à son entreprise, il s'engage à faire exécuter les dites conditions par son Successeur et s'il cédait son bail avant le 1er Mars 1834, il paierait à M. Scribe, avant son départ, les deux mille cinq cents restant dûs sur la prime de cinq mille francs.

Art^e. 5.

Dans le cas où M. Scribe n'aurait pas terminé les cinq actes du dit opéra le quinze Octobre prochain, il consent à payer à M. Véron un dédit de trois mille francs, sauf le cas de maladie grave constatée par les médecins.

    fait double à Paris le *25 Août 1833*
dix mots rayés nuls
    approuvé l'écriture ci dessus
    /s/ Véron
/s/ Scribe

25 August 1833
Académie royale de musique

Between the undersigned.
    Louis Désiré Véron, Director and entrepreneur of the Académie royale de musique, residing in Paris, rue Pinon, N° 8, as the first party;
    And M. Eugène Scribe, man of letters, residing in Paris, rue Olivier S^t. Georges, N°8, as the second;
    Have agreed to the following:

Article 1.

M. Scribe is contracted to write* the words of an opera in five acts entitled *La Juive*, for which he has submitted the scenario to M. Véron, who

*crossed-through phrase follows in original: "within two months of today's date"

adopts it and approves it. M. Scribe will read the first act on the first of September, the second on the fifteenth of the same month, and the last three acts on the fifteenth of next October.

Art^e. 2.

M. Véron is contracted to pay to M. Scribe as a bonus, in addition to the royalties fixed by the usual rules, a sum of *five thousand francs* payable, as follows: *two thousand five hundred francs* at the moment when M. Scribe submits to him the five acts of the said opera, and *two thousand five hundred francs* on the first of March eighteen hundred and thirty-four, whether the said opera has been performed or not by this time; seeing that M. Véron is the master to perform the said work when he thinks best.

Art^e. 3.

Furthermore, for each performance of the said opera, M. Scribe will have a box of *six seats facing the stage on the third level* and, with his signature, he will have the right to give *two tickets* of *two seats each* wherever he wishes, except seats reserved in advance.

Art^e. 4.

If M. Véron cedes or renounces his lease or his enterprise, he is contracted to have the said conditions executed by his successor, and if he cedes his lease before 1 March 1834, he will pay to M. Scribe, before his departure, the two thousand five hundred [francs] that remain due on the bonus of five thousand francs.

Art^e. 5.

If M. Scribe does not finish the five acts of the said opera on the fifteenth of next October, he agrees to pay M. Véron a debt of three thousand francs, except in the case of serious illness confirmed by physicians.

executed in duplicate in Paris on *25 August 1833*
the ten words scored out are null
approve the above writing
/s/ Véron
/s/ Scribe

Appendix D

Rough chronology of the genesis and early performances of *La Juive*, c. 1832/3–1835

c. December 1832 – early 1833	Sketch of plot outline of "la belle juive" in Scribe *carnet*
25 August 1833	Contract for libretto of *La Juive* between Véron and Scribe
1 September 1833	Date stipulated in contract for Scribe "to read" the first act to Véron
15 September 1833	Date stipulated in contract for Scribe "to read" the second act to Véron
16 September 1833	Scribe begins work on draft verse of Act III (F-Pn, Ms., n.a.fr. 22562)
21 September 1833	Scribe begins work on draft verse of Act III, Scene v (F-Pn, Ms., n.a.fr. 22562)
15 October 1833	Date stipulated in contract for Scribe "to read" the last three acts to Véron
January 1834	Date in Leborne's *registre* indicating the beginning of copying of performing parts and, shortly thereafter, of soloists' rehearsals
July 1834	Date of itemized records for costumes and staging materials (F-Pan, AJ^{13} 202); *La Gazette musicale de Paris* (6 July 1834) announces the rehearsing of Act I
13 and 14 July 1834	Dates of payments to Halévy from Schlesinger for full score and piano-vocal score, respectively, suggesting completion of first-draft musical score (sale price for each score = 15,000 francs)
17 August 1834	Last acts in rehearsal, as reported in *La Gazette musicale de Paris*

late November – early December 1834	Beginning of *répétitions générales*
	Leborne reports "Successive cuts, restorations, and changes made after each of the 15 full rehearsals" ($37^{1}/2$ days of copy work) (F-Pan, AJ^{13}289)
9 December 1834	Fifth *répétition générale*
11 January 1835	*La Gazette musicale de Paris* reports that Acts I–III are in rehearsal
mid-January 1835	Projected date of première, as reported in *La Revue musicale* (28 December 1834)
1 February 1835	Acts IV and V back in rehearsal "au quatuor"
12 February 1835	Rehearsal of Acts I and III with scenery and costumes
16 February 1835	*Répétition générale* of Act V with costumes
18 February 1835	Scheduled première; postponed
23 February 1835	Première of *La Juive*, Académie royale de musique
[24] February 1835	Leborne *atelier* begins cuts (totaling $16^{1}/2$ days of copy work after each of the first three performances) (F-Pan, AJ^{13} 289)
25 February 1835	Second performance of *La Juive*; Act III numbers omitted
27 February 1835	Third performance of *La Juive*; alterations continue
28 February 1835	Report in *Le Moniteur universel* of sale of score to Schlesinger for 30,000 francs
9 August 1835	Advertisement for sale of Schlesinger full score in *La Gazette musicale de Paris*
September 1835	Copying of overture performing parts by Leborne *atelier*
16 October 1835	First performance of overture, as reported in *La Gazette musicale de Paris* (11 October 1835)
16 January 1836	Letter from Fromental Halévy to Charles Valter, Rouen, mentioning engraved orchestral score and supplement

Appendix E

Description of the genesis of *La Juive* by Léon Halévy

F. Halévy: Sa Vie et ses oeuvres, 23–5

Peu de poëmes d'opéras subirent plus de transformations que celui de *la Juive*, cette heureuse création de Scribe. Dans le plan primitif, la scène se passait à Goa, et l'inquisition tenait la place qu'occupe aujourd'hui dans l'ouvrage le concile de Constance. La conception musicale primitive fut elle-même changée, car une distribution de rôles qui avait été projetée, mais non maintenue, eût donné à la partition un tout autre caractère: dans ces bases premières, qui furent abandonnées, Adolphe Nourrit, au lieu d'être le père, était l'amant, et le rôle du père devait être confié à la voix de basse, à Levasseur. Nourrit, l'artiste supérieur, homme de si excellent conseil et de tant de goût, prit beaucoup de part à ces remaniements du fond. Combien de fois mon frère et lui vinrent-ils discuter, régler près de moi ces modifications consenties par Scribe, qui, comprenant avec un tact exquis le véritable rôle du poëte dramatique à l'Opéra, s'effaçait pour se subordonner aux inspirations du compositeur et à celles des artistes éminents, ses interprètes! C'était dans l'été de 1834; mon frère eut bientôt les deux premiers actes de *la Juive*, et successivement les trois autres. Quand l'on fut d'accord sur le fond, alors commença cette refonte partielle de l'oeuvre à laquelle mon frère soumettait ses poëmes, car il se les assimilait, il en faisait sa chose propre et individuelle; il s'y incarnait pour ainsi dire; il les absorbait dans sa création musicale: ici, c'était une scène dont il fallait changer le mouvement, parce qu'il ne répondait pas à sa pensée; là, au lieu du récitatif, il fallait un air; ici, au lieu du récit, un choeur (et il avait le don rare de faire intervenir admirablement les masses vocales). Il avait aussi l'éminente faculté de fondre le récitatif dans le tissu mélodique de l'oeuvre, tout en lui conservant son caractère; là, il fallait que le duo fût un trio ou qu'un air vînt se placer dans un finale; ici, il fallait exprimer un sentiment que le poëte avait omis de rendre, et qui lui inspirait un chant pathétique. Venaient ensuite les détails du vers, les innombrables modifications prosodiques, les exigences, pour lui absolues, du rhythme. "Des vers cadencés, modulés, disait-il sans cesse; pas de coupe uniforme!" De là l'extrême variété de rythmes qui caractérise sa manière, et qui lui a fait porter si haut l'un des mérites les plus distinctifs de l'école française.

Un mot d'explication devient ici nécessaire.

Scribe, homme vraiment supérieur, du commerce le plus charmant et du caractère le plus sûr, avait, avec la passion du théâtre, celle du travail, mais du travail toujours nouveau. C'est une de ces fantaisies dans la passion, qu'on peut facilement pardonner, comme la passion elle-même est digne de tout honneur et de toute louange. Il n'aimait donc pas à s'appesantir longtemps sur le même ouvrage, et sa merveilleuse facilité de conception et d'exécution ne le lui eût pas permis. On ne pouvait, du reste, raisonnablement exiger que cet homme si occupé, si surchargé d'engagements et de travaux, et dont deux ou trois théâtres attendaient sans cesse les oeuvres promises et exigibles par traités, après avoir livré un poëme au compositeur qu'il avait choisi, se mît pendant une année, pour d'incessantes modifications, au service de ses exigences, de ses caprices ou même des nécessités de son art. Certes il n'aurait pas refusé à mon frère, qu'il aimait, ce sacrifice, si celui-ci l'eût réclamé; mais mon frère avait près de lui un coopérateur toujours prêt: j'évite à dessein le mot de *collaborateur*, et j'emploie l'expression la plus propre à la modeste mission que je m'étais assignée, mission qui, je puis le dire, n'était pas exempte d'abnégation, et dont le moindre mérite fut le désintéressement. Un accord tacite s'était donc naturellement formé sur ce point entre nous. De précédents rapports s'étaient d'ailleurs établis entre Scribe et moi, et une circonstance nouvelle vint un peu plus tard les resserrer: Scribe avait été nommé à l'Académie française en remplacement d'Arnault, l'auteur de *Marius à Minturnes*, de *Germanicus* et des *Fables*; il avait bien voulu, pour son discours de réception, me demander quelques documents, quelques aperçus sur la vie et les ouvrages d'un homme qui m'avait voué une constante et affectueuse bienveillance, et dont j'avais été, jusqu'au jour de sa mort, le répétiteur et le suppléant à l'Ecole polytechnique, dans la chaire de littérature où, pendant trois années, il avait remplacé Andrieux. Scribe n'oublia pas ce léger service, qu'il m'avait été si doux de lui rendre, et il manifesta toujours le plus complet assentiment, la plus franche et la plus cordiale adhésion aux changements qu'à la demande de mon frère j'apportais aux poëmes dont il écrivait la partition, retouches de détails sans doute, mais importantes pour le compositeur, parce qu'il lui suffit souvent de huit vers et même de quatre lignes rimées selon son oreille et accentuées selon son coeur pour tenir le public en haleine par un magnifique choeur ou un *andante* passionné. Je débarrassais, il est vrai, d'un grand soin le fécond et ingénieux écrivain, mais il m'honorait d'une confiance dont j'étais touché, en même temps que j'appréciais vivement la faculté de contribuer au succès d'oeuvres qui m'étaient chères. Que l'on ne croie pas du reste que Scribe y mît de l'indifférence: il n'aurait jamais accepté un changement mal fait ou qui, dans ses idées, pût nuire à l'ouvrage. Mais, quand il reconnaissait que la pièce et le musicien trouvaient également leur compte à ce qui avait été ajouté ou modifié, il applaudissait le premier et remerciait avec effusion. J'en fis mille fois l'épreuve.

Few opera libretti were subjected to more transformations than that of *La Juive*, this lovely creation of Scribe's. In the original scenario, the action was set in Goa, and the Inquisition held the place that the Council of Constance occupies in the work today. The original musical conception itself changed, because the distribution of roles that had been planned, but not retained, would have given the score an entirely different character: in these first drafts, which were abandoned, Adolphe Nourrit was the lover instead of the father, and the role of the father was to be given to a bass voice, to Levasseur. Nourrit, the superior artist, a man of such excellent counsel and good taste, was very involved in these basic revisions. How many times my brother and he came to discuss and sort out with me these modifications agreed to by Scribe, who, understanding with exquisite tact the true role of the dramatic poet at the Opéra, would step aside in order to give way to the inspirations of the composer and to those of eminent artists, his interpreters! It was in the summer of 1834; my brother soon had the first two acts of *La Juive* finished, and, successively, the next three. When there was agreement on the fundamentals, there began this revision of sections of the work to which my brother subjected his librettos, because he assimilated them, they became his own, individual thing; he was embodied in them, so to speak; he absorbed them into his musical creation: here, there was a scene in which the tempo had to change because it did not match his conception; there, in place of recitative, an air was necessary; here, in place of recitative, a chorus (and he had the rare gift of making massed voices work admirably). He also had the eminent faculty of melding the recitative into the melodic fabric of the work, while keeping its character; there, the duo had to be a trio or an aria had to be placed in a finale; here, it was necessary to express a feeling which the poet had failed to render and which inspired in him a moving melody. Then came the details of the verse, the innumerable modifications of prosody, the exigencies of rhythm, which for him were absolute. He was always saying: "Rhythmic, inflected lines; no uniform length!" Hence, the extreme variety of rhythms which characterize his style, and which allowed him to take to such heights one of the most distinctive merits of the French school.

A word of explanation is necessary here.

Scribe, a truly superior man, the most charming and the most trustworthy in character, had a passion for the theatre and for work, but the work had to be always new. It is one of those fantasies in his passion, which can be easily forgiven, as passion itself is worthy of all honor and praise. He did not like to dwell a long time on the same work, and his marvelous ease of conception and execution would not have allowed it. Besides, it would not be reasonable to demand that a man so busy, so overloaded with engagements and work (whose promised works payable by contract were expected constantly by two or three theatres), occupy himself, over the course of a year after having already delivered a poem to the composer he had chosen, with incessant modifications in the service of his requirements, his caprices, or even the necessities of his art. Certainly he would not have refused this sacrifice for my brother, whom he loved, if he had asked for it; but my brother had at his side a cooperator who was always ready: I purposely avoid the term *collaborator*, and I use the most appropriate expression for the modest task that I assigned myself, a task which, I may say, was not without self-sacrifice and whose least merit was selflessness. A tacit agreement, then, had come about naturally between us on this point. Moreover, previous relations had been established between Scribe and me, and a new circumstance drew us closer a little later: Scribe had been appointed to the Académie française [in 1834] to succeed Arnault, the author of *Marius à Minturnes*, *Germanicus*, and the *Fables*; for his reception speech, he was kind enough to ask me for some documents, some anecdotes on the life and works of a man who had devoted a constant and affectionate goodwill towards me, and to whom I had been tutor and assistant at the Ecole polytechnique up to the day of his death, in the chair of literature in which he had replaced Andrieux for three years. Scribe did not forget this small favor, which had been such a pleasure for me to do, and he always demonstrated the fullest approval, the frankest and heartiest support for the alterations that I introduced, at the request of my brother, in the libretti for which he was writing the score, alterations of details no doubt, but important to the composer, because eight lines or even four lines often suffice, rhymed according to his ear and accentuated according to his heart, to keep the public's attention with a magnificent chorus or a passionate *andante*. I freed the fecund and ingenious writer from a great care, it is true, but he honored me with a trust that touched me; at the same time, I deeply appreciated the freedom to contribute to the success of works that were dear to me. Besides, don't think that Scribe was indifferent about it: he would never have accepted a change that was badly made or that, in his view, could harm the drama. But, when he could see that the work and the musician profited equally from what had been added or modified, he was the first to applaud and was very thankful. I experienced this a thousand times.

Appendix F

Rapport from the Secrétaire, Commission de Surveillance, to the Ministre de l'Intérieur, recommending authorization of the première of *La Juive*

F-Pan, AJ[13]202

Commission de Surveillance
auprès de l'Académie Royale
5 du
Conservatoire de Musique

Paris, le 13 février 1835

Monsieur Le Ministre,

La Commission de Surveillance a assisté hier, conformément à vos instructions à la répétition avec décors et costumes des 1er et 3e actes de la *Juive*, nouvel opéra en cinq actes, que M. Véron se propose de donner incessamment sur le théâtre de l'Académie royale de musique.

A la lecture qui lui avait été faite de cet opéra, la Commission n'avait trouvé rien qui ne fut très digne et très convenable, et s'étoit réservé, toutefois, de juger, par elle-même, de l'effet que pourroient produire sur les spectateurs les scènes principales des 1er, 3e, et 5e actes dans lesquelles des cérémonies religieuses devoient avoir lieu avec une sorte de solennité.

La Commission, Monsieur Le Ministre, a vu les 1er et 3e actes; les cérémonies qui ont lieu sont de celles que nos moeurs ont repoussées depuis de longues années heureusement. On y voit figurer effectivement les membres les plus marquans du clergé, et notamment des Cardinaux; mais dans des costumes qui ne sont plus ceux d'aujourd'hui; on y voit aussi des croix, des bannières; mais tous ces emblèmes sont toujours dans la pièce, aussi bien que le clergé, l'objet de la vénération des populations, et tout ce qui se passe est tellement pris au sérieux, qu'il y aura impossibilité pour les esprits les plus mal intentionnés de rien tourner en dérision. L'opéra de Robert le diable, joué sur les théâtres de toutes les capitales de l'Europe, présente certainement dans la résurrection des soeurs du couvent de Ste Eulalie, et dans leurs danses, des inconvenances qu'on ne trouve pas dans l'opéra nouveau. Que seroit-ce donc si l'on rappeloit ici ces tems [sic] anciens, où la foi pourtant étant plus grande et le respect pour les choses saintes poussé bien plus loin que de nos jours, on alloit jusqu'à jouer les mystères, non sur un théâtre de premier ordre, mais dans de véritables parades, plus burlesques les unes que les autres?

La Commission, Monsieur Le Ministre, n'a pas encore vu le 5e acte de la *Juive*; mais elle s'est assurée que tout s'y passe avec autant de dignité et de convenance que dans les 1er et 3e actes; on y voit seulement figurer de plus des pénitents, cortège obligé d'un auto-da-fé.

En conséquence, Monsieur Le Ministre, la Commission, à l'unanimité, a l'honneur de vous proposer d'autoriser la représentation de la *Juive*, opéra en cinq actes, paroles de M. Scribe, musique de M. Halévy.

> J'ai l'honneur d'être avec un profond respect,
> Monsieur Le Ministre,
> Votre très humble serviteur,
> Le Sec^{re} Membre de la Commission
> de Surveillance,
> /s/ F. de M[oncey?]

Paris, 13 February 1835

Monsieur Le Ministre,

Following your instructions, the Commission de Surveillance attended the rehearsal yesterday with scenery and costumes of the first and third acts of *La Juive*, the new opera in five acts that M. Véron plans to put on the stage of the Académie royale de musique.

When the opera was read to them, the Commission found that everything was very dignified and suitable, but nonetheless reserved the right to judge for itself the effect the principal scenes of the 1st, 3rd, and 5th acts, in which religious ceremonies were to take place with some solemnity, might produce on the spectators.

The Commission, Monsieur Le Ministre, has now seen the 1st and 3rd acts; the ceremonies which take place are among those that our customs have rejected, fortunately, for many years. In fact, one sees in them the most prominent members of the clergy, and notably cardinals, but in costumes that are no longer those of today; there are also crosses, banners; but in the drama all these emblems, as well as the clergy, are always the object of the people's veneration, and everything that happens is taken so seriously that it would be impossible for the most badly intentioned to turn anything into derision. The opera *Robert le diable*, played in the theatres of all the capitals of Europe, certainly presents in the resurrection of the sisters of the Convent of St. Eulalie, and in their dances, problems that are not found in the new opera. What would it be like, then, if in conjuring up those olden times when faith was in fact greater and respect for saintly things went far beyond that of today, one went so far as to present mystery plays, not in a principal theatre, but in actual parades, each one more burlesque than the last?

The Commission, Monsieur Le Ministre, has not yet seen the 5th act of *La Juive*; but it has ascertained that everything in it occurs with as much dignity and appropriateness as in the 1st and 3rd acts: it only adds penitents, the obligatory cortège of an *auto-da-fé*.

Consequently, Monsieur Le Ministre, the Commission unanimously has the honor of advising that you authorize the performance of *La Juive*, opera in five acts, words by M. Scribe, music by M. Halévy.

> With deep respect,
> Monsieur Le Ministre,
> Your very humble servant,
> The Secretary Member of the
> Commission de Surveillance
> /s/ F. de M[oncey?]

Appendix G

Records of payments to Fromental Halévy from Maurice Schlesinger for the musical scores of *La Juive*

F-Po, "Lettres autographes," Halévy folder

MAURICE SCHLESINGER, EDIT^r DE MUSIQUE

97, rue Richelieu

Paris, le 13 juillet 1834

Reçu de Monsieur Maurice Schlesinger la Somme de Six Cent francs a compte de mon Opéra La Juive dont je lui ai vendu la Propriété [des] paroles et [de la] musique moyennant la Somme de Quinze mille francs

/s/ F. Halévy

Reçu de Monsieur Maurice Schlesinger la Somme de Deux mille francs en 2 Effets chacun de mille francs payable

le 1er fin Novembre	1000 fr
le 2ème Le 10 Janvier	1000
	2000

a compte de mon Opera La Juive, dont je lui ai vendu la Propriété des paroles et de la musique moyennant la Somme de Quinze mille francs. Il est bien entendu que si par circonstance de force majeure ou autre l'opéra ne serait pas representé a cette epoque, je rendrai l'argent reçu de Mr Schlesinger.

Paris le 13 juillet   approuvé l'Ecriture ci dessus

1834   /s/ F. Halévy

MAURICE SCHLESINGER, EDIT^r DE MUSIQUE

97, rue Richelieu

Paris, 13 July 1834

Received from M. Maurice Schlesinger the sum of six hundred francs for my opera *La Juive* of which I have sold him the ownership of the words and music in return for the sum of fifteen thousand francs.

/s/ F. Halévy

Received from M. Maurice Schlesinger the sum of two thousand francs in
two notes each of one thousand francs payable

the first, the end of November	1000 fr.
the second, 10 January	1000
	2000

for my opera *La Juive*, of which I have sold him the ownership of the words
and music in return for the sum of fifteen thousand francs. It is understood
that if by circumstance of *force majeure* or for some other reason the opera is
not performed in this period, I will return the money received from M.
Schlesinger.

Paris, 13 July	Approve the above writing
1834	/s/ F. Halévy

Appendix H-1

Excerpt from a review of *La Juive* in *Le Constitutionnel*, 25 February 1835

Dossier de presse parisienne, ed. Leich-Galland, 9–10

Le concile de Constance est fameux parmi les conciles, par le nombre de princes ecclésiastiques et séculiers qui y concourent, par l'importance des questions que les passions religieuses y provoquèrent, et par les tristes bûchers qu'y éleva l'intolérance. Vaste, magnifique et lugubre arène qui s'ouvrit en des pompes solennelles et dans des splendeurs d'un luxe inouï, se prolongea en subtiles arguties et en brillans exercices de science théologique, et finit cruellement par deux supplices lamentables. Ainsi, toute la physionomie et toute l'histoire du quinzième siècle se réfléchissent dans ce célèbre conclave, comme dans un immense miroir. Les richesses et les prodigalités des prélats y témoignent leurs moeurs cupides et corrompues, lèpre de l'église, contre laquelle Wicleff et Jean Hus, ces deux précurseurs de Luther, provoquaient déjà les sévérités de la réforme. La prédominance de l'esprit dogmatique et ascétique du temps, y éclate en longues paraphrases, où non seulement les cardinaux, les évêques et les abbés, mais les rois et les barons entrent tout cuirassés d'argumens, et se montrent diserts. Dans les querelles et les intrigues qui firent flotter le concile, de la papauté de Jean à celle de Benoît, de celle de Benoît à celle de Grégoire, on retrouve les marques de la lutte des anti-papes, cet autre scandale et cette grande plaie du 14e et 15e siècles. Enfin pour attester le fanatisme de cette curieuse et déplorable époque, le cruel aveuglement et la foi cruelle des persécuteurs et des victimes, voyez Jean Hus et Jérôme de Prague, attaqués et condamnés comme deux criminels, défendant leurs doctrines et montant intrépidement au bûcher comme deux martyrs.

Le concile dura quatre ans, de 1414 à 1418; pendant quatre ans, l'Europe fut attentive à ce merveilleux spectacle, où les plus singuliers contrastes se trouvent réunis, l'orgueil et le luxe de l'église à côté de la simplicité de son institution primitive, l'intolérance hautaine et barbare en regard des dogmes de charité et de fraternité, les saints hymnes et les saintes prières mêlés aux ruses et aux jeux d'esprit des docteurs et des clercs, le temple et l'autel de Dieu de miséricorde tout voisins des fagots ardents et de la hache du bourreau. Constance, la ville impériale, était alors tout à la fois une vaste église, un tribunal, une Sorbonne, un camp, un bazar, une immense salle de fêtes et de festins, et un cirque pour les martyrs.

. . .

On n'imaginerait pas la grande et singulière émigration qu'amena après elle à Constance cette foule armée ou tonsurée, portant le glaive ou l'Evangile, la dalmatique ou le manteau royal: il arrivera à sa suite plus de soixante orfèvres pour la parer d'or ou de pierreries, quatre cent cinquante marchands de toutes espèces, deux cent cordonniers, quatre-vingt-six pelletiers, trois cent six barbiers, soixante-douze banquiers, soixante-cinq apothicaires; et ce qui donne une haute idée de la chasteté du concile, près de huit cent courtisanes.

The Council of Constance is famous among the councils for the number of ecclesiastical and secular princes who converged there, for the importance of the questions that the religious passions provoked, and for the dreadful burnings at the stake that intolerance brought about. A vast, magnificent, and lugubrious arena that opened in solemn pomp and in displays of extraordinary wealth, it persisted in subtle quibbles and in brilliant exercises of theological science and ended cruelly with two appalling executions. Thus, the entire physiognomy and history of the fifteenth century are reflected in this famous conclave, as in an immense mirror. The riches and the extravagances of the prelates reveal their greedy and corrupt morals, leprosy of the Church, against which Wycliffe and Jan Hus, these two precursors of Luther, were already advocating severe reforms. The predominance of the dogmatic and ascetic spirit of the time explodes in long paraphrases, in which not only the cardinals, bishops, and priests, but also the kings and barons argue combatively and eloquently. In the quarrels and intrigues that made the Council drift, from the papacy of John to that of Benoît, from that of Benoît to that of Gregory, one recognizes the traces of the struggle of the antipopes, that other scandal and that great affliction of the 14th and 15th centuries. Finally, to attest to the fanaticism of this curious and deplorable epoch, the cruel blindness and the cruel faith of persecutors and victims, consider Jan Hus and Jerome of Prague, attacked and condemned like two criminals, defending their doctrines and intrepidly walking to the stake like two martyrs.

The Council lasted four years, from 1414 to 1418; for four years, Europe watched this marvelous spectacle, in which the strangest contrasts come together, the pride and luxury of the Church next to the simplicity of its primitive institution, haughty and barbarous intolerance opposite the dogmas of charity and fraternity, saintly hymns and prayers mixed with the trickery and intellectual games of professors and clerics, the church and the altar of the God of mercy, next to the burning fires and the executioner's axe. Constance, the imperial city, was thus, at one and the same time, a vast church, a tribunal, a Sorbonne, a camp, a bazaar, an immense hall of celebration and feasts, and a circus for martyrs.

. . .

One could not imagine the great and unique emigration that this armed or tonsured crowd brought with it to Constance, carrying the sword or the gospel, the dalmatic or the royal mantle: it was followed by more than 60 goldsmiths in order to adorn it in gold or gems, 450 tradesmen of all types, 200 cobblers, 86 furriers, 306 barbers, 72 bankers, 65 apothecaries, and, giving a good idea of the chastity of the Council, almost 800 courtesans.

Appendix H-2

Excerpt from a review of *La Juive* in *La Gazette de France*, 27 February 1835

Dossier de presse parisienne, ed. Leich-Galland, 58–9

La chose est de grave conséquence; on ne ment pas impunément à l'égard de l'institution la plus nécessaire à l'ordre social. Où M. Scribe a-t-il pris que les conciles prononçassent des condamnations, choisissent des supplices, et assistassent aux derniers momens de ceux qu'on exécutait? Les conciles ont jugé des doctrines et condamné des erreurs, mais jamais ils n'ont prononcé d'arrêt contre les hommes. Son drame pêche donc dans sa base principale, la vérité historique. Il est un grand outrage à la religion et il lui attribue précisément ce que les lois de l'église interdisaient à la juridiction ecclésiastique: l'effusion de sang, les arrêts capitaux. Les pouvoirs politiques ont pu à cet égard outrepasser les lois de l'humanité et les règles de la modération; mais ce n'est pas la religion qu'il faut en accuser. Le concile de Constance a fait des efforts inouïs pour sauver Jean Hus qui était non-seulement un hérétique, mais encore un factieux, un chef d'émeute; l'obstination de cet homme et les violences de ses partisans ont seules obligé le pouvoir temporel à sévir contre lui.

Ce n'est pas ici le lieu de faire un cours de théologie et d'histoire ecclésiastique et si j'ai pris la liberté de me moquer de M. Scribe parce qu'il a travesti sous les oripeaux de l'Opéra les choses de la religion, je ne veux pas lui donner lieu de se moquer de moi si je traitais trop sérieusement ses tromperies historiques, ses anachronismes et sa philosophie voltairienne . . .

. . . Il faut qu'un écrivain comme M. Scribe soit bien malheureux lorsque, tourmenté du besoin de mettre en scène les principes de l'église, des évêques, des prêtres et un peuple chrétien, il ne trouve dans son imagination qu'une action atroce, dégoûtante, ridicule et fausse par dessus le marché, au lieu de tant d'exemples d'héroïsme, de vertus, de charité sublime et de dévouement à la cause de l'humanité.

Ce qui est odieux dans toutes ces élaborations voltairiennes, c'est la mauvaise foi avec laquelle on attribue à la religion ce qui appartient aux pouvoirs politiques, aux partis et aux passions du temps.

The matter is of grave consequence: one does not lie with impunity in relation to the institution that is the most necessary to the social order. Where did M. Scribe find that the councils pronounced condemnations, chose capital punishment, and witnessed the last moments of those who were executed? The councils judged doctrines and condemned errors, but they never passed sentence against anyone. Thus his drama errs in its principal foundation, historical truth. It is a great insult to religion and it attributes to it precisely what the laws of the Church prohibited in ecclesiastical jurisdiction: bloodshed and death sentences. The political powers may have exceeded in this regard the laws of humanity and the rules of moderation; but it is not religion that should be accused. The Council of Constance made unprecedented efforts to save Jan Hus, who was not only a heretic, but also a troublemaker, a ringleader; only the obstinacy of this man and the brutalities of his followers forced temporal authority to deal with him severely.

This is not the place to give a course in theology and ecclesiastical history and if I have taken the liberty of making fun of M. Scribe because he has made a travesty of religious matters under the tinsels of the Opéra, I do not want to give him reason to make fun of me for taking his historical frauds, anachronisms, and Voltairean philosophy too seriously . . .

. . . A writer like M. Scribe must be truly unhappy if, tormented by the need to stage the principles of the Church, bishops, priests, and a Christian people, he finds in his imagination only an atrocious, distasteful, ridiculous, and false action into the bargain, in place of so many examples of heroism, virtue, sublime charity, and devotion to the cause of humanity.

What is odious in all these Voltairean elaborations is the bad faith with which one attributes to religion that which belongs to the political powers, parties, and passions of the times.

Appendix I-1

Letter from Fromental Halévy to Charles Valter, *chef d'orchestre*, Rouen, with addendum of Maurice Schlesinger

F-Pn, Ms., n.a.fr. 14346, fols. 352–3

Paris, 16 janvier 1836

Mon cher ami,

Il m'est impossible de faire ce que vous demandez; c'est-à-dire de remplacer les cors à pistons par des cors ordinaires. J'ai dû, pour supprimer les cors à pistons, distribuer leurs parties entre plusieurs instruments soit ceux à vent ou au quatuor. Je suis fâché de la peine que cela va vous donner pour faire régulariser les parties d'orchestre; mais je crois avoir arrangé tout cela de manière à produire le meilleur effet désirable, ne m'en veuillez donc pas, de vous donner tant de mal, il est de votre intérêt comme du mien que tout cela aille le mieux possible. Je ferai tous mes efforts pour aller vous voir et entendre votre dernière répétition. Je vous prie de ne pas égarer les feuilles de partition gravées que je vous envoie, sur lesquelles j'ai fait les changements; voulant conserver ce travail et le publier en supplément à la fin de la partition, pour la commodité des directeurs qui voudront bien monter La Juive.

Votre bien dévoué

/s/ F. Halévy

Paris, 16 January 1836

My dear friend,

It's impossible for me to do what you ask; that is, to replace the valve horns with natural horns. To omit the valve horns, I had to distribute their parts among several instruments, wind and strings. I'm sorry for the trouble that that is going to give you in adjusting the orchestral parts; but I think that I have worked it all out so as to produce the most desirable effect; please don't be angry with me for causing you such trouble; it's in your interest as in mine that everything works out for the best. I will make every effort to see you and to hear your last rehearsal. Please don't lose the sheets of the engraved score that I'm sending you, on which I have made changes; I want to keep this work and publish it as a supplement at the end of the score, for the convenience of directors who might wish to produce *La Juive*.

Your very devoted
/s/ F. Halévy

[Schlesinger addendum]
Mon cher Monsieur,

Je vous recommande tout particulièrement de me conserver les corrections et les feuilles d'observations que je vous envoie. J'en aurai besoin pour les faire graver en supplément à la partition. C'est un travail trop ennuyeux pour espérer le faire recommencer à M. Halévy. Ainsi soyez assez bon pour me renvoyer cela dès que vous n'en aurez plus besoin.

La partie de tambour est peu considérable, elle n'est pas gravée, faites la copier dans la partition.

Tout à vous
Pour M. Maurice Schlesinger   A. Lard

Je vous envoie le reste de la partition de *Cornaro*.

My dear Sir,

In particular, please be sure to retain the corrections and the pages with observations that I'm sending you. I'll need them to have them engraved as a supplement to the score. It's such a tedious job that I can't expect M. Halévy to do it all over again. And please be good enough to send all of it back when you no longer need it.

The part for drum is not very significant; it isn't engraved; have it copied into the score.

Yours truly,
For M. Maurice Schlesinger   A. Lard

I'm sending you the rest of the score for *Cornaro*.

Appendix I-2
Note from Fromental Halévy to Adolphe Nourrit
Fromental Halévy: Lettres, ed. Galland, 14

[early 1836]

Mon cher Adolphe,

Au lieu de jouer *la Juive* samedi, croyez-vous pouvoir la jouer vendredi? De la part du directeur Duponchel, dans son lit et dans l'embarras.

Votre tout dévoué ami,
F. Halévy

N.B. Mon cher Adolphe, je suis tout prêt à commettre un assassinat quelconque, si cela peut vous être agréable.

[early 1836]

My dear Adolphe,

Instead of performing *La Juive* on Saturday, do you think you could perform it on Friday? On behalf of director Duponchel, in his bed and in his predicament.

Your always devoted friend,
F. Halévy

N.B. My dear Adolphe, I am quite willing to murder anyone of your choice, if that would please you.

Appendix J

Excerpt from "L'Artiste, le savant, et l'industriel: Dialogue" by Léon Halévy

Saint-Simon *et al.*, *Opinions littéraires*, 341–4 (translation adapted from Locke, *Saint-Simonians*, 38–41)

C'est nous, artistes, qui vous servirons d'avant-garde: la puissance des arts est en effet la plus immédiate et la plus rapide. Nous avons des armes de toute espèce: quand nous voulons répandre des idées neuves parmi les hommes, nous les inscrivons sur le marbre ou sur la toile; nous les popularisons par la poésie et le chant; nous employons tour-à-tour la lyre ou le galoubet, l'ode ou la chanson, l'histoire ou le roman; *la scène dramatique nous est ouverte, et c'est là surtout que nous exerçons une influence électrique et victorieuse* [my emphasis]. Nous nous adressons à l'imagination et aux sentiments de l'homme, nous devons donc exercer toujours l'action la plus vive et la plus décisive; et si aujourd'hui notre rôle paraît nul ou au moins très secondaire, c'est qu'il manquait aux arts ce qui est essentiel à leur énergie et à leurs succès, une impulsion commune et une idée générale.

. . .

Sans doute l'imagination aura long-temps encore un grand empire sur les hommes; mais son règne exclusif est passé; et si l'homme est aussi avide que jamais des jouissances que les beaux-arts procurent, il exige que sa raison trouve aussi son compte dans ces jouissances: ainsi les arts risqueraient de perdre pour toujours leur importance, et, loin de diriger la marche de la civilisation, ils ne seraient plus rangés parmi les besoins de la société, s'ils s'obstinaient à suivre une direction où ils n'ont plus rien à exploiter, celle de l'imagination sans objet, de l'imagination rétrograde. Mais au contraire, s'ils secondent le mouvement général de l'esprit humain, s'ils veulent aussi servir la cause commune, contribuer à l'accroissement du bien-être général, produire sur l'homme des sensations fructueuses, telles qu'il convient à son intelligence développée d'en ressentir, et propager, à l'aide de ces sensations, des idées généreuses qui soient *actuelles*; aussitôt ils verront s'ouvrir devant eux un avenir immense de gloire et de succès; ils pourront reconquérir toute leur énergie, et s'élever au plus haut point de dignité qu'ils puissent atteindre: car la force de l'imagination est incalculable, quand elle s'élance dans une direction de bien public.

It is we artists who will be your avant-garde: the power of the arts is in fact the most immediate and the most rapid. We have arms of all kinds: when we want to spread new ideas among mankind, we inscribe them on marble or canvas, we popularize them in poetry and song; we use in turn the lyre or the fife, the ode or the chanson, the historical account or the novel; *the dramatic stage is open to us, and it is there, above all, that we exert an electric and victorious influence* [my emphasis]. We address ourselves to the imagination and to the sentiments of mankind, we must therefore always exercise the most vivid and decisive action; and if today our role appears to be nil or at least truly secondary, it is because the arts were missing what is essential to their spirit and success, a common impulse and a widely shared idea.

. . .

No doubt imagination will hold sway over mankind for a long time yet, but its exclusive reign is over. And while we are still as avid as ever for the delights that the fine arts procure, we insist that our reason should also find profit in these delights. Otherwise, the arts would risk losing their importance forever, and, far from leading the march of civilization, they would no longer be ranked among the needs of society, were they to insist on following a direction in which they have little to gain: that of imagination without purpose, of reactionary imagination. But if, on the contrary, they promote the general movement of the human spirit, if they also wish to serve the common cause, to contribute to the improvement of the general welfare, to produce such fruitful sensations in mankind as are appropriate for our developed intelligence to experience, and to propagate, by means of those sensations, generous ideas that are *timely,* immediately they will see an immensely glorious and successful future opening before them. They will be able to take possession of all their energy again and rise to the greatest heights of dignity that they can attain. For the power of the imagination is incalculable when it launches itself in the direction of public good.

Appendix K

Public notice of the candidacy of Fromental Halévy to the Assemblée nationale, 1848

Translation adapted from Hansen, *Ludovic Halévy*, 9–10

République Française
Liberté, Egalité, Fraternité

ASSEMBLEE NATIONALE

Aux Citoyents Electeurs du
Département de la Seine.

Citoyents,

Les belles lettres, le théâtre, les arts
libéraux réclament une part dans vos
suffrages. Le pauvre leur doit ses
consolations, l'homme laborieux ses
délassements, la France une partie
de sa gloire.

C'est par sa pensée que la France
brille entre toutes les nations, c'est de
sa pensée que s'inspirent les
peuples de l'Europe, chacun de ses
mouvements est une secousse
donnée au monde.

Les trônes s'écroulent: les idées
restent et grandissent. Il n'y a point
eu de traités de 1815 pour la
puissance intellectuelle de la
France. Il est donc juste de choisir
quelques représentants de cette
pensée toute-puissante parmi
ceux qui la conçoivent ou
l'interprètent, qui l'expriment

French Republic
Liberty, Equality, Fraternity

NATIONAL ASSEMBLY

To the Citizen-Electors
of the Department of
the Seine,

Citizens,

The humanities, the theatre,
and the liberal arts claim a
portion of your vote. The poor
man is indebted to them for his
enjoyment, the working man
for his diversions, and France
for a part of her glory.

It is because of her ideas
that France shines among
nations, it is her ideas that
inspire the peoples of Europe,
each of her movements shakes
the entire world.

Thrones are collapsing; only
ideas remain and grow. There
were never any treaties of 1815
for the intellectual power of
France. It is only right then to
choose some representatives of
these all-powerful ideas from
among those who conceive or
interpret them, who express

par la plume, la voix, les accords ou le pinceau.

Les hommes qui se sont voués à la culture des lettres et des arts ont formé plusieurs associations dont les services sont incontestés. Ces associations se confondent dans un sentiment de fraternité, et ne forment plus qu'une famille. Pour représentants à l'Assemblée nationale, elles ont choisi cinq candidats aussi recommandables par le patriotisme que par le talent.

Nous avons réuni nos votes sur ces candidats. Isolés, ces votes seraient impuissants. Citoyents, nous vous demandons de les rendre forts par votre sympathie. Ouvriers, nos frères, quand il s'agit d'accomplir l'oeuvre sociale, faites une place aux ouvriers de l'intelligence.

them through the pen, the voice, the chord, or the brush.

The men who are devoted to the cultivation of literature and art have organized several groups whose functions are clear. These groups merge in a feeling of brotherhood, no longer existing as separate bodies. For representatives to the National Assembly they have chosen five candidates, as commendable for their devotion to country as for their talent.

We have combined all our votes in these candidates. Alone, these votes would be powerless. Citizens, we ask you to make them strong by your support. Workers, our brothers, since social reform is to be accomplished, give a place to the workers of the mind.

CANDIDATS DES ASSOCIATIONS:

Le citoyen VICTOR HUGO, homme de lettres.
Le citoyen MICHELOT, artiste dramatique.

Le citoyen ALPHONSE ESQUIROS, homme de lettres.
Le citoyen F. HALEVY, compositeur.
Le citoyen DELAITRE, peintre.

CANDIDATES OF THE GROUPS:

Citizen VICTOR HUGO, man of letters.
Citizen MICHELOT, actor.

Citizen ALPHONSE ESQUIROS, man of letters.
Citizen F. HALEVY, composer.
Citizen DELAITRE, painter.

PRIMARY SOURCES

Archival sources

Paris, Archives Nationales (F-Pan), AJ¹³176. "Rapports et ordonnances.
1815–1828"; "A.R.D.M. Liste des pensionnaires de l'Opéra au 1ᵉʳ Janvier
1841: Extrait du budget de l'Intérieur de 1842/Mai 1841."
F-Pan, AJ¹³180. Dossier I, Letter from Duponchel to the Ministre de
l'Intérieur, June 1836; "Démission de the Directeur [Véron]," 15 August
1835; Dossier II, "Cahier des charges de l'Opéra," 28 February 1831,
"Supplément du cahier des charges de l'Opéra," 30 May 1831; letter
from the Commission de Surveillance to the Ministre de l'Intérieur,
15 August 1835.
F-Pan, AJ¹³183. Letter from the duc de Choiseul to the Ministre de
l'Intérieur, 2 March 1836.
F-Pan, AJ¹³184. Letter from the duc de Choiseul to the Ministre de
l'Intérieur, 29 March 1836; letter from the Ministre de l'Intérieur to the
duc de Choiseul, [n.d.].
F-Pan, AJ¹³185. Draft letters from the Ministre de l'Intérieur to the duc de
Choiseul, May 1834, 20 May 1834; letter from the duc de Choiseul to
the Ministre de l'Intérieur, 25 May 1834.
F-Pan, AJ¹³187. "Arrêté," 15 August 1835; "2ᵉ Supplément au cahier des
charges de l'Opéra," 14 May 1833.
F-Pan, AJ¹³192. "Actes de naissance"; "Actes de l'état civil."
F-Pan, AJ¹³202. Printed Schlesinger libretto, 23 February 1835; 2d ed., with
handwritten emendations, Paris: Jonas, 1835; printed Schlesinger
libretto, 18 February 1835; fair copy of libretto in unknown hand [fall
1834]; draft letter from the Ministre de l'Intérieur to the duc de
Choiseul, 3 February 1835; letter from Louis Véron to the Ministre de
l'Intérieur, 4 February 1835; draft letter from the Ministre de l'Intérieur
to the duc de Choiseul, 12 February 1835; letter from the duc de
Choiseul to the Ministre de l'Intérieur, 12 February 1835; letter and fair

copy from the Commission de Surveillance to the Ministre de l'Intérieur, 13 February 1835; letter from the duc de Choiseul to the Ministre de l'Intérieur, 15 February 1835; draft letter from the Ministre de l'Intérieur to the duc de Choiseul, 16 February 1835; letter from the Secrétaire Membre de la Commission de Surveillance to the Ministre de l'Intérieur, 10 March 1835; inventories of costumes used in first production at Paris Opéra, 1834–5; "Chant, La Juive," list of printed names of singers, 8 September 1847; "Autorisation pour les marchandises nécessaires de la confection des costumes et des accessoires de la scène pour l'opéra de la Juive," 7 July 1834; "Mémoire des décorations composées et exécutées pour Mons' Véron, directeur de l'Académie royale de musique, par MM Séchan Feuchères et Cie," February 1835; "Résumé du présent mémoire pour la décoration seulement" [February 1835]; "Tableau de la dépense faite pour La Juive, opéra en 5 actes," 1834–5; "Mémoire des peintures faites pour l'opéra de la Juive" [Act III], 1835.

F-Pan, AJ^{13}287. "Décomptes" and "Appointemens" of Opéra artists, May 1834–June 1835.

F-Pan, AJ^{13}289. "Fourniture de copie de musique," January–February 1835, inventory of copying of Opéra performing parts and scores of *La Juive* by Leborne *atelier*.

F-Pan, AJ^{13}293. "Fourniture de copie de musique," December 1835–February 1836, inventory of copying of Opéra performing parts and scores of *Les Huguenots* by Leborne *atelier*; "Etat d'émargement pour servir au paiement des musiciens externes employés," June 1835–June 1836; "Copie de musique," notice of copying of *La Juive* overture, 10 September 1835; "Fourniture de copie de musique," September 1835, inventory of copying of Opéra performing parts and score of *La Juive* overture by Leborne *atelier*; "Jetons de présence des artistes externes: Année de gestion 1835–36 (Juin 1835–Mai 1836)"; "Honoraires des auteurs et compositeurs: Année de gestion 1835–36."

F-Pan, AJ^{13}507, II. Letter from Emile Perrin to Vernoy de Saint-Georges, 29 June 1866; letter from Vernoy de Saint-Georges to Emile Perrin, 30 June 1866; letters from Léon Halévy to Emile Perrin, 31 May 1866 and 4 June 1866; note from Emile Perrin to Service de l'habillement, 6 June 1866; miscellaneous documents related to 1866 production of *La Juive*.

F-Pan, F^{18}664. Libretto manuscripts submitted to censors.

F-Pan, F^{18}669. Libretto manuscripts submitted to censors.

F-Pan, F¹⁹11013–14. "Culte israélite de France."

F-Pan, F²¹741–2. Fromental Halévy, "Marche funèbre pour le retour des cendres de Napoléon" (15 December 1840), score and *matériel*.

F-Pan, F²¹960. Dossier v, letters from the duc de Choiseul to the Ministre de l'Intérieur, 21 May and 23 May 1834; Dossier vi, "Opéra, et Conservatoire, notte [*sic*] relative sur l'organisation de la Commission de Surveillance" by the duc de Choiseul, 10 April 1834; letter from the duc de Choiseul to the Ministre de l'Intérieur, 29 April 1834; notes of the duc de Choiseul on reorganization of the Commission de Surveillance; "Rapport à Monsieur le Ministre Secrétaire d'Etat au département de l'Intérieur" from Cavé; letter from the duc de Choiseul to the Ministre de Surveillance, 30 September 1836.

F-Pan, F²¹969. "Procès-verbaux de la censure."

F-Pan, F²¹1296. Conservatoire, Dossier Halévy.

F-Pan, Minutier central, Etude cxvii/1058. Dossier Halévy.

F-Pan, Minutier central, Etude cxvii/1288. De la Palme papers. Inventory of Halévy's estate.

Paris, Archives de Paris, Archevêché, Notre-Dame-de-Lorette, Registres 3331, 3333, 3335, 3337; "Naissances antérieur à 1860," 5 Mi 2/1002.

Paris, Bibliothèque Nationale de France, Bibliothèque de l'Arsenal (F-Pa), Ms. 7782/56. Letter from Eugène Scribe to Père Enfantin, n.d. [*circa* 1849–55].

F-Pa, Ms. 7817/121. Letter from Adolphe Nourrit to Monsieur Léroux, editor of *Le Globe*, 10 December 1830.

F-Pa, Ms. 7817/183. Acknowledgment of money received by Adolphe Nourrit from *Le Globe*, 8 January 1831.

F-Pa, Ms. 7860/2. Michel Chevalier *et al.*, "Encyclopédie, Procès-verbaux des séances du comité séance du 26 déc. 1862," unpublished manuscript.

F-Pa, Ms. 7860/3–9. Michel Chevalier. Unpublished offprints of articles for Saint-Simonian *encyclopédie*.

F-Pa, Ms. 7860/18. "Musique par F. Halévy." Unpublished offprint of article for Saint-Simonian *encylopédie*.

F-Pa, Ms. 14379/41. Letter from Fromental Halévy to Gustave d'Eichthal, n.d.

F-Pa, Ms. 14379/42. Letter from Geneviève Halévy-Bizet to Gustave d'Eichthal, n.d.

F-Pa, Ms. 14381. Journal of Gustave d'Eichthal.

F-Pa, Ms. 14393/1. Gustave d'Eichthal, "Note sur le dogme."

F-Pa, Ms. 14393/2. Gustave d'Eichthal, "Le Chant d'Ahasvérus."

F-Pa, Ms. 14393/3–5. Gustave d'Eichthal, "Extrait d'une lettre à M^r. ... à Paris," n.d.

F-Pa, Ms. 14393/19, 20; Ms. 14396/50. Letters from Gustave d'Eichthal to Adolphe d'Eichthal, 7 October 1836, 10 October 1836, 29 March 1838.

F-Pa, Ms. 14394/1. Gustave d'Eichthal, "Notice sur ma vie, 1875."

F-Pa, Ms. 14394/9. Letter from Gustave d'Eichthal to Charles Duveyrier, 30 April 1830.

F-Pa, Ms. 14404/6, 112. Letters from Eugène d'Eichthal to Gustave d'Eichthal, 28 August 1868, 11 January 1871.

F-Pa, Ms. 14404/111. Letter from Geneviève Bizet to Eugène d'Eichthal, 9 January 1871.

F-Pa, Ms. 14717. Gustave d'Eichthal, "Souvenirs d'enfance."

Paris, Bibliothèque Nationale de France, Département des Manuscrits (F-Pn, Ms.), n.a.fr. 10177, fols. 296–7. Letter from Fromental Halévy to "Mon cher & illustre confrère."

F-Pn, Ms., n.a.fr. 14346. Letters to Georges Bizet and family. Fols. 352–3, letter from Fromental Halévy to Charles Valter, director in Rouen, with addendum of Maurice Schlesinger, 16 January 1836.

F-Pn, Ms., n.a.fr. 14347. Letters to Fromental Halévy.

F-Pn, Ms., n.a.fr. 14349. Journal of Fromental Halévy, 1821–2.

F-Pn, Ms., n.a.fr. 14350. Journal of Geneviève Halévy-Bizet.

F-Pn, Ms., n.a.fr. 19806. Journal of Ludovic Halévy, "Premier cahier du 1er août 1862 au 16 octobre 1862."

F-Pn, Ms., n.a.fr. 19914, fols. 127–9, 136–42. Letters to and from Fromental Halévy.

F-Pn, Ms., n.a.fr. 22502, vol. XXIII (Opéras-Ballets). 1°:1°, "2 petites notes volantes au crayon sur *La Juive*," unknown hand; 1°:2°, draft scenario of *La Juive* in hand of Eugène Scribe; 1°:3°, draft verse of Acts IV and V in hand of Eugène Scribe; 1°:4° and 5°, partial fair copies of libretto, Acts IV and V; 2°:2°, draft scenario of *Les Huguenots*, with notes by Meyerbeer; 2°:4°, letter to Scribe from Nourrit, including draft verse.

F-Pn, Ms., n.a.fr. 22539. Eugène Scribe, "Oeuvres inédites – Fragments et plans divers."

F-Pn, Ms., n.a.fr. 22543, vol. LXIV. Eugène Scribe, "Plans et fragments de drames et comédies," loose-leaf draft verse of *La Juive*.

F-Pn, Ms., n.a.fr. 22562. Eugène Scribe, "*Vade mecum*, notes diverses," vol. II (1833–6), full and partial draft libretti.

F-Pn, Ms., n.a.fr. 22571. Eugène Scribe "Plans de pièces de théâtre, opéras-comiques, vaudevilles, etc."

F-Pn, Ms., n.a.fr. 22584, vols. I–XLV. Eugène Scribe, "Carnets de notes et de voyages en France, Suisse et Italie, 1826–1852."

F-Pn, Ms., n.a.fr. 22839, vol. I, fol. 276. *Traité* of *La Juive*, 25 August 1833.

F-Pn, Ms., n.a.fr. 24378. Letters from Eugène Scribe to various correspondents. No. 40, "Discours prononcé par M. Eugène Scribe, Président de l'Association des Auteurs et Compositeurs dramatiques dans l'Assemblée générale du 11 Mai 1855: Réunie pour procéder à la réélection du Président et au remplacement des membres sortant de la commission."

Paris, Bibliothèque Nationale de France, Département de la Musique (F-Pn, Mus.), "Fichier des lettres vendues."

F-Pn, Mus., "Lettres autographes." Vol. IX, No. 53, note by Henri-Montan Berton; vol. XXXVI, No. 193, letter from Cornélie Falcon to Fromental Halévy, [n.d.]; vol. L, No. 1, letter from Fromental Halévy to Salvador Cherubini, 7 May 1829; No. 2, note from Fromental Halévy to Luigi Cherubini, n.d.; No. 6, letter from Fromental Halévy to Eugène Scribe, 5 January 1849; No. 16, letter from Fromental Halévy to Vernoy de Saint-Georges with addendum from Eugène Scribe, 4 December 1849; No. 57, printed invitation to funeral of Fromental Halévy (d. 17 March 1862); Nos. 60–64, 89–93, 95–9, letters from Fromental Halévy to Gilbert Duprez; vol. LXXXI, letter from Adolphe Nourrit to M. Pley, Paris, 13 July 1835.

F-Pn, Mus., Ms. 14264. Fromental Halévy, "Juillet 1830," manuscript bifolios.

Paris, Bibliothèque Nationale de France, Bibliothèque-Musée de l'Opéra (F-Po), A.509a, vols. I–II, supplément. Autograph full score of *La Juive*.

F-Po, A.509b, vols. I–VI. Archival full score of *La Juive*, copied by Leborne *atelier*.

F-Po, [D. 216 (10)-II, fols. 70–111. Paul Lormier, watercolor and pencil sketches of costumes for *La Juive* [1834].

F-Po, [D. 216 (O²). Eugène du Faget, watercolor sketches of costumes for *La Juive*.

F-Po, Dossier d'artiste: Fromental Halévy.

F-Po, Dossier d'oeuvre: *La Juive*.

F-Po, [Esq. Cambon 65–7; [Esq. Cicéri 13–14; [Esq. 19 (91). Preliminary sketches of sets for *La Juive* by Charles Cambon, Pierre-Luc-Charles Cicéri, and Charles Séchan.

F-Po, Est. Sc. N° 6. Lithograph by Eugène Cicéri, Philippe Benoist, and Gaildrau of stage set for Act I of *La Juive* designed by Charles Séchan, Léon Feuchère, Edouard Despléchin, and Jules Diéterle.

F-Po, "Lettres autographes." Halévy folder. Receipts for Halévy's sale of scores of *La Juive* to Maurice Schlesinger.

F-Po, Livr. 19[274. Libretto, 23 February 1835, Paris: Maurice Schlesinger, 1835.

F-Po, Mat. 19e[315 (1)–(183), (231)–(268), (479), (505)–(540), (547)–(548), (551)–(607). *Matériel* for performance of *La Juive* at the Académie royale de musique, including solo, choral, and instrumental parts for 1835 production.

F-Po, Opéra Arch. 19/229. "Dépenses de matériel relatives à la mise en scène de divers ouvrages."

F-Po, RE 38. "Régie: Nombre des représentations par ouvrage, 1831–1849."

F-Po, RE 235. "Registre de copie" of Leborne *atelier.*

F-Po, Rés. 135, 1–3. Autograph fragments of *La Juive.*

F-Po, Rés. 658 (1)–(5). "Chroniques de l'Académie royale de musique: Les Cancans de l'Opéra en 1836[–1848]. Extraits du journal tenu par une habilleuse concernans les choses qui sont venues à sa connaissance durant l'année 1836[–1848]." Vols. I–III.

F-Po, ♭4387. Score fragment of *La Juive* in unknown copyist's hand.

New York, New York Public Library, Performing Arts Division, Research Library (US NYp), *MGZMB-Res. "Chroniques de l'Académie royale de musique: Les Cancans de l'Opéra en 1836[–1848]. Extraits du journal tenu par une habilleuse concernans les choses qui sont venues à sa connaissance durant l'année 1836[–1848]." Vol. IV.

New York, Pierpont Morgan Library (US NYpm), Mary Flagler Cary Collection, Koch 681 (Box 98). Letters from Fromental Halévy, Madame Fromental Halévy, and Léon Halévy to various correspondents.

US NYpm, Koch 914.5. Letter from Léon Halévy to Georges Bizet, 30 September [1868?].

Editions of *La Juive*

Score

Halévy, (Jacques-François-) Fromental (-Elie). *La Juive: Libretto by Eugène Scribe, Music by Jacques-François Halévy*. With an introduction by Charles

Rosen. 2 vols. Facsimile of Schlesinger orchestral score, 183[5]. New York: Garland Publishing, 1980.

La Juive: Opéra en cinq actes d'Eugène Scribe, musique de Fromental Halévy. Edited by Karl Leich-Galland. Saarbrücken: Musik-Edition Lucie Galland, 1985.

La Juive: Opéra en cinq actes, paroles de Mr E. Scribe, musique de F. Halévy, à son illustre maître et ami L. Cherubini . . . représenté pour la première fois à Paris, sur le théâtre de l'Académie royale de musique le 23 février 1835. Paris: Maurice Schlesinger, 183[5] (M.S. 2000).

La Juive: Opéra en 5 actes, paroles de Mr E. Scribe, musique de F. Halévy [morceaux détachés]. Paris: Maurice Schlesinger, 1835 (M.S. 2003, 1–18).

La Juive: Opéra en cinq actes, paroles de M. Scribe, musique de F. Halévy de l'Institut. Paris: Henri-Lemoine, n.d. (4504 HL)

Ouverture à grand orchestre de l'Opéra: La Juive (Die Jüdin) composée par F. Halévy. Berlin: Schlesinger, 183[?] (S. 2012).

Libretto

Scribe, Eugène. *La Juive: Opéra en cinq actes d'Eugène Scribe, musique de Fromental Halévy.* Edited by Marthe Galland. Saarbrücken: Musik-Edition Lucie Galland, 1990.

La Juive: Opéra en cinq actes, paroles de Mr E. Scribe, musique de F. Halévy, divertissemens de M. Taglioni, représenté, pour la première fois, sur le théâtre de l'Académie royale de musique, le 18 février 1835. Paris: Maurice Schlesinger, 1835.

La Juive: Opéra en cinq actes, paroles de Mr E. Scribe, musique de F. Halévy, divertissemens de M. Taglioni, représenté, pour la première fois, sur le théâtre de l'Académie royale de musique, le 23 février 1835. Paris: Maurice Schlesinger, 1835.

La Juive: Opéra en cinq actes, paroles de Mr E. Scribe, musique de F. Halévy, divertissemens de M. Taglioni, représenté, pour la première fois, sur le théâtre de l'Académie royale de musique, le 23 février 1835. 2d ed. Paris: Jonas, Libraire de l'Opéra; J. N. Barba, Libraire, Palais-Royal, 1835.

Nineteenth-century periodicals

Les Archives israélites: Revue mensuelle historique, biographique, bibliographique et littéraire
Le Constitutionnel

Le Courrier français

L'Entr'acte

Le Figaro

La France: Journal des intérêts monarchiques de l'Europe

La France musicale

La Gazette de France

La Gazette musicale de Paris

Le Globe: Journal littéraire

L'Israélite français: Ouvrage moral et littéraire

Journal de Paris et des départemens

Journal des débats politiques et littéraires

Le Ménestrel

Le Moniteur universel

L'Opinion: Journal des moeurs, de la littérature, des arts, des théâtres et de l'industrie

L'Organisateur

Le Producteur: Journal de l'industrie, des sciences et des beaux-arts

La Quotidienne

Le Réformateur: Journal des nouveaux intérêts matériels et moraux, industriels et
    politiques, littéraires et scientifiques

Le Rénovateur, courrier de l'Europe

La Revue de Paris

Revue des deux mondes

La Revue et gazette musicale de Paris

La Revue musicale

Le Temps: Journal des progrès politiques, scientifiques, littéraires et industriels

L'Univers israélite

L'Univers religieux, politique, scientifique et littéraire

Published sources

Archives parlementaires de 1787 à 1860: Recueil complet des débats législatifs et
    politiques des chambres françaises, seconde série. Edited by J. Mavidal and
    M. E. Laurent. Paris: Société d'Imprimerie et librairie
    administrative / Paul Dupont, 1887.

Berlioz, Hector. *A travers chants: Etudes musicales, adorations, boutades et*
    critiques. Paris: Michel Lévy Frères, 1862.

    Grand Traité d'instrumentation et d'orchestration. Paris: Henri Lemoine et
    Cie, 1843.

Mémoires de Hector Berlioz, comprenant ses voyages en Italie, en Allemagne, en Russie et en Angleterre, 1803–1865. Paris: Michel Lévy Frères, 1870. *The Memoirs of Hector Berlioz, 1830–1868*. Translated and edited by David Cairns. London: Panther, 1970.

Berr, Michel. *Du rabbinisme et des traditions juives*. Paris: Sétier, 1832.

Lettre sur les israélites et le judaisme au directeur du panorama des nouveautés parisiennes. Paris: Sétier, 1825.

Beulé, Charles-Ernest. "Eloge de F. Halévy à l'Institut de France." *Les Archives israélites* 23, no. 2 (November 1862): 643.

Notice sur la vie et les ouvrages d'Halévy, l'Académie des Beaux-Arts de l'Institut de France. Paris: Didot, 1862.

Blanc, Louis. *The History of Ten Years, 1830–1840*. 2 vols. New York: Augustus M. Kelley. 1969. Reprint, London: Chapman & Hall, 1845.

Blaze de Bury, Henri. "Lettres sur les musiciens français," part 1: "M. Halévy: Guido et Ginevra." *Revue des deux mondes* 13 (15 March 1838): 768–85.

Meyerbeer et son temps. Paris: Heugel et Cie, 1865.

Musiciens contemporains. Paris: Michel Lévy Frères, 1856.

Musiciens du passé, du présent et de l'avenir. Paris: Michel Lévy Frères, 1880.

"Portraits d'hier et d'aujourd'hui," part 1: "Scribe et Auber." *Revue des deux mondes* 35 (1879): 43.

Boigne, Charles de. *Petits Mémoires de l'Opéra*. Paris: Librairie nouvelle, 1857.

Bulwer, Henry Lytton. *France, Social and Political*. 2 vols. London: Richard Bentley, 1834.

Cahen, S[amuel]. "De la littérature hébraïque et juive en France." *Les Archives israélites* 1 (1840): 33–52.

Carnot, Hippolyte. *Sur le Saint-Simonisme: Lecture faite à l'Académie des sciences morales et politiques*. Paris: Alfonse Picard, 1887.

Castelino, A. *François Halévy*. Paris: Michel Lévy Frères, 1862.

Castil-Blaze, François. *L'Académie impériale de musique: Histoire littéraire, musicale, chorégraphique, pittoresque, morale, critique . . . de 1645 à 1855*. 2 vols. Paris: Castil-Blaze, 1855.

Mémorial du grand-opéra. Paris: Castil-Blaze, 1847.

Sur l'opéra français, vérités dures mais utiles. Paris: Castil-Blaze, 1856.

Catelin, Adolphe. *F. Halévy: Notice biographique*. Paris: Michel Lévy Frères, 1863.

Chefs-d'oeuvre des théâtres étrangers . . . traduits en français. Lessing, Nathan le Sage, avec une notice signée P. B. Emilie Galotti, traduit par M. le c^{te} de

Sainte-Aulaire. Minna de Barnhelm, avec une notice signée Merville. Paris: Rapilly, 1827.

Chopin, Frédéric. *Correspondance de Frédéric Chopin.* Edited and translated by Bronislas Edouard Sydow, with Suzanne and Denise Chainaye. 3 vols. Paris: Richard-Masse, 1981.

Chorley, Henry Fothergill. *Music and Manners in France and Germany.* 3 vols. London: Longman, 1841.

Thirty Years' Musical Recollections. 2 vols. London: Hurst & Blackett, 1862.

Cohen, H. Robert. *The Original Staging Manuals for Twelve Parisian Operatic Premières/Douze Livrets de mise en scène datant des créations parisiennes.* Stuyvesant, NY: Pendragon Press, 1991.

Comettant, Oscar. *Les Compositeurs illustres de notre siècle.* Paris: Calmann-Lévy, 1883.

Créhange, Abraham. *La Sentinelle juive: Réponse à la dix-septième lettre de la correspondance dite israélite de Tsarphati.* Paris: Chez l'auteur, 1839.

Cs. [*sic*]. "Académie française: Réception de M. Scribe." *Journal des débats* (30 January 1836): 3.

Dairnvaell, Georges. *Histoire édifiante et curieuse de Rothschild Ier, roi des juifs, par Satan.* 2d ed. Paris: L'Editeur, 1846.

"De l'état actuel des Beaux-Arts." *L'Organisateur* 1, no. 7 (26 September 1829): 1–2.

Deldevez, Ernest-Marie-Edouard. *Mes Mémoires.* Le Puy: Imprimerie de Marchessou fils, 1890.

Dumas, Alexandre. "La Juive." *La Gazette musicale de Paris* 2, no. 17 (26 April 1835): 141–6; 2, no. 18 (3 May 1835): 149–54.

My Memoirs. Translated by A. Craig Bell. Philadelphia: Chilton Co., 1961.

Duprez, G[ilbert]. *Souvenirs d'un chanteur.* Paris: Calmann-Lévy, 1880.

Escudier, Léon. *Mes Souvenirs.* Paris: E. Dentu, 1863.

Escudier, Marie-Pierre-Yves. *Etudes biographiques sur les chanteurs contemporains, précédées d'une esquisse sur l'art.* Paris: J. Tessier, 1840.

Fétis, François-Joseph. *Biographie universelle des musiciens et bibliographie générale de la musique.* 8 vols. Brussels: Leroux (and Méline); Paris: H. Fournier (and Royer), 1835–44.

"Curiosités historiques de l'Opéra de Paris." *La Revue musicale* 13 (1833): 233–6.

"Halévy (Jacques-François-Fromental-Elie)." *Biographie universelle des musiciens et bibliographie générale de la musique,* 8 vols. 2d ed. Paris: Firmin-Didot, 1878.

Fiorentino, P. A. *Les Grands Guignols*. Paris: Michel Lévy Frères, 1872.

Fourier, Charles. *La Fausse Industrie morcelée, répugnante, mensongère, et l'antidote, l'industrie naturelle, combinée, attrayante, véridique, donnant quadruple produit*. 2 vols. Paris: Bossange Père; L'auteur, 1835–6.

Galérie illustrée des célébrités contemporaines: Les Théâtres de Paris. Texte par une société de gens de lettres, dessins par Eustache Lorsay. Lithographies par Collette. 4 vols. Paris: Administration/Martinon Libraire, 1854.

Gautier, Théophile. *Histoire de l'art dramatique en France depuis vingt-cinq ans*. 6 vols. Leipzig: Edition Hetzel, 1858–9.

Gautier, Théophile, Jules Janin, and Philarète Chasles, eds. *Les Beautés de l'Opéra; ou, Chefs-d'oeuvre lyriques*. Paris: Soulié, 1845.

Gorse. "Enseignement public, pensée philosophique: Cours de droit naturel par M. Jouffroy; Cours d'histoire du seizième siècle par M. Michelet." *L'Univers religieux* 3, no. 359 (3 January 1835): cols. 614–17.

Gouder, A. *Discours prononcé aux funérailles d'Halévy*. Paris: O. J., Institut Impérial de France, 1862.

Gounod, Charles François. *Memoirs of an Artist*. Translated by Annette E. Crocker. Chicago and New York: Rand, McNally & Co., 1895.

Grégoire, Abbé Henri-B. *Discours sur la liberté des cultes, nouvelle édition, augmentée du décret rendu le 3 ventose*. Paris: Chez Maradan, An III de la République.

Essai sur la régénération physique, morale et politique des juifs, ouvrage couronné par la Société royale des sciences et des arts de Metz, le 23 août 1788. Metz: Devilly, 1789.

Halévy, Elie. *Ha-Shalom: Hymne à l'occasion de la paix par le Cen. Elie Lévy, chanté en hébreu et lu en français, dans la grande synagogue, à Paris, le 17 Brumaire An X*. Paris: Imprimerie de la République, An X [1801].

Instruction religieuse et morale à l'usage de la jeunesse israélite. Paris: Chez l'auteur; Metz: Chez Gerson-Lévy, 1820.

Halévy, Elie, trans. *Discours prononcé dans le Temple de la rue Ste.-Avoye*. Paris: De l'Imprimerie de Ballard, imprimeur du Consistoire central des israélites, 1808.

trans. *Discours prononcé par M. Abraham Cologna, Membre du Collège électoral des Savans du royaume d'Italie, Grand-Rabbin du Consistoire central des Israélites, le 13 mai 1809, dans le Temple de la rue Ste.-Avoie, à l'occasion de la cérémonie célébrée en actions de graces, pour les victoires remportées par l'armée française aux champs de Tann, Eckmühl, Ratisbonne, etc. etc., suivi d'une prière composée en Hébreu, par M. le Prés. du dit Consistoire,*

D. Sintzheim, traduit par M. Elie Halévy. Paris: De l'Imprimerie de
    Ballard, [1809].

trans. *Prière composée par M. Mardoché Roque-Martine Grand Rabbin de la
    Circonscription de Marseille. Pour être récitée à l'occasion de l'inauguration
    du nouveau Temple israélite de la ville de Lyon (en mars 1813), administré par
    M. Isaac Helft, Commissaire délégué de la Synagogue consistoriale de
    Marseille, traduite en Français par M. Elie Halévy, traducteur spécial du
    Consistoire central des israélites, et de celui de la Circonscription de Paris.*
    Paris: De l'Imprimerie des Langues Orientales de L.-P. Sétier Fils,
    1813.

Halévy, (Jacques-François-) Fromental (-Elie). *Derniers Souvenirs et portraits,
    précédés d'une notice par P.-A. Fiorentino.* Paris: Michel Lévy Frères, 1863.

Fromental Halévy: Lettres. Edited by Marthe Galland. Heilbronn: Musik-
    Edition Lucie Galland, 1999.

*Marche funèbre et de profundis en Hébreu, à 3 voix et à grand orchestre (avec une
    traduction italienne et accompagnement de piano).* Paris: Chez Ignaz Pleyel
    et Fils aîné, [1820].

Souvenirs et portraits: Etudes sur les beaux-arts. Paris: Michel Lévy Frères,
    1861.

Halévy, Léon. *Au roi: Ode sur la mort de S. A. R. Monseigneur le duc d'Orléans.*
    Paris: Maulde et Renou, 1842.

*Chant funèbre, exécuté au Temple consistorial israélite de Paris le 26 juillet 1842,
    au service célébré pour le repos de l'âme de S. A. R. Ferdinand-Philippe, duc
    d'Orléans.* Paris: Imprimerie de Wittersheim, 1842.

"Du mot littérature." *L'Opinion* 1, no. 9 (9 December 1825): 1.

F. Halévy: Sa Vie et ses oeuvres. 2d ed. Paris: Heugel et Cie, 1863.

*Hommage à F. Halévy: Intermède lyrique exécuté sur le théâtre impérial de
    l'Opéra-comique, le 27 mai 1864, pour l'anniversaire de la naissance d'Halévy.*
    Paris: Heugel et Cie, 1864.

*Hymne national en l'honneur des morts et des blessés des grandes journées de
    juillet 1830.* Paris: Imprimerie de Pihan Delaforest (Morinval), n.d.

"Instruction publique: Des améliorations introduites par M. Cousin dans
    l'instruction publique." *Les Archives israélites* 1 (1840): 464–7.

Luther: Poème dramatique en cinq parties. Paris: Dépôt Central de la
    Librairie, 1834.

La Marseillaise de 1830, dédiée à la Garde nationale. Paris: Imprimerie de
    David, n.d.

Martin Luther; ou, La Diète de Worms: Drame historique en quatre actes, en vers, imité de Zacharias Werner, reçu au Théâtre-Français, non-représenté. Paris: A. Le Chevalier, 1866.

Résumé de l'histoire des juifs anciens. Paris: Lecointe et Durey, 1825.

Résumé de l'histoire des juifs modernes. Paris: Lecointe, 1828.

Saint-Simon, ode. Paris: Levasseur, Delangle, 1831.

"Souvenirs de Saint-Simon." *La France littéraire* 1 (1832): 521–46.

Les Trois Jours d'un grand peuple. Paris: Levasseur, 1830.

Halévy, Léon, Gustave Drouineau, and Louis-Marie Fontan. *L'Espion: Drame en cinq actes, en prose . . . représenté pour la première fois, sur le théâtre de l'Odéon, par les Comédiens du Roi, le 6 décembre 1828.* Paris: Riga et Jeannin Editeurs, 1828.

Halévy, Léon, E. Jaime, and Adolphe de Ribbing Leuven. *Grillo; ou, Le Prince et le banquier: Comédie-vaudeville en deux actes, représentée pour la première fois, sur le théâtre des Variétés, le 22 décembre 1832.* Paris: J. N. Barba, 1833.

Hallays-Dabot, Victor. *Histoire de la censure théâtrale en France.* Paris: E. Dentu, 1862.

Hallez, Théophile. *Des Juifs en France: De leur état moral et politique depuis les premiers temps de la monarchie jusqu'à nos jours.* Paris: G.-A. Dentu, 1845.

Heine, Heinrich. "De l'Allemagne depuis Luther." *Revue des deux mondes* 1 (1 March 1834): 473–505; 4 (15 November 1834): 373–408; 4 (15 December 1834): 633–78.

Heinrich Heine: Selected Works. Translated and edited by Helen M. Mustard and Max Knight. New York: Random House, 1973.

Lutèce: Lettres sur la vie politique, artistique, et sociale de la France. 5th ed. Paris: Michel Lévy Frères, 1855.

Hugo, Victor. *Théâtre complet.* Paris: Gallimard, 1963–4.

La Juive de Pantin; ou, La Friture manquée, folie en trois actes et en vers, mêlée de couplets, imitée d'un opéra très-sérieux; par M. . . . représentée pour la première fois, sur le Théâtre du Gymnase, à Lyon, le 25 Avril 1836. Lyon: Imprimerie de Gabriel Rossary, 1836.

Lamothe-Langon, Etienne de. *Histoire de l'Inquisition en France, depuis son établissement au XIIIe siècle, à la suite de la croisade contre les Albigeois, jusqu'en 1772, époque définitive de sa suppression.* 3 vols. Paris: J.-G. Dentu, 1829.

Leich-Galland, Karl, ed. *Fromental Halévy, "La Juive": Dossier de presse parisienne (1835).* Saarbrücken: Musik-Edition Lucie Galland, 1987.

Lorbac, Charles de. *Fromental Halévy: Sa Vie, ses oeuvres*. Paris: Heugel et Cie, 1862.

Mainzer, Joseph. *Chronique musicale de Paris*. Paris: Au Bureau de Panorame de l'Allemagne, 1838.

"Vienne et la synagogue juive pendant les années 1826, 1827 et 1828." *La Gazette musicale de Paris* 1, no. 16 (20 April 1834): 125–8; no. 18 (4 May 1834): 143–6.

Meyerbeer, Giacomo. *Giacomo Meyerbeer: A Life in Letters*. Edited by Heinz Becker and Gudrun Becker. Translated by Mark Violette. Portland: Amadeus Press, 1989.

Giacomo Meyerbeer: Briefwechsel und Tagebücher. Edited by Heinz Becker, Gudrun Becker, and Sabine Henze-Döhring. 5 vols. Berlin: Walter de Gruyter & Co., 1960–99.

Michelet, Jules. *Histoire de France*. 6 vols. Brussels: Louis Hauman et Cie, 1834.

Histoire de la révolution française. 7 vols. Paris: Chamerot, 1847–53.

Mémoires de Luther, écrits par lui-même. 2 vols. Brussels: Société Belge de Librairie, 1837.

Monnais, Edouard [under pseud. Paul Smith]. "F. Halévy." *La Revue et gazette musicale de Paris* 29, no. 12 (23 March 1862): 93.

Monnais, Edouard. *F. Halévy: Souvenirs d'un ami pour joindre à ceux d'un frère*. Paris: Imprimerie Centrale des Chemins de Fer, 1863.

"Musée grotesque et sérieux de Dantan, considéré sous son rapport musical." *La Gazette musicale de Paris* 2, no. 33 (16 August 1835): 269–71.

Musset, Alfred de. "La Loi sur la presse." *Revue des deux mondes* 3 (1 September 1835): 609–16.

Naumbourg, Samuel, ed. *Nouveau Recueil de chants religieux*. Paris: Chez l'auteur, 1866.

Recueil de chants religieux et populaires des israélites des temps les plus reculés jusqu'à nos jours. Paris: Chez l'auteur, 1875.

Semiroth Israël: Chants religieux des israélites. Paris: Chez l'auteur, 1847.

Palianti, L., ed. *Collection de mises en scène de grands opéras et d'opéras-comiques représentés pour la première fois à Paris. Rédigées, et publiées par M. L. Palianti*. Paris: Chez l'auteur et chez MM. les Correspondants, n.d.

Palliet, J. B., ed. *Manuel de droit français*. 4th ed. Paris: Chez Th. Desoer, 1819; 8th edition, Paris: Chez Th. Desoer, 1838.

Pougin, Arthur. *Fromentin Halévy, écrivain*. Paris: A. Claudin, 1865.

Quicherat, Louis Marie. *Adolphe Nourrit: Sa Vie, son talent, son caractère, sa correspondance.* 3 vols. Paris: L. Hachette, 1867.

Quinet, Edgar. "Ahasvérus." *Revue des deux mondes* 4, no. 2 (1823): 5–41.

"Un Mot sur la polémique religieuse." *Revue des deux mondes* 2 (1 April 1842): 332–9.

Rodrigues, Eugène. *Lettres sur la religion et la politique.* Paris: Calmann, 1832.

Rousseau, Auguste, Marc-Antoine-Madeleine Désaugiers, and Jean-Baptiste Mesnard. *Le Juif: Comédie anecdotique en deux actes, mêlée de vaudevilles, par MM. A. Rousseau, Désaugiers et Mesnard, représentée, pour la première fois, sur le théâtre de la porte Saint-Martin, le 14 mai 1823.* In *Fin du répertoire du théâtre français.* Paris: Mme veuve Dabo, 1824.

Saint-Saëns, Camille. *Ecole buissonnière: Notes et souvenirs.* Paris: Pierre Lafitte & Co., 1913.

Saint-Simon, cte. Claude-Henri de, and Enfantin. *Oeuvres de Saint-Simon et d'Enfantin.* 47 vols. Paris: E. Dentu, 1865–78. Reprint, Aalen: Otto Zeller, 1963–4.

Saint-Simon, cte. Claude-Henri de, Léon Halévy, Olinde Rodrigues, *et al. Opinions littéraires, philosophiques et industrielles.* Paris: Galerie de Bossange Père, Libraire de S. A. R. M^{on} le duc d'Orléans, 1825.

Sainte-Beuve, Charles-Augustin. *Correspondance générale recueillie, classée et annotée par Jean Bonnerot.* Paris: Stock, 1935.

Portraits contemporains. 5 vols. Rev. ed., Paris: Michel Lévy Frères, 1869–71.

Sand, George. *Correspondance.* Edited by Georges Lubin. 25 vols. Paris: Garnier Frères, 1964–91.

[Schlesinger, Maurice], "Les Feuilletons musicaux des journaux politiques de Paris." *La Gazette musicale de Paris* 2, no. 31 (2 August 1835): 253–4.

Scott, Sir Walter. *Ivanhoe.* Edited by A. N. Wilson. London: Penguin Books, 1984.

Scribe, Eugène. *Correspondance d'Eugène Scribe et de Daniel-François-Esprit Auber.* Edited by Herbert Schneider. Sprimont, Belgium: Mardaga, 1998.

Oeuvres complètes de M. Eugène Scribe. 5 vols. Rev. ed., Paris: Furne & Cie / Aimé André, 1840–41.

Théâtre de Eugène Scribe dédié par lui à ses collaborateurs. 10 vols. Paris: Bezou & Aimé André, 1828.

Scudo, Pierre. "Revue des théâtres: Théâtres lyriques." *Revue des deux mondes* (15 March 1855): 1315–17.

Séchan, Charles. *Souvenirs d'un homme de théâtre 1831–1855*. Edited by
    Adolphe Badin. Paris: Calmann-Lévy, 1883.
Sécond, Alberic. *Les Petits Mystères de l'Opéra*. Paris: G. Kugelmann, 1844.
Shakespeare, William. *The Merchant of Venice*. Edited by Louis B. Wright.
    New York: Washington Square Press, 1957.
    Twenty-three Plays and the Sonnets. Edited by Thomas Marc Parrott, with
    Edward Hubler and Robert Stockdale Telfer. Rev. ed. New York:
    Charles Scribner's Sons, 1953.
Stendhal. *Racine et Shakespeare*. Paris: Bossange, 1823.
Tamvaco, Jean-Louis. *Les Cancans de l'Opéra: Le Journal d'une habilleuse,
    1836–1848*. 2 vols. Paris: CNRS Editions, 2000.
    "Les Cancans de l'Opéra: Première édition critique intégrale du
    manuscrit dit: 'Les Cancans de l'Opéra' ou 'Les Mémoires d'une
    habilleuse' de 1836 à 1845." 3 vols. Ph.D. diss., Université de la
    Sorbonne Nouvelle [Paris III], Institut d'études théâtrales, 1995.
Toussenel, Alphonse. *Les Juifs, rois de l'époque: Histoire de la féodalité financière*.
    2 vols. Paris: Gabriel de Gonet, 1847.
Trollope, Frances. *Paris and the Parisians in 1835*. 2 vols. Paris: Baudry's
    European Library, 1836.
Véron, Louis. *Mémoires d'un bourgeois de Paris comprenant la fin de l'empire, la
    restauration, la monarchie de juillet, la république, jusqu'au rétablissement de
    l'empire*. 6 vols. Paris: Libraire Nouvelle, 1856–7.
    L'Opéra de Paris, 1820–1835. Paris: Editions Michel de Maule, 1987.
    Preface, *La Revue de Paris* 1 (1829): iii–vi.
Voltaire, François-Marie Arouet de. *Oeuvres complètes de Voltaire*. 11 vols.
    Paris: Chez Th. Desoer Libraire, 1817.
Wagner, Cosima. *Cosima Wagner's Diaries*. Edited by Martin Gregor-Dellin
    and Dietrich Mack. Translated by Geoffrey Skelton. 2 vols. New York
    and London: Harcourt Brace Jovanovich, 1978–[80].
Wagner, Richard. "Bericht über eine neue Pariser Oper: La Reine de Chypre
    von Halévy." *Dresdener Abend-Zeitung* (26–9 January 1842). In *Wagner:
    Prose Works*, translated by W. A. Ellis, 8 vols., vol. VII, 207–22. New York:
    Broude Bros., 1969.
    "Halévy et 'La Reine de Chypre.'" *La Revue et gazette musicale de Paris* 9,
    no. 9 (27 February 1842): 75–8; no. 11 (13 March 1842): 100–102; no. 17
    (24 April 1842): 179–80; no. 18 (1 May 1842): 187–8. In *Wagner: Prose
    Works*, translated by W. A. Ellis, 8 vols., vol. VIII, 175–200. New York:
    Broude Bros., 1969.

SECONDARY SOURCES

Ages, Arnold. *The Image of Jews and Judaism in the Prelude to the French Enlightenment.* Sherbrooke, Quebec: Editions Naaman, 1986.

Allévy, Marie-Antoinette. *La Mise en scène en France dans la première moitié du dix-neuvième siècle.* Paris: Librairie E. Droz, 1938.

Armstrong, Alan. "Meyerbeer's *Le Prophète*: A History of its Composition and Early Performances." 4 vols. Ph.D. diss., Ohio State University, 1990. Ann Arbor, MI: UMI Press, 1990.

Arvin, Neil Cole. *Eugène Scribe and the French Theatre, 1815–1860.* Cambridge, MA: Harvard University Press, 1924.

Atwood, William G. *The Parisian Worlds of Frédéric Chopin.* New Haven and London: Yale University Press, 1999.

Auberry, Pierre. "Montesquieu et les Juifs." *Studies on Voltaire and the Eighteenth Century* 87 (1972): 87–99.

Bailbé, Joseph Marc. *La Musique en France à l'époque romantique: 1830–1870.* Paris: Flammarion, 1991.

Le Roman et la musique en France sous la monarchie de Juillet. Paris: Calmann-Lévy, 1969.

Baron, John H. "A Golden Age for Jewish Musicians in Paris: 1820–1865." *Musica Judaica* 12 (1991–2): 30–51.

Bartlet, M. Elizabeth C. *Etienne Nicolas Méhul and Opera: Source and Archival Studies of Lyric Theatre during the French Revolution, Consulate and Empire.* 2 vols. Heilbronn: Musik-Edition Lucie Galland, 1999.

Bartlet, M. Elizabeth C., ed. *Guillaume Tell, opéra en quatre actes di Victor Joseph Etienne de Jouy e Hippolyte Louis Florent Bis, musica di Gioachino Rossini.* Pesaro: Fondazione Rossini, 1992.

Bartlet, M. Elizabeth C., with Mauro Bucarelli. *Guillaume Tell di Gioachino Rossini: Fonti iconografiche.* Pesaro: Fondazione Rossini, 1996.

Barzun, Jacques. *Berlioz and the Romantic Century.* 2 vols. Boston: Little Brown & Co., 1950.

Becker, Hans Ulrich. "'Dieu de nos pères': Grosse Oper auf authentischem Hintergrund." In *Halévy: La Juive*, 36–42, program booklet for the 1999/2000 production of *La Juive* at the Vienna Staatsoper.

Becker, Heinz. "Die Couleur locale als Stilkategorie der Oper." In *Die Couleur locale in der Oper des 19. Jahrhunderts*, edited by Heinz Becker, 23–46. Regensburg: Gustav Bosse, 1976.

"Die historische Bedeutung der Grand Opera." In *Beiträge zur Geschichte der Musikanschauung im 19. Jahrhundert*, edited by W. Salmen, 151–67. Regensburg: Gustav Bosse, 1965.

Beecher, Jonathan. *Charles Fourier: The Visionary and His World*. Berkeley, Los Angeles, and London: University of California Press, 1986.

Beik, Paul H. *Louis Philippe and the July Monarchy*. Princeton, NJ: D. Van Nostrand Co., 1965.

Bellaigue, Camille. "Les Epoques de la musique: Le Grand Opéra français." *Revue des deux mondes* 35, no. 5 (September–October 1906): 612–49.

Berg, Roger. *Histoire des juifs à Paris de Chilpéric à Jacques Chirac*. Paris: Les Editions du Cerf, 1997.

Berkovitz, Jay R. *The Shaping of Jewish Identity in Nineteenth-Century France*. Detroit: Wayne State University Press, 1989.

Billaz, André. "Les Ecrivains romantiques et Voltaire: Essai sur Voltaire et le romantisme en France (1795–1830)." 2 vols. Ph.D. diss., Université de Paris IV, 1974. Université de Lille III: Service de Reproduction des Thèses, 1974.

Bloch, Maurice, "La Femme juive dans le roman et au théâtre." *Conférence faite à la Société des études juives le 23 janvier 1892, extrait de la Revue des études juives* xxxiii. Paris: Librairie A. Durlacher, 1892.

Bloom, Peter, ed. *Music in Paris in the 1830s*. Stuyvesant, NY: Pendragon Press, 1987.

Blume, Friedrich, ed. *Die Musik in Geschichte und Gegenwart*. 14 vols. Kassel and Basel: Bärenreiter Verlag, 1949–67. S.v. "Halévy, Jacques François Fromental (Fromentin) Elias (eigentlich Elias Levy)" by Wilhelm Pfannkuch.

Blumenkranz, Bernhard. *Histoire des juifs en France*. Paris: Edouard Privat, 1972.

Bo Bramsen, Michèle. *Portrait d'Elie Halévy*. Amsterdam: B. R. Grüner, 1978.

Bonnaure, Jacques. "Monsieur Scribe ou le romantisme du juste milieu." *L'Avant-scène opéra* 100 (July 1987): 88–93.

Bonnefon, Paul. "Les Métamorphoses d'un opéra. Lettres inédites de Eugène Scribe." *Revue des deux mondes* 41, no. 6 (1917): 877–99.

"Scribe sous la monarchie de Juillet d'après des documents inédits." *Revue d'histoire littéraire de la France* 28 (1921): 60–99, 241–60.

"Scribe sous l'Empire et sous la Restauration d'après des documents inédits." *Revue d'histoire littéraire de la France* 27 (1920): 321–70.

Bourdrel, Philippe. *Histoire des juifs de France*. Paris: A. Michel, 1974.

Bouvier, Jean. *Les Rothschild*. 2d ed. Paris: Fayard, 1967.

Brandes, George. *Main Currents in Nineteenth-Century Literature*. 6 vols. New York: Haskell House Publishers, 1975.

Brent Smith, Alexander. "The Tragedy of Meyerbeer." *Music and Letters* 6 (1925): 248–55.

Brisson, Jules, and Félix Ribeyre. *Les Grands Journaux de France*. Paris: Bureau, 21, rue de Hanovre, 1862–3.

Brockhaus Enzyklopädie. 24 vols. Mannheim: F. A. Brockhaus, 1986. S.v. "Siegmund, Sigismund."

Cahen, Isidore. "Actualités: Quelques Notes sur Léon Halévy." *Les Archives israélites* 44, no. 37 (13 September 1883): 296–9.

Cardwell, Douglas. "Eugène Scribe (1791–1861)." In *Dictionary of Literary Biography*, vol. CXCII: *French Dramatists, 1789–1914*, edited by Barbara T. Cooper, 358–72. Detroit, Washington, DC, and London: Gale Research, 1998.

Carlson, Marvin. *The French Stage in the Nineteenth Century*. Metuchen, NJ: Scarecrow Press, 1972.

Charléty, Sébastien. *Histoire du Saint-Simonisme (1825–1864)*. Paris: Hachette, 1896.

Charlton, David. "Orchestration and Orchestral Practice in Paris, 1789–1810." 2 vols. Ph.D. diss., Cambridge University, 1974.

Chase, Myrna. *Elie Halévy: An Intellectual Biography*. New York: Columbia University Press, 1980.

Chouquet, Gustave. *Histoire de la musique dramatique en France depuis ses origines jusqu'à nos jours*. Paris: Firmin Didot, 1873.

Clark, Maribeth. "Understanding French Grand Opera through Dance." Ph.D. diss., University of Pennsylvania, 1998.

Cobban, Alfred. "The 'Middle Class' in France, 1815–1848." *French Historical Studies* 5 (1967): 41–52.

Cohen, H. Robert. "Berlioz on the Opera, 1829–1849: A Study in Music Criticism." Ph.D. diss., New York University, 1973.

"La Conservation de la tradition scénique sur la scène lyrique en France au XIXᵉ siècle: Les Livrets de mise en scène et la Bibliothèque de l'association de la régie théâtrale." *Revue de musicologie* 64 (1973): 253–67.

"The Nineteenth-Century French Press and the Music Historian: Archival Sources and Bibliographical Resources." *Nineteenth-Century Music* 7, no. 2 (fall 1983): 136–42.

Cohen, H. Robert, and Marie-Odile Gigou. *Cent Ans de mise en scène lyrique en France, env. 1830–1930/One Hundred Years of Operatic Staging in France.* New York: Pendragon Press, 1986.

Collingham, H. A. C., with R. S. Alexander. *The July Monarchy: A Political History of France, 1830–1848.* London and New York: Longman, 1988.

Collins, Irene. *The Government and the Newspaper Press in France, 1814–1881.* London: Oxford University Press, 1959.

Collins, Irene, ed. *Government and Society in France, 1814–1848.* London: Edward Arnold, 1970.

Coudroy, Marie-Hélène. *La Critique parisienne des "grands opéras" de Meyerbeer: "Robert le diable," "Les Huguenots," "Le Prophète," "L'Africaine."* Saarbrücken: Musik-Edition Lucie Galland, 1988.

"La Critique parisienne et le grand opéra meyerbeerien." *Revue internationale de musique française* 17 (June 1985): 29–40.

Crosten, William L. *French Grand Opera: An Art and a Business.* New York: King's Crown Press, 1948.

Curtiss, Mina. *Bizet and His World.* New York: Alfred A. Knopf, 1958.

"Fromental Halévy." *Musical Quarterly* 39 (1953): 196–214.

Czyba, Lucette. "Misogynie et gynophobie dans *La Fille aux yeux d'or.*" In *La Femme au XIXe siècle: Littérature et idéologie,* edited by Jean-François Têtu et al., 139–47. Lyon: Presses Universitaires de Lyon, 1978.

Mythes et idéologie de la femme dans les romans de Flaubert. Lyon: Presses Universitaires de Lyon, 1983.

Dahlhaus, Carl. *Nineteenth-Century Music.* Translated by J. Bradford Robinson. Berkeley and Los Angeles: University of California Press, 1989.

Dantan, Jean-Pierre. *Dantan jeune: Caricatures et portraits de la société romantique.* Paris: Paris-Musées, 1989.

Dauriac, Lionel. *La Psychologie dans l'opéra français (Auber–Rossini–Meyerbeer).* Paris: F. Alcan, 1897.

Dayot, Armand P. *Journées révolutionnaires: 1830, 1848, d'après des peintures, sculptures, dessins, lithographies, médailles, autographes, objets . . . du temps.* Paris: E. Flammarion, 1897.

Dean, Winton. *Bizet.* London: Dent, 1975.

Debré, Moses. *The Image of the Jew in French Literature from 1800 to 1908.*
Translated by Gertrude Hirschler, with an introduction by Anna
Krakowski. New York: Ktav, 1970.

Devries, Anik, and François Lesure. *Dictionnaire des éditeurs de musique
français.* 2 vols. Geneva: Editions Minkoff, 1979.

Döhring, Sieghart. "Giacomo Meyerbeer: Grand Opera als Ideendrama."
Lendemains 31 /2 (1983): 11–22.

"Multimedia Tendenzen in der französischen Oper des
19. Jahrhunderts." IMS Report, Berkeley 1977, 497–500. Kassel:
Bärenreiter, 1981.

Döhring, Sieghart, and Sabina Henze-Döhring. *Oper und Musikdrama im 19.
Jahrhundert.* Laaber: Laaber-Verlag, 1997.

Dresch, Joseph Emile. *Heine à Paris, 1831–1856, d'après sa correspondance et les
témoignages de ses contemporains.* Paris: M. Didier, 1956.

DuBled, Victor. *Histoire de la monarchie de juillet de 1830 à 1848.* 2 vols. Paris:
E. Dentu, 1877–9.

Ellis, Katharine. *Music Criticism in Nineteenth-Century France: La Revue et
gazette musicale de Paris, 1834–1880.* Cambridge: Cambridge University
Press, 1995.

Encyclopaedia Britannica, 32 vols. New York: Encyclopaedia Britannica Inc.,
1910. S.v. "Hussites."

Encyclopaedia Britannica. 24 vols. Chicago: Encyclopaedia Britannica, 1973.
S.v. "Jerome of Prague," by F. M. Bailey.

Encyclopaedia Judaica. 18 vols. Jerusalem: Macmillan, 1971. S.v. "Music" by
Bathja Bachrach and Hanoch Avenary; "Rabbi, Rabbinate" by Godfrey
Edmond Silverman; "Saint-Simonism" by Hans G. Reissner.

Encyclopaedia Judaica. 16 vols. New York: Macmillan, 1971–2. S.v. "Halévy" by
Moshé Catane; "Elie Halfon Halévy" by Gerald E.Tauber; "Jacques
(François) Fromental Elie Halévy" by Josef Tal.

Evans, David-Owen. *Le Drame moderne à l'époque romantique.* Geneva:
Slatkine Reprints, 1974.

Social Romanticism in France, 1830–1848, with a Selective Critical Biography.
Oxford: Clarendon Press, 1951.

Le Théâtre pendant la période romantique (1827–1848). Paris: Les Presses
Universitaires de France, 1925.

Evans, Raymond Leslie. *Les Romantiques français et la musique.* Paris: Honoré
Champion, 1934.

Everist, Mark. "Giacomo Meyerbeer, the Théâtre Royal de l'Odéon, and Music Drama in Restoration Paris." *Nineteenth-Century Music* 17, no. 2 (fall 1993): 124–48.

Fajon, Robert. *L'Opéra à Paris*. Geneva: Slatkine, 1984.

Fath, Rolf. "Bielefeld." *Opéra International* (November 1989): 39–40.

Ferguson, Niall. *The House of Rothschild: Money's Prophets, 1798–1848*. New York: Viking Penguin, 1998.

Ferris, George T. "Méhul, Spontini and Halévy." In *Great Italian and French Composers*, 175–95. New York: D. Appleton & Co., 1878.

Finscher, Ludwig. "Aubers *La Muette de Portici* und die Anfänge der Grand-opera." In *Festschrift Heinz Becker*, edited by Jürgen Schläder and Reinhold Quandt, 87–105. Berlin: Laaber-Verlag, 1982.

Fitzgerald, Gerard, ed. *Annals of the Metropolitan Opera: The Complete Chronicle of Performances and Artists*. 2 vols. New York: Metropolitan Opera Guild; Boston: G. K. Hall, 1989.

Forbes, A. de. "Scribe, son répertoire, ses collaborateurs." *Le Ménestrel* 42 (1876): 67–8.

Friedmann, Aron. *Der synagogale Gesang: Eine Studie*. Berlin: C. Boas Nacht, 1904.

Fulcher, Jane F. *French Cultural Politics and Music: From the Dreyfus Affair to the First World War*. New York and Oxford: Oxford University Press, 1999.

———. "French Grand Opera and the Quest for a National Image: An Approach to the Study of Government-Sponsored Art." *Current Musicology* 35 (1983): 34–45.

———. "Meyerbeer and the Music of Society." *Musical Quarterly* 67, no. 2 (April 1981): 213–29.

———. *The Nation's Image: French Grand Opera as Politics and Politicized Art*. Cambridge: Cambridge University Press, 1987.

Ganvert, Gérard. "La Musique synagogale à Paris à l'époque du premier Temple consistorial (1822–74)." Ph.D. diss., Université de Paris-Sorbonne, 1984.

Gay, Peter. *Voltaire's Politics: The Poet as Realist*. New Haven and London: Yale University Press, 1988.

Gerhard, Anselm. "Die französische 'Grand Opéra' in der Forschung seit 1945." *Acta musicologica* 59, no. 3 (1987): 220–70.

———. *Die Verstädterung der Oper: Paris und das Musiktheater des 19. Jahrhunderts*. Stuttgart: J. B. Metzler, 1992. *The Urbanization of Opera: Music Theater in Paris in the Nineteenth Century*. Translated by Mary Whittall. Chicago and London: The University of Chicago Press, 1998.

Gilman, Sander L. *Jewish Self-Hatred: Anti-Semitism and the Hidden Language of the Jews*. Baltimore: Johns Hopkins University Press, 1986.

Girard, Louis. *Les Libéraux français, 1814–1875*. Paris: Aubier, 1985.

Girard, Patrick. *Les Juifs de France*. Paris: B. Huisman, 1983.

Les Juifs de France de 1789 à 1860: De l'émancipation à l'égalité. Paris: Calmann-Lévy, 1976.

La Révolution française et les juifs. Paris: R. Laffont, 1989.

Gossett, Philip. "The Operas of Rossini: Problems of Textual Criticism in Nineteenth-Century Opera." Ph.D. diss., Princeton University, 1970.

Gossett, Philip, and Charles Rosen, eds. *Early Romantic Opera*. 44 vols. New York: Garland, 1978–84.

Gourret, Jean. *Ces Hommes qui ont fait l'Opéra*. Paris: Albatross, 1984.

Dictionnaire des cantatrices de l'Opéra de Paris. Paris: Albatross, 1987.

Histoire des salles de l'Opéra de Paris. Paris: G. Tredaniel, 1985.

Gourret, Jean, with Jean Giraudeau. *Dictionnaire des chanteurs de l'Opéra de Paris*. Paris: Eds. Albatross, 1982.

Graetz, Heinrich. *History of the Jews*. 6 vols. Philadelphia: The Jewish Publication Society of America, 1895.

Graetz, Michael. "Une Initiative Saint-Simonienne pour l'émancipation des juifs." *Revue des études juives* 129 (1970): 67–84.

Les Juifs en France au XIXe siècle de la révolution française à l'alliance israélite universelle. Paris: Ed. du Seuil, 1989.

Grand Larousse de la langue française. 6 vols. Paris: Libraire Larousse, 1971–8. S.v. "Ducat"; "Ecu"; "Florin."

Greene, Christopher. "Romanticism, Cultural Nationalism and Politics in the July Monarchy: The Contribution of Ludovic Vitet." *French History* 4, no. 4 (December 1990): 487–509.

Grout, Donald J., and H. W. Williams. *A Short History of Opera*. 3d ed. New York: Columbia University Press, 1989.

Gruber, Alexander. "Gang der Handlung." In *Halévy, Die Jüdin*, edited by Heiner Bruns, 16–29, program booklet for the 1989/90 production of *La Juive* by Bühnen der Stadt Bielefeld. Bielefeld: Kramer Druck, 1989.

Guex, Jules. *Le Théâtre et la société française de 1815 à 1848*. Ph.D. diss., Université de Lausanne, 1900. Paris: Vevey, Imprimerie de Säuberlin and Pfeiffer, 1900. Reprint, Geneva: Slatkine, 1973.

Guichard, Léon. *La Musique et les lettres au temps du romantisme*. Paris: Presses Universitaires de France, 1955.

Hagan, Dorothy. "Music Criticism between the Revolutions." Ph.D. diss., University of Illinois, 1965.

Halévy, Elie. *La Doctrine économique de Saint-Simon et des Saint-Simoniens.* Paris: Editions de la *Revue du mois*, 1908.

Hallman, Diana R. "The French Grand Opera *La Juive* (1835): A Socio-Historical Study." 2 vols. Ph.D. diss., City University of New York, 1995.

Review of *Fromental Halévy: His Life and Music*, by Ruth Jordan, *Notes: Quarterly Journal of the Music Library Association* 54, no. 1 (fall 1997): 83–4.

Hansen, Eric C. *Ludovic Halévy: A Study of Frivolity and Fatalism in Nineteenth-Century France*. Lanham, MD: University Press of America, 1987.

Hartmann, Rudolf, ed. *Les Grands Opéras: Décor et mise en scène.* Translated by Michel R. Flechtner, Marie-Claire Gérard-Zai, and Antoine Golea. Freiburg and Paris: Office du Livre-Vilo, 1977.

Hertzberg, Arthur. *The French Enlightenment and the Jews: The Origins of Modern Anti-Semitism*. New York: Columbia University Press, 1990.

Hoog, Marie-Jacques. "Ces Femmes en turban." In *Women in French Literature*, edited by Michel Guggenheim, 117–23. Saratoga, CA: ANMA Libri, 1988.

Huebner, Stephen. "Opera Audiences in Paris 1830–1870." *Music and Letters* 70, no. 2 (1989): 206–25.

The Operas of Charles Gounod. Oxford: Clarendon Press, 1990.

Review of *Fromental Halévy, "La Juive": Dossier de presse parisienne (1835)*, edited by Karl Leich-Galland, Saarbrücken: Musik-Edition Lucie Galland, 1987. *Music and Letters* 71, no. 4 (November 1990): 579–80.

Idelsohn, A. Z. *Jewish Music in its Historical Development*. New York: Henry Holt & Co., 1929.

Iggers, Georg G. "The Social Philosophy of the Saint-Simonians, 1825–1832." Ph.D. diss., University of Chicago, 1951.

Indy, Vincent d'. *Cours de composition musicale*. 3 vols. Paris: Durand & Cie, 1903–50.

Ionescu, Ghita, ed. *The Political Thought of Saint-Simon*. London and New York: Oxford University Press, 1976.

Jardin, André, and André-Jean Tudesq. *Restoration and Reaction, 1815–1848*. Translated by Elborg Forster. Cambridge: Cambridge University Press, 1973.

The Jewish Encyclopedia. 12 vols. New York: Ktav Publishing House, 1976–82. S.v. "Elie (Halfan) Halévy" by M. Seligsohn; "Jacques François Fromenthal Elie Halévy" by Joseph Sohn; "Léon Halévy" by Victor R. Emanuel; "Heinrich Heine" by Joseph Jacobs.

Johnson, James H. "Antisemitism and Music in Nineteenth-Century France." *Musica Judaica* 5, no. 1 (1982–3): 79–96.

Johnson, Janet Lynn. "Rossini in Bologna and Paris during the Early 1830s: New Letters." *Revue de musicologie* 79, no. 1 (1993): 63–81.

Join-Diéterle, Catherine. *Les Décors de scène de l'Opéra de Paris à l'époque romantique*. Paris: Picard, 1988.

"Evolution de la scénographie à l'Académie de musique à l'époque romantique." *Romantisme* 38 (1982): 65–76.

"L'Opéra et son public à l'époque romantique." *L'Oeil* 288–9 (July–August 1979): 30–37.

Jordan, Ruth. *Fromental Halévy: His Life and Music, 1799–1862*. London: Kahn and Averill, 1994; New York: Proscenium Publishers, 1996.

Kahane, Martine, ed. *L'Ouverture du nouvel opéra, 5 janvier 1875*. Paris: Ministère de la culture et de la communication, 1986.

Katz, Jacob. *From Prejudice to Destruction: Anti-Semitism, 1700–1933*. Cambridge, MA: Harvard University Press, 1980.

Klein, John William. "Halévy's *La Juive*." *Musical Times* 114, no. 1560 (February 1973): 140–41.

"Jacques Fromental Halévy (1799–1862)." *Music Review* 23 (1962): 13–17.

Koon, Helene, and Richard Switzer. *Eugène Scribe*. Boston: Twayne Publishers, 1980.

Krakovitch, Odile. *Hugo censuré: La Liberté au théâtre au XIXᵉ siècle*. Paris: Calmann-Levy, 1985.

Kruse, Joseph A., and Michael Werner, eds. *Heine à Paris, 1831–1856*. Düsseldorf: Droste, 1981.

L. C. "De l'histoire du juif errant." *L'Israélite français* 1 (1817): 109–21.

Labat-Poussin, Brigitte. *Archives du Théâtre national de l'Opéra: Inventaire*. Paris: Archives Nationales, 1977.

Lajarte, Théophile de. *Bibliothèque musicale du théâtre de l'Opéra: Catalogue historique, chronologique, anecdotique*. Paris: Librairie des bibliophiles, 1878. Reprint, Paris: Hildesheim, 1969.

Landau, Chief Rabbi Judah Leo. *Judaism in Life and Literature*. London: Edward Goldston Ltd., 1936.

Larousse, Pierre. *Grand Dictionnaire universel du XIXᵉ siècle, français, historique, géographique, mythologique, bibliographique, littéraire, artistique, scientifique.* 17 vols. Paris: Administration du Grand Dictionnaire universel, 1866–79. Reprint, Geneva and Paris: Slatkine, 1982. S.v. "Bourgeois, -oise"; "(La) Juive"; "(Augustin-Eugène) Scribe."

Lasalle, Albert de. *Meyerbeer: Sa Vie et le catalogue de ses oeuvres.* Paris: Dentu, 1864.

Lathers, Marie. "Posing the 'Belle Juive': Jewish Models in Nineteenth-Century Paris." *Woman's Art Journal* 21, no. 1 (spring–summer 2000): 27–32.

Legouvé, Ernest. *soixante Ans de souvenirs.* 2 vols. Paris: J. Hetzel, 1886–7. *Sixty Years of Recollections.* Translated by Albert D. Vandam. 2 vols. London: Eden, Remington & Co., 1893.

Leich-Galland, Karl. "*La Juive*: Commentaire musical et littéraire." *L'Avant-scène opéra* 100 (July 1987): 32–87.

———. "Quelques Observations sur les autographes des grands opéras de Fromental Halévy." In *Les Sources en musicologie,* ed. Michel Huglo, Actes des journées d'études de la Société française de musicologie à l'Institut de recherche et d'histoire des textes d'Orléans-La Source, 9–11 September 1979.

———. "'Scheut Ihr die Erinnerung?' Zur Wirkung von Halévys *La Juive*." In *Halévy: La Juive,* 19–26; program booklet for the 1999/2000 production of *La Juive* at the Vienna Staatsoper.

Leppert, Richard, and Susan McClary, eds. *Music and Society: The Politics of Composition, Performance and Reception.* Cambridge and New York: Cambridge University Press, 1987.

Locke, Ralph P. *Music, Musicians and the Saint-Simonians.* Chicago: University of Chicago Press, 1986.

Loewenberg, Alfred. *Annals of Opera 1597–1940.* 2 vols. 2d ed. Geneva: Societas Bibliographica, 1955.

Longyear, Rey M. "La Muette de Portici." *Music Review* 19 (1958): 37–46. *Nineteenth-Century Romanticism in Music.* 3d ed. Englewood Cliffs, NJ: Prentice-Hall, 1988.

———. "Political and Social Criticism in French Opera, 1827–1920." In *Essays on Bach and Other Matters: A Tribute to Gerhard Herz,* edited by Robert L. Weaver, 245–54. Louisville, KY: University of Kentucky Press, 1981.

Loyrette, Henri, ed. *Entre le théâtre et l'histoire: La Famille Halévy (1760–1960).* Paris: Librairie Arthème Fayard, 1996.

Lyons, Martyn. *Le Triomphe du livre: Une Histoire sociologique de la lecture dans la France du XIXe siècle*. Paris: Promodis, 1987.

Macdonald, Hugh. "Grandest of the Grand." Notes to the 1989 Philips recording of *La Juive*, 18–23 (CD 420 190-2).

Magraw, Roger. *France, 1815–1914: The Bourgeois Century*. New York: Oxford University Press, 1986.

Mehta, Binita. "Jean-François Casimir Delavigne (1793–1843)." In *Dictionary of Literary Biography*, vol. CXCII: *French Dramatists, 1789–1914*, edited by Barbara T. Cooper, 65–70. Detroit, Washington, DC, and London: Gale Research, 1998.

Ménétrier, Jean-Alexandre. "L'Amour triste: Fromental Halévy et son temps." *L'Avant-scène opéra* 100 (July 1987): 4–12.

Moatti, Jacques. *The Paris Opera*. New York: Vendome Press, 1987.

Modder, Frank Montagu. *The Jew in the Literature of England to the End of the Nineteenth Century*. Cleveland and New York: The World Publishing Co., 1960.

Moindrot, Isabelle. "Le Geste et l'idéologie dans le 'grand opéra' *La Juive* de Fromental Halévy." *Romantisme* 28, no. 102 (1998): 63–79.

Mongrédien, Jean. *La Musique en France: Des Lumières au romantisme (1789–1830)*. Paris: Flammarion, 1985.

Moynet, M. J. *French Theatrical Production in the Nineteenth Century*. Edited by Marvin A. Carlson. Translated and augmented by Allan S. Jackson with M. Glen Wilson. Binghamton, NY: Max Reinhardt Foundation with the Center for Modern Theatre Research, 1976.

Muhlstein, Anka. *Baron James: The Rise of the French Rothschilds*. New York and Paris: Vendome Press, 1987.

Murphy, Kerry. *Hector Berlioz and the Development of French Music Criticism*. Ann Arbor, MI: UMI Research Press, 1988.

Newark, Cormac. "Ceremony, Celebration and Spectacle in *La Juive*." In *Reading Critics Reading: Opera and Ballet Criticism in France from the Revolution to 1848*, edited by Roger Parker and Mary Ann Smart. Oxford: Oxford University Press, 2001.

"Staging Grand Opéra: History and the Imagination in Nineteenth-Century Paris." Ph.D. diss., University of Oxford, 1999.

Newman, Ernest. *More Stories of Famous Operas*. New York: Alfred A. Knopf, 1968.

Nochlin, Linda, and Tamar Garb, eds. *The Jew in the Text: Modernity and the Construction of Identity*. London: Thames & Hudson, 1995.

Ockman, Carol. "Two Large Eyebrows à l'orientale: Ethnic Stereotyping in Ingres's *Baronne de Rothschild.*" *Art History* (December 1991): 521–39.

Pendle, Karin. *Eugène Scribe and French Opera of the Nineteenth Century.* Ann Arbor, MI: UMI Research Press, 1977.

Perris, Arnold. "French Music in the Time of Louis-Philippe: Art as a Substitute for the Heroic Experience." Ph.D. diss., Northwestern University, 1967.

Pierrakos, Hélène. "Chrétienté, judaïté et la musique." *L'Avant-scène opéra* 100 (July 1987): 20–23.

Piette, Christine. *Les Juifs de Paris (1808–1840): La Marche vers l'assimilation.* Quebec: Presses de l'Université Laval, 1983.

Pinkney, David H. *The French Revolution of 1830.* Princeton: Princeton University Press, 1972.

Radice, Mark A., ed. *Opera in Context: Essays on Historical Staging from the Late Renaissance to the Time of Puccini.* Portland: Amadeus Press, 1998.

Rather, L. J. *Reading Wagner: A Study in the History of Ideas.* Baton Rouge and London: Louisiana State University Press, 1990.

Reeves, John. *The Rothschilds: The Financial Rulers of Nations.* New York: Gordon Press, 1975.

Reininghaus, Frieder. "Religion als Trumpf und Trauma: Glaubensfragen and Kirchenbilder in musikalischem Gewand." In *Halévy: La Juive,* 48–52, program booklet for the 1999/2000 production of *La Juive* at the Vienna Staatsoper.

Rieger, D. "*La Muette de Portici* von Auber/Scribe: Eine Revolutionsoper mit antirevolutionarem Libretto." *Romanistische Zeitschrift für Literaturgeschichte* 10 (1986): 349–59.

Roberts, John H. "The Genesis of Meyerbeer's *L'Africaine.*" Ph.D. diss., University of California at Berkeley, 1977.

Rosenberg, Edgar. *From Shylock to Svengali: Jewish Stereotypes in English Fiction.* Stanford: Stanford University Press, 1960.

Rothmueller, Aron Marko. *The Music of the Jews.* South Brunswick, NJ: Thomas Yoseloff, 1967.

Runyan, William Edward. "Orchestration in Five French Grand Operas." Ph.D. diss., Eastman School of Music, 1983.

Sadie, Stanley, ed. *The New Grove Dictionary of Music and Musicians.* 20 vols. London: Macmillan, 1980. S.v. "Gaetano Donizetti" by William

Ashbrook and Julian Budden; "(Jacques-François-) Fromental
[Fromentin] (-Elie) [-Elias] Halévy" by Hugh Macdonald.

The New Grove Dictionary of Music and Musicians. 2d ed. 29 vols. London:
Macmillan; New York: Grove's Dictionaries, 2001. S.v.
"(Jacques-François-) Fromental (-Elie) Halévy" by Hugh
Macdonald.

Sadie, Stanley, ed. *The New Grove Dictionary of Opera.* 4 vols. London:
Macmillan, 1992. S.v. "Laure (Cinthie) Cinti-Damoreau" by Philip
Robinson; "Gaetano Donizetti" by William Ashbrook and Julian
Budden; "Julie (-Aimée-Josephe [Josephine]) Dorus-Gras [née Van
Steenkiste]" by Elizabeth Forbes; "(Marie) Cornélie Falcon" by
Philip Robinson; "Grand opéra" by M. Elizabeth C. Bartlet;
"(Jacques-François-) Fromental (-Elie) [Fromentin (-Elias)] Halévy" by
Hugh Macdonald; "Les Huguenots" by Steven Huebner; "La Juive" by
Hugh Macdonald; "Nicolas (Prosper) Levasseur" by Philip Robinson;
"La Muette de Portici" by Herbert Schneider; "Sacred opera" by
Graham Dixon and Richard Taruskin.

Sadler, Graham. "A Re-examination of Rameau's Self-Borrowings." In
*Jean-Baptiste Lully and the Music of the French Baroque: Essays in Honor of
James R. Anthony,* edited by John Hajdu Heyer. Cambridge: Cambridge
University Press, 1989.

Said, Edward W. *Orientalism.* New York: Vintage Books, 1979.

Sammons, Jeffrey L. *Heinrich Heine: A Modern Biography.* Princeton:
Princeton University Press, 1979.

Shulman, Laurie C. "Music Criticism of the Paris Opera of the 1830s." Ph.D.
diss., Cornell University, 1985.

Silbener, Edmund. "Charles Fourier on the Jewish Question." *Jewish Social
Studies* 8 (1946): 245–66.

Simon, W. M. "The 'Two Cultures' in Nineteenth-Century France: Victor
Cousin and Auguste Comte." *Journal of the History of Ideas* 26
(January–March 1965): 45–58.

Slatin, Sonia. "Opera and Revolution: *La Muette de Portici* and the Belgian
Revolution of 1830 Revisited." *Journal of Musicological Research* 3 (1979):
45–62.

Smart, Ninian, and John Clayton, Steven Katz, and Patrick Sherry, eds.
Nineteenth-Century Religious Thought in the West. 3 vols. Cambridge:
Cambridge University Press, 1985.

Smith, Marian E. *Ballet and Opera in the Age of Giselle.* Princeton and Oxford: Princeton University Press, 2000.

———. "Music for the Ballet-Pantomime at the Paris Opéra, 1825–1850." Ph.D. diss., Yale University, 1988.

———. "'Poésie lyrique' and 'Choréographie' at the Opéra in the July Monarchy." *Cambridge Opera Journal* 4, no. 1 (1992): 1–19.

Spitzer, Alan B. *The French Generation of 1820.* Princeton: Princeton University Press, 1987.

Szajkowski, Zosa. "French Jews during the Revolution of 1830 and the July Monarchy." *Historia Judaica* 22 (1960): 1017–42.

———. "The Growth of the Jewish Population of France: The Political Aspects of a Demographic Problem." *Jewish Social Studies* 8, no. 3 (July 1946): 179–96.

———. *Jewish Education in France, 1789–1939.* Edited by Tobey B. Gitelle. New York and London: Columbia University Press, 1980.

———. "The Jewish Saint-Simonians and Socialist Antisemites in France." *Jewish Social Studies* 9, no. 1 (January 1947): 33–60.

———. *Jews and the French Revolutions of 1789, 1830 and 1848.* New York: Ktav Publishing House, 1970.

———. "Judaica-Napoleonica: A Bibliography of Books, Pamphlets and Printed Documents, 1801–1815." *Studies in Bibliography and Booklore* 2, no. 3 (June 1956): 107–47.

Taylor, Gary. *Reinventing Shakespeare: A Cultural History from the Restoration to the Present.* New York: Oxford University Press, 1989.

Thomson, Joan Lewis. "Meyerbeer and His Contemporaries." Ph.D. diss., Columbia University, 1972.

Tomlinson, Gary. "The Web of Culture: A Context for Musicology." *Nineteenth-Century Music* 7, no. 3 (3 April 1984): 350–62.

Trésor de la langue française: Dictionnaire de la langue du XIXe siècle (1789–1860). 15 vols. Paris: Gallimard, 1973–92. S.v. "Ducat," "Ecu," "Florin."

Van Moere, Didier. "*La Juive* au feu de la presse." *L'Avant-scène opéra* 100 (July 1987): 99–105.

Weill, Georges. "Les Juifs et le Saint-Simonisme." *Revue des études juives* 31 (1895): 261–80.

Weinstock, Herbert. *Rossini: A Biography.* New York: Alfred A. Knopf, 1968.

Wellington, Marie. *The Art of Voltaire's Theater: An Exploration of Possibility.* New York: Peter Lang, 1987.

Werner, Eric. "Jews around Richard and Cosima Wagner." *Musical Quarterly* 71, no. 2 (1985): 172–99.

Wilberg, Rebecca S. "The *mise en scène* at the Paris Opéra Salle Le Peletier (1821–1873) and the Staging of the First French *grand opéra*: Meyerbeer's *Robert le diable*." Ph.D. diss., Brigham Young University, 1990.

Wild, Nicole. *Décors et costumes du XIXe siècle*. 2 vols. Paris: Bibliothèque Nationale, Département de la Musique, 1987.

——. *Dictionnaire des théâtres parisiens au XIXe siècle: Les Théâtres et la musique*. Paris: Aux Amateurs de Livres, 1989.

Wilson, Derek. *Rothschild: The Wealth and Power of a Dynasty*. New York: Charles Scribner's Sons, 1988.

Wolff, Hellmuth Christian. "Halévy als Kunst- und Musikschriftsteller." In *Musicae scientiae collectanea: Festschrift Karl Gustav Fellerer*, edited by H. Hüschen, 697–706. Cologne: Volk, 1973.

——. "Der Orient in der französischen Oper des 19. Jahrhunderts." In *Die Couleur locale in der Oper des 19. Jahrhunderts*, edited by Heinz Becker, 371–86. Regensburg: Gustav Bosse, 1976.

Wolff, Stéphane. *L'Opéra au Palais Garnier (1875–1962): Les Oeuvres, les interprètes*. Paris: Déposé au journal *L'Entr'acte*, n.d.

Yon, Jean-Claude. "Eugène Scribe, la fortune et la liberté." 2 vols. Ph.D. diss., Université de Paris-Sorbonne, 1993. Saint-Genouph: Edition A. G. Nizet, 2000.

INDEX

Abigail (*The Jew of Malta*), 210, 211, 231, 237

absolutism, 5, 125, 296

Académie des beaux-arts, 2, 9, 65, n 133, 84

Académie française, 31, 59, 60, 61, 85, App. E *320, 322*

Académie royale de musique, *see* Opéra, Paris

affaire Damas, l', 101, 253, 286, 301

Aguado, Alexandre-Marie, marquis, 276, 277

Ahasvérus, *see* "juif errant, le"

Albert (*La Juive*), 118, 155, 160, 162

ancien régime, 5, 39, 301, 302

anti-authoritarianism, 130, 143, 302, 304

anti-capitalism, 263–9

"anti-capitalist antisemitism," 10, 254–5, 263–9, 288–9

anticlericalism, 5–6, 23
    of *La Juive*, 116, 143, 302, 304
    during July Monarchy, 143
    of liberal writers, 130
    during Restoration, 38–9, 42, 148
    of Scribe and Halévys, 42–6, 130

antisemitism, 10, 75, 257, 261, 263–70, 280, 287, 304
    of Christians, 254, 291
    during July Monarchy, 257, 261, 270, 292
    at Paris Opéra, 273–5, 280
    of *philosophes*, 7, 287–9
    in theatre and music circles, 271–80

Antonio (*The Merchant of Venice*), 236, 243

apostasy, *see* Jews, conversion of

Archives israélites, Les, 101, 102 n. 103, 253, 270, 286, 289

Arnault, Antoine-Vincent, 31, 47, 60, 62 n. 121, App. E *320, 322*

Assemblée nationale, 65, 106, App. K *339–40*

assimilation, *see* Jews, acculturation / assimilation

Auber, Daniel, 30, 52 n. 87
    Le Maçon, 158 n. 10
    La Muette de Portici, 30, 41, 51, 52, 63, 68

Aumer, Pierre, 26

auto-da-fé, l', 116, 134
    in *La Juive*, 1, 3, 116, 140–41, 152, 215, App. F *325, 326*
    Voltaire's discussion of, 127–8

Avignon, 43, 115, 128, 247

Ballanche, Pierre-Simon, 133

Balzac, Honoré de, 39, 128, 216 n. 19, 242 n. 78, 248

Barabas (*The Jew of Malta*), 210, 235, 237, 243 n. 81, 244, 246

Barder (Bardet), Stephanie, 86 n. 48, n. 49

Barrault, Emile, 67

Barthélemy, Saint, *see* St. Bartholomew's Eve

Bayard, Jean-François, 29